Habitus of the Hood

Habitus of the Hood

Edited by Chris Richardson and Hans A. Skott-Myhre

intellect Bristol, UK / Chicago, USA

First published in the UK in 2012 by
Intellect, The Mill, Parnall Road, Fishponds, Bristol, BS16 3JG, UK

First published in the USA in 2012 by
Intellect, The University of Chicago Press, 1427 E. 60th Street,
Chicago, IL 60637, USA

A catalogue record for this book is available from the
British Library.

Cover designer: Holly Rose
Copy-editor: MPS Ltd
Typesetting: Mac Style, Beverley, E. Yorkshire
Production manager: Tim Mitchell

ISBN 978-1-84150-479-7

Printed and bound by Hobbs, UK.

Contents

Chapter 1

Introduction

Chris Richardson and Hans A. Skott-Myhre

"The hood" embodies both the utopian and dystopian aspects of low-income urban areas. It represents an awareness of community, an enclosed space in which residents are united in their daily struggles. It also signifies an isolated, marginalized, and often-criminalized space that appears frequently in popular media representations, legal discourses, and public discussions. The popularity of the word *hood*, here slang for *neighborhood*, is generally associated with the emergence of hip-hop culture in the 1980s. The word also became highly visible after a series of "hood films" were produced in the early 1990s. The most popular of these films were John Singleton's *Boyz N the Hood* (1991), Ernest Dickerson's *Juice* (1992), and the Hughes brothers' *Menace II Society* (1993). Today, however, "the hood" signifies much more than the young, predominantly black subculture in North America from which it originated. The chapters in this collection demonstrate that the hood has now expanded to Europe, Australasia, and many spaces in between, incorporating a plurality of ethnicities and subcultures as global capital and new media technologies collapse previous notions of time and space.

The concept of the hood can be both liberating and limiting. Residents associate certain life possibilities with their surroundings, which they internalize and act upon. This conception has both real and symbolic consequences for individuals inside as well as outside the hood. It pushes people in certain directions and creates values, practices, and judgments that are often shared within similar communities. As the saying goes, "you can take me out of the hood but you can't take the hood out of me." This internalizing of one's environment, its implications, and its representations, are what we seek to interrogate in the following chapters.

We argue that Bourdieu's (2007 [1977]) notion of *habitus*, a "system of durable, transposable dispositions" that form "principles which generate and organize practices and representations" (p. 72), is a valuable theoretical tool for analyzing the hood. While the term *habitus*, a Latin word meaning habitude, mode of life, or general appearance, may be as old as the ancient philosophers, we use the term as promoted by Bourdieu, particularly in *Outline of a Theory of Practice* (2007).[1] In this book, we also expand Bourdieu's concept through a reading of Robin Cooper's (2005) "dwelling place," which she explains as "a kind of knowing one's way about ... [that] implies a freedom to move in some domain or other, which is more akin to sure-footedness" (p. 304). In addition, Cornel West (1999a) provides a useful distinction between *hood* and *neighborhood*, which he argues represents the difference between extreme individualism and collective identity. Finally, we approach the hood as a concept *à la* Deleuze and Guattari (1994), as a space that is perpetually *becoming*, a space constituted by "revolutions and societies of friends, societies of resistance; because to create is to resist; pure becomings, pure events on a plane of immanence" (p. 110).

This collection explores how the hood is conceived within the lived experiences of residents and within mediated representations in popular culture.[2] Whether fictional or documentary, representations of the hood embody potentialities. Like habitus, the hood is "a past which survives the present and tends to perpetuate itself into the future" (Bourdieu, 2007, p. 82). The relationship of individual subjects with the social conditions in which they live is explored in this collection through methodologies such as (auto) ethnography, textual analysis, and critical discourse analysis. By examining this relationship through different lenses and with different focal points, we illuminate the similarities between (neighbor)hoods while also examining the particularities of hoods populated by multiracial, multisexual, and multicultural families (Skott-Myhre, Chapter 2), youth along the Gold Coast in Australia (Baker, Bennett, & Wise, Chapter 5), and young women in the inner suburbs of Los Angeles (Nicol & Yee, Chapter 8). As Hagedorn (2007) argues, the elements of crime that were once considered part of the twentieth-century North American hood now inhabit "the global city." In other words, confining "the hood" to cities like New York, Chicago, and Los Angeles is no longer accurate. One telling example of this change is evident in Wacquant's (2008) introduction to his recent study of urban marginality. He begins by pointing out the similarities and differences between what can roughly translate as the global hood – the American ghetto, the French *banlieue*, the Italian *quartieri periferici*, the Swedish *problemomrade*, the Brazilian *favela*, and the Argentinian *villa miseria*. Evidently, while "the hood" may continue to hold distinctly American connotations, there is something in virtually every country on the globe that knows marginality, poverty, and stigma. We intend to address this expanded definition of the hood through our exploration of the hood as habitus.

Before turning to these studies, we would first like to explore what is at stake. How is the hood related to Bourdieu's concept of habitus? Is there a clear difference between neighborhood and hood? Is the hood a spectacle or a dwelling place? In the following chapters, we reflect upon what these questions imply, how we might negotiate them, and the importance of such intellectual work. At a time when inquiries such as these can very easily be pushed aside by more "prestigious" or "empirical" work (often by individuals and institutions with no connection to hoods in their communities and who remain dismissive of such research *tout court*), this exploration is incredibly important. The publication of this book broadens the intellectual scope of previous arguments in the fields of cultural studies, sociology, critical pedagogy, and child and youth work. Perhaps, more importantly, it recognizes a situation that has been increasing in scope and severity over the last few decades. As transnational corporations and capital markets struggle to extend their reach and the middle classes that formed in the late twentieth century quickly dissolve, the hoods are becoming more populated (see Hollander & Hollander, Chapter 7), residents are growing more desperate, and youth are becoming increasingly frustrated. We feel this exploration could not be more important, necessary, and timely.

The hood as habitus

The forging of a relationship between individuals and their environments is an important and complex part of socialization. The experiences and attitudes one witnesses first-hand at home, on the streets, and in schools shape practices and beliefs that are likely to be repeated in the future. Bourdieu (1984) writes of this connection as a relationship "between the two capacities which define the habitus, the capacity to produce classifiable practices and works, and the capacity to differentiate and appreciate these practices and products" (p. 170). In essence, habitus is a cyclical – but alterable – series of behaviors that determines how individuals see and act within their environments. Bourdieu notes that "the 'eye' is a product of history reproduced by education" (p. 3). In other words, the way we see the world is learned. And we learn to see by participating and interacting within our communities. We might say, then, that habitus (re)creates the social spaces that we call hoods by teaching insiders and outsiders how to see it, classify it, work within it, and understand it.

The habitus of the hood plays a crucial role in teaching residents what is and is not acceptable, achievable, and dreamable. It "makes coherence and necessity out of accident and contingency," writes Bourdieu (2007, p. 87). Habitus naturalizes the attitudes and behaviors of residents in particular areas, street corners, and meeting places and makes them appear natural, as if they were innate parts of our being. Habitus can also make certain practices seem inherent to the spaces in which they occur, as if these practices were only possible in these spaces and other possibilities for acting are out of the question. This aspect of culture, as situated in geography, is often confused for nature. Bourdieu's concept allows us to recognize that these "essential" practices are the result of experiences, mediations, representations, and dialogues that have taken shape within these spaces. It is a "nature" that must be constantly reiterated as "natural."

Habitus is a way of seeing and acting that links certain groups in society. While all individuals form a habitus, this acquired skillset is not always the same. The experiences of one resident in one neighborhood can be very different from a resident of another neighborhood, even within the same city. What one sees and looks for may be completely different. The practices of one group may even be incomprehensible to others. For example, in *Menace II Society* (1993), the character O-Dog is famously described by his friend Caine as "America's nightmare: young, black, and [does not] give a fuck." But what does this mean? To an affluent, white resident of Beverly Hills, this description might provoke fear, indicating that O-Dog, as a young person, is reckless and rude; as a black person, is uncultured and prone to violence; and, finally, as someone who "doesn't give a fuck," he may be seen as disrespectful – particularly of private property rights. All these characteristics are negative and threatening to mainstream values – to mainstream habitus. Why one would adopt these behaviors may be baffling to the average person. On the other hand, to O-Dog's friends, this description may be flattering. As a young person, he could be seen as energetic, passionate, and unbroken. As a black person, he can be viewed as conscious of racial prejudices and protective of his friends and family. And as someone who "doesn't give a fuck," O-Dog speaks his mind, regardless of the consequences. In other words, O-Dog is unlike those who have become reliant upon social norms; those who have according to West (2008) become "well-adjusted to injustice" (p. 16). O-Dog is not afraid to lash out at oppressors, to take what he feels he is entitled to, and he does not hesitate to challenge others. In most hoods, these are admirable qualities.

We are not arguing for or against O-Dog and the group of young, black men that he represents. What this example highlights is the difference between people in various communities and the conflict between the ways many of them see the world. Because habitus is a naturalized way of thinking, we tend to assume that *our* habitus is the only habitus that exists. O-Dog is raised within a community – Watts, California – in which attributes such as toughness are privileged and respected by his peers while traditional Judeo-Christian values like patience and "turning the other cheek" are not as admirable – in fact, those traits are more likely to get one hurt. Bourdieu's concept of habitus helps us understand why this is so.

The fact that people within various communities tend to share values, practices, and beliefs means that our experiences within a certain space are often similar enough to create a sort of group habitus. Bourdieu (2007) argues that habitus presupposes a "community of 'unconsciouses'" (p. 80). Each collective habitus is a product of events and circumstances that become naturalized and therefore unrecognized (i.e., unconscious) in the minds of community members. O-Dog is no more natural than the law-abiding, affluent, white person we hypothesized above. The only thing that is natural is the ability to form a habitus in which members of a community act in a sort of "regulated improvisation" (p. 79). One way of thinking through this idea is with the metaphor of a game. The rules of the game can be different in any community. But *every* community plays a version of this game.

People learn how to act as they grow within their environment. Each individual comes into contact with people and situations that illustrate the "right" way and the "wrong" way to do things. Seeing this repeated over and over again eventually guides residents toward common practices, allowing them to know what to expect from situations before they arise. We develop a set of linguistic and cultural competences through this process much like the way accents are formed between people in various parts of the country. Because neighbors are used to speaking with each other, they begin to sound similar. This is why no one thinks of themselves as having an accent. Accents are something *other* people have. One only notices the difference in dialect when traveling or when strangers come to town.[3]

Local practices are often internalized and repeated without ever being consciously examined. By continuing to act in a way that seems completely natural and unquestionable, individuals perpetuate these practices within the community. Bourdieu (2007) refers to this as "the dialectic of the internalization of externality and the externalization of internality" (p. 72). People internalize the culture of their surroundings. Simultaneously, these actions influence the characteristics of their neighborhoods. One's hood does not determine how one acts, nor does one's action determine the hood. Together, however, a symbiotic relationship arises and customs and practices become difficult to separate from the communities in which they occur. Thus, Bourdieu (2007) writes about "a community of dispositions" (p. 79). Although not everyone experiences the same events, and therefore generates a different habitus, growing up in a similar class, with similar education, similar ethnic backgrounds, and similar values means that similar habituses are likely to develop. This is why we can talk about the hood as a collective habitus, even though individuals maintain their capacity to act differently, to challenge norms, and to think for themselves.

Hood or neighborhood?

We do not use the term "hood" to specifically denote a space with negative or positive connotations in this collection. It may bring up a whole web of connotations, but the only characteristics that make a hood a hood for us is the marginalized relationship it shares with the mainstream; the working-class or sub-working-class existences of the majority of its residents; and the often high population of visible minorities living within it. In this way, the hood is a particular kind of neighborhood.

The first lines of Lance Freeman's *There Goes the Hood* (2006) may provide the best description of what the hood has become in popular culture:

> The Ghetto, the inner city, the hood – these terms have been applied as monikers for black neighborhoods and conjure up images of places that are off-limits to outsiders, places to be avoided after sundown, and paragons of pathology. Portrayed as isolated pockets of deviance and despair, these neighborhoods have captured the imagination of journalists and social scientists who have chronicled the challenges and risks of living in such neighborhoods.
>
> (p. 1)

This may be an accurate account of modern perceptions of the hood. In this book, however, we hope to probe more deeply the ways in which the hood is different from *and* similar to common notions of neighborhood and community. Clearly, the answer is not a simple matter of definitions nor causes and effects. As Freeman indicates throughout his book, the hood often teeters between self-destruction and upward mobility. In Lawrence Fishburne's famous speech on gentrification in *Boyz N the Hood* (1991), he asks "Why is it that there's a gun shop on almost every corner in this community? … For the same reason that there's a liquor store on almost every corner in the black community. Why? They want us to kill ourselves." He explains how the property values of a neighborhood, like the one in South-Central Los Angeles depicted in the film, is driven down so that houses can be purchased by developers and later sold at a profit when they "clean up" the hood (which is often a euphemism for transferring the problems elsewhere). Freeman's research seems to support this argument.[4] In this case, the *hood* is inherently self-destructive while a *neighborhood* is built to support the community.

Cornel West argues for this kind of differentiation between a "hood" and a "neighborhood." The former, he argues, is filled with gangsters while the latter is filled with friends. "I grew up in a neighborhood, not a hood," writes West (2008, p. 155).[5] "Our neighborhood was a place where there were wonderful ties of sympathy and bonds of empathy. The folk who lived there kept track of you." In contrast, he writes that a "hood is survival of the slickest. They're obsessed with their 11th commandment, 'Thou shalt not get caught.'" While this is a provocative distinction, we feel that defining the hood as a completely negative, selfish, and destructive place may be too simplistic. If the hood were truly devoid of strong bonds and close-knit social relationships, there would not likely be so many nostalgic references to it in popular culture. In music alone, everyone from 2Pac and Nas to Alicia Keys and Jennifer Lopez make references to their respective hoods and the ways those experiences have shaped them as individuals. Whether these claims are authentic or disingenuous is another story. The sheer number of references to the hood, however, points to the importance of this space as a community of shared experiences and a point of connection with others. This is not to say that the hood is an easy or ideal place to live. Often times, it is the enduring struggles of the residents that unite them. It is not a sense of love or joy but a shared understanding of the injustice imposed on residents from outside the hood that creates a bond. This formation of a group habitus, based on specific geographical spaces, should not be underestimated both for its power to shape ideas and its power to unite a community – even if members are only united in their anger and distrust of outsiders.

West (1999a) argues that the hood has become an extended metaphor for America in general "as it undergoes gangsterization from the White House all the way down" (p. 94). He asserts, however, that even in the black community the major difference between now and then "is that even behind the veil of color, you had more of a neighborhood than a hood then. And this meant that you had flowing a certain kind of love, care, concern, and nurture behind that veil that allowed you to deal with the gangsterism coming at you – namely white America treating you like a dog" (West, 1999a, pp. 93–94). Whether or not one subscribes to this distinction of the hood or the neighborhood, it seems clear that the hood cannot be an island. It exists only in relation to the mainstream neighborhoods that define themselves in opposition to the working-class, predominantly black areas of major cities that we call hoods. The closer one looks at any discourse of the hood, the more obvious it becomes that the statements presuppose another space, an "elsewhere" in relation to the mainstream. Ultimately, the American dream of prosperity and large homes surrounded by white picket fences and like-minded neighbors can only exist in contradistinction with spaces defined as "low-income," "high-immigrant," or "crime-ridden." It then becomes evident that the idea of the hood lurks behind every image of happy nuclear families, luxury housing complexes, and Hollywood happy endings that we have become accustomed to seeing in popular culture.

For the most part, the hood is represented only in rap lyrics and newspaper crime coverage. When communities known as hoods actually *do* appear in government reports or other texts, they signify their existence with two distinct movements. On the one hand, they highlight what is different, out of place, or abnormal (and therefore what must be fixed). On the other hand, they allude to what it means to be central and to belong. Such depictions, as Cameron (2006) writes, "are now used to identify, define (i.e., to produce) and map the socially excluded – but, importantly, *not the socially included*" (p. 400, emphasis in original). Cameron argues that "social inclusion is most commonly defined only *negatively* – as whatever is *not socially excluded*" (p. 397, emphasis in original). These discourses tend not to address forms of inclusion, power, and knowledge because attention is directed toward the Other. This play of visibility and invisibility is central to how the hood is signified. As Cameron highlights, any investigation of the hood must also explore the socially included sites that work to make the hood a marginal space.

The hood as dwelling place

The hood is a place of residence. It is where people live their lives in the most mundane of fashions: buying groceries, cooking meals, washing dishes, talking with friends, and all the other banal activities of life. These events comprise the fabric of any lived space and, moment to moment, vastly outnumber the spectacles and anomalies that produce a space as social exception. The question then is how does community as spectacle and carceral space, with all the resonances of Debord,[6] and the panopticism of Foucault,[7] recover itself as simply lived space?

Writing about another spectacular community, the world of the asylum and the project of deinstitutionalization, Robin Cooper (2005) offers an avenue toward producing the hood as a space of residence. Commenting on R. D. Laing's constructed community of the antiasylum at Kingsley Hall, Cooper notes that Laing's experimental community failed, in part, because it could not resist the social production of the community as a spectacular space. She tries to offer an alternative that addresses the specific material failings of Laing's project. Cooper starts by leaving the entire notion of asylum aside and instead discusses a space where "human beings reside ... a dwelling" (pp. 301–302).

Indeed, we might begin here. One of the authors in this volume, Kitossa (Chapter 6) suggests that we resist the seduction of the term "hood" with all its sociohistorical baggage. Instead, he argues that we need to produce new terminology that posits the space as mundane. This is not to step aside from the struggle of communities defined as hoods. Instead, it returns them to themselves as sites of daily material struggle with the force of lived experience as the grounds for political action.

Rather than producing the hood as a spectacular space – as dramatically evoked in many song lyrics and film images – Cooper (2005) proposes a focus on the "hospitality of dwelling" and an interest in "the ordinary and in ordinary human dwellings" (p. 302).

The space that Cooper and her colleagues have produced eschews the dramatic language of sociology and psychology with their pronouncements of social dysfunction as well as the heroic language of those who would rescue the hood from itself. There is a move, instead, toward the adoption of a language that operates on a local scale, what she calls ordinary language.

This should be distinguished from the language of reality or rationality referred to as normal down-to-earth speech, deployed by the worst ideological machine of capture within postmodern capital (this is to say, the discourse of the dominant masking itself as the language of the common).[8] Cooper refuses the role of resistance or "addressing ourselves too much to the tyranny of the other," by using terms such as the "hood." She uses the term "dwelling" because "dwelling is much more to do with us. With all of us" (p. 302). Cooper notes that Laing was insistent that "we should worry less about them and more about us." In a dwelling space, we enter somewhere that is constituted for us and by us. It is a space designed for our own purposes. Here, we can go through those effects we experience such as "fears, terrors and weaknesses" not as extraordinary events in need of social remediation, nor as tutelary events in which we can learn how to manage such feelings so that we can be better workers, lovers, students, and so on. Instead, the dwelling is a space in which we live such things "precisely because they are so day to day, so commonplace, so ordinary" (pp. 303–304).

This world of the ordinary, however, is largely obscured from our common perception by the machinery of global capitalism. Cooper suggests that the people who seek to live within what she and her colleagues call "dwelling spaces" have been served by life experience with a painful opportunity. They have been removed from the familiar through their social marginalization and "find themselves, in one way or another, isolated; alienated or disarticulated from *ordinary human belonging*" (Cooper, 2005, p. 304, emphasis in original). They have lost their "sure footedness" in the world and no longer know how to comfortably negotiate the social as though it were familiar. They hold themselves at constant risk of having no concrete sense of belonging and are, according to Cooper, homeless. Although they may have homes, there is no space that belongs to them.[9]

Cooper cites Goffman's work, describing the way psychiatric patients within the asylum create small spaces for themselves: along a wall, on top of a radiator, or a corner of the room. Such a space is defended against all comers with a fierce sense of territoriality. She suggests that the ability to have a space of one's own is central to the production of human dignity. We would argue that it is instead the rupture of desire within the carceral that demands a space, no matter how limited, for creative production. The patient in the corner refers to his space as an office, a space of work and production. The patient seated on the radiator has a space free of intrusion for his mental productions. This kind of space, which Cooper refers to as "free inhabitation within which … some patients are able to carve out for themselves some little pockets of free space in what is essentially occupied territory" (p. 307), has immense implications for the ways people living in "the hood" might take free inhabited space under a different set of territorial imperatives.

In trying to describe how a dwelling functions, Cooper tells a story of a resident who was sometimes so afraid that she would hide in her room. She would stay there in a state of high anxiety. However, while there,

> The sounds of the house waft up to her, they hold her, they place her. We can probably imagine, without too much difficulty, something of the complex chorus of concordant and discordant meanings that the house sings out. We could think of this as just one modality of what I would call the textures of the household into which a person (even the person who withdraws) becomes woven. This is the household, to use Winnicott's unforgettable phrase, "going on being."
>
> (p. 307)

Here we might think of those forgotten residents of the hood, those whose lives are notably mundane and whose fabric of community is composed of life together. We might propose that this life together is one fabric produced in the daily living of subjects together, infinite in capacity, woven out of time and space that "goes on being." The hood, exploded out of its carceral form, becomes specifically a desiring assemblage of bodies together in all states of affect, all modes of history, all compositions of personality, and all singular expressions of form. Creating such dwelling spaces of desire is, we would argue, a central political project of returning the hood to itself.

Revolutions and societies of friends

In their final book, *What is Philosophy?* Deleuze and Guattari (1994) reflect on what they term "geophilosophy;" that is, the relation between the earth and the concept. This relation is critical in our exploration of the production of the hood. How is the physical space of the hood related to its conceptual form? Deleuze and Guattari point out that the relation of any area of the earth to the conceptual frameworks produced on it, by it, and from it is complex. It is, they say, a process of territorialization and deterritorialization; the production of territories and peoples and their dissolution and reconstitution. The constant process of what they say is the immanent machinery of the earth as a relentless force of deterritorialization is composed of both the transcendent and immanent forces of the social world. Let us then situate the hood, historically, within this context.

In referring to the Holocaust, Deleuze and Guattari (1994) state that "There is indeed catastrophe" (p. 107). In our age, one might say that given the poverty, violence, and carceral status of the hood, it may well constitute a certain kind of catastrophe as well. But what exactly do Deleuze and Guattari mean by this term? They state that catastrophe consists of "the society of brothers or friends having undergone such an ordeal that brothers and friends can no longer look at each other or each at himself, without a 'weariness,' perhaps a 'mistrust'" (p. 107). The hood may be just such a product of catastrophe. Precisely, the catastrophe of colonialism and slavery morphing into the postcolonial settler colonies with their endemic racism and brutal policing of those constituted outside the anticulture of whiteness, affluence, and respectability. As in all carceral spaces, from the prison to the hood, a deep distrust is built between the inmates, the guards, and those citizens on the outside who support the prison in its existence and function. In a society premised on the denial of the traumas of the colonial enterprise and its subsequent formations within the realm of global capitalism, indeed a certain weariness and mistrust becomes the rule of the day. In this sense, the hood is emblematic but not solely constitutive of the catastrophe of the late capitalist empire and builds on the social diagrams of the camp, the prison, and the madhouse. Deleuze and Guattari, however, offer us a glimpse of something else when they say that this mistrust does "not suppress friendship but gives it its modern color" (p. 107).

Deleuze and Guattari (1994) suggest that our friendships are colored with shame. They argue that the history of human catastrophe that makes up the past 400 years cannot be remedied through "forming a universal opinion as 'consensus' able to moralize nations, States and the Market" (p. 107). This is because universal declarations, such as human rights, designed to protect us from catastrophe are premised in a system of law that can suspend such rights when they conflict with such things as property rights or the sovereignty of the state. As Deleuze and Guattari point out:

> Who but the police and armed forces that coexist with democracies can control and manage property and the deterritorialization-reterritorialization of shanty towns? What social democracy has not given the order to fire when the poor come out of their territory or ghetto?
>
> (p. 107)

Of course, this is where relationships and organizations such as the Black Panther Party form within the early apparitions of the hoods, the ghettos, as self-defense against catastrophe. Such friendships are composed of the very weariness and distrust noted above. The hood, one might argue, is indeed a nexus for these kinds of friendships.

Friendships formed through networks premised on distrust and exhaustion cannot provide us with a full explication of the productive possibilities of the hood. Deleuze and Guattari (1994) call for a revolution premised on creativity and what they term "resistance to the present" (p. 108). They say that we need a "future form … a new earth and a people that does not yet exist." Where might we find these new people? They suggest we investigate spaces such as those found in the abominable sufferings that they argue create a people through their "resistance to death, to servitude, to the intolerable, to shame and to the present" (p. 110). Where might we find the signs of such a coming people who do not yet exist? Deleuze and Guattari suggest that such traces can be found in books of philosophy and works of art that "also contain their sum of unimaginable sufferings that forewarn the advent of a people." They suggest that the revolution to come is more "geographical than historical" and will be composed of "societies of friends, societies of resistance because to create is to resist: pure becomings, pure events on the plane of immanence" (p. 110). Such a revolt, which produces itself in an infinitude of deterritorializations, is manifest here in all the creative forms of lived experience, works of the mind, and impressions of events and struggles. The revolution is produced through the creative force of all life within the bounded space of the hood itself. It is in the networks of self-production no longer constrained by the axiomatic discipline of the dominant media, the state, or the market. New societies of friends can be formed wherein resistance ceases to be against the forces of domination and control and becomes instead resistance for its own ends as a form of pure becoming. For this we must all become artists and philosophers. Not in the sense of academics or aesthetes but as those sets of social relations that produce concepts and new forms of life not seen before. This event needs to be explicated in any new politics of the hood as a liberatory space – as a space that produces liberation rather than a space from which one must be liberated.

Preview

The hood as lived practice

This collection is divided into two sections, each with a short introduction by the editors. The authors in this section question the notion of the hood by calling upon their own experiences and the documented experiences of others to explore how individuals and communities come to embody a lived practice. Each of the authors comes from a particular geography with specific concerns. They are from Canada, the United States, and Australia and they write about and from those locales at the same time commenting on the global forms of the hood such as the *favela*, the barrio, and what Morton and Smith call the spaces of precarious life such as tent cities and homeless encampments. They are activists, pedagogues, artists, and scholars. They consider the hood from multiple perspectives including class, race, gender, age, geography, and the very personal space of autoethnography.

Skott-Myhre begins by exploring the hood as a place both mundane and revolutionary. Deploying a textual and discursive analysis of Dead Prez's video "It's Bigger than Hip Hop," Skott-Myhre explores the connection between the absolute materiality of residence, where everyday activities vastly outnumber the spectacular events and the anomalies that produce a space as social exception. Focusing on Dead Prez's critique of capitalism's appropriation of hip hop, which obscures the lived experiences of what they term "Ghettos Everywhere," the chapter explores the possibilities inherent in Cooper's (2005) concept of the dwelling place. He proposes that rather than producing the hood as a spectacular space – as evoked in many song lyrics and film images – political interventions should focus on the "hospitality of dwelling" and take interest in "the ordinary and in ordinary human dwellings" (Cooper, 2005, p. 302). He uses the imagery and lyrics of the Dead Prez video to argue for the utility of valorizing those forgotten residents of the hood, those whose lives are notably mundane and whose fabric of community is composed of life together. He suggests that the video uses the discourse of materiality and lived experience as the ground for creating a dwelling place. Creating such "dwelling spaces," he argues, is a central political project of returning the hood to itself. To this end, Skott-Myhre explores Deleuze and Guattari's (1994) call for a revolution premised on creativity and what they term "resistance to the present" (p. 108). He draws connections between the iconic referencing of suffering and revolt in the Dead Prez video and Deleuze and Guattari's suggestion that we investigate spaces found in sufferings that create a people through their "resistance to death, to servitude, to the intolerable, to shame and to the present" (p. 110). He deploys an analysis of the video's lyrics and visual representations to make an argument that such a revolt is manifest in all the creative forms of lived experience, works of the mind, and impressions of events and struggles.

In Chapter 3, Muzzatti probes how an important distinction between lived experiences in "neighborhoods" and lived experiences in "hoods" is the fluid construction of ethnicity that is afforded to the latter. Whereas neighborhoods are constructed as rigid, stratified, homogeneous spaces of class privilege and comfort, he argues that "the hood" is a far more active site of class unrest and resistance. The pressures of marginalization in the hood foster alliances between ethnicities that are not possible in idyllic suburban life. The chapter employs autoethnographic methods to explore how the instability of the working- and under-classes leads to opportunities of shared spaces between ethnicities. A narrative about 1980s working-class Toronto depicts how shared spaces and the intersecting histories that inform them allow for sites where fugitive knowledge is shared, where cooperation is encouraged, and where ethnicity becomes less a restrictive border and more an avenue for resistance and collective acts of revolution.

In Chapter 4, Morton and Smith examine the questions surrounding how informal community settlements are mediated as social spaces under the conditions of globalization. They explore the mired acceptability of claiming territory through presence and human strength alone. They argue that the precariousness of life in contested social spaces pushes the boundaries of mobility and movement within the discourse of globalization theory. The chapter focuses on two recent examples of contemporary art that pushed the boundaries of "safe" social space: Robert Jelinek's "State of Sabotage" and Vessna Perunovich and Boja Vasic's "Parallel Worlds: The Architecture of Survival." Through interviews with Jelinek, Perunovich, and Vasic, the chapter probes their representations of informally settled communities and questions the ability of artistic intervention to foster critique without reproducing dominant frameworks. The insights gleaned from these artistic works are easily translatable to the global implications of using community, architecture, and movement as sites of resistance and survival.

In Chapter 5, Baker, Bennett, and Wise examine the status of Australia's Gold Coast. In the past 50 years, the region has grown from a cluster of scattered suburban towns into a thriving urban conurbation. The population of the Gold Coast, although still predominantly white and Anglo-Saxon, is becoming more ethnically and demographically diverse. Within this rapid socioeconomic change are vestiges of the original Gold Coast neighborhoods. Often sandwiched between the highway and the beach, many of these neighborhoods are literally fighting for survival as prospectors mark their ocean-side locations for Riviera style redevelopment. Notwithstanding such pressures and paradoxes, however, vibrant expressions of community can – and do – manifest themselves. Such manifestations are pluralistic – yet each in their own way portrays a sense of belonging. Alongside local expressions of community, the spatial construction of the region is also increasingly exposed to mediatized representations such as *The Strip*, a fictionalized television series that focuses on crime and other deviant underworlds in and around Surfers Paradise, the key tourism and entertainment district of the Gold Coast. This chapter considers how local groups negotiate the rapidly shifting physical and cultural landscapes of the region in an effort to assert and re-assert particular expressions and associated rituals of neighborhood and community.

Kitossa, in Chapter 6, examines "the ghetto" as an internal colony. In both academia and popular culture, "the hood," a euphemism for "the ghetto," is imagined to constitute particular spatial/political/geographical coordinates as well as behaviors and creative expressions. While this book is comfortable with the usage of "the hood," Kitossa refers to this real and imagined place as a "ghetto." He argues that something analytically vital (descriptive and normative) is lost in the translation when well-meaning outsiders publicly adopt the affectionate *lingua franca* of this place. Kitossa suggests that the habitus of the "ghetto," self-generating, dynamic, and creative, are adaptations to impositions from the state, capitalism, and white supremacy. Some have taken to imagining, even when meaning well, that the ghetto lacks a variety of capitals: cultural, social, and above all human. But, as Kitossa points out, the ghetto is not created and kept in existence by some happy accident, as much as liberalism would want us to believe it was. In structural terms, the ghetto exists in dynamic relation to centers of privilege and power that feed off it parasitically. To pursue this structural account of the ghetto as a place that constitutes capital, the chapter focuses on issues surrounding youth epidemiology and gangs.

In Chapter 7, Hollander and Hollander explore how modern cities throughout the world are facing population decline at an unprecedented scale and the implications of such changes for marginalized communities. The authors suggest that present-day notions of the hood will change as more and more of the urban American landscape is decimated by population loss. Over the past 50 years, 370 cities throughout the world with populations over 100,000 have shrunk by at least 10 percent. They describe these changing neighborhoods through the lens of community activists and the literacy artifacts they produce. They ask: what are the discourses and values embedded in the work of activists in the hood and how can that work be used in neighborhood classrooms to help empower youth? To answer this, the authors have collected literacy artifacts from community organizations, which include newsletters, brochures, historical notes, and webpages. They then employ critical discourse analysis in order to understand the key values, discourses, and subject positions made available by each literacy artifact. This research brings them to community-based organizations operating in three US cities with persistent population decline: Pittsburgh, Pennsylvania; New Bedford, Massachusetts; and Richmond, Virginia. Their analysis reveals how literacy artifacts can be used in the classroom to engage students in the challenges their cities face.

In Chapter 8, Nicol and Yee use autoethnography to investigate how two "girls" from Compton, which is often perceived as a breeding ground for gang members, drug dealers, and rappers, could earn doctorate degrees and become faculty members at the largest campus in the California State University system. This project describes how their experiences in Compton influence their attitudes toward education, their sense of community, and their politics. Nicole and Yee explore how they use these "teachable moments" to challenge students' assumptions about what life is like for people in "the hood" and to help students develop a multilayered and multidimensional examination of Compton in order to frame discussions about larger social issues. They recount how their stories, though rooted in the same geography, are neither identical nor common and have helped them form their particular habitus, which has been informed by their personal and familial experiences with poverty, racism, sexism, educational achievement, domestic violence, and drug addiction. The authors contend that Compton enriched their cultural and social capital by allowing them to become "bi-cultural," where they could enter and operate in a variety of social spaces and be able to communicate in the language of their particular audience.

Representing the hood in music, film, and art

In this section, we argue that the creative works produced within the hood and outside of it (re)present a cultural politics. These creative moments are infused into the debates about the lived hood, its residents' experiences, and the dominant power structures that surround it. None of the following authors would claim that representations of the hood are neutral. And through methodologies falling into the broad categories of textual analysis, critical discourse analysis, and ethnography, the authors interrogate how meanings circulate in relation to the hood through its representations and the political implications of these creations.

In Chapter 9, Richardson analyzes the rapper Tupac Shakur's popular single "Changes" (1998) to explore the habitus that the artist vocalizes. Through this reading, he demonstrates how Tupac's lyrics articulate the process of habitus formation as described by Bourdieu and interrogates how the recognition of a group habitus, like the one Tupac presents in the song, is an important step in the process of making concrete changes in the hood. Without a conscious recognition of such formations, Richardson argues, it is unlikely that the vicious cycles that the habitus of the hood tends to produce will ever be significantly altered. By exploring the contemporary rapper Nas's single "Black President" (2008), which samples Tupac's "Changes," Richardson looks at how the habitus that was being formed ten years earlier with Tupac continues to transform and adapt to new circumstances and social conditions as it is adopted by new artists. The chapter demonstrates how readings of a habitus described through hip hop and other popular forms of expression can help those both inside and outside the hood understand the way practices are established and outlooks are formed, perpetuated, and/or changed.

In Chapter 10, Britt examines the hood as both an evolving mobile entity and as a space for multiple temperaments through a reading of one of rap music's most malleable figures, Game (née Jayceon Terrell Taylor). Britt argues that Game has succeeded largely by defying music conventions that rely on the creation of an immutable, undefeatable distance between artist and audience, adherence to a narrow subgenre or geographical space, and/or a disavowal of musical forms that undermine the attempt to self-define. The author suggests that Game's formula for "realness" involves an ability to acknowledge the inherent mobility and mutability of the habitus of the hood. The chapter traces Game's career and how he constructs his claims with several illustrative measures of realness that feature his unique street virtues while self-reflexively exposing the commercial context and consequences of that persona. Although the primary focus of the chapter is Game, the author also explores the ownership of "realness" in modern rap to question the artistic worth and commercial staying power of hood icons in an increasingly segmented industry.

In Chapter 11, Sciurba examines the arguments for incorporating popular culture into school curricula. She investigates the notion that students, especially "urban" or "disenfranchised" students, will identify with the material that is taught and, consequently, become more deeply invested in their educations. This type of instruction falls under the "culturally relevant" umbrella, by which teachers are encouraged to tap into children's cultures to better meet students' educational needs. She points out that the theoretical basis of this discussion rests on assumptions about the "subversive" or counter-hegemonic nature of youth culture. What has not been considered, she argues, is the degree to which youth cultural interests are varied and that they often transform and may in fact produce resistance once they are used in the classroom. This chapter draws upon data collected from a national study on black and Latino adolescent males to analyze the ways in which youth cultural interests are (re)conceptualized in the classroom. It examines the degree to which there are differences in the perceptions of educators and students about the inclusion of popular culture in the classroom and the extent to which it contributes to student empowerment. The author seeks to understand whether elements of "pop culture" maintain their counter-countercultural stance once they become part of the school curriculum, and how the use of elements of popular culture mesh with contemporary ideas about the purpose of schooling.

In Chapter 12, deWaard considers the cycle of early-1990s hood films, particularly *Boyz N the Hood* (1991) and *Menace II Society* (1993), as operating primarily within the melodramatic mode. Beyond proving how versatile the melodramatic mode really is, these films use melodrama in two unique ways: First, they put the "melos" back in melodrama, argues deWaard, with hip hop playing a major role in establishing the hood chronotope (as well as providing intertextual "cross-pollination"). Second, these films shift that key concern of melodrama – the home – to the hood as a whole. deWaard demonstrates that the implications of such a shift are indicative of the issues facing the African-American urban community.

In Chapter 13, Mann looks at the death and resurrection of Chicago's hood in the American visual imagination. During the latter half of the twentieth century, most popular media coverage depicted Chicago's housing projects as a dystopia of crime and terminal poverty. Today, as the Plan for Transformation – the Chicago Housing Authority's (CHA) controversial urban renewal initiative – implodes the last of the city's public housing buildings, the first part of this chapter seeks to address the ways in which the projects have been mythologized in popular visual culture as sites that *deserve* to be razed. Mann first considers *Judgment Night* (1993), arguing that the film constructs public housing as a site of repression and social isolation through textual references to its cartography. She then compares it to the horror film *Candyman* (1992), which offers a more democratic vision of spatial justice. Smashing through *Judgment Night's* seemingly insurmountable sociospatial barriers, *Candyman* reconceptualizes public housing as a site of negotiation. Through this examination, Mann challenges notions of black sociopathy that render public housing residents "marginal to," existing "on the edges of" (West, 2002, p. 80), or "socially isolated" from the wider urban matrix (Wilson, 1989). Supported by onsite interviews conducted with activist groups who oppose the Plan for Transformation, the author highlights the need to recognize some tenants as "spatial actors" who mobilize, resist, and challenge by "using the space" of public housing as a productive site of social action (Gotham & Brumley, 2002; Gotham, 2003). In depicting Chicago's public housing as a fantastical psycho-topographical landscape where sociospatial divides *can* be conquered, *Candyman* demythologizes the one-dimensional mythological terrain of stereotypes, assumptions, and moral panics presented in *Judgment Night*.

In Chapter 14, Drissel examines the role of graffiti in urban areas, tracing the subcultural origins of the art form within America's inner-city neighborhoods, particularly those of New York City and Philadelphia. Emerging from a multifaceted environment of dwindling economic opportunities, urban renewal campaigns, racial stigmatization of "ghetto youth," and the widespread dissemination of hip hop/rap music, the practice of graffiti writing is examined as an underground phenomenon that is utilized for the purpose of framing resistance to urban spatial hegemonies. The importance of the local neighborhood to graffiti crews is addressed in this context. He explores the various reasons why many young people continue to engage in writing graffiti, given probable legal and social sanctions. Theories of deviance are considered in conceptualizing and assessing the subterranean values and collective identities of graffiti crews found in the hood.

Notes

1. "Habitus" was also used a number of times by Marcel Mauss (1872–1950) to describe *les techniques du corps* (body techniques).
2. Bourdieu (1984) argues that the evocation of lived experience "is most often merely a thinly disguised projection of the researcher's 'lived experience'" (p. 100). Though our experiences growing up in working-class neighborhoods east of Toronto and in Seattle may influence our work, we attempt to ground our understandings of residents' lived experiences through descriptions in literature,

music, art, and film. We also acknowledge that lived experiences are often represented through popular culture and popular culture often influences lived experiences. This distinction between lived experiences and mediated representations, therefore, may not be as easily recognizable as one might think.

3. Of course, this idea is not unique to Bourdieu. In *Philosophical Investigations* (1963), Wittgenstein wrote that "We also say of some people that they are transparent to us. It is, however, important as regards this observation that one human being can be a complete enigma to another. We learn this when we come into a strange country with entirely strange traditions; and, what is more, even given a mastery of the country's language. We do not *understand* the people. (And not because of not knowing what they are saying to themselves.) We cannot find our feet with them" (p. 223). Where Bourdieu becomes indispensable is in his theorization of *how* and *why* these differences and inabilities to understand others occur.

4. Whether or not gentrification in the hood is a positive or negative thing for residents is a separate debate that Freeman negotiates in his book.

5. Interestingly, in an interview conducted in 1992, West (1999b) speaks of the ironic occurrence that he should find such familiarity in a "radically secular Budapest-born Marxist [Lukacs] even though I come from 'the hood'" (p. 230). Whether this reflects a change in West's conceptualizing of the hood or if he is just poking fun at the idea that he comes from the hood is unclear.

6. We refer here to Debord's (1983) concept of late-stage capitalist society in which life becomes dominated by representations as spectacle or media event.

7. We refer here to Foucault's (1995) reading of Jeremy Bentham's panopticon as internalized discipline enforced through constant surveillance or the belief that one is under constant surveillance.

8. Bourdieu (1990) argues that often times the reclamation of slang or common speech perpetuates the distinction that leads to the dominant language remaining dominant. "Those who rebel against the effects of domination that are exercised through the use of the legitimate language often arrive at a sort of inversion of the relation of symbolic force and think they are doing the right thing by consecrating as such the dominated language, for instance in its most autonomous form, namely slang. This reversal from *for* to *against* ... is still an effect of domination" (p. 154, emphasis in original).

9. Said (1993) provides an important twist to this idea and reminds us that being a stranger (or homeless) in the world has advantages as well as disadvantages. Referring to a quotation from a twelfth-century monk, he writes that the person "who finds his homeland sweet is still a tender beginner; he to whom every soil is as his native one is already strong; but he is perfect to whom the entire world is as a foreign place" (p. 335). In other words, while feeling like a stranger in the world is often a horrible burden, it forces one to become critical of his or her surroundings which results in an attempt to change them for the better.

References

Bourdieu, P. (1984). *Distinction: A Social Critique of the Judgement of Taste.* (R. Nice, Trans.) Cambridge, MA: Harvard University Press.

Bourdieu, P. (1990). *In Other Words: Essays Towards a Reflexive Sociology.* (M. Adamson, Trans.) Stanford: Stanford University Press.

Bourdieu, P. (2007 [1977]). *Outline for a Theory of Practice.* (R. Nice, Trans.) Cambridge: Cambridge University Press.

Cameron, A. (2006). Geographies of Welfare and Exclusion: Social Inclusion and Exception. *Progress in Human Geography, 30* (3), 396–404.

Cooper, R. (2005). Seeking Asylum: R. D. Laing and the Therapeutic Community. In S. Raschid (Ed.), *R. D. Laign: Contemporary Perspectives* (pp. 297–312). London: Free Association Books.

Debord, G. (1983). *Society of the Spectacle.* (K. Knabb, Trans.) London: Rebel Press.

Deleuze, G., & Guattari, F. (1994). *What is Philosophy?* New York: Verso.

Foucault, M. (1995). *Discipline and Punish: The Birth of the Prison.* (A. Sheridan, Trans.) New York: Vintage Books.

Freeman, L. (2006). *There Goes the Hood: Views of Gentrification from the Ground Up.* Philadelphia: Temple University Press.

Gotham, K. F. (2003). Toward an Understanding of the Spatiality of Urban Poverty: The Urban Poor as Spatial Actors. *International Journal of Urban and Regional Research, 27* (3), 723–737.

Gotham, K.F. & Brumley, K. (2002). Using Space: Agency and Identity in a Public Housing Development. *City & Community,* 1 (3), 267–289.

Hagedorn, J. M. (Ed.). (2007). *Gangs in the Global City: Alternatives to Traditional Criminology.* Urbana: University of Illinois Press.

Said, E. W. (1993). *Culture and Imperialism.* New York: Vintage Books.

Wacquant, L. (2008). *Urban Outcasts: A Comparative Sociology of Advanced Marginality.* Cambridge: Polity Press.

West, C. (1999a). *Restoring Hope: Conversations on the Future of Black America.* Boston: Beacon Press.

West, C. (1999b). The Indispensability yet Insufficiency of Marxist Theory. In C. West, *The Cornel West Reader* (pp. 213–230). New York: Basic Civitas Books.

West, C. (2002). *Prophesy Deliverance!: An Afro-American Revolutionary Christianity.* Louisville, KY: Westminster John Knox Press.

West, C. (2008). *Hope on a Tightrope.* Carlsbad, CA: Smiley Books.

Wilson, W. J. (1989). The Underclass: Issues, Perspectives, and Public Policy, *The Annals of The American Academy of Political and Social Science,* 501, 182–192.

Wittgenstein, L. (1963). *Philosophical Investigations.* Malden, MA: Blackwell.

Part I

The Hood As Lived Practice

Chris Richardson and Hans A. Skott-Myhre

What does it mean to experience the hood as lived practice? To the authors in section one it is to live a geography of conflict, hybridity, contestation, creativity, survival, warfare, unrest, resistance, and the mundane. The authors in this section question the notion of the hood by calling upon their own experiences and the documented experiences of others to explore how individuals and communities come to embody a lived practice. Each of the authors comes from a particular geography with specific concerns. They are from Canada, the United States, and Australia and they write about and from those locales as well as commenting on the global forms of the hood such as the *favela*, the barrio, and the spaces of what Morton and Smith call precarious life such as tent cities and homeless encampments. They are activists, pedagogues, artists, and scholars and they consider the hood from multiple perspectives including class, race, gender, age, geography, and the very personal space of autoethnography.

Indeed, autoethnography is an important methodology within these writings. Muzzatti and Samarco (2006) argue that autoethnography provides authors with an opportunity to "explore the boundaries of their experiences … without being obliged to conform those experiences to prevailing conventions" (p. 3). For this reason, it is "an outsider's methodology" that works as an effective "tool for exploring difference and for offering resistance to dominant paradigms" (ibid.). Parker (2005) writes that autoethnographic narratives form a sense of identity that emerges "as 'figure' against the 'ground' of culturally given images of the self" (pp. 71–72). He asserts that "because individual lives are made possible by material conditions and social networks, the discussion of any particular narrative should connect with broader narratives" (p. 81). Therefore, while the authors speak to their own experiences, they also outline the situations that may arise as others work, live, and practice in the hood.

In his chapter, Muzzatti reflects on growing up in a working-class Italian "hood" in Toronto. He argues for a recovery of space lost to the abstractions of generalization and calls for recognition of class – not just race – as a defining factor in producing the hood. Skott-Myhre reflects on his own experience of moving into the hood with his family and how he came to know the hood as a living community full of revolutionary potential – a site of what Muzzatti calls fugitive knowledge. Nicol and Yee write of how their disparate and yet common experiences of growing up in the prototypical American hood shaped their identities as border dwellers constantly negotiating between the hood and their academic identities as Ph.D holding professors. Each of these authors calls for a recognition of the hood as a source of activism and liberatory possibility.

This sentiment is echoed in the activism promoted by the authors in this section who write from outside of the hood. In these works, the question of how the hood is represented in art, media, state ideology, and schooling becomes both constraining and full of alternative lines of force. Mortin and Smith take on our suggestion in the introduction that we should become artists in explicating the role of art as an activist enterprise that challenges outside state order by reclaiming the right of representation and claims to territory. Wise et al. challenge the ways in which hoods as spaces and places are configured in essentialist sorts of discourses. They discuss the world of young people on the Australian Gold Coast as a highly contested space made up of a hybridity of descriptions that shift and flow depending on the multiple constituencies that collide within that space. The question of who gets to define the space and whether any definition can hold within the current global social realm takes on significant meaning here. Kitossa delineates what he calls the hyper-hood, as a space of warfare in which global capital produces social decay. Within that decay, however, are forces of resiliency and resistance. For Hollander and Hollander the question of literacy and what role Frierian activism has for the hood is central to any discussion of lived experience.

In each author's work, we find the hood as a dynamic space of creative force that is built on a certain kind of survivorship and mutual suffering. The role of activism, personal experience, art, and day to day living are combined in this section to produce a portrait of the hood as a dwelling space and a site of liberation and revolution. It is a space appearing to be an established and inevitable site of social struggle in many discourses while also entering into a constant state of becoming and reinvention. Where the future of this dwelling space lies, none of these authors can say for certain. A cautious optimism, however, seems to be a common theme that runs throughout these projects.

References

Muzzatti, S. L., & Samarco, C. V. (Eds) (2006). *Reflections from the Wrong Side of the Tracks: Class, Identity, and the Working Class Experience in Academe.* Lanham: Rowman & Littlefield.

Parker, I. (2005). *Qualitative Psychology: Introducing Radical Research.* Berkshire: Open University Press.

Chapter 2

Resistance to the Present: Dead Prez

Hans A. Skott-Myhre

This predominantly African-American neighborhood in St. Paul was displaced in the 1960s by freeway construction. In the 1930s, Rondo Avenue was at the heart of St. Paul's largest black neighborhood. African-Americans whose families had lived in Minnesota for decades and others who were just arriving from the South made up a vibrant, vital community that was in many ways independent of the white society around it. The construction of I-94 in the 1960s shattered this tight-knit community, displaced thousands of African-Americans into a racially segregated city and a discriminatory housing market, and erased a now-legendary neighborhood.

(Minnesota Historical Society, 2009)

In 2000 I moved with my family into a large old Victorian house within the area of St Paul, Minnesota referred to locally as "the hood." We were a multiracial, multisexual, and multicultural assortment of adults and young people only some of whom were biologically related. The street onto which we moved was a mix of old established African-American families, gangs, drug dealers, and young families. There were cars that circled the block all night purchasing drugs, gunshots were heard at fairly regular intervals, people tended their gardens, took their children for walks, kids rode bikes, and people sat on their porches. Within the immediate few blocks, there was a barbeque joint, community agencies, community activists, a barber shop, an Afrocentric art gallery, a community market, grade school, and a local coffee shop that served as a community hub and gathering place. There were also crack houses and corner stores that were fronts for drug dealing and gambling.

The parade on Rondo

There were three events that occurred while we lived there that I will note as the chapter unfolds. The first event occurred a few months after we had moved in. One morning we awoke to the sound of a parade on the main thoroughfare one street over. We headed out the front door to see what was going on, only to discover that our street was full of people walking toward the park at the end of the street and to the parade. There were hundreds of people, 99 percent of whom were African-American. Our neighbors up and down the street were barbequing and the smell of roasting meat filled the air. The parade was full of African-American marching bands and dance groups, and went on for blocks and blocks with groups from all over the United States.

As the day proceeded, we learned that this was a celebration of the old Rondo neighborhood. Rondo Avenue was a street at the heart of a thriving self-contained black community that was destroyed by freeway construction in the 1960s. With its destruction, the community was split in two and its functional integrity significantly impacted. The residents displaced by the freeway found themselves unable to relocate in the heavily, although covertly, segregated city of St Paul. As a result, a diaspora occurred as residents left the city to find housing in black communities across the segregated United States. However, every year these former residents and their families return to St Paul to the old neighborhood in an affirmation of community continuity in the face of all odds.

On this day my neighbors set up tables in front of their homes with barbeque, pies, greens, cornbread, and chicken for the crowds that passed up our street to the park and school at the end of the block. In the park, old friends greeted each other and families were reunited as they strolled among booths with crafts and clothing, community agencies, and music.

In our introductory chapter, we asserted that the hood is a place of residence. We stated that it is where people live their lives in the most mundane of fashions: buying groceries, cooking meals, washing dishes, talking with friends, and all the other banal activities of living. Certainly, this was true of the hood as we experienced it. However, as Kitossa will assert later in his chapter, the hood as a term for neighborhood is one of two aspects that the geography of race has produced in these post-colonial times. The other aspect is that of the ghetto. Of course, both the hood and the ghetto are lived and embodied spaces that are the products of historical trajectories and social discourses. The geography composed of these lines of history and ordering definitions have delineated a machinic composition that produced both a life lived from within and a view from without.

In the age of industrial capitalism, the segregated communities composed of people of African descent functioned as an internally defined and enclosed space largely invisible to the dominant white culture surrounding it. In this aspect, it produced communities such as the Rondo neighborhood with tremendous integrity and social cohesion. The double aspect of segregation was the ghetto, which functioned as a space of exclusion and domination: a space bounded by the disciplinary codes of racism and brutal exploitation that were the hallmarks of colonial capitalism.

In the 1960s the configuration of the hood/ghetto doublet began a massive transformation as capitalism transitioned into its global and postmodern formations. While a detailed exposition of this shift in capitalism's configuration is beyond the scope of this brief chapter, several key elements are of particular interest here. The first is the complicated intersection of the discourse of civil rights and judicial challenges to the colonial structures of racism. This juridical reform is produced simultaneously with the continuance of functional racism in the absolute truncation of financial possibility for the black blue-collar worker. Put in another term, at precisely the moment that a public discourse was emerging that appeared to grant equal opportunity and rights to those African-Americans living in the ghetto, the functional capacity of neighborhoods to financially sustain themselves was placed under fatal assault.

What this meant was while civil rights leaders were petitioning the government for redress, legal representation, and protection, the communities from which these leaders derived were being destroyed in two ways. The first mode of community destruction occurred in the early to mid-sixties with the massive layoffs of black blue-collar workers all across the industrialized United States. Of course, this was a harbinger of what would come with the emergence of global capitalism. Black workers were clearly the canaries in the coalmines. As unrest grew in the neighborhoods and living conditions deteriorated as a result of this economic disenfranchisement, the economic distress was compounded by the literal destruction of housing infrastructure by freeways being put through the center of black communities across the United States, as well as what was euphemistically called "urban renewal."

Indeed, with the advent of emergent global capitalism, the functioning communities of African-Americans were eviscerated both economically and geographically, specifically at a time when they appeared to be obtaining their greatest degree of legal and civil rights. Of course, we can see in retrospect that this social diagram, first executed in these communities, was to become increasingly prevalent across the rest of the global capital. The wholesale destruction of the industrial working class, and increasingly the middle class, has spread to all sectors of American society. The obliteration of neighborhoods and collapse of housing infrastructure is now endemic. The resulting erosion of cultural integrity and the introduction of widespread violence, crime, drug addiction, familial dissolution, and corruption that marked the transition from the neighborhood to the hood is now found across all segments of American society. The most severe effects, however, are still being exercized on those areas with the longest history of socioeconomic disenfranchisement.[1]

It was Marx (1978) who noted early on that one of the inevitable results of capitalism was the destruction of the cultures it exploited. Hardt and Negri (2000) have noted that with the development of capitalism as a global empire, corruption is an integral component of rule. Capitalism as a thoroughly abstract system of value that produces, as Luhmann (1995) points out, a society that operates on a logic separate from living things and their interests has a long history of strip mining communities at every level. Indeed, one might argue that Agamben's (1998) notion of bare life or life that can be killed without protection or consequence is the ideal subject for capitalism's proliferation. In this sense, it is not surprising to find the hood/ghetto in both its aspect as social diagram and in its actuality as a living space resembling a clear-cut forest or an open pit mine. Without a doubt, the ecology of the community is filled with residual toxic waste and limited nutrients.

The question becomes how to rebuild a healthy ecology in the face of ongoing assaults on its functional integrity. It is in answer to this that I would like to make some preliminary proposals. To do this, I bring together a diverse and possibly unlikely combination of resources: a French philosopher, a French anti-psychiatrist, a Scottish psychoanalyst, and the hip hop duo Dead Prez.[2] I argue that what this heterogeneous array holds in common is an interest in recovering lived space from the abstractions of dominant systems – in particular capitalism. In this respect, each of them is a performer who, in his or her own vernacular, proposes and performs an alternative line of force leading into the fabric of lived space and the moment to moment, away from the spectacular events and anomalies that produce a space as social exception. The question at hand then is how does the hood/ghetto recover itself as lived space? Further, in what ways is lived space a revolution in and of itself?

Getting together, crossing borders

Here, I would like to return briefly to our own history of the hood and note another event that took place about a year after we had been there. Our neighbors had been friendly from a distance, but had not really engaged with us. Without a doubt we seemed a bit suspicious and decidedly not typical of the community. We were neither an old established black family nor affiliated with any illegal commerce. Instead, we were a fluid group of regularly shifting membership as we took in young people without stable homes, friends who had lost work or relationships, relatives in need of a place to stay, and, of course, our own core family of myself, my wife, and our children. At the height of the house we had upwards of twelve people living in assorted spaces (with one bathroom!).

One day, my neighbor from across the street, whom I guess one could call the patriarch of the block, came to the front door. When I answered, he declined to come in but said he had something to tell me. He told me that the neighbors had been watching us for the past year. They had noticed that we were taking care of kids who needed caring for. He told us that the neighborhood had decided that we were okay and that they would watch out for us. He shook my hand and left. We later learned that most of the established families on the block had thought we were pretty crazy to be the only white folks living in the hood and felt that we clearly needed looking out for, as we obviously had no sense. We were now living – not just residing – in the hood.

"Now that we have your attention": revolution as lived practice

In the video "It's Bigger Than Hip-Hop," Dead Prez presents an intricate weaving of critique and proposal that offers a vision of revolution as lived practice rather than spectacular political event. The video proposes a fundamental distinction between the commercial world of contemporary hip hop and the possibility of founding life as foundational revolutionary practice. Using neo-Garvian iconography to subvert the traditional hip-hop video format, Dead Prez presents an overtly political message that operates through a complex interweaving of bodies, lyrics, objects, and visual tropes. The images of gangster rap are taken and turned back on themselves beginning with the opening shot of a woman's hips as she slowly walks away accompanied by the sound of a radio bouncing across channels. The image is then frozen and digitized and the message "Now that we have your attention" is inserted into the frame that immediately breaks into the message in bold black on white:

"Ghettos Everywhere." This then cuts to a shot of three young black men with black and red kerchiefs worn more like Commander Zero of the Zapatistas than rap gangsters. The images throughout the video are stripped back to bare walls and open rooms, conveying archetypal Black Nationalist colors and slogans that deploy gangster rap iconography to convey a message deeply critical of the commercialization of the hip hop video form.

> Shit is real out here, don't believe those videos
> This fake ass industry gotta pay to get a song on the radio
> Really though DP'z gon' let you know
> It's just a game of pimps and hoes
> And it's all 'bout who you know
> Not who we are or how we grow

It is this juxtaposition of lived experience and mediated popular culture that is of particular interest. There is a call throughout the video for attention to the actual struggles of real people within the black community rather than what they call the "slave ship" of the capitalist media machine. Dead Prez calls for a materialist reading of the black community as it is lived under conditions of economic disenfranchisement and what they have referred to as open warfare with the police designated to monitor and control the ghetto. Notable here is the replacement of the term "hood" with "ghetto" in a step away from the spectacular media circus of film, music, and video that comprises the geography of black experience. Clearly, at times Dead Prez is reaching back to the Black Nationalist movements of the nineteenth and twentieth century in order to deconstruct and reassemble them as a new kind of politics premised in the question of how to live now.

In his interview with Antonio Negri, "Control and Becoming," Gilles Deleuze (1995) raises the importance of creating a people on the basis of the creative force of day to day interactions. He states that what "we lack most is a belief in the world, we've quite lost the world, it's been taken from us" (p. 176). Dead Prez echoes this in their reading of commercialized hip hop as a discourse emptied of all substance related to the actuality of ghetto life and struggle.

> Back the beats, it don't reflect on how many records get sold
> On sex, drugs, and rock and roll, whether your project put on hold
> In the real world, these just people with ideas
> They just like you and me and when the smoke and camera disappear
> Again the real world (world), it's bigger than all these fake ass records

The ghost in the machine here is, of course, capitalism and its appropriation of the creative impetus of that which is and was rap and hip hop. Certainly the function of capital as a kind of social machinery that takes the active material productions of living subjects and turns their force into thoroughly mediated abstraction that operates directly in opposition to the best interests of those it appropriates has been delineated by Marx and his postmodern antecedents Foucault, Deleuze and Guattari, and Hardt and Negri among others. Here, however, we have a critique from within the community of those directly impacted by this appropriation. What might possibly be an artistic response to Spivak's inquiry as to whether the subaltern can speak.[3]

Geophilosophy and the hood

The loss of what Dead Prez calls the real world is precisely the slippage that Deleuze and Guattari (1994) reflect on when they explore what they term geophilosophy; that is, the relation between the earth and the concept. What is the relation between the geography of the ghetto and the concept of the hood as spectacular media event? What is at stake in the production of the hood as an abstraction that deploys the creative impetus of resistance itself to produce capital? Deleuze and Guattari point out that the relation of any area of the earth to the conceptual frameworks produced on it, by it, and from it is complex. It is, they say, a process of territorialization and deterritorialization – the production of territories and peoples and their dissolution and reconstitution. The constant process of what they say is the immanent machinery of the earth as a relentless force of deterritorialization is composed of both the transcendent and immanent forces of the social world.

In the case of the hood as a site of immanent production, or production through the lived creative force of those bodies within that geography (i.e., the productions of life itself), we have what Dead Prez refer to as, "do what you got to do." That is to say, the actual engagement with the struggles for survival demonstrated throughout the video by the flash screens that state "gotta eat" and "welfare ain't working" or by the repetitive clips of a crowd waving a placard that calls for "food, shelter, clothing." It is the drive for survival and the creative force of people in struggle that initially produced rap and hip hop as music forms which can be connected to the long history of struggle for survival of peoples subject to the dominant rule of the evolving forms of global colonial and postmodern capitalism.

This immanent force, however, is dissembled and reproduced as a world of what Dead Prez refer to as a "fake thug r & b rap scenario, same scenes in the video, monotonous material." It is the transcendent world of the purely symbolic money form in which the actual world of poverty and struggle for survival is reproduced as a fantasy land of "Lexuses" and "necklaces." In a singularly powerful verse, Dead Prez state:

> These record labels slang our tapes like dope
> You can be next in line and signed, and still be writing lines and broke
> Would you rather have a Lexus, some justice, a dream or some substance?
> A beamer, a necklace or freedom?

The juxtaposition and complex interplay of the world of abstraction and delusion signified through dope and money underscores the common addictive properties of both as systems that promise, but do not deliver, a way out of the ghetto and its struggles. It is on this terrain that we enter the central discourse of "Bigger than Hip Hop." Through acknowledgment of the deterritorializing force of capitalism and the music industry on the geography of the ghetto, Dead Prez propose an alternative discourse that reterritorializes a new organizing set of concepts with the possibility of revolutionary force or in Deleuzian terms the capacity to seize back the world.

Taking back the world

It is interesting to note that the video operates its critique and proposals at two distinct levels. The critique is offered in the lyrics, while the proposal is carried visually throughout. This split between the role of language in developing a critique of the world of capital-driven media as spectacular event and the use of iconography, placards, photos, slogans, and bodies in motion and collaboration (dancing, doing martial arts, laughing, shouting) carries within it an acknowledgment of the importance of acts in addition to articulation. The combination of an alternate iconography that challenges the status-driven imagery of capitalist hip hop with a linguistic pastiche of spoken word and polemic signage and bodies engaged in both community and self-construction produces the video as a multilayered challenge to the single-minded consumption-driven imagery of the music industry video. For example, there are shots of crowds of people dancing together including children, men, and women who are dressed simply, carrying placards calling for "food, shelter and clothing," while Dead Prez exhorts the crowd over a megaphone with the lyrics of the critique, interspersed with full-screen signage carrying political slogans such as "their system does not work for us," and Polaroid shots of people's faces with statements underneath them such as "needs food."

The early part of the video makes a powerful case regarding the poverty, violence, and carceral status of the hood. The critique of media-driven hip hop speaks to the catastrophe that is the assault by the dominant capitalist system as a process of personal, cultural, and community bankruptcy. In referring to the Holocaust, Deleuze and Guattari (1994) state that, "There is indeed catastrophe" (p. 107). But what exactly do Deleuze and Guattari mean by this term? They state that catastrophe consists of "the society of brothers or friends having undergone such an ordeal that brothers and friends can no longer look at each other or each at himself, without a 'weariness,' perhaps a 'mistrust'" (p. 107). The critique leveled by Dead Prez against the hood as media event may be just such a product of catastrophe. It is, of course, the catastrophe of drugs, violence, and nihilistic consumption. However, perhaps even more pressing in the work of Dead Prez is the catastrophe of relations disrupted and community capacity deferred or eviscerated. It is the disruption of the potential and possibilities of bodies together that is at stake here. In the early part of the video the weariness and mistrust between those Deleuze and Guattari refer to as "brothers[4] and friends" is addressed as a question of survival in a war zone. The trope of the warrior as a mode of self-defense is deployed in place of the gangster. Where the gangster is positioned specifically as the penultimate figure of paranoia and lack who misapprehends the nature of the threat and turns his violence against his own community, the warrior in the video is exhorted to "know yourself" and "know your enemy." In this sense, there is an acknowledgment of the wisdom of distrust and vigilance but only if, as Deleuze and Guattari say, this mistrust does "not suppress friendship but gives it its modern color" (p. 107).

What is the modern color of friendship proposed by Dead Prez? It is an immanent or self-productive set of relations that operates in the thoroughly material realm of those actions that protect, valorize, and celebrate life. In this sense, there is no appeal in the video to an outside such as money, government programs, or legal recourse as a mode of escape. This position, it could be argued, is because, as Deleuze and Guattari point out, the history of human catastrophe that makes up the past four hundred years cannot be remedied through "forming a universal opinion as 'consensus' able to moralize nations, States and the Market" (p. 107). Universal declarations designed to protect us from catastrophe, such as human rights, are premised in a system of law that can suspend such rights when they conflict with such things as property rights or the sovereignty of the state. As Deleuze and Guattari point out, "Who but the police and armed forces that coexist with democracies can control and manage property and the deterritorialization-reterritorialization of shanty towns? What social democracy has not given the order to fire when the poor come out of their territory or ghetto" (p. 107).

Dead Prez draw directly on this contestation between the representatives of the dominant state form (i.e., the police) and the history of resistance and self-defense represented by groups such as the Black Panther Party whose imagery appears throughout the video. However, friendships premised solely or primarily on self-defense and protection are recipes for disaster and self-immolation. While survival is necessary as a basic ground for capacity, it cannot provide us with a full explication of the productive possibilities of the hood. This is another lesson in the dichotomy of the warrior vs. the gangster. The tradition of the warrior as portrayed in the video involves a production of the self through the mastery of the self, "strength," "endurance," "rhythm," "balance," and last of all, "power." This is a revolution of subjectivity that exceeds the limits of self-defense. It requires what Foucault (1971) called for when he proposed that the first political task is to undo the "habits and beliefs of one's own age" within oneself. Here the call is for a reconstitution of the subject through bodies together in mutual transformation as warriors not gangsters.

Deleuze and Guattari (1994) call for a revolution premised in creativity and what they term "resistance to the present" (p. 108). Clearly, "Bigger than Hip Hop" is calling for just that. In eschewing what can only be termed in the strongest Gramscian sense of the word, the false consciousness of "fake thug videos," Dead Prez is proposing the production in the hood of what Deleuze and Guattari refer to as a "future form … a new earth and a people that does not yet exist."

Like Deleuze and Guattari, "Bigger than Hip Hop" draws its impetus and inspiration from an investigation into spaces that are founded in what Deleuze and Guattari (1994) call abominable sufferings, where a people are created through their "resistance to death, to servitude, to the intolerable, to shame and to the present" (p. 110). This is very clearly the space of "ghettos everywhere" under the conditions of capitalist appropriation and exploitation. The video is what Deleuze and Guattari refer to as a trace that "contain(s) their sum of unimaginable sufferings that forewarn the advent of a people." In this trace, the community of those living together under these conditions constitutes a revolution to come that is more "geographical than historical" and composed of "societies of friends, societies of resistance because to create is to resist" (p. 110). The revolt proposed by Dead Prez is manifest in all the creative forms of lived experience, works of the mind, and impressions of events and struggles. The revolution is produced through the creative force of all life within the bounded space of life under domination itself. It is in the networks of self-production no longer constrained by the axiomatic discipline of the dominant media, the state, or the market.

Dwelling spaces

In what way does this revolt of the creative force of bodies together formulate a new relation to the geography of space that is the historical doublet of the hood/ghetto? One possible response is to be found in the lineage of anti-psychiatrist R. D. Laing. Robin Cooper (2005) who worked with Laing in producing alternative living spaces outside psychiatric incarceration, argues that central to any reterritorialization of a carceral space is a sense of a "space where human beings reside … a dwelling" (pp. 301–302). That is to say, in order to reclaim a geography of oppression and appropriation, there must be a functional re-alignment of the space that reconstitutes it as a place where the central function becomes for life to reside there and produce itself. Quite clearly, life can exist under extremely adverse conditions and produce itself in the face of ongoing genocidal assault. This is the history and legacy of the hood/ghetto doublet. Indeed, like any other ecology that is threatened by cataclysmic intrusions and extractions, life continues to find spaces in which to extend itself in the cracks and corners of the terrain in question. So, to reclaim the "lost world … taken from us," as Deleuze and Guattari suggest, it is not necessary to produce something that does not exist. Instead, what becomes the necessary political act is an extension of modes of living truncated or marginalized by the dominant overlay of abstract value. That is to say, to create spaces in which dwelling can occur and new societies of friends can be produced.

Cooper (2005) suggests that this can be done through engaging an interest in "the ordinary and in ordinary human dwellings" (p. 302); that is to say a focus on the actualities of daily living. She argues that it is important to adopt language that focuses on a local scale in describing the geography of dwelling. In another term, this is what Dead Prez is referring to by what they call "real world" that emerges when all the media constructions are removed.

41

Cooper also calls for a repudiation of heroic language in favor of a discourse of the ordinary in the construction of a dwelling space. She argues that since it is in the lived experience of the mundane that dwelling is produced, language which reflects that kind of life holds more force than the hyperbolic language structures of the heroic form. Here, it might be argued that with the calls for warrior training Dead Prez is engaging in a polemic of the spectacular. Without a doubt, the video deploys highly charged and polemical injunctions that use metaphors of war and self-defense. However, this rhetoric is tempered by the repeated reminders borrowed from the martial arts displayed in the video that call for self-discipline and the building of a community premised on the realities of life as lived together.

At another level, however, one must account for the experiential difference in the work of Dead Prez and Cooper that are projected in the use of certain tropes and linguistic conventions. The production of free and alternative living spaces for those deemed psychiatrically marginal as in Cooper's project, while a profound and difficult struggle, seldom involves the casualty rate suffered by residents of the hood/ghetto. To respond to the conditions of an undeclared and unacknowledged war zone may require a language that appears from the outside to be spectacular when, in fact, it is the ordinary day to day speech of battle.

In relation to struggle and forces of outside domination, Cooper (2005) calls for a dwelling space to be a geography that refuses the role of resistance or "addressing ourselves too much to the tyranny of the other." She argues for dwelling as a term "that is much more to do with us. With all of us" (p. 302). Cooper notes that Laing was insistent that "we should worry less about them and more about us." In a dwelling space, we enter somewhere that is constituted for us and by us. It is a space designed for our own purposes. The dwelling is a space in which to live through experiences "precisely because they are so day to day, so commonplace, so ordinary" (Cooper, 2005, pp. 303–304).

Clearly, there is merit in this proposal. Too many revolutionary movements have become reactionary precisely because they spent far too much time resisting and far too little time creating spaces where dwelling could occur. That said, as we have noted previously, "Bigger Than Hip Hop" operates at two levels; the critique and call for resistance as well as a proposal for reconstituting subjectivity in a way that would allow for ordinary living. However, it is important to note the double nature of the geography that is the hood/ghetto. It is both a space of ordinary life and a space of war and struggle for survival. In this sense, the trope of martial arts deployed throughout the latter half of the video is particularly appropriate. Martial arts is a form developed during periods of political instability and threat. Such arts are designed to function at multiple layers, as a mode of self-defense, a healing regime, and a mode of self-reflection. In a war zone one must be able to defend oneself so as to survive, however, it is equally important to cultivate oneself and one's community for a world to come. In a zone of conflict, I would argue, this ceases to be resistance as an act of agency and instead engages resistance in the Foucauldian sense: the inevitable and simultaneous response of life to subjugation. To live in such a way as to repudiate addiction and valorize self-cultivation, to refuse alienation in favor of bodies creating together, to step away from mindless consumption toward a production of common desire are all acts of resistance that are not against an outside but towards a production of dwelling.

Cooper (2005) also proposes a focus on the "hospitality of dwelling," by which she means an open and accepting invitation to dwell together. The impetus to live in a dwelling space of the ordinary and mundane in which one might seek a space in which the "balance" and "rhythm" of life suggested by Dead Prez might be re-established or produced is a response to life on the margins. Cooper suggests that to be forced to the margins of the social is to be presented with what she terms a painful opportunity. She argues that such subjects "find themselves, in one way or another, isolated; alienated or disarticulated from *ordinary human belonging*" (p. 304, emphasis in original). They have lost their "sure footedness" in the world and no longer know how to comfortably negotiate the social as though it were familiar. They hold themselves at constant risk of having no concrete sense of belonging and are, according to Cooper, homeless. Although they may have homes there is no space that belongs to them.[5]

Clearly, in the world of the ghetto there may be homes but in the central areas of the war zone these seldom constitute any concrete sense of belonging. Indeed, to live in a zone under constant surveillance and threat most certainly unsettles any sense of "sure footedness." Hence, the call by Dead Prez for not simply a rhetoric of revolutionary response but the reconfiguration of the rhythms and habits of the body and mind in a collective bid for re-appropriating a sense of lived community. The dominant culture will never serve as a template for "ordinary human belonging" and so a new space of belonging must be produced. This is the iconography in the video of all the bodies collectively acting together in a form redolent with Hardt and Negri's (2005) concept of the multitude. That is, a collectivity of subjects each operating out of his or her own singular creative force for the good of a common project. Such a form always holds itself as open and hospitable for dwelling.

As we have noted, Deleuze and Guattari (1994) cite the important relation between geography and the concept of a people to come or a new world. In the production of dwelling, geography and space also hold a central function. Cooper talks about how psychiatric patients take small spaces for themselves within the institution: along a wall, on top of a radiator, a corner of the room. She discusses how such a space is defended against all comers with a fierce sense of territoriality. We have already discussed the role of self-defense in the rhetoric and proposal's of the Dead Prez video and certainly the defense of a space of one's own is a central component. In a very interesting way, however, it is not just physical space, as in the asylum, but the very space of subjectivity and creative force that is being re-appropriated. It is, in this sense, more than self-defense of a territory claimed because the territory is one that has been emptied by media-driven capitalism and produced as a fantasy. In this sense, the Dead Prez proposal is a re-assertion of the actuality of the space, an active production of the realities of struggle and ordinary life. Cooper (2005) refers to claimed space within the institution as "free inhabitation within which … some patients are able to carve out for themselves some little pockets of free space in what is essentially occupied territory." In the case of the ghetto/hood doublet the capacity to carve spaces of the mundane into the landscape of the spectacular has immense implications for the ways people living in "the hood" might take free inhabited space under a different set of territorial imperatives. This is the new terrain of "free inhabitation" constituted within "Bigger than Hip Hop."

Conclusion

In the opening of this chapter, I shared vignettes of my life in the "hood." Parades, barbecues, neighborly interactions, and the sharing of one's home may not seem the stuff of revolution. Indeed, as the video points out, there are stronger and more complex strategies of the mundane to be deployed. However, I would argue that without the underpinnings of daily interactions of bodies successfully achieving the living of the mundane, no revolution is worth its struggle.

In closing, I would like to add one last event to our own history in the hood. The final story is about my next-door neighbor and took place about two years after we had moved in. I was sitting on my front porch drinking beer and watching life go by. My neighbor walked up to the porch steps and initiated a conversation. This was pleasantly surprising as we had waved to each other but never spoken. I invited him up on the porch to join me for a beer. He came up and we sat and drank for a minute in silence. After a bit, my neighbor, a black man of fifty or so, said that this was the first time he had ever been on a white man's porch. It seemed okay, he said. In fact, sometime in the future he might even work up the courage to go inside the house.[6]

Like the video I would like to propose here that it is specifically a focus on those forgotten residents of the hood, those whose lives are notably mundane and whose fabric of community is composed of life together that is crucial and imbedded throughout the Dead Prez video in Polaroid camera shots, the collectivity of bodies, and the call for clothing, food, and shelter. It is the desire to live and persist in living that is central and irreducible. The hood, exploded out of its carceral form, becomes specifically a desiring assemblage of bodies together in all states of affect, all modes of history, all compositions of personality, and all singular expressions of form. Creating such dwelling spaces of desire is, I would argue, a central political project of returning the hood to itself.

Notes

1. Of course, this includes similar configurations with unique histories of struggle such as the Rez and the Barrio.
2. There will be some who will suggest that this array is inherently suspect and runs the risk of incurring the kind of critique leveled by Spivak against French intellectuals theorizing about

subaltern groups and their capacities. However, I think that the tools offered by the pastiche of unlikely comrades holds a force worthy of explication.

3. I am referring here to Spivak's (1988) argument that groups who, under colonial conditions, have only mediated access to power, are unable to articulate their desires in their own language. Spivak argues that whenever they speak, the mediation by the group in power will always translate what they say into the dominant vernacular seriously compromising if not evacuating its original meaning.

4. It is important to note that the term "brothers" in Deleuze and Guattari has a very problematic gender exclusion. The video on the other hand overtly is inclusive of women as central performers as martial artists, head shots, and members of the crowd. They are portrayed as both powerful and dynamic throughout the video in obvious contradistinction to their roles in the traditional hip hop format.

5. Said (1993) provides an important twist to this idea and reminds us that being a stranger (or homeless) in the world has advantages as well as disadvantages. In a quotation from Hugo that he uses in *Culture and Imperialism*, he writes "the person who finds his homeland sweet is still a tender beginner; he to whom every soil is as his native one is already strong; but he is perfect to whom the entire world is as a foreign place" (p. 335). In other words, while feeling a stranger in the world is often a horrible burden, it forces one to become critical of his or her surroundings and attempt to change them for them better.

6. Indeed, it was a year before he did come inside the house. We were having a party and invited him. He came, got a beer, and walked straight through the house from the front door to the back. It seemed to take a lot of courage.

References

Agamben, G. (1998). *Homo Sacer: Sovereign Power and Bare Life*. Stanford, CA: Stanford University Press.

Cooper, R. (2005). Seeking Asylum: R. D. Laing and the Therapeutic Community. In S. Raschid (Ed.), *R. D. Laing: Contemporary Perspectives* (pp. 297–312). London: Free Association Books.

Deleuze, G. (1995). *Negotiations: 1972–1990*. (M. Joughlin Trans.) New York: Columbia University Press.

Deleuze, G., & Guattari, F. (1987). *A Thousand Plateaus: Capitalism and Schizophrenia*. Minneapolis: University of Minnesota Press.

Deleuze, G & Guattari, F. (1994). *What is Philosophy?* London: Verso.

Foucault, M. (1971) *Human nature: Justice vs power*. Retrieved from http://www.chomsky.info/debates/1971xxxx.htm. (Retrieved August 12, 2010.)

Hardt, M., & Negri, A. (2000). *Empire*. Cambridge, MA.: Harvard University Press.

Hardt, M. and Negri, N. (2005). *Multitude: War and Democracy in the Age of Empire*. New York: Penguin.

Luhmann, N. (1995). *Social Systems. Writing Science*. Stanford, CA: Stanford University Press.

Marx, K. (1978). "The German Ideology Part One." In R. C. Tucker (Ed.), *The Marx-Engles Reader* (pp. 146–202). New York: Norton.

Minnesota Historical Society. (1990). Rondo Neighborhood and the Building of I-94, http://www.mnhs.org/library/tips/history_topics/112rondo.html (accessed August 3, 2011).

Spivak, G. (1988) "Can the Subaltern Speak." In C. Nelson and L. Grossberg (Eds), *Marxism and the Interpretation of Culture* (pp. 271–316). Urbana: University of Illinois Press.

Chapter 3

Sì Siamo Italiani!:[1] Ethnocultural Identity, Class Consciousness, and Anarchic Sensibilities in an Italian-Canadian Working-Class Enclave

Stephen L. Muzzatti

Only slowly did I understand that if some of my most banal reactions were often misinterpreted, it was often because the manner – tone, voice, gestures, facial expressions, etc. – in which I sometimes manifested them, a mixture of aggressiveness, shyness and a growling, even furious bluntness, might be taken at face value, in other words, in a sense too seriously, and that it contrasted so much with the distant assurance of well-born Parisians that it always threatened to give the appearance of uncontrolled, querulous violence to reflex and sometimes purely ritual transgressions of the conventions and commonplaces of academic or intellectual routine.

(Bourdieu, 2007, p. 89)

In the late 1980s, American minister Robert Fulghum published his collection of short essays titled, *All I Really Need to Know I Learned in Kindergarten* (1988). Axioms such as, "Play fair," "Put things back where you found them," and "Clean up your own mess" from the lead essay are frequently cited (often unknowingly, without attribution, or indeed, even knowledge of the source) and circulate widely on the Internet. At best folksy and saccharine and at worst downright trite, Fulghum's "pearls of wisdom" no doubt occupy a place of honor alongside recyclable episodes of *Oprah* and *Dr. Phil* and on the ambiguous "Religion & Spirituality" shelves of used bookstores. They are, however, an interesting, useful, and admittedly convenient starting point for this chapter; how the habitus of my "hood" set the stage for the critical sociology and social justice work that has come to define not only my work as a university professor, but my practices in everyday/night life.

I, like Bourdieu (2007), am cautious of autobiography as a conventional, illusory, and self-indulgent practice. As such, I have attempted to avoid it, instead offering what he terms a "self-socioanalysis" (p. 1). My approach takes the form of a retrospective autoethnography; specifically, it is a narrative through which I hope to provide some insight into the collective habitus of a group of young, first-generation Italian-Canadian working-class men in Toronto's Keele and Eglinton neighborhood during the 1980s and early 1990s. The use of personal narratives to qualitatively flesh out the intricacies of systemic order is a useful tool for exploring difference, and for understanding tastes, attitudes, and behaviors. It is also, perhaps most significantly, a strategy for offering resistance to dominant paradigms; in this case paradigms of working-class immigrant neighborhoods as bastions of violence, drugs, and crime. Ferrell (2011) theorizes that such narratives are both an account of oneself and one's own experiences, as well as an account of the particular social situation and physical spaces in which those experiences occur. Following the insights of Bourdieu and Ferrell,

I am acutely cognizant that the process of constructing such a narrative occurs *in situ* – embedded in particular places and situations – and these spaces and conditions that the authors choose to occupy, or in which they find themselves caught, define their accounts of self and self-experience.[2]

As Richardson and Skott-Mhyre's introductory essay in this collection illustrates with great aplomb, habitus (re)creates the "hood," teaching insiders and outsiders how to see, classify, work within, and understand it. Rather than addressing the specifics of the mediascape's highly problematic scripting of working-class Italians in North America as criminals (e.g., *The Godfather, The Sopranos*), good hearted but dodgy scam-artists (e.g., *My Cousin Vinny, Boiler Room*), or vacuous narcissists (e.g., *Growing Up Gotti, Jersey Shore*), this chapter focuses on a vital uncovering of truths hidden not only by the corporately owned mass media, but also by traditional academic discourses.

Throughout this chapter, I use "I," but in reality I am writing of a "we;" John, Rob, Giuliano, Sal, Martin, Sandro, Dino, Vince, Marcello, Peter, Dave, Giacomo, Franco, Joe, Nunzio, Chris, Danny, Livio, Nick, and a dozen or more other friends and neighbors. It is as much reclamation of us as it is an analysis of the habitus of our hood. I position us as subjects in society rather than the passive objects of someone else's history, thereby becoming the "text," rather than the "footnotes" of history (Presdee, 1992). As such, I hope to illustrate the habitus of the hood as an active site of unrest and resistance. In my experience, the marginalization of the hood's residents in combination with a highly controlled yet unstable situation fosters alliances and creates opportunities for spaces where fugitive knowledges are shared, where cooperation is encouraged, and where ethnicity becomes less a restrictive border than an avenue for resistance and collective transgression (Muzzatti, 2010).

The sections that follow are organized around the major themes of antiracism, masculinity, class-consciousness, and anticonsumerism that permeated the habitus of my hood. Neither fully comprehensive, nor wholly chronological, they are anchored in anecdotes which continue to inform my life and work as well as that of many of my neighborhood friends and family. More so than seeing these as simply entertaining (and possibly offensive) anecdotes, I hope that the reader will be able to read within them particular intersections of biography and history, self and society, that illuminate the paradoxical lives of young men caught "in-between" spatial, economic, as well as ethnocultural lines.

Italiani Nel Mondo:[3] Italy to Toronto

I am the child of Italian immigrants. My mother's family languished for several years under Benito Mussolini's brutal fascist rule until they were able to flee Pisa for Toronto in the late 1930s. She was the only child of a truck driver and seamstress and grew up in a small flat near Ossington and Dupont. Though her parents were committed anti-Fascists in Italy and regular readers of Antonio Gramsci's socialist weekly *Ordine Nuovo*, the family was treated with considerable suspicion by the Canadian government. While on the whole they did not suffer as greatly as the Japanese (see Sugiman, 2009), Italians experienced significant discrimination and state violence during the war. My grandparents were regularly harassed by the police and my grandmother's brother-in-law was interred as an "Enemy Alien" for a year and a half despite the fact that he had lived in Canada for almost twenty years before the war began.

My father's family were poor tenant farmers, known as *farmioglo* or *contadino* from Bannia, a rural village in the Friuli region of northeastern Italy. Unlike my mother and her family who paid a heavy price, as did other "undesirable" immigrants in the "Dominion of Canada," my father and his family became what is now euphemistically referred to as "collateral damage" – the fate of civilian populations during the war in Italy (see Lamberti & Fortunati, 2009). His family suffered acutely as Udine, an industrial city located nearby, was heavily bombed, alternately by the American, British, and German forces, over the course of the war. Bannia bore a heavy toll because it was alleged to be the home of many "communists," my grandfather included. Their village was routinely pillaged by German and Italian Fascist troops and *Squadristi* (blackshirted pro-Fascist militias) who delighted in terrorizing the populace and stealing what little food they had. Any resistance, or indeed, any behavior deemed "un-cooperative" on the part of villagers was met with vicious brutality by the soldiers. Among the village's numerous dead was the family's oldest child, Edda, then only a teenage girl. My father's earliest memories involve running into the fields with his siblings and hiding as Fascist troops entered the village, or trembling with fear at the realization that the "thunder" they heard was a column of tanks rolling toward them from ten kilometers away. In 1951 my father, his parents, and his surviving siblings immigrated to Toronto and shortly thereafter set up a home at Keele and St. Clair.

The Toronto of the 1950s that my parents grew up in bore little resemblance to the diverse cosmopolitan city today. The Census Metropolitan Area's population was barely over one million with fewer than 9,000 foreign-born Italians residing in the City of Toronto (Census Canada, 1961; Iacovetta, 1992). Put bluntly, it was very white, very British, and not an easy place to live if you were a working-class Italian immigrant. At this time, the Orange Order was still prominent in business, politics and civic life; paraded openly; and among other things elected most of Toronto's mayors into the 1950s (Wilson, 2007). Like many Italian newcomers of that generation, including the parents of my neighborhood friends, my parents and grandparents suffered from bigotry, prejudice, and discrimination at the hands of these *Inglese*.[4] My mother's parents both struggled to find work. They literally had doors slammed in their faces, and in one instance were thrown bodily from the premises of a business because of the pervasive anti-immigrant/anti-Italian sentiment. My grandfather eventually found work driving and operating a cement-mixer, a job he held until he retired 30 years later. My grandmother held a succession of domestic jobs, primarily cleaning the houses of wealthy *Inglese* before she was able to secure work in a garment factory located in what is now Toronto's Entertainment District. My paternal grandfather originally worked on a farm north of the city in what is now Vaughan, but soon entered the construction trade as a bricklayer because the pay was better and the work allowed him to remain closer to home. My grandmother, by this time the mother of nine children ranging in age from late teens to toddlers, understandably, worked only sporadically outside the home. In addition to being the primary caregiver, she worked both "legally" as a part-time cleaning lady at a Catholic church in the neighborhood and participated in the informal economy, primarily taking in mending, washing, and preparing packed lunches for many of the single Italian-immigrant men who lived nearby or worked on sites with my grandfather.

Like their parents and my father's older siblings, both my mum and my dad faced considerable discrimination and violence. As a man, my father endured more frequent physical attacks, though my mum was often harassed, threatened, and was on a few occasions set upon by *Inglese* girls. Even mundane activities such as walking to the corner shop or waiting on a street corner were potentially dangerous; at best they were verbally assailed as "Wops" or "I-Tys," and at worst they were accosted and assaulted (see also DeMaria-Harney, 1999 and Stanger-Ross, 2009). Not surprisingly, neither of my parents completed high school – pushed out of Ontario's public education system as a result of a vicious blend of a language barrier, discrimination (at the hands of teachers as well as other students), and economic necessity. Both my parents had been working for several years, my mum in a factory making flatware, my dad as a plasterer/painter when they met. They married in 1958 and rented a series of small flats before eventually moving into the basement of a small semidetached house near Keele and Eglinton with my maternal grandparents in 1963. I was born several years later.

Ragazzi:[5] growing up in the Italian hood

Painful as these experiences were for my parents, and for other Italian immigrants of their generation in our neighborhood, they did not, for the most part, breed long-term resentment or bitterness. Instead their experiences instilled in them a plethora of virtues and valuable lessons; among them solidarity, cooperation and mutual aid, tolerance, compassion, respect for human dignity, and a belief in the importance of lifting those around you as you climb. As I explore, it was this set of beliefs, proclivities, and associated tastes and manners that constituted the habitus of my hood.

When I was growing up in the 1980s, Keele and Eglinton was not Toronto's Little Italy, nor for that matter was it the "new Little Italy" that emerged at Dufferin and St. Clair, and it certainly was not Woodbridge – but our neighborhood was heavily populated by postwar Italian immigrant families. It was a neighborhood where working-class immigrants both lived and worked. The industrial track to the immediate north-east provided many factory jobs for both men and women. The City of Toronto's Ingram Transfer Station (i.e., garbage dump and incinerator) and the adjacent York Steel mill employed a virtual army of Italian sanitation and steel workers. So too, what was then called Northwestern General Hospital's housekeeping, maintenance, shipping-receiving, food-service, and central stores departments were all heavily staffed by Italian immigrants.[6] It was a neighborhood that was acutely class conscious – one where labor activism and ethnicity blended into one (Iacovetta, 1992). As grade school children, we aspired to employment at the nearby Hilroy Paper plant, Canada Post's local station or the Snyder furniture factory – and the concomitant union memberships because that was the work-life of our parents, neighbors, and *paesani*. The neighborhood was a vibrant, exciting place, where neighbors knew each other and helped each other. One rarely saw contractors' vans parked on the streets during the day because most people did their own roof repair, masonry, plumbing, drywall, or electrical work. And if they could not do the work themselves, they certainly had a cousin, in-law, *paesan*, or *compare* who could.[7] It was a neighborhood where people who had lawns took great pride in them and where the garden was as much a vital source of fresh fruits and vegetables (pears, apples, plums, tomatoes, beans, scarolla, peppers, radicchio, zucchini, and cucumbers) as it was a place of recreation, kinship, and intergenerational cooperation. It was a place in which we first-generation Canadians explored and negotiated the tenets of social justice and praxis along with the implications of our "Italian-ness."

Though a few of my friends were born in Italy, most, like me, were Canadian-born children of Italian immigrants. Regardless of our country of birth, acquiring "Italian-ness" was easy. As Bourdieu (1998) notes, in a differentiated society like the 1980's Toronto, our ethnicity was *a percipi*: a perceived quality that functioned as positive symbolic capital in our neighborhood. As young men, it seemed as though almost everyone we knew was Italian. Our clothes came from Albina's Smart Fashions, shoes from Calzolaio Veneto, bread from Commisso Bros and Racco Bakery, produce from Lanzarotta grocers, other staples from Darrigo's Supermarket. The doctor's office was Italian. Church was Italian. The bank was Italian. Given as we were to the typical misbehaviors of working-class male youth, we discovered relatively quickly that the Metro Police were not Italian – though thankfully our parents knew lawyers who were. In short, it was some time before we realized that the majority of Toronto's population was not Italian, nor were all Toronto's Italians working-class folks who lived in our neighborhood.

Speaking Italian to our parents and grandparents, patronizing Italian businesses, utilizing Italian professional services, buying Italian goods, receiving home delivery of the *Corriere Canadese*,[8] hanging an Italian flag and shouting "*Forza Azzurri*" during World Cup constituted the seamless and routinized process of our tutelage in Italian-ness. Far more subtle and nuanced, though no less ever-present was our socialization in the values our parents paired with their identity as working-class Italian immigrants: peace, solidarity, and resistance.

La Gente Soffrono Più Di Noi:[9] standing together

My parents' direct experience with the suffering that war and imperialism inflicts upon civilian populations significantly influenced the ways they conceptualized the State, other recent immigrants to Canada, and racialized peoples, and played a major role in the ways they interacted with these entities and social groups. As I noted in the previous section, while postwar Italian immigrants constituted the largest single group in my neighborhood, it was quite ethnically diverse, comprised almost entirely of immigrant families. Although we literally lived next door to the Joneses, a Canadian-born couple who were senior citizens, most of the other "non-Italians" were more recent immigrants from Latin America and the Caribbean. Fewer in number but still a presence were Asian, Middle-Eastern, and North-African immigrants.

My experiences growing up in the neighborhood starkly contradicted the images of Italians as overtly xenophobic if not racist that feature prominently in Hollywood-generated mediations. While sheer numbers and a common first language determined that the majority of my parents' friends were other Italians, they had many close friends with whom they frequently socialized from the aforementioned groups. As a child, I was taught that the "non-Italians" in the neighborhood were the same as us. For my parents, it was always *il popolo* (the people), never *quelle personi* ("those" people).[10] As the title of this section indicates, my parents believed, correctly or not, that civilian populations in contemporary wars, particularly those in Central America, suffered even more greatly than we did when Nazis and *squadristi* ran roughshod over Italy and proto-Fascists congregated in Toronto's Orange Halls. Hence, in addition to a shared economic condition as working class, my parents empathized with the experiences of peoples displaced by military conflicts and colonialism.

My parents also recognized the power of whiteness. They knew that despite their status as immigrants and our class disadvantages, our whiteness afforded power and some protection. Because my mum spent all but her infancy in Toronto, she eventually spoke English fluently, though always with a slight Italian accent because it was her first language and the language spoken in the home with her parents. Because my dad immigrated in his early teens and had virtually no formal education in Canada, he spoke English somewhat haltingly with a pronounced Friulan accent. For them, literally remaining silent (i.e., not speaking) or when necessary, only whispering in public places such as while riding the bus masked their otherness, allowing others only to see whiteness – and hence "Canadianess."[11] This knowledge, reassuring in that it offered them some respite, also saddened them because they knew it was not something their racialized friends, either immigrant or Canadian born, could rely upon.

As a preteen, long before the school board instituted any form of "antiracist" curriculum, my parents, in various ways attempted to illustrate for me the subtle and insidious ways racism manifested itself. While many of these examples came from American televisions' lifeworlds, such as the ghettoized-buffoonery of George Jefferson, the wild (or rarely, noble) savagery of First Nations in rerun Westerns and the caricature of wrestling's "Hossein the Arab," others were Canadian-grown and much closer to home, like the complete absence of racialized players in the NHL or as teachers at my schools. Possibly one of the most powerful lessons in white privilege that I received involved my dad and his friend Shig. Shig was a friend and workmate of my dad's for almost 40 years. He was of Japanese descent, but was born in Canada – in an internment camp in Alberta where the Canadian government imprisoned his parents during World War II (see Sugiman, 2009). In and of itself, the story of Shig's parents would have been a powerful lesson in state racism, but it was made all the more poignant around the time that I was fourteen years old. Unable to work "legally," I frequently accompanied my father to work during the summer and on weekends for which he paid me out of his wage. I learned some useful skills, made a bit of money, and one day, caught a revealing glimpse of white privilege and normalized racism. At the end of the day, when my dad, Shig, and I were standing on the street talking about hockey, we were approached by a man whom my dad recognized as another worker from the area but whom he did not know personally. He joined the conversation and after a few minutes turned to Shig and, in a complete nonsequitor, stated, "You speak English very well. How long have you lived in Canada?" Shig, whose first language was English, and who spoke only a little French, and no Japanese, responded nonchalantly, "Oh, I was born here," before turning back to the topic of conversation. My father began to say something to the man, but was cut off by Shig's stern glance and the speed with which he resumed talking about the Toronto Maple Leafs. During the ride home, my dad and I discussed the incident, white privilege, and his deference to Shig's "non-confrontational" response.

As a sociology undergraduate in the late 1980s and early 1990s, many of the lessons learned from my parents about racism in Canada were reinforced. Critically examining Canadian immigration policy, globalization, ethnographic methods, standpoint epistemology, identity politics, and similar perspectives resulted in a more sophisticated and nuanced comprehension of the issue, though I always saw it as supplemental to the first-hand fugitive knowledges I had gleaned in my hood.

Recordate Millecinquecento E Undici:[12] the State and the working class

On the morning of February 27, 1511, thousands of starving peasants, artisans, and militiamen in Udine surrounded and then burned the Della Torre Palace. As word of the event spread, peasants throughout Friuli attacked rural castles and the nobles who resided within them. By the time the revolt was put down a few weeks later by the Venetian cavalry, approximately 50 nobles and a large number of their retainers had been killed, their corpses dismembered and fed to animals. My father loved this story and told it to me many times, in part because it coincided with my birthday. I think that he also liked the story of this peasant uprising and its vicious suppression because it helped him understand the reasons Friuli languished from the Renaissance through the middle of the twentieth century as "one of the most backwardly agrarian and feudal areas in northern Italy" in the words of one American historian (Muir, 1998, p. xxi). Ultimately, I think he liked this story because it was a metaphor for the State's relationship with its vulnerable populations. My father knew that his relationship to the State was not the same as that of the Friulan peasants to the nobles of the Venetian Republic, or any of the numerous overlords that ruled the region since then, but he also knew that four-and-a-half centuries of "advancement" in civic life and "democracy" did little to significantly alter the fundamental power imbalance between the rulers and working people.

My parents loved being Italian and enthusiastically embraced many aspects of the habitus that they formed through this identity. However, they felt no affinity for the State of Italy, even when it was at its most politically "progressive." It was for this reason, more so even than their financial hardships, that they never returned to Italy for a holiday. So too, they loved being in Canada, and eventually, as did three out of four of my grandparents, took Canadian citizenship. "*Canada è la mia casa*" (Canada is my home) they would say. My mum and dad enjoyed, in some respects, a folksy sort of "Canadiana;" Pierre Burton, hockey, *Front Page Challenge*, fishing, *Royal Canadian Air Farce*, Don Harron's comical "Charlie Farquharson" character, and car trips to Niagara Falls. But they were ever suspicious of the State and the elite, particularly the way they treated working-class people, immigrants, and racialized people at home and abroad. They detested Prime Minister Brian Mulroney and US President Ronald Regan, openly referring to them as *fascisti*. They also disliked several Italian-Canadian politicians, such as John Nunziata, Michael Colle, and Joseph Volpe whom they viewed as opportunists who used their ethnic heritage to garner votes, but did little for their working-class constituents once elected.

War and militarism, the most obvious manifestations of the State as violence, were things very close to my parents, and to many Italians of their generation in the neighborhood. As children, neither I, nor any of my friends were ever permitted to have toy guns, nor allowed to play "war." While there was no way around the former prohibition, we sometimes, at least when we were younger, circumvented the latter – provided we were beyond the gaze of our parents and grandparents. Avoiding the gaze of adults, however, was often difficult. When I was nine or ten years old, Signora Lucci, the mother of two neighborhood boys that were friends of mine caught us playing war in a parking lot when she was returning from work. She screamed at us, taking off her shoe and proceeding to hit me, her sons, and at least two or three other boys until some of us gathered our wits enough to run away. I ran toward my home crying, in part because her blows hurt, but perhaps equally so because I knew that I had done wrong – very wrong. As I approached home, I deliberately slowed in an attempt to obscure evidence of tears and red eyes. I did not want to be asked about why I had been crying. To this day I am not sure if the physical evidence of my pain and shame showed; Signora Lucci, even dragging her two sons and one other boy with her, had arrived at her home and telephoned my mother before I got to my house. Upon entering, I was repeatedly spanked with a wooden mixing spoon by my mother while my grandmother shouted encouragement – "*Cattivo! Vergogna te.*"[13] And though I do not remember all of the details, I do recall that several of my friends suffered similar fates.

That night, after my father had returned home from work and we finished our supper, my parents sat me down for a long talk about the day's events. I understood, as best as a nine or ten year old child could, that war was horrible and not something out of which a game should be made. In the days before sophisticated videogame consoles and slick, "Fight with the Canadian Armed Forces" TV commercials, playing war, like playing "cops and robbers" or "cowboys and Indians" was a gender-specific exercise in socialization that normalized, legitimized, and indeed glorified the violence of the State. It also, as I will endeavor to briefly illustrate below, potentially had a very specific class dynamic that my parents, Signora Lucci, and other postwar Italian immigrants in the neighborhood were not prepared to leave unchallenged (see Presdee 2006, 2009).

Because World War II was so central to the experiences of people from my parents' and grandparents' generations, Remembrance Day was always treated with great solemnity in our neighborhood. Wherever we were, regardless of what we were doing, people stopped at 11 O'clock for two minutes of silence. For several years when I was young, neighbors walked en masse to York's Borough Hall[14] on Eglinton just west of Keele for wreath-laying ceremonies. They were emotional ceremonies that brought many of the adults I knew, both men and women, to tears. Many of us cried too, not because we knew anyone killed in war, but because we saw the suffering of our parents and grandparents, and extrapolated from that the suffering of people in El Salvador, Nicaragua, Panama, Somalia, and other places ravaged by war in any given year. When I was about twelve, following a Remembrance Day service that we watched on TV, my mum gave me one of the most emotionally charged pieces of advice she ever imparted. I vividly recall that she turned off the TV and asked that I come to sit on her lap. I felt somewhat uncomfortable, thinking that I was "too big" to sit on my mum's lap because I was almost a teenager. After some brief posturing, I acquiesced, though not without some affectation. I quickly knew it was serious and ceased my adolescent resistance when she took my chin in her hand and turned my head toward her. Tears welling in her eyes, she said in a quavering voice that she tried to steel, "Look at me. Listen. Never, never … no matter what they say, no matter what they promise or threaten … never go into the military. The military is where boys like you go to kill and die for rich men. Promise me you'll never go into the military."

That event, perhaps more so than all the other discussions of war's atrocities before or since, solidified my antiwar resolve. While I will not self-aggrandize by calling myself a "peace activist," an antimilitarism praxis has been a core element of my life since I was a teenager. To this day I rip down or otherwise vandalize any piece of military recruitment propaganda I see, usually surreptitiously, but occasionally with great dramatic flare, including those that appear on my own university's campus. As a professor, I have written and publicly lectured about war and other forms of State violence. Recognizing my own position of privilege, and well aware of the class dynamics and economic imperatives that govern the lives of some of my students, I have on every occasion in which the matter has arisen, spoken privately with them in an attempt to dissuade them from enlisting in the armed forces. These activities did not make me particularly popular during my time as a professor in the United States between 2001–2004, even among some of my "liberal" sociology colleagues. Indeed, while not the only reason, America's proclivity to war was a significant factor in my decision to return to Toronto and the vicinity of my old hood.

Io Lavoro Con Le Mie Mani:[15] aspirations to "manliness"

Most of the men in my neighborhood, including all of my friends' fathers were skilled tradespeople. Their job skills were not simply employed while they were "on the clock," but also utilized in their homes and in the neighborhood on evenings and weekends. These proficiencies were also defining elements of who they were as men, both in their own eyes and in those of the neighborhood's multiple audiences. Our fathers repaired and maintained our homes and vehicles, renovated long before Home & Garden Television's (HGTV's) hyperconsumption ethos made it a "lifestyle" requisite, and on occasion undertook to fix public infrastructure in the neighborhood that they felt the city was unduly remiss in completing or had done, in their opinion, "improperly." As such it is not surprising that as young boys we grew up acquiring both some of these trade skills and adopting the definitions of working-class Italian manliness of which they were such a vital component.

We learned from our parents at a very young age that because tools were "very expensive" and essential to our fathers' livelihoods (more so than because they were "dangerous") they were to be treated with respect. By the time we were in Grade 6 most of us had experience using hand tools, and a few of us had even ventured to use small power tools. Because there was no "real" work that we could do with the tools we began to conceive of "projects" to build. Though we all fantasized about building tree houses like the ones enjoyed by the upper-middle-class kids who populated TV's lifeworlds, we soon abandoned the notion, resigned to the facts that our backyards were too small, that the only trees we had were fruit trees – which none of our parents would allow us to potentially damage with hammering and climbing – and that even if we concentrated our efforts we were never going to be able to "steal" enough pressboard and lumber from our garages to construct anything bigger than a large bird house. Instead, we spent a couple of weeks that summer digging a hole in the "forest;" two brush-covered vacant lots surrounded by a three-foot barbed wire fence adjacent to my friend Danny's house. It was not a tree house, but we got to use men's tools – shovels, a pick, a wheelbarrow, and a sledgehammer. We schemed for a few days about using a jackhammer that one of my friend's father owned, but dropped the matter when we realized that while we might be able to sneak off with the jackhammer, there was no way to use the compressor needed to operate it without getting caught. Once the hole was completed, it measured several feet in diameter and was over six feet deep. At some point during the process we decided that we would cover it with branches and sticks in an effort to conceal it as we saw in TV programs about stoneage trappers and hunters. Our prey was not mastodon, but three Grade 9 boys, Sabino, Joe, and Peter who regularly bullied and occasionally beat the shit out of us. We knew that they often snuck onto the property at night to drink and smoke and we wished that they would fall into the hole and break their bloody necks. For better or worse, it never happened and a few months later during a moment of pre-adolescent impetuousness, we decided to fill in our hole.

Over the course of the next several years, despite our best intentions and a modicum of effort, outside of a few lopsided hockey nets and some small ramps for bicycle and skateboard jumps, none of us really built anything. We did, however, work extensively on our bicycles; swapping out seats, forks, and handlebars, eventually becoming competent enough to change sprockets and adjust the gearing – but little else. In retrospect, I realize that the same working-class habitus that spawned our dreams of "building things" and doing "men's work" all but determined that such things would not come to pass when we were adolescents. The adults never trusted us enough to do this kind of unsupervised work around the house – nor, to be fair, should they have. Though we had the desire, we did not have sufficient skills. And unlike the upper-middle-class kids we saw on TV, or indeed real-life kids that lived outside our hood in more affluent areas of Toronto, we simply did not have the money to buy the supplies we needed to make motorized go-carts, let alone a place to ride them.

In a process indicative of the education system's class bias, most of the kids I grew up with were pushed out of secondary school (MacLeod, 1987; Muzzatti and Samarco, 2006). Few of the boys and only slightly more of the girls in my neighborhood ever completed their Ontario Secondary School Diploma. Of the almost two-dozen guys with whom I regularly socialized, only two others were able to enroll in university, and just one other graduated.[16] Pushed out of formal education before the prospect of university, or indeed even community college could materialize, most of my friends began informal apprenticeships with their fathers, uncles or older siblings, eventually acquiring the skills to which we all aspired.

In the years between high school and university the dynamic tension between positive and negative cultural capital grew immensely. By the standards of the neighborhood my friends developed and refined valuable skills of plastering, drywalling, and framing, flushing transmissions and rebuilding carburetors, laying pipe and repairing furnaces. Not unlike Willis' (1977) "lads" they embodied masculinity, particularly an aggressive sharpness of wit, creativity, and defiance (pp. 99–106). In this arena, I languished – in their eyes submitting myself to the authority of the biased education system and pretentious tweed-coated, pipe-smoking professors. My developing skills as a researcher and writer, while not truly negative cultural capital in their eyes, simultaneously marked a muting of my true self and lost opportunities at gaining the positive social capital valued in our neighborhood. It took several years for even three of my four closest friends to fully understand what I was doing at university. They eventually realized, more through my community organizing, op-ed pieces, and occasional radio interviews and TV appearances than my "scholarship" that my academic endeavors were not given to esoterica (e.g., "The Gothic tradition was neither 'gothic,' nor a 'tradition.' Discuss."), but instead focused on promoting in word and in deed many of the values that marked the habitus of our neighborhood.

Now, most of my friends have long-established careers as skilled tradespeople. Included among them are a few mechanics, a building maintenance man, a construction supervisor, a HVAC repairman, a mason, a tile-fitter, an electrician, and a carpenter (see Willis, 1977). Though I am far more adept *con la mie mani*[17] than any of my university colleagues and do quite a bit of my own home and motorcycle maintenance, I am woefully inept compared to my friends and our fathers.

One night a few years ago, several of us from the neighborhood were hanging out in a coffee shop. As it frequently does, the conversation turned to the vicissitudes of late modernity, as we lamented the banality and viciousness of lifestyle consumerism. It was late, we were all tired, and inevitably the wildly speculative, profanity-laced discussion of, "When the revolution comes ..." ensued. We quickly established that everyone at the table but me would bring much-needed skills to the new socialist utopia. After a few minutes of searching in vain for a role that I could play, they collectively determined that my talents would best be put to use scavenging dumpsters, collecting wood, and growing the tomatoes – as they begrudgingly (with tongues firmly planted in their cheeks) admitted that I had in fact gained and retained some valuable social capital from the hood.

Il Giardino:[18] environmental stewardship and sustainability in the hood

Early on a Saturday morning several weeks ago one of my elderly neighbors' sons, Jim, himself a Canadian-born child of Greek immigrants was on the roof of his parents' home two houses over from mine replacing broken shingles. Standing in my backyard I called out to him and we bantered for a few minutes, mainly about the poor performances of our respective Greek and Italian soccer squads in the recent World Cup. From his vantage point two stories up, he had a very good view of my backyard and complimented me on the "big [vegetable] garden." He qualified further, saying that, "Gardening is in your blood, eh!" As Bourdieu theorizes, for Jim, our habitus normalized the practice of raising vegetables, making it appear as though it was an innate part of being Italian, when it was in fact a product of the economic necessity and cultural traditions of families in my hood.

For as long as I can remember, our family has raised vegetables in the backyard (and the front yard, until a city by-law officer enforcing the middle-class domestic aesthetic repeatedly threatened us with a fine). Every spring I was enlisted to help my parents and maternal grandparents prepare the soil. As a very young child, my duties were somewhat limited – laying out sticks for beans and tomatoes, untangling the hose, moving empty pots about, and similar "gopher" duties. As I grew older, my responsibilities increased to turning over the soil, digging trenches, and carrying the 20L mosto pails in which we collected rain water. So too, by the time I was in my early teens, the physical work of gardening was augmented by an imparting of edaphological folk knowledge (e.g., "This is why the finocchio should be planted here this year, not over there like we did last year"), the logic of neighborhood agrarian bartering (e.g., "Signora DiSanti always plants too much Swiss chard and gives us her surplus. We should plant less Swiss chard this year and instead use the extra space for more arugula"), and an understanding of global commodities markets (e.g., "We have eleven rows of green peppers so that we will be able to can them – because in February they cost $3.99/kg at the grocery store").

We practiced what is today fashionably called "organic gardening." We used neither pesticides/herbicides nor chemical fertilizers not because they were too expensive (though relative to my family's income, they were) but because they were unnecessary and unhealthy. My grandfather in particular was adamantly opposed to the use of what he called *veleno* (which is literally translated from Italian as "poison," but which he used as a catch-all term for commercially engineered pesticides). His favorite adage on the matter was, "*Se si uccide un insetto che ti uccidera*" (loosely, "If it will kill a bug, it will eventually kill you"). My mum once rhetorically added that some of the same companies, such as Dow that produced chemical garden sprays also made chemical weapons used in wars. Weeds were pulled by hand, except chiccoria, some of which was allowed to "grow wild" for salads, while vermin and insects were kept away by the strategic location of certain herbs (e.g., chives and rosemary) and homemade liquid mixtures of crushed hot peppers and vinegar. Likewise, replenishing the soil every couple of years was accomplished "naturally." While we occasionally would travel to a farm north of Highway 7 to collect manure from a farmer my dad knew, we usually simply tilled-under a winter cover crop, such as rye, a few weeks before our annual May planting. We also used our own compost, which, before the city made compost bins available, entailed keeping our food scraps in a homemade trunk my father constructed from salvaged sheet metal, cinder blocks, and 2x4s in the backyard. Affectionately referred to by us as "the slop pile," this compost heap proved a valuable source of soil-enriching nutrients, and was soon adopted by several of our neighbors.

In addition to our vegetable garden, we had several homemade planter and window boxes in which we grew herbs like parsimmon, oregano, and basil, as well as certain varieties of lettuce and some smaller plants such as tiny tim tomatoes. In addition to allowing us to reserve our somewhat limited garden space for more "vital crops" (like the aforementioned green peppers), these boxes afforded us the opportunity to bring plants inside, and hence to extend the growing season. We also had some fruit trees, but fewer than most of our neighbors. As in the case of the vegetables, fruit was freely exchanged with neighbors.[19] For example, we had apples and pears which we gave to the Boffos next door, who in turn gave us cherries and grapes. We made a particular point to give produce to people we knew in the apartments up the street who did not have gardens. Over the course of the winter, in a practice one may be more likely to expect of a rural community in the early 1900s than of a late twentieth-century working-class hood, neighbors exchanged among themselves seeds they saved from their biggest and best plants.

Now that I have my own home, I continue to garden avidly, even though as a university professor I am, demographically at least, exactly the type of bourgeois prat to whom costly commercially produced "organic" vegetables are marketed and whom one might expect to see overpaying for fruit at a "specialty" grocery store. For me, gardening is not an economic necessity as it was for my parents, but it is certainly more economical than the aforementioned consumer follies. It is also equally, if not more, politically and environmentally sound now than it was when I was growing up. I currently have a fairly large garden, a few fruit trees, and almost two dozen planters and pots (a number that seems to increase incrementally year by year, and at present is threatening to encroach upon my neighbors' half of our shared drive). Over the last several years, a combination of good planning and cooperative weather has meant that I am only using the last of the canned, dried, and frozen vegetables from the previous season just as this year's batches mature. I typically also have enough to freely share with my neighbors, many of whom also have gardens, and reciprocate in kind. Like my parents, I make a point to give produce to people without gardens. Of course, Toronto's climate necessitates that I buy some of my produce. However, whenever possible, I only purchase locally (or "Ontario") grown produce – and ideally through local vendors at nearby Toronto West Flea Market. Ultimately, I enjoy gardening because it keeps me connected to the memory of my parents, facilitates relationships with my neighbors, and allows me, in a very small way, to resist massive grocery conglomerates and multinational agribusinesses. In short, it is yet another way I maintain the ties to my working-class Italian heritage.

Non È Mai Scompare:[20] concluding remarks

The quotation from Bourdieu that opens this chapter succinctly encapsulates the relationship I have had with most of my colleagues, and even much of the discipline of sociology in my "university life." As the site of the internalization of externality and the externalization of internality, the multiple habituses of my colleagues, myself, and the university intersect and transmogrify into a conflagration wherein any true liberty of thought or deed on my part is scripted and marginalized as "fugitive."

Early in my career as a professor, I sometimes resorted to "silence" both as a form of resistance and self-preservation in my interactions with senior colleagues and administrators. Like my suddenly quiet-as-mice parents riding Toronto's public transit pretending to be "Canadian," I thought that by not talking I could obfuscate my habitus. It did not work. Apparently my actions spoke louder than the words I consciously stifled. Maybe someone noticed the grease under my fingernails or the cuts and calluses on my hands. It might have been when I first pulled a butterfly-knife from my pocket to help an administrative assistant cut open a package she was struggling to open. Perhaps it was because I drank my beer from the bottle and spent more time chatting with the administrative support staff than obsequiously flocking about the Dean and Provost as they "circulated" during a university party. Perchance my disdain for unwarranted and misplaced academic elitism, my scorn for the unapologetic and arrogant behavior of many of my colleagues, and my contempt for the sense of entitlement and consumerist attitude toward education on the part of some of the more economically privileged students showed. I am unsure if I ever "passed," but if I did, I knew that my veneer was gone barely a year into my career as a professor when a dean with whom I had numerous confrontations disparagingly referred to me and another working-class Italian professor as "Sacco and Vanzetti" in front of an auditorium filled with 80 of our university colleagues.[21]

In a decade as a university professor, I have authored approximately 30 journal articles and book chapters, along with some shorter entries, research notes, and invited essays.[22] Of these publications, in only one did I explicitly address my working-class roots, and in one other my working-class, Italian-immigrant background. All of my publications, irrespective of the "research topic," focus on social justice by challenging authority (not only its capricious exercise, but the very legitimacy of its existence), and demythologizing power. It is not false modesty or self-effacement to point out that few if any of my colleagues, save perhaps some members of hiring, tenure, and promotions committees, have ever read these publications. Yet despite my minimal accounts of my own history, and despite my colleagues' general lack of engagement with my work challenging authority, I am certain that they know that my habitus was that of a working-class, Italian immigrant. As with Bourdieu, their knowledge has derived not from my academic writings, but from my being in the world, and the subtleties of class and ethnic heritage that it continues to carry. And yet, sadly, I suspect that their "knowledge" of my habitus is a caricatured malformation – one that fails, perhaps because of their own habitus, to appreciate the empathic class consciousness and the anarchic spirit that was so central to the history and future of my hood's residents.

Notes

1. Translation.: "Yes, we're Italian."
2. So too should the reader.
3. Translation: "Italians in the World."
4. Literally translated as "English," this is a catch-all term used by many Italian-Canadians to refer to people of British descent, or others of northern European descent, whose families have lived in Canada for multiple generations.
5. Translation: "Young boys."
6. In the mid-late 1990s, the Conservative government of Mike Harris reorganized (i.e., "gutted") the province's healthcare system. This resulted in the consolidation (i.e., severe cutbacks and closings) of several hospitals. Northwestern General, located in a working-class immigrant neighborhood with a long history of electing Liberal candidates, was one of the affected hospitals. Once a fully functioning eight-floor, two-wing hospital, it now operates as little more than a glorified "walk-in" clinic as one of Humber River Regional Hospital's "Health Resource Centre, Keele Street Site."
7. The "contractors' vans" usually appeared between 6–8 p.m.–when the contractors themselves returned home. The vans typically vanished by 6.30 a.m.
8. Toronto's Italian-language daily newspaper.
9. Translation: "There are people who suffer worse than us."
10. I should point out, here, that my parents were neither well-intentioned but naïve "liberals," nor were they given to parroting the rhetoric of Immigration and Citizenship Canada. They realized that the experiences of more recent immigrants and of Canadian-born racialized people were not the same as their own. But they understood that many of our "non-Italian" neighbors were refugees or otherwise found themselves in Canada as a result of the brutal legacy of imperialism.
11. As a young child, I never fully comprehended why my parents, who I always felt spoke too loudly, too quickly, and too brashly to us in the house, or with friends on the street, suddenly became quiet as mice when we were in public outside the neighborhood. Nor for that matter, why I was often enlisted to make phone calls on their behalf.
12. Translation: "Remember 'The Carnival' of 1511."

13. Translation: "Bad boy! Shame on you."
14. It has since been renamed the York Civic Centre.
15. Translation: "I work with my hands."
16. He is currently a practicing defense attorney who works extensively with Ontario's legal aid, and for The Association in Defence of the Wrongly Convicted (AIDWYC).
17. Translation: [Working] "with my hands."
18. Translation: "The vegetable garden."
19. See Bourdieu's (1998) lectures on the economy of symbolic goods.
20. Translation: "It is always there."
21. The Dean was an arrogant, overbearing lout who constantly badgered faculty. Like many bullies, he felt he could hide his malfeasance beneath artifice; in his case, of a fatherly "Southern gentleman." My response to his antics usually consisted of subtle defiance.
22. I provide this information not to "give you my cv," as academics are wont to do; I seek neither accolades nor shame, but rather wish to provide context.

References

Bourdieu, P. (1998). *Practical Reason: On the Theory of Action*. Stanford: Stanford University Press.

Bourdieu, P. (2007). *Sketch for a Self-Analysis*. Chicago: University of Chicago Press.

DeMaria Harney, N. (1999). *Eh, Paesan! Being Italian in Toronto*. Toronto: University of Toronto Press.

Iacovetta, F. (1992). *Such Hardworking People: Italian Immigrants in Postwar Toronto*. Montreal: McGill-Queen's University Press.

Ferrell, J. (2012). Autoethnography. In D. Gadd, S. Karstedt, & S. Messner (Eds), *The Sage Handbook of Criminological Research Methods*. London: Sage

Fulghum, R. (1988). *All I Really Need to Know I Learned in Kindergarten*. New York: Villard Books.

Lamberti, E. & Fortunati, V. (Eds) (2009). *Memories and Representations of War: The Case of World War I and World War II*. New York/Amsterdam: Rodopi.

MacLeod, J. (1987). *Ain't No Making It: Leveled Aspirations in a Low-Income Neighborhood*. Boulder, CO: Westview Press.

Muir, E. (1998). *Mad Blood Stirring: Vendetta in Renaissance Italy*. Baltimore: The John Hopkins University Press.

Muzzatti, S. L. (2010). Consumer Culture, Criminology and the Politics of Exclusion. In M. Maguire and D. Okada (Eds), *Critical Issues of Crime and Justice: Thought, Policy and Practice* (pp. 119–131). Thousand Oaks: Sage.

Muzzatti, S. L. and Samarco, C. V. (2006). Working Class Need Not Apply: Reflecting on the Academic Job Hunting Experience. In S. L. Muzzatti and C. V. Samarco (Eds), *Reflections from the Wrong Side of the Tracks: Class, Identity, and the Working Class Experience* (pp. 69–80). Lanham, MD. Rowman & Littlefield Publishers.

Presdee, M. (Ed.) (1992). *Working it Out: Recounting, Reclaiming and Reworking Reality*. Canterbury: Canterbury Christ Church College.

Presdee, M. (2006). Working it Out. In S. Muzzatti and V. Samarco (Eds), *Reflections from the Wrong Side of the Tracks: Class, Identity, and the Working Class Experience* (pp. 23–36). Landham: Rowman and Littlefield.

Presdee, M. (2009). *The Muck of Ages: A Working Class Upbringing in Gloucester*. Canterbury: Puckle Lane Publishing.

Stanger-Ross, J. (2009). *Staying Italian: Urban Change and Ethnic Life in Postwar Toronto and Philadelphia*. Chicago: University of Chicago Press.

Statistics Canada. (1961). *Distribution of the Population, by Ethnic Group, Census Years, 1941, 1951 and 1961*. Ottawa: Government of Canada.

Sugiman, P. (2009). Life is Sweet: Vulnerability and Composure in the Wartime Narratives of Japanese Canadians. *Journal of Canadian Studies, 43*(1), 186–218.

Willis, P. (1977). *Learning to Labour: How Working Class Kids Get Working Class Jobs*. New York: Columbia University Press.

Wilson, D. A. (Ed.) (2007). *The Orange Order in Canada*. Dublin: Four Courts Press.

Chapter 4

Precarious Life: On Dwelling, Mobility, and Artistic Intervention

Erin Morton and Sarah E.K. Smith

I was the 13th person to move into Tent City. It was the Canada Day weekend in 1998. We were evicted in 2002, four years and two months later … Up to the first 75 residents we still had a sense of community. I think most of us at Tent City felt we had a home and weren't homeless … The day we were evicted was the worst day of my life.

Marty Lang, quoted in Cathy Crowe, *Dying for a Home*, 2007

The active process of making spatial sites significant – or the active transformation of space into place – involves the investment of subjective value and the attribution of meanings to components of the socially constructed environment … It emerges as a meaningful domain through experience, perception, and the visceral contact that occurs as one interacts with the physical and social environment. One's sense of place is the product of a particular proximity and familiarity with the environment of one's routine circulation and is encompassing of those elements that are frequently described as the "practices of everyday life," accounting for the minutiae and subordinated details that may be overlooked due to their apparent insignificance.

Murray Forman, *The Hood Comes First*, 2002

But what is a "slum"?

Mike Davis, *Planet of Slums*, 2006

Precarious life

In a recent article in the *New York Times* travel section, journalist Eric Weiner details the tourist experience of Michael Cronin, a US college admissions officer whose job took him to India on business a few times each year. Titled "Slum Visits: Tourism or Voyeurism?" the article outlines the growing desire of experienced tourists such as Cronin to move beyond a given region's "usual" tourist sites (in this case, the temples, monuments, and markets that Cronin already felt familiar with from his previous visits to South Asia). And so, Cronin remembers, his interest was piqued when he came across an advertisement for "slum tours," an idea that, as he puts it, "resonated with me immediately" (quoted in Weiner, 2008). Cronin soon found himself "skirting open sewers and ducking to avoid exposed electrical wires" as he toured Dharavi, a 213-hectare area of Mumbai that is home to over a million people (quoted in Weiner, 2008). According to Weiner's article, "slum tourism" or "poorism" seems to be catching on, from "the favelas of Rio de Janerio to the townships of Johannesburg to the garbage dumps of Mexico" (Weiner, 2008), raising a number of questions regarding how urban dwelling places are conventionally conceptualized in the age of global tourism. Mike Davis's 2006 book *Planet of Slums* articulates a now relatively commonplace assertion that

> the cities of the future, rather than being made out of glass and steel as envisioned by earlier generations of urbanists, are instead largely constructed out of crude brick, straw, recycled plastic, cement blocks, and scrap wood. Instead of cities of light soaring toward heaven, much of the twenty-first-century urban world squats in squalor, surrounded by pollution, excrement, and decay.
>
> (p. 19)

Most recently, Danny Boyle's feature film *Slumdog Millionaire* brought images of this new urbanity to Hollywood. In the words of one travel writer, the film "shines the spotlight on Mumbai it had long deserved" (Hampton, 2009). "It may seem voyeuristic," the author continues, "but a tour of Mumbai's Dharavi district allows you to judge for yourself. The largest slum in Asia … this is the India that brochures never show" (Hampton, 2009).

The social distancing that takes place between tourists such as Cronin, who possess the capital to travel for leisure, and Dharavi residents, who are conventionally understood to be trapped within the new millennium's global urban squalor, is an important entry point through which to discuss the habitus of the hood. These various popular representations of the hood as global slum ultimately serve to construct the hood as simultaneously liberating and limiting, a conceptualization that holds both actual and symbolic consequences for resident insiders and tourist outsiders. Weiner, for example, proposes that slum tourism simply requires moral regulation, noting, "The crucial question … is not whether slum tours should exist but how they are conducted. Do they limit the excursions to small groups, interacting respectfully with residents? Or do they travel in buses, snapping photos from the windows as if on safari" (Weiner, 2008)? For those of us who recognize the "slum" as a demographic, legal, and territorial construct (Rao, 2006), such questions bring to mind the mired acceptability of claiming one's dwelling place, "the place to which all other places bear reference" (Cooper, 2005, p. 313), outside of the state order and of maintaining this claim through presence and human strength alone. If a community lacks the conventional mechanisms of gatekeeping, which allow insiders to regulate interlopers of all kinds, including tourists, what impact does this have on how this place is conceived? Does it affect, for example, perceptions of residents' permanence, stability, belonging, and safety in their dwelling place?

One only has to think of the demolition of Toronto's Tent City in 2002, a community that residents began erecting on the downtown waterfront in 1996 and which quickly became a source of social and political tensions surrounding squatter's rights to the land – in this case, land that was legally owned by the US-based corporation Home Depot (Gilbert &

Phillips, 2003). This situation escalated during the 2002 City of Toronto municipal workers' strike, when, according to resident Marty Lang, "people would come down and dump their garbage and construction waste at Tent City because the dumps were closed and we were just off the highway. That's when the rat problem began" (quoted in Crowe, 2007). That same year, private security guards and Toronto police officers flooded Tent City without warning during an 11:00 a.m. raid on September 24, while a team of workers erected a wire fence around the community's perimeter to keep residents out, leaving those who returned only 72 hours to collect their belongings before the entire area was leveled (Welsh & Shephard, 2002). As Home Dept reclaimed Tent City's land and suddenly evicted the people who had been living there for six years, former resident Rainer "Dri" Driemayer commented to reporters as he stood outside the newly constructed fence: "It's surprising they'd do it in this manner, with no warning. But when you're living in a situation like this, this is something you expect each and every day. If you go somewhere to do something … every time you come back, you're hoping you're going to be able to go home" (quoted in Welsh & Shephard, 2002, p. A1).

Mainstream media coverage of the Tent City eviction focused on the precariousness of life in a contested dwelling place, emphasizing the conventional boundaries between mobility and settlement and making apparent the vulnerability of residents who are sometimes left without the strong authority to control changes in their own community (CBC News, 2002; Immen & Rusk, 2002). In this chapter, we will explore such conceptualizations of "precarious life" in dwelling places established outside the state order with greater profundity. Judith Butler (2006) has recently articulated the concept of "precarious life" in relation to the ethics of non-violence, "one that is based upon an understanding of how easily human life is annulled" (p. xvii). We will make use of this concept differently in this chapter, by examining how the conceptualization of the precariousness of human life affects the conceptualization of home and away. In short, we question what dwelling places are considered precarious and who considers them thusly. We approach these dwelling places by critically examining their representations in contemporary art practice, since, much like mainstream media reporters, visual artists are among those pushing ideas about mobility and settlement as far as they can (sometimes to the point of transgression).

As both the Mumbai tourism and the Tent City eviction cases make clear, parsing the relationship between outsiders' perceptions of community dwelling places, including those advanced in artistic representations, and the lived experiences of resident insiders foregrounds "the sites and places of reified social space" (Bourdieu 1999, p. 126). To tackle this relationship, this chapter will explore two artists' projects that address ideas about dwelling and belonging outside of the state's legitimatization through citizenship or inherited rights to the land: Vessna Perunovich and Boja Vasic's multimedia installation "Parallel World: The Architecture of Survival" and Robert Jelinek's State of Sabotage project. Perunovich's photography and Vasic's video work examine resident life in a Romani community on the outskirts of urban Belgrade, the resulting installation providing a means to interrogate current issues of mobility and survival that are increasingly complicated by global patterns of informal settlement (Davis, 2007). Jelinek's multifaceted artistic practice centers on his autonomous and utopian micronation, which he has named the State of Sabotage (SoS). Using performance as one strategy among many to mimic the apparatus of the state, Jelinek claims geopolitical territory in various locations and identifies citizens through the issuing of passports, all the while using acts of sabotage veiled by artistry to establish the SoS as nation-state, which might also be considered through the competing lenses of dwelling and mobility. Each of these artists seeks to intercede notions of community and challenge conventional understandings of dwelling and mobility in the context of late capitalism, to varying degrees of success in our reading of the situation.

There often exists a notable economic, social, and symbolic disparage between the artist who travels to various dwelling places and the people who get represented by the artist's project, since, as Bourdieu (1999) suggests, one's "lack of capital intensifies the experience of finitude: it chains one to a place" (p. 127). We would therefore like to make clear our motivation for analyzing these artists' projects as they intersect with the dual mechanisms of dwelling and mobility. There are quite obviously fundamental differences between actually settling dwelling places outside of the state order and representing the struggle to appropriate these places for the audiences of contemporary art. If dwelling places are produced, to borrow Murray Forman's (2002) words, "according to rhythms of movement and patterns of use" (p. 28), then these rhythms and patterns also affect the ways in which these places get treated in media and artistic representations. To explore the nature of these representations, this chapter will make use of Bourdieu's concept of habitus, as the form and structure of the embodied practices that shape, and are shaped by, social practice (Bourdieu, 1977; Postone, LiPuma, & Calhoun, 1993). In considering habitus as both the "habit" and the "habitat" of social life – as Kim Dovey (2005) puts it, "the sense of 'place' and the sense of one's 'place' in a social hierarchy" (p. 283) – we will examine how artists engage with the dual frameworks of domination and empowerment in dwelling places, especially when it comes to certain methods of artistry assuming a particular and unquestioned habitus. In particular, Bourdieu's conceptual framework provides a way to examine how artistic representations of places established outside the state order often assume that "a habitat can be occupied physically without really being inhabited in the full sense of the term" (Bourdieu, 1999, p. 128).

On dwelling

Examining ideas about "precarious life" in informal settlements requires parsing the competing dualities of liberation and limitation commonly used to conceptualize so-called slum dwelling. As Jeremy Seabrook has recently articulated, "It would be foolish to pass from one distortion – that the slums are places of crime, disease and despair – to the opposite: that they can be safely left to look after themselves" (quoted in Davis, 2007, p. 70). Bourdieu's (1977) conceptual framework provides a way to think beyond this duality, by considering dwelling places according to their habitus – "a way of being, a habitual state (especially of the body) and, in particular, a predisposition, tendency, propensity, or inclination" (p. 214). The dwelling place in which such systems of embodied dispositions take place also structures its community's habitus, since particular struggles over economic, social, cultural, and symbolic capital help shape the principles around which a community organizes itself. For inhabitants of a given social world, these dispositions may go virtually unnoticed. Yet for interlopers, such dispositions often strike a chord, since the ways in which inhabitants make a living, organize their daily activities, conceptualize their community, and conduct themselves within it also reveals something about the social world in which they live. It is at precisely this juncture that Vessna Perunovich and Boja Vasic conceptualize their multimedia installation "Parallel World: The Architecture of Survival," which visually surveys the artists' own perceptions of Gazela, a Romani settlement on the outskirts of downtown Belgrade.[1]

After filming and photographing the people and places of Gazela, Perunovich and Vasic showcased "Parallel World" at the Modern Fuel Artist Run Centre (Kingston, ON, Canada) in the spring of 2008. The resulting exhibition consisted of twenty photographs, a multimedia sculptural installation, and a double-channel video, components that come together to present Gazela as a provisional neighborhood in between the relative permanence of the city's high-rise buildings and beside the Belgrade neighborhood where the artists themselves lived for many years. Perunovich and Vasic, who are currently based in Toronto, collaborated on this project after returning to Belgrade from Canada and, as Perunovich puts it, noticing their own shift in perspective as they began to see Gazela "in a different way" (Perunovich & Vasic, 2008). Perunovich elaborates:

> The whole thing started very intuitively, it wasn't really preconceived. This is very familiar territory because the whole settlement is very close to where we used to live in Belgrade and has been there for over twenty-five years. For us, it was like something that is subconsciously inside of you, but that you don't notice. While we were living in Belgrade we didn't pay attention to the settlement.

For Perunovich and Vasic, Gazela exists in a world parallel with their own in Belgrade, which is economically structured by market capitalism, socially structured by liberal property ownership, and symbolically structured by a belief in the permanence of the city's urban built environment. For the artists, Gazela functions as an invisible city within a city, geographically within Belgrade's city limits but separate from its municipal state governance and civil society (A Space Gallery, 2007). As a stark contrast to urban Belgrade's habitus, in which people have legal claim to their homes and have their trash removed by city workers, Gazela residents' ability to survive on Belgrade's periphery despite their geographical, social, and economic segregation from its core appeared remarkable to the artists.

According to Perunovich and Vasic, many Gazela residents make their living through the informal economic practice of sorting through refuse and selling scrap materials – materials that also serve to construct their homes. The connection between Gazela residents' everyday labor practices and the settlement architecture is Perunovich and Vasic's primary inspiration for the "Parallel Worlds" project. In the foreground of each photograph in the installation, for example, Perunovich portrays unnamed Gazela residents in front of their homes against a digitally altered background, creating a blurred exposure that erases the surrounding community from the visual frame (see Figure 1).

As the background environment around Gazela's homes is removed, Perunovich's photographs exemplify what Bourdieu (1999) describes as "sites that are fundamentally defined by an *absence* – basically, that of the state and of everything that comes with it, police, schools, health care institutions, associations, etc" (p. 123). The viewer is invited to focus on the settlement architecture, rather than on elements that surround it, which might, first, socially bind the Gazela settlement to the rest of Belgrade and, second, offer landmarks with which to contextualize individual homes. As a result, the photographs have the effect of situating a particular Gazela home not in a position that is relative to other sites, but "by the distance separating it from them" (Bourdieu, 1999, p. 124). Visually, the distance between the people in the photographs, the artist behind the camera, and the viewer in the gallery space is stark, since the images contain very few elements that could identify the actual site of the shot. As such, Perunovich and Vasic present Gazela residents as what Mike Davis (2006) describes as the universal "human symbol, whether as victim or hero, of the Third World city" (p. 90). The geophysical site of this human symbol becomes almost insignificant in the context of Perunovich's image.

The decision to unframe the images of Gazela homes is important to consider in relation to the remaining elements of the "Parallel Worlds" installation. The photographs line the gallery walls and provide the viewer with the documentary context to interpret the second component of the installation, in which Perunovich and Vasic assemble a structure made of found materials to mimic the architecture of Gazela homes (see Figure 2). The performative act of recreating Gazela's architecture, which the artists undertake by searching for discarded materials near the town or city hosting their exhibition, allows the viewer to engage spatially with the structure of Gazela's homes. As social space transforms into physical space by way of the gallery, Perunovich and Vasic's photographic representations of Gazela are retranslated in a new context. Such translations between the social and the physical, as Bourdieu (1999) reminds us, are always "more or less *blurred*: the power over space that comes from possessing various kinds of capital takes the form in appropriated physical space of a certain relation between the spatial structure of the distribution of agents and the spatial structure of the distribution of goods and services, private or public" (p. 124). In this case, appropriating Gazela's architecture by recreating it in a gallery space further displaces Gazela residents from both the artists and the viewer, since the residents' system of embodied dispositions that serves to physically and symbolically construct their homes is reasserted as art practice rather than as survival strategy. The resulting home-*cum*-art object operates somewhere between veiled social critique and appropriation.

Figure 1: Vessna Perunovich and Boja Vasic. Photograph from the installation "Parallel World: The Architecture of Survival," 2008.

Figure 2: Vessna Perunovich and Boja Vasic. Installation view of "Parallel World: The Architecture of Survival," 2008.

On the whole, the installation highlights the struggle of Gazela residents to eke out a livelihood in the face of poverty, while at the same time attempts to showcase Gazela as "a sort of 'favela' which is home to people rejected by mainstream society" (Vasic quoted in Kemeny, 2007, n.p.). This representation of Gazela-as-*favela* is one that advances the settlement as unconventional, outside the mainstream, and peripheral in contrast to the rest of Belgrade, trapping its Romani residents in a "vicious cycle" of poverty (Perunovich & Vasic, 2008). As Vasic notes,

> It's socially and economically and politically unacceptable that the community is in this vicious cycle because they're poor. Because they're poor and self-sufficient, they need to work for themselves and they need help from their kids to work. So their kids don't go to school and because they don't receive conventional education they cannot work outside of their settlement context. So it becomes a closed circle that exists parallel to the official society, where you have all the conventional mechanisms associated with employment and education.

This conceptualization suggests that as Gazela residents' daily activities structure their community, such activities also restrict residents' ability to move freely outside of their own settlement. According to this line of thinking, Gazela Romanies are both victims to larger systemic disadvantages beyond their control and heroic in their ability to navigate this system for survival. If we consider this representation in relation to Bourdieu's (1990) conceptualization, then, habitus "is a kind of transforming machine that leads us to 'reproduce' the social conditions of our own production, but in a relatively predictable way, in such a way that one cannot move simply and mechanically from knowledge of the conditions of production to knowledge of the products" (p. 77; quoted in Reay, 2004, p. 433). Yet this "projection of the poor" as resilient hero-victims, who, despite their resourcefulness, cannot escape their lot in life because of their embodied, learned behaviors falls far short of critiquing "the areas of social life abandoned by the neoliberal state – health care, labor, poor neighborhood development, street children and the homeless – [and the way this is often turned] into an agenda for organizing civil society" (Yúdice, 2003, pp. 123, 88). Instead, the implications of the "Parallel World" project are that Gazela's habitus will further its continual instability. Perunovich articulates:

> What is interesting to me as an artist is how [Gazela residents] are forced nomads. They don't travel anymore in the same way that they once did and are forced to settle in one place. I am interested in how they use materials and how these materials reflect this sensibility, of something that is not permanent and that is really fragile, structures that are built but not intended to stay there forever. It's not traditional architecture in the way that traditional architecture is built and presented to be solid and last forever. The way the Roma in this settlement build their houses and their sense of architecture reflects that sensibility of being impermanent.

> (Perunovich & Vasic, 2008)

Figure 3: Vessna Perunovich and Boja Vasic. Photograph from the installation "Parallel World: The Architecture of Survival," 2008.

Figure 4: Vessna Perunovich and Boja Vasic. Photograph from the installation "Parallel World: The Architecture of Survival," 2008.

Perunovich's description of Gazela Romanies as "forced nomads" emphasizes the Serbian state's subjugation of Romani communities and implies that Romani people will remain perpetual outcasts in Belgrade, while precarious life in Gazela is perceived to be the source of the residents' continued subjugation.[2] What is more, the idea of forced nomadism is based on the Romanies' current lack of legal claim to the Gazela settlement, which suggests that Gazela Romanies are further trapped behind the rigid boundaries of class division, racialized segregation, and only travel because of changes in the social order that are beyond their control (Conlon, 2005). The overall implication here is that, as George Yúdice (2003) argues, "civil society must be *managed* in the interest of maximizing political stability and economic transformation" – otherwise, places such as Gazela will continue to result in "the strengthening of 'uncivil society'" (p. 96).

A case in point is the logic behind the "Parallel World" photographic series. Perunovich's photographs all display a common feature in the homes they depict: a large painted house number on the front of each dwelling, indicating a form of determined community organization (see Figures 3 and 4). Perunovich and Vasic remain uncertain as to whether Belgrade officials employ the numbers to assign Gazela's residents a legal address, or to determine certain homes for demolition by the city, or both (Perunovich & Vasic, 2008). Originally, the artists intended to document a sampling of homes in numbered order, from one to 100, but eventually abandoned this project because the local government had already destroyed several Gazela houses (Perunovich & Vasic, 2008). The impact of the municipal state's management of Gazela through this numbered signage remains equally ambiguous in the remaining photographs in the installation. Is this numbered system creating a linkage between Gazela residents and municipal governance? Might this system be at best understood as surveillance and, at worst, as a plan for eviction and erasure? Reading this numbered sequence in combination with the third component of the exhibition, Vasic's double-channel video loop, which he filmed as one long shot through the village to capture "a stroll through the settlement with the camera recording the reality of whatever happens there" (Perunovich & Vasic, 2008), these images speak not to the Romani residents' strategies for community coordination, but become an arbitrary image of state control (see Figure 5).

As such, the installation's critique of the state remains veiled by its critique of Gazela's habitus, which the artists' work ultimately positions as the primary source of oppression in the Gazela residents' lives. It is in this regard that we see the "Parallel World" installation underscoring Deleuze and Guattari's (1994) notion of *zones de voisinage* – that is, the ambiguous borderlines that designate a lived environment and which speak to the potential for both collaboration and confrontation between insider residents and outsider visitors. While we have already been upfront about our reading of confrontation between the artists, viewers, and subjects of the "Parallel World" installation, we also see marked potential for collaboration in Perunovich and Vasic's planned extension of the project, in which they would like to work with Gazela residents to build similar installations in the future (Perunovich & Vasic, 2008). This proposal for collaboration, in which, should they choose

Figure 5: Vessna Perunovich and Boja Vasic. Installation shot of video still from "Parallel World: The Architecture of Survival," 2008.

to participate, Gazela Romanies could control the means of their own representation and involvement in this project, will no doubt shift the artists' visual treatment of the Gazela settlement and, as a result, its reception. More importantly, though, such collaboration has the capability to dismantle narratives of Romani victimization, making it possible to forge a dialogic relationship between artist and subject, visitor and resident, and, perhaps, sparking conversations about both the restrictions of social space and their potential as sites for resisting the state order.

On mobility

If Perunovich and Vasic's art project falls just short of critically addressing the habitus of the hood in relation to broader fields such as nation and civil society, Robert Jelinek's art practice actually mimics the embodied dispositions that structure, and are structured by, these fields. Specifically, his explorations take place in the realm of his self-declared micronation, the State of Sabotage (SoS). Embedded in Jelinek's declaration of the SoS as "micronation," that is, as a self-proclaimed state, are ideas about dissatisfaction with an established political system and the activist potential of recreating the birth of a nation on one's own terms (Blackson, 2007). In 2006, the travel company Lonely Planet picked up on these ideas by offering a broad overview of self-declared states in the style of a tourist guidebook: *Micronations: The Lonely Planet Guide to Home-Made Nations*. "Bored of visiting the same old UN-recognized countries? Ready to explore somewhere unique and perhaps a little wacky?" reads the book's back cover, "For a world succumbing to globalization and international blanding, micronations are the perfect antidote." This travel guide posits micronations as the new site of consumption for the seasoned tourist struggling with the leveling effects of globalization, surveying 30 "home-made" states (including the SoS) and affirming Jelinek's position as "Non-President." While *Micronations* presents these sites as the latest frontier in tourism, at the same time it reads them as social experiment. The SoS micronation therefore operates somewhere between a field in which to enact a particular habitus, mimicking the embodied practices of citizenship within established nation-states, and symbolic project, which uses the habitus of citizenship as a site of social critique.

A given habitus is always galvanized in relation to a field, whether it is defined, in Melanie White's (2006) words, as "a network or configuration of objective relations between positions that offers an alternative way to conceptualize general terms such as society, nation or state; moreover, a field may also express civil society and the complex of associations, community centers, and bowling halls of which it is comprised" (p. 113). When it comes to the habitus of citizenship, White continues, "the capacity to conduct oneself 'appropriately' implies that one has learned to *recognize* these pre-reflexive assumptions that organize 'effective,' 'normal' or 'accepted' conduct in the social world" – in this case, the nation-state (ibid.). Jelinek's SoS project aims to critique the regulatory structures of the nation-state and civil society under neoliberal globalization, by questioning the habitus of citizenship and its relationship to these interrelated fields. In other words, Jelinek uses the embodied practices of citizenship conventionally associated with the nation-state to question the continued relevance of the field of nationhood in an increasingly globalized world. Since citizenship can no longer be wholly defined according to the legal rights and practices that designate belonging to a nation-state, the habitus of citizenship is constructed in relation to fields such as nation or civil society, but also in relation to others, such as the global economy, the Internet, or the micronation (White, 2006). We might, however, question the effectiveness of Jelinek mimicking the habitus of citizenship as his primary means of critique.

Officially inaugurated in Helsinki at the Summit of Micronations in 2003, the SoS has since gained de facto recognition internationally by Australia, Hungary, Monaco, Switzerland and the United Nations, amongst others (Jelinek, 2003a). The SoS serves as the basis for Jelenik's larger artistic practice, taking the form of performative interventions into public space, providing the basis for the creation of material objects such as currency and stamps, and generating the content for many of Jelenik's writings (Jelinek, 2005; Jelinek & Giger, 2003). It also provides a means for Jelenik to address the acquired patterns of thought and behavior that correspond with the historical formation of the nation-state. In mimicking the everyday performances of citizenship through such actions as the *SoS Stoning* (a performance which also establishes the borders of the state's territory) and the SoS passports (artistic multiples that act as SoS citizens' identifying documents), Jelinek's project both critiques and reinforces the system of embodied dispositions of the liberal democratic state. Much like Perunovich and Vasic, Jelinek understands his art practice as goading the boundaries of conventional dwelling (in this case, at the macro level, in the form of the nation). Jelinek uses the term sabotage to mean "the breaking of conventions" and "the artistic interruption of processes of thinking" (2003d). As he puts it: "Sabotage is the experiment to [break] up incrustation of an organized ... society that insulates itself against all changes and tries to make thinkable new possibilities" (Jelinek & Giger, 2003, p. 5).

Guided by these principles, the SoS seeks to intervene in the public realm through such acts of sabotage, as a means to foster new understandings of global order. In our reading of the SoS project, a central paradox lies in the fact that Jelinek's approach is at odds with this proclamation. In mimicking the habitus of the liberal state (albeit with a critical and even activist lens), the SoS comes into being by claiming territory through public performances, proclaiming this territory as part of its autonomous state, engaging in diplomatic relations, setting up embassies and consulate offices across the globe, and issuing passports to citizens. National signifiers for the state are abundant, in the form of a state constitution, currency, art collection, flag, and national anthem. By asserting SoS legitimacy through these embodied actions and recognized symbols, Jelinek limits his artistic intervention to mimicry and ultimately reduces the nation-state to its most conventional and clichéd form (Comaroff & Comaroff, 2001). As such, Jelinek's art practice critically assesses what Bourdieu describes as "the mere fact of taking the world for granted, of accepting the world as it is, and of finding it natural because *their mind is constructed according to cognitive structures that are issued out of the very structures of the world*" (Bourdieu & Wacquant, 1992, p. 168, emphasis in original;

quoted in White, 2006, p. 114). At the same time, it is well established that in order to enact disavowal, mimicry must effectively distinguish itself from what it means to critique; thus, in effect, the SoS project reinforces the habitus of state structures by employing these same forms without adequate disparity (Bhabha, 1994).

In this respect, the critical outcome of Jelinek's art practice is limited because the SoS project actually reinforces the system of embodied dispositions that constitutes the field of nationhood in the first place. A case in point is Jelinek's 2007 enactment of the SoS in conjunction with the Modern Fuel Artist-Run Centre, when he claimed territory on Wolfe Island in the name of the micronation. In choosing this particular site, which is located just a short ferry ride away from the city of Kingston, Ontario, and acts as a gateway to the Canada-US border, Jelinek references the region's historical connections to state projects that have come into being atop established patterns of indigenous settlement. Titled *SoS Stoning*, this official state ceremony marked the SoS's first territory in Canada with the help of approximately sixty new citizen-participants. Jelinek chose a large piece of fallow land on the island's north shore for the site of this performance, which he conducted with the solemnity of a state ritual. Upon their arrival at the location, Jelinek led the participants across the site to form a circle before taking his place on a small patch of land in the center, where he had gathered a large pile of rocks, each painted gold and labeled with the initials "SoS." Jelinek then claimed the territory where he and his citizens stood in the name of the SoS, while playing the state's national anthem from a portable stereo (see Figure 6). As the performance's culmination, SoS citizens were invited to hurl the painted rocks in all directions across the field and away from the center of the circle (see Figure 7). After a quarter of an hour, the stones were scattered across the field and acted to define the boundaries of the new state's terrain. Jelinek later drew the exact borders of the SoS territory by tracing the points where the stones had landed. To date, using a range of different means and performance strategies, the SoS has claimed over 650 acres of territory across the globe in such places as Australia, Austria, Czech Republic, and Finland (Horwatt, 2007).

In claiming land through an act of artistry and mimicking the violence of colonial expansion in the name of the state, Jelinek relegates the *SoS Stoning* to the performative realm. This artistic intervention thus provides a striking contrast to the contested land claims surrounding Tent City introduced at the beginning of this chapter. Significantly, both the SoS citizens and the Tent City residents were united in their use of the habitus of citizenship as a basis from which to claim territory and form communities. While the Canadian state denied the Tent City residents' claim on the grounds of their "homelessness," that is, based on their inability to fully embody the state sanctioned conventions of liberal citizenship through the tenets of individual property ownership, the residents themselves expressed political mobilization as citizens against the governance of the state (Gilbert & Phillips, 2003). In contrast, the fact that many of the SoS's Kingston-based citizens have full access to state-sanctioned citizenship outside of Jelinek's performance makes their claim to country largely uncontested.[3]

Figure 6: SoS citizens stand for the national anthem. SoS Stoning, Wolfe Island, 2007.

Figure 7: SoS citizens claim territory through stoning. SoS Stoning, Wolfe Island, 2007.

More broadly, the limits of the *SoS Stoning* are apparent in that Jelinek's appropriation, despite its rhetoric of critique, fails to question the larger structure of citizenship and the behaviors and norms that define it. As White (2006) explains, citizenship is formed from the relationship between habitus and a specific field, a role that "we actively constitute and create ... in specific contexts under determinate objective conditions" (pp. 188, 120). The relationship between habitus and field, or, in this case, the act of claiming territory and the relationship of this action to the structure the SoS state, was not illuminated by Jelinek's performance, nor was the active construction of the embodied practices of citizenship mined critically to any degree. In contrast, the Tent City residents issued a direct challenge to constructions of citizenry within a capitalist liberal order in their political mobilization, thus illuminating the fact that liberal citizenships are formed by various participations in society that often either defend existing democratic principles or claim new ones that would expand democratic spaces (Friedmann, 2002; Gilbert & Phillips, 2003). Since it might be argued that the *SoS Stoning* is limited to the realm of art performance, in contrast to the supposed "precarious" reality of the Tent City action, we suggest that examination of art which blurs the boundaries between performative intervention and everyday practices of citizenship be considered. Here, we would specifically like to draw attention to the SoS passports, another facet of Jelinek's SoS project, which offers potential in expanding the SoS project beyond the realm of the performative. The production and circulation of SoS passports demonstrates the extent to which art practice can impact the lived experiences of SoS citizens, ultimately contesting the habitus of citizenship by enabling SoS citizens to resist the restrictions of their previous home states when it comes to practices of migration and settlement.

The SoS widely promotes its citizenship internationally and has granted over 8,000 passports since its inception (Horwatt, 2007). These passports serve a dual function, as both a means to identify SoS citizens and as works of art created as part of an artistic edition by Heimo Zobernig (see Figures 8 and 9) (Jelinek, 2003c). In Kingston, Jelinek opened a SoS consulate office at the Modern Fuel where prospective citizens could educate themselves about the SoS through printed materials, videos, and by engaging with Jelinek as he processed the individual passport requests (see Figure 10). The quality of the SoS passports is masterful and they bear a striking resemblance to genuine identification papers. They are also freely available to all applicants who request them, which points to the passports' potential to affect material, sociopolitical consequences. In fact, these documents exist in a tenuous legal situation, for example, in February 2005, when the US Department of Homeland Security confiscated Jelinek's SoS materials (including the passports) while he was en route to exhibit his work at Cincinnati's Contemporary Arts Center (Paice, 2005). Homeland Security justified the confiscation, stating that the items were "produced by an anarchy group called Sabotage which does not believe in international borders" (quoted in Paice, 2005, p. 43). The SoS passports were thus subject to US state control because they had the potential to act as actual legal documents. Once the US government authorities returned the confiscated items to Jelinek, he did not issue any new passports at the Cincinnati exhibition (Paice, 2005).

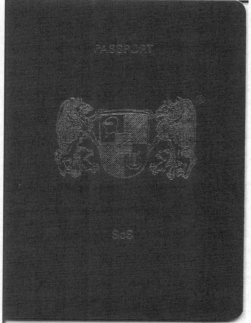

Figure 8: SoS passport (exterior view).

Figure 9: SoS passport (interior view).

This incident demonstrates the extent to which mimicking the habitus of citizenship, in this case, by issuing state identification documents, can challenge the state's regulatory power to mediate movement across national borders. In this way, the SoS passports transgress the realm of cultural citizenship (which includes the freedom to engage in cultural activities such as Jelinek's SoS performance) and provide a means to secure political and civil rights (such as the right to regulate one's own movement across the borders of a particular state), effectively expanding the conventional limits of art making (Yúdice, 2003). This transgression is particularly evident when considering the passport's disruption of conventional migration privileges, beginning in 2005 when Jelinek began issuing passports to residents of Nigeria, Ghana, Togo, South Africa, Benin, Cameroon, Burkina Faso, Libya, Gambia, Liberia, Uganda, Senegal, and Zambia (Jelinek, 2003b). Jelinek initiated an art exchange instead of accepting a monetary payment for the materials used to create the passports, which added to the SoS official state art collection. However, very shortly, the influx of African citizenship applications overwhelmed Jelinek. "Within a few months," he explains, "news of this cultural exchange had spread like wildfire to several other African countries and many more works, along with applications, arrived at SoS headquarters. This time, they were articles of street art" (Jelinek, 2003b). According to Jelinek, this spike in applications was related to the African applicants' successful use of these documents as

Figure 10: SoS Consulate Office. Modern Fuel Artist-Run Centre, 2007.

official pieces of identification, providing these new SoS citizens with the credentials they needed for civil services such as marriage and banking (Jelinek, 2007). Moreover, Jelinek contends that the SoS passports allowed the African applicants to cross national borders their home states had once denied them access to (Jelinek, 2005).

Consequently, the passports were valuable beyond their function in Jelinek's art practice and became a means by which to transgress the regulations of state governance, challenge the norms of state citizenship, and provide the SoS citizens of African origin with access to rights previously denied to them. The events surrounding the issuing of SoS passports have also had serious implications for Jelinek. After the demand for the passports skyrocketed, in March 2006 Jelinek learned that third parties in Nigeria were appropriating SoS passport forms and posing as official agents in order to sell them for profit (Jelinek, 2003b). Jelinek ceased to issue SoS passports at this point, but between June and August 2006 appeals for SoS citizenship only increased, eventually capturing the attention of the Austrian Customs Office and the Criminal Investigation Department. Austria's Office of Public Prosecutor assessed the case but later declined to file charges against Jelinek (Jelinek, 2003b). Nonetheless, Jelinek's difficulties traveling to the US combined with the Austrian government's investigation greatly reduced SoS passport distribution. Currently, Jelinek only issues passports in person through such venues as the SoS Consulate Office at the Modern Fuel, which raises further questions about the continued ability of these passports to transcend the limits of performative intervention based on the select audiences who would attend such gallery openings.

Returning to the Tent City action, there are a number of important considerations for Jelinek's SoS project when it comes to examining the habitus of the hood. In their reading of the case, Liette Gilbert and Catherine Phillips (2003) argue that Tent City's "practices of urban environmental recognition, appropriation and citizenship demonstrate the everyday struggles of and within urban society by exposing the tensions between the promise and the reality of neoliberal democratic governance" (p. 328). It could be argued that in reducing the habitus of citizenship to one of its most common forms, membership to a liberal democratic state, Jelinek's SoS project simultaneously promotes and resists this type of governance. Most importantly, in the specific instance where SoS documents were used by African migrants, the SoS passports provided a means to challenge the embodied dispositions of citizenry, for example, in their ability to confirm, negotiate, and contest the associated state legislated rights (Gilbert & Phillips, 2003). As a result, the precariousness of an art project turned self-declared micronation ironically calls attention to its own limitations in fostering mobility and also in expanding the boundaries of democratic social space. As both the Tent City and SoS examples make clear, there exist significant gaps between constitutional and performative citizenships, making apparent the necessity of examining the relationship between a given habitus and the field in which it takes place.

Conclusion: on artistic intervention

As we have argued throughout this chapter, there is an important distinction to be made between representing so-called precarious settlements (for instance, in Perunovich and Vasic's photographs of Gazela), performing claims to community (as in the *SoS Stoning*), and challenging the disconnect between the rights granted by a state government and the everyday practices of citizenship (in this case, through the use of SoS passports as civil documents) (Gilbert & Phillips, 2003). We therefore distinguish between those who claim rights according to government legislation and those who seek to expand these rights, whether these claims are made through artistic practice or through human presence alone. Gilbert and Phillips (2003) put it best when they explain that "performative citizenship is not something outside of constitutional citizenship; rather it is a set of actions, practices and claims that reveal the gap between an assumed equality of individual citizens within a self-governing nation-state and aspirations for appropriate or even alternative forms of government" (p. 314). In this respect, we give credit to Perunovich, Vasic, and Jelinek as artists since their work allows us to question who belongs where and why. It also allows us to examine the habitus of citizenship and the construction of "precarious life," as both intersect with dwelling and mobility, with greater complexity.

These projects also help to visualize the ways in which the embedded habitus of citizenship is continually being redefined (Gilbert & Phillips, 2003). We see great possibility in the audiences of these art projects, since, like the artists themselves, these participants in contemporary culture make important contributions to these discussions; they too are in the process of questioning, affirming, negotiating, and enacting the everyday habits and habitats of citizenry (Gilbert & Phillips, 2003; Rogoff, 2002b). Much like the collective activism that can emerge from contexts such as the Tent City eviction, wherein residents and their partners (including academics, journalists, and homelessness activists) challenged the confines of liberal citizenry, the audiences of contemporary art practice can also enact change through their engagement with these projects (Rogoff, 2002b). Such collaboration facilitates the use of art as a stage for political action, where, as Irit Rogoff argues, "the potential to engage with [art] as a form of cultural participation rather than as a form of either reification, or representation or contemplative edification, comes into being" (p. 132). By way of conclusion, we would like to suggest here that approaching Perunovich and Vasic's and Jelinek's projects also involves examining the meaning that unfolds in the conversations that follow their installations, performances, and interventions.

And so, in our attempt here to provide critical inquiry into artistic engagements with dwelling and mobility, we recognize the importance of trying to inhabit a problem rather than simply analyze it (Rogoff, 2006). Acknowledging the relationship between contemporary art and its audiences can help to push this discussion beyond the idea that art practice exists in a realm separate from everyday lived reality (Stallabrass, 2004). We ourselves are guilty in this chapter of making the perceived disjuncture between art and everyday life seem like a complete certainty. And so, the potential of work by artists such as Perunovich, Vasic, and

Jelinek, which questions the embodied dispositions that constitute settlement and mobility in relation to a particular field and provides a platform to expand democratic spaces through audience intervention, reminds us of Bourdieu's suggestion that meaning is never produced in isolation (Rogoff, 2006; White, 2006). Not only does this imply bridging the gap between those who are being represented in art practice and those conjuring up the representations, but it also helps to collapse the boundaries between those being studied and those doing the studying (Rogoff, 2002a; 2006). In our minds, looking between these boundaries invites us to reinvestigate notions of citizenship, rights, and belonging and, perhaps, suggests new cultural exercises in the process.

Notes

1. Throughout this essay, we use the term *Romani* (plural *Romanies*) as opposed to *Roma*. As Mayling Simpson-Herbert et al. (2005) write, "Roma is the term that people, who were formerly called 'Gypsies' or 'Cigani', today use for themselves. The term refers to their quite variable ethnic group. It includes people who speak the Romani language as well as those who do not but who know they are of Roma origins" (p. xvii). Ian F. Hancock (2002), a leading Romani activist and academic, notes that although the term *Roma* has recently gained increased usage to describe populations who speak the Romani language and their descendents, many Romanies do not accept this term since the root of the word (*Rom*) typically connotes a married Romani male or, literally, "husband." Therefore, following Hancock, we employ the term *Romani* in keeping with "the common practice of using adjectival forms as nouns (e.g., she is a Bulgarian, he is a Hungarian)" (p. xx).

2. Hancock (2002) discusses the *gadže* (non-Romani) tendency to understand Romani culture as permanently unsettled, wherein "A home means stability and permanence; it means being part of a community, where your neighbors can recognize you and know exactly where you fit into their social structure. Outsiders meet none of these criteria and, being an unknown quantity, pose a potential threat. At best a people without a country must forever be guests in another's homeland, and at worst unwelcome intruders" (p. 55). As Hancock points out, contemporary versions of the traveling "gypsy" persona are "the result of a dynamic which got out of hand in the last century and which then took on a life of its own. It was stimulated by a combination of the responses to industrialization, colonialism and emerging nineteenth century ideas of racial hierarchy" (p. 65). Similarly, the European Roma Rights Centre notes that the "nomad" theory "is used time and again as the justification for excluding the Roma from the responsibility for decision-making normally afforded adult human beings" (quoted in Sigona, 2003, p. 74).

3. While this certainly risks homogenizing Jelinek's Kingston audience, to the best of our understanding, the majority of the *SoS Stoning* participants on Wolfe Island were either residing in or legally visiting Canada.

References

A Space Gallery. (2007). Aberrations (ex situ). *A Space Gallery*. Retrieved from http://www. aspacegallery.org/index.php?m=programdetails&id=42.

Bhabha, H. K. (1994). *The Location of Culture*. New York: Routledge.

Blackson, R. (2007). Once More … With Feeling: Reenactment in Contemporary Art and Culture. *Art Journal*, 66(1) (Spring), 28–40.

Bourdieu, P. (1977). *Outline of a Theory of Practice*. London: Cambridge University Press.

Bourdieu, P. (1990). *Sociology in Question*. Cambridge: Polity Press.

Bourdieu, P. (1999). Site Effects. In P. Bourdieu et al., *The Weight of the World: Social Suffering in Contemporary Society*. Stanford, CA: Stanford University Press.

Bourdieu, P. and Wacquant, L. (1992). *An Invitation to Reflexive Sociology*. Chicago: Chicago University Press.

Butler, J. (2006). *Precarious Life: The Powers of Mourning and Violence*. London: Verso.

CBC News. (2002). Homeless Evicted from Toronto's "Tent City." *CBC*, September 25. Retrieved from http://www.cbc.ca/canada/story/2002/09/24/tentcity_eviction020924.html.

Comaroff, J. and Comaroff, J. L. (2001). Millennial Capitalism: First Thoughts on a Second Coming. In J. Comaroff and J. L. Comaroff (Eds), *Millennial Capitalism and the Culture of Neoliberalism* (pp. 1–56). Durham and London: Duke University Press.

Conlon, J. (2005). Nature, Heritage and Spatial Technologies of Fear: Uncanny Experiences in Kruger National Park. *CTheory*, November 11. Retrieved from www.ctheory.net/articles.aspx?id=497.

Cooper, R. (2005). Seeking Asylum: R. D. Laing and the Therapeutic Community. In S. Raschid (Ed.), *R. D. Laing: Contemporary Perspectives* (pp. 297–312). London: Free Association Books.

Crowe, C. (2007). *Dying for a Home: Homeless Activists Speak Out*. Toronto: Between the Lines.

Davis, M. (2006. *Planet of Slums*. London: Verso.

Deleuze, G. and Guattari, F. (1994). *What is Philosophy?* H. Tominson and G. Birchill (Trans). 4th edn. London: Verso.

Dovey, K. (2005). The Silent Complicity of Architecture. In J. Hillier and E. Rooksby (Eds), *Habitus: A Sense of Place* (pp. 283–296). London: Ashgate.

Forman, M. (2002) *The Hood Comes First: Race, Space, and Place in Rap and Hip-Hop*. Minnesota: Wesleyan University Press.

Friedmann, J. (2002). *The Prospect of Cities*. Minneapolis: University of Minnesota Press.

Gilbert, L. and Phillips, C. (2003). Practices of Urban Environmental Citizenships: Rights to the City and Rights to Nature in Toronto. *Citizenship Studies*, 7(3), 313–330.

Hancock, I. F. (2002). *We Are the Romani People*. Hatfield, UK: University of Hertfordshire Press.

Hampton, M. (2009). Slumdogs and Millionaires: Tours in Mumbai's Dharavi District. *Travel Weekly*, February 19. Retrieved from http://www.travelweekly.co.uk/Articles/2009/02/19/30303/slumdogs-and-millionaires-tours-in-mumbais-dhavari.html.

Horwatt, E. (2007). Robert Jelinek. *Visible City Project and Archive*. Retrieved from http://www. visiblecity.ca/home/index.php?option=com_content&task=view&id=140&Itemid=65.

Immen, W. and Rusk, J. (2002). Toronto's Tent City Sealed Off, Squatters Ejected. *Globe and Mail*, September 25, A1.

Jamieson, Lynn. Migration, Place and Class: Youth in a Rural Area. *Sociological Review* 48, no. 2 (May 2000): 203–223.

Jelinek, R. (2003a). DE FACTO–DE JURE Forms of State Recognition. *The State of Sabotage*. Retrieved from www.sabotage.at/sos/defacto.php.

—— (2003b) Notice to Applicants from Africa. *The State of Sabotage*. Retrieved from http://www. sabotage.at/sos/notice_for_african_de.php.

—— (2003c). SoS Passports. *The State of Sabotage*. Retrieved from www.sabotage.at/sos/passport.php.

—— (2003d). What is Sabotage? *The State of Sabotage*. Retrieved from http://www.sabotage.at/sos/ what.php.

—— (2005). The African Chamber. In *TOUCH DOWN Africa/USA*, 5. Vienna.

—— (2007). Interview by Sarah Smith. September 13, 2007. Modern Fuel Artist-Run Centre, Kingston.

Jelinek, R. and Giger, H. R. (2003). Roots of Sabotage. In *The Formation*, 5. Vienna.

Kemeny, M. (2007). The Spirit of Serbia's Roma People Shines in Glendon Exhibit. *YFile: York's Daily Bulletin*, October 31. Retrieved from http://www.yorku.ca/yfile/archive/index.asp?Article=9341.

Paice, K. (2005). Artistic License. *Art on Paper* (May/June), 42–43.

Postone, M., LiPuma, E. & Calhoun, C. (1993). Introduction: Bourdieu and Social Theory. In C. Calhoun, E. LiPuma, & M. Postone (Eds), *Bourdieu: Critical Perspectives* (pp. 1–13). Chicago: University of Chicago Press.

Rao, V. (2006). Slum as Theory: The South/Asian City and Globalization. *International Journal of Urban and Regional Research, 30*(1) (March), 225–232.

Reay, D.(2004). "It's All Becoming a Habitus": Beyond the Habitual Use of Habitus in Educational Research. *British Journal of Sociology of Education, 25*(4). 431–444.

Rogoff, I. (2002a). Hit and Run – Museums and Cultural Difference. *Art Journal, 61*(3) (Autumn), 63–73.

—— (2002b). We – Collectivities, Mutualities, Participations. In D. von Hantelmann & M. Jongbloed (Eds), *I Promise It's Political* (pp. 127–133). Cologne: Museum Ludwig.

—— (2006). "Smuggling" – An Embodied Criticality. *Transform* (European Institute for Progressive Cultural Politics, 5. Retrieved from http://transform.eipcp.net/transversal/0806/rogoff1/en.

Ryan, J., Dunford, G. & Sellars, S. (2006). *Micronations: The Lonely Planet Guide to Home-Made Nations*. Oakland, CA: Lonely Planet Publications Pty Ltd.

Stallabrass, J. (2004) *Art Incorporated: The Story of Contemporary Art*. Oxford: Oxford University Press.

Sigona, N. (2003). How Can a "Nomad" be a "Refugee"? Kosovo Roma and Labelling Policy in Italy. *Sociology, 37*(1), 69–79.

Simpson-Herbert, M., Mitrovic, A., Zajic, G., & Petrovic, M. (2005). *A Paper Life: Belgrade's Roma in the Underworld of Waste Scavenging and Recycling*. Loughborough, UK: Water, Engineering, and Development Centre, Loughborough University.

Perunovich, V. and Vasic, B. (2008). Interview by Erin Morton and Sarah Smith. March 15. Modern Fuel Artist-Run Centre, Kingston.

Weiner, E. (2008). Slum Visits: Tourism or Voyeurism? *New York Times*, March 9. Retrieved from http://www.nytimes.com/2008/03/09/travel/09heads.html.

Welsh, M. and Shepard, M. (2002). Owners Send in Guards to Remove Residents. *Toronto Star*. September 25, A1.

White, M. (2006). The Dispositions of "Good" Citizenship: Character, Symbolic Power, and Disinterest. *Journal of Civil Society, 2*(2), 111–122.

Yúdice, G. (2003). *The Expediency of Culture: Uses of Culture in the Global Era*. Durham, NC and London: Duke University Press.

Chapter 5

Living "The Strip": Negotiating Neighborhood, Community, and Identity on Australia's Gold Coast

Sarah Baker, Andy Bennett, and Patricia Wise

During the last 50 years, the Gold Coast region of south-east Queensland has grown from a cluster of scattered suburban towns, stretching from State capital Brisbane down to the New South Wales border, into a thriving conurbation. Over the last twenty years, the rate of growth in the Gold Coast region has been unprecedented. According to the Australian Bureau of Statistics, between the 2001 and 2006 census dates alone, total growth was 23.5 percent, an average of 3.7 percent per annum, and "472,279 persons were usual residents of Gold Coast City on Census night in 2006" (GCCC/First Release ABS 2006 Census data). Given that the Bureau expected a continued annual growth rate of at least 13,000 residents, the Gold Coast City Council estimates the current population to have passed 500,000 and "this is expected to double over the next 20 years" (GCCC "Centre Improvement Program"). The population, although still predominantly white, is becoming more ethnically and demographically diverse. Alongside an increasing student population due to the rapid expansion of the region's two universities, Griffith and Bond, the Gold Coast attracts high numbers of pensioners and retirees due to its moderate climate and high standard of living as well as people attracted by work in the construction and hospitality industries. Similarly, increasing numbers of professionals are relocating to the Gold Coast to take up positions in the burgeoning cultural and IT industries (while a second major public training hospital adjacent to Griffith University will create a new demand for medical professionals in the region). Within this scenario of rapid socioeconomic change, are vestiges of the original Gold Coast neighborhoods. Often sandwiched between the Gold Coast Highway and the beach, many of these neighborhoods are literally fighting for survival as prospectors mark their ocean-side locations for high-end redevelopment.

The speed and scale of development – and redevelopment – on the Gold Coast has had significant effects on notions of community and place within the region. Indeed, as Wise (2006) observes,

conventional notions of community and neighborhood do not sit well on the Gold Coast … Communities – in the sense of affinity groups – appear and disappear, depending on how committed people are to particular interests and regional issues; how long a locale remains physically intact; and whether residents see themselves as "passing through" as they exchange one property upgrade for another.

(p. 180)

Notwithstanding such pressures and paradoxes, however, vibrant expressions of community can and do manifest themselves along and across the Gold Coast. Such manifestations are predictably pluralistic – yet each in their own way portrays a sense of belonging; the "Palmy Army" a youth gang from Palm Beach (an older Gold Coast neighborhood) whose territorial sensibilities sometimes extend to random violence against "outsiders;" the local woman turned author whose recently published book chronicles the friends she has made through walking her dog on local beaches; the numerous Surf, Bowls, and RSL clubs along the Gold Coast that function as social hubs for citizens of the region; and, indeed, the many residents who form their sense of belonging to the region, of being "Gold Coasters," not so much out of any particular sites or locales, but out of the city's representations of itself in terms of "international resort style" and a globalized set of aesthetic, economic, and sociocultural participations as developed by city marketing and real estate sales discourses.

The purpose of this chapter will be to consider how a range of multiple, dispersed, fragmented yet increasingly "characteristic" qualities of the Gold Coast play out as local groups of residents negotiate the rapidly shifting physical and cultural landscapes of the region in an effort to assert and re-assert particular expressions – and associated rituals – of neighborhood, community, and identity. We also suggest that for many Gold Coast citizens there is no necessary or actual coalescence between these ideas, that is, that notions of neighborhood, community and identity may be as likely to be determined stylistically, contingently, or strategically as to arise out of a sense of or a desire for continuity, sedimentation, "heritage," or stasis.

The Gold Coast as a multiply articulated space

Over the last twenty years, concepts of "space" and "place" have become subject to significant new interpretations invoking pertinent questions of sociocultural agency. Space and place are now regarded not merely as physical manifestations of natural and man-made sites; rather they are seen as socially – and culturally – constructed by those individuals who inhabit or cross them. This, in turn, has a considerable bearing on the meanings attached to space and place in late modern social contexts. Such meanings can no longer be regarded as in any way fixed or essentialist. Rather, social constructions of space and place give rise to what Bennett (2000) refers to as multiple narratives of the "local." In socially situating themselves, individuals perceive and define space and place in highly specific ways – ways that provide varying and distinctly pluralistic means of engagement with concepts of neighborhood, community, locality, and other common descriptors for collective life.

It follows that if space and place are multiply constructed in this way, then they are also apt to become matters of contestation. Thus, as Doreen Massey (1993) observes:

If it is now recognized that people have multiple identities, then the same point can be made in relation to places. Moreover, such multiple identities can be either, or both, a source of richness or a source of conflict.

(p. 65)

Such contestation and conflict in relation to issues of space and place may take a number of forms, from the territoriality of youth cultures and gangs to the constitutionalized lobbying of pressure groups in response to proposed urban re-development and so on. Common to these and other examples of spatial conflict, however, is the operationalization of highly particularized knowledges and discourses pertaining to issues of ownership, belonging, and identity. Despite the arguments of postmodern and globalization theorists that the world is becoming increasingly uniform and placeless, counterarguments suggest that projects of territorialization and reterritorialization remain a key driver of everyday social and cultural process (see for example, Lull, 1995). The ensuing fictions of collective life (Chaney, 1993) become powerfully inscribed in spatial metaphors. Individuals draw upon the physical and discursive properties of space and place as means of socially and culturally situating themselves. A useful model for understanding the value of space and place in this respect is Keith and Pile's concept of "spatialization." According to Keith and Pile (1993) "spatialization" serves

to capture the ways in which the social and spatial are inextricably realized one in the other; to conjure up the circumstances in which society and space are simultaneously realized by thinking, feeling, doing individuals and also to conjure up the many different conditions in which such realizations are experienced by thinking, feeling, doing subjects.

(p. 6)

Given the rapidly shifting social and physical terrain of the Gold Coast region, the process of spatialization as described by Keith and Pile is particularly apparent. Vestiges of traditional Gold Coast neighborhoods stand side by side with new building projects and developments. These contesting physical articulations of space and place harbor distinctive groups of individuals who often pursue radically different lifestyles, both socioeconomically and culturally, the latter in turn giving rise to very different cultural perceptions of the Gold Coast as a "social" space. For many long-term residents of the Gold Coast, their perception of place and belonging is couched in a long-term sense of neighborhood and community, albeit one subject to the encroachment of property developers and rapid urban transformation – or "churn." For other, more newly arrived residents, an understanding of space and place on the Gold Coast is paradoxically motivated by the frenetic temporality of the Gold Coast as a twenty-first-century city which, due to socioeconomic and environmental factors, has an acutely unstable and uncertain future.

Intermeshed with such locally experienced versions of the Gold Coast, "locals" and temporary residents of the region alike also engage with another set of representations of the Gold Coast as a mediated space. Globally speaking, the Gold Coast is firmly entrenched in a mediascape (Appadurai, 1990) of highly desirable holiday destinations and has consequently become a potent symbol of Australia within the tourist gaze (Urry, 1990). A further dimension of the Gold Coast's re-presentation as a mediatized space is seen in the recently broadcast serialized TV drama *The Strip*, the latter weaving its own sensationalized fiction of the Gold Coast as an LA-style center for crime and corruption set against a backdrop of glamour, wealth, exquisite beaches and coastal scenery. *The Strip* is discussed in more detail below.

The Gold Coast as hood

Such pluralistic, and often fragmented or fragmenting, narratives of the local suggest the need for a revised definition of the hood as this applies to the Gold Coast. Indeed, it could be argued that the concept of the hood is itself an idealized construct – one that bespeaks a sociocultural need to identify and consolidate a notion of place and belonging rather than any essential or given quality of a place. That said, if we are to accept Massey's (1993) interpretation of places as both distinctive and infinitely contested, it follows that the complexities – and contradictions – of the hood as both a naming and situating device is open to scrutiny at the micro-social level. To transpose the concept of the hood onto a particular space is to begin a journey of exploration into the particular socioeconomic and cultural forces that come together in shaping the discourses of place and belonging that coexist there and in many cases compete – overtly or covertly – against each other.

In dealing specifically with the Gold Coast, it should be clear from what precedes that we perceive the region as acutely difficult to quantify in terms of any singular notion of community, neighborhood, and so on. Across a series of critical bases – socioeconomic, cultural, historical, spatial – the Gold Coast comprises a range of collective groupings and attendant expressions of sociality that are inherently out of step with each other. Beaches, bars, clubs and shopping centers may appear to register as common nodal points, but in reality these may say more about fragmentation than cohesion within and among the Gold Coast population. Each of these and other points of convergence say much more about the transience than the stability of Gold Coast life – and about the plurality rather than cohesiveness of local narratives of space and place on the Gold Coast. Undoubtedly, older Gold Coast neighborhoods, notably Palm Beach, which have to a greater extent escaped – or await – the transforming hand of property developers, engender vestiges of "community" that adhere more readily with conventional notions of the hood. Even here, however, it is clear that transience and instability have begun to take hold; indeed, expressions of neighborhood, for example the territoriality of local youth gangs, would seem to highlight a perceived loss of community and resistance to change.

Both empirically and conceptually, the Gold Coast presents a complexly rich, yet highly contradictory, sociocultural universe. On the one hand, working-class youth cultures and gangs who appear to exhibit those same subcultural yearnings for magical recovery of community identified among East London youth by Phil Cohen in the early 1970s (Cohen, 1972). On the other hand, transient middle-class and leisure-based social groupings whose temporal bonds and rituals of conspicuous consumption and lifestyle adhere more readily with Maffesoli's (1996) notion of the neotribe. To this, of course, must be added a swelling population of ageing baby boomers and younger workers attracted to the Gold Coast region due to its sub-tropical climate, beachside living, and general quality of life. While each of these, and other, elements of the diffuse local population consider themselves Gold Coast residents, the knowledges, sensibilities, and everyday discourses that they bring to bear in situating themselves as such bespeak very different understandings of what it means to be a resident – and, by definition, a citizen – of the Gold Coast. At the same time, there may also be an emergent experience of being a "Gold Coaster" that does not lodge in conventional questions of citizenship or community, but more in people's engagements with representations of regional "milieu," "stylistics," and "ways of living." This experience is clearly and strongly mediated by commercially produced versions of "Gold Coast lives" and "lifestyle," but it is an experience that is, it would seem, becoming embodied and expressed by a surprising range of people in their own ideas of "life in the Gold Coast style." If we refuse a nostalgia for forms of community and citizenship (romantically) undetermined by media, consumerism, and property development, it may well be possible to discover the potential for something of a shared understanding of what it means to be a resident and citizen of the Gold Coast that takes account of the ubiquity of mediated representations of the city and its residents.

Youth culture on the Gold Coast

Unlike the neighboring city of Brisbane, set on the Brisbane River some distance from the ocean, the most readily identifiable youth culture on the Gold Coast centers around the beach – most notably the highly vibrant local surfing scene. Among the many chapters of youth style documented over the years, surf culture has remained conspicuously absent from the literature (for exceptions, see Evers, 2004; Ford & Brown, 2005). Precisely why this should be the case is unclear but undoubtedly it has some relation to the dominant emphasis on stylized inner-city and street-based urban youth cultures. Along the Gold Coast, surf culture is both a crossclass and multiethnic phenomenon. To some degree surfing is also a crossgender phenomenon although it is accurate to say that it is still a predominantly male activity.

Arguments against the until-quite-recently dominant paradigm of subcultural theory have gone to lengths to point out the problems inherent in conceptualizing all youth cultural activities as class-based (see, for example, Clarke, 1981; Bennett, 1999; Muggleton, 2000). Surfing culture offers an interesting example of how an ostensibly cohesive youth cultural activity can, in fact, encapsulate a range of different sensibilities encompassing aspects of class, locality, together with style, technique and other forms of knowledge and expertise defined by Thornton (1995) as subcultural capital.

That said, other elements of Gold Coast youth do exhibit a strongly class-based, gang structure. A significant example of this is the "Palmy Army," a localized youth culture located in an old, originally working-class suburb of Palm Beach. During recent years, there have been a number of reports in the local media concerning incidents of violence involving members of the Palmy Army and other youth gangs in the region. Similarly, attacks on temporary and transient Gold Coast residents – young tourists, backpackers, and students – connote a strong sense of territoriality on the part of the Palmy Army and members of other local youth gangs. In this sense, the Palmy Army exhibit behavior not unlike classic British working-class youth cultures such as the Teddy Boys and Skinheads for whom issues of turf and territory were key to their rituals of male bonding and collective shows of violence against members of other gangs and newly arrived immigrant groups (see Clarke, 1976; Jefferson, 1976). In the case of the Palmy Army then, we see a clear example of a discourse of space and place in the Gold Coast region grounded in notions of traditional neighborhood and local community. For members of the Palmy Army, the perceived threat to neighborhood and community cohesion by socioeconomic and demographic change becomes a key driver for the gang's ritual displays of violence.

Dramatizing "the hood" in *The Strip*

The media is important in other ways too. With its vast expanses of water and expensive real estate the Gold Coast is a cinematographer's dream and as such it is used regularly as a location for international film productions. Its diverse geography, from the beach and ocean, rivers, and canals, to cane fields to the hinterland's mountains and escarpments, makes the region highly adaptive to being a stand-in for on-screen movie settings. Home to the Warner Roadshow Studios, whose theme park, Warner Brothers Movieworld is dubbed "Hollywood on the Gold Coast," the region is promoted internationally by local and state government as an attractive and affordable place to film and make movies. It has also been the setting of home-grown television dramas. In the nineties drama serials *Paradise Beach* and *Pacific Drive* were both filmed and set on the Gold Coast, depicting its aspirational lifestyle which was at that time widely represented in the increasingly sophisticated material produced by the booming development industry. More recently the city has become the setting of a thirteen-part crime drama, *The Strip*, commissioned and broadcast by Network Nine and produced by Sydney-based production company Knapman Wyld who were previously the makers of gritty Australian crime series like *Wildside* and *White Collar Blue*. *The Strip* is particularly interesting for discussion in that it depicts the glamour and high-end real estate of the Gold Coast as currently marketed but as a crime drama it also explores what is noticeably absent in such advertising and in glossy Gold Coast publications like *Panache* magazine – that is, the darker elements that all neighborhoods can possess.

As described by the series co-producer, the first episode of *The Strip* begins with "a chopper shot coming in off the Pacific Ocean on to a character hanging 50 stories up on the tallest building on the Coast which is reflecting all the other buildings, the sky and the sea" (Knapman in "Gold Coast stars …" 2008, para 8). It is visually exciting and effortlessly captures the fragmented beauty of the beach strip. The program's aesthetic is akin to American crime series like *CSI: Miami* and as the production company states "Like LA and Miami for Americans, we want to make *The Strip* a national icon for Australians": "a place the audience will want to revisit every week" (Wyld in Nine Network 2008, para 6). The Gold Coast and *The Strip*, as the Coast's mediated representation, then, share the same characteristic – they are experienced as a visitor's respite; "somewhere that others c[o]me to enjoy, and leave" (Wise & Breen, 2004, p. 164). This is a region that encourages its residents to emulate the tourist (see also Wise & Breen, 2004, p. 163) and *The Strip* tacitly asks the Gold Coast television audience to view the series in this same light. That is, like the real estate advertising, the real Gold Coasters are invited to fold themselves into their own representations unproblematically, and to (re)produce themselves – to-a-point – according to how they see themselves in the images of them. When the on-location filming moved to the Gold Coast's southern beachside suburb of Coolangatta locals and tourists intermingled to watch scenes being shot ("TV Drama Hits Town," 2008), and the local media coverage of the event participated enthusiastically in the proliferation of inter-implicated image-production.

At the time of writing Baker lived in Surfers Paradise. The view from her high-rise apartment took in the hinterland, shrouded in a sunny haze, the sparkling waters of the Nerang River and, through the other high rises of Surfers Paradise (the closest thing that this sprawling region has to a downtown), glimpses of the deep blue sea. From this position in the strip, the Gold Coast can only be described as a richly cinematic neighborhood – something that works on-screen and for tourism. As one Gold Coast resident wrote in an online forum dedicated to the series: "Being a Gold Coaster myself (if that term ever existed), I feel the constant scene changes remind me of segments for a Gold Coast Tourism Video" (Chef_24, 2008). However, a tourism video would not then show a window cleaner falling in suspicious circumstances from one of the region's iconic high-rise apartment buildings as happened in the first episode of *The Strip*. Weekly on-screen murders in Australia's postmodern playground "will deter tourists" according to one viewer who wrote to the regional newspaper (Austen, 2008, p. 26). The Gold Coast Tourism Corporation (GCTC) does not share this view, saying depictions of crime will not "harm the area's reputation as a leading family destination" because "audiences know how to distinguish what's true from what is fiction" (Pole in Jensen, 2008, para 7, p. 9). Obviously, deterring tourists was never Knapman Wyld's intention. Rather, the production company states that its premise for the series was "all that glitters is not gold … People come up here with a dream, and what if they don't fulfil it?" (Knapman in Idato, 2008, para 11). In a place such as the Gold Coast, which the coproducer describes as "a temple of materialism," the answer for *The Strip* is that such people turn to crime (ibid.).

The Strip centers on the detectives of the fictitious Main Beach CIB (offscreen location is Fifty Cavill Avenue, an office block in Surfers Paradise) who investigate organized crime on the Gold Coast. Though, as stated above, the GCTC see *The Strip* as a fictional portrayal of the Coast, stating that the producers chose the region "not because of the criminal element but because it's a distinct city" (Pole in Jensen, 2008, para 8), offscreen reviews of the series and interviews with actors and "real" Gold Coast police officers blur the "fiction" of this mediation of the community of crime. One real Gold Coast police officer, when asked for his opinion on the first episode, was reported as commenting that *The Strip* "realistically portrays the Coast's crime landscape" and that the producers have "done some research on the local criminals and Gold Coast identities" (Doneman, 2008, para 2, p. 4). In media interviews, Frankie J. Holden, who plays one of the detectives in the series, is particularly vocal about the seedier side of the Gold Coast. Holden reported that on first arriving on the Gold Coast for filming, co-star Jeffery "found a gram of coke in the lift of his hotel" (in Braithwaite, 2008, para 4). And television critic Graeme Blundell (2008), observes that the Gold Coast is a "playground of excess" and the "languid sleaze" of its onscreen representation shows it to be "a world of lurking dangers" (paras 3, 9, 10). What *The Strip* gives us, then, is "the city as a surface of specious and ambiguous glamour hiding depths of corruption" (Blundell, 2008, para 23). But does "the strip" give us that too? Holden believes it does:

> I think it's really fertile ground for a show of this type because it's got a lot of elements there in real life that lend themselves to drama … You've got all that money, there is so much money floating around up there, you've got a transient population, there is sleaze up there, people go up there to have "a good time," so there's strip clubs and all that sort of thing there. There's a lot of money gets washed through there, I know that for a fact.
> (Holden in Braithwaite, 2008, para 13–15)

Though Holden was initially concerned that having one major crime incident per show would seem excessive, this concern dissipated once he arrived on the Gold Coast where sitting "on his condo balcony at night after rehearsals … all he could hear was the sound of sirens" (Blundell, 2008, para 7).

The Gold Coast of *The Strip*, then, is perhaps as close as we get to the region as hood in the contemporary ghetto sense of that term. The cinematic vision might be one of urban and natural beauty but this is marred by bodies buried in the sand or falling from high-rise buildings. The image of paradise is pierced by the sound of wailing sirens. Can these mediated representations overwhelm the "real" spatializations as experienced by a community? To what extent does the "real" community enact such a dramatization of the hood? And how does this gel with the more glamorous depiction by real estate advertising and in the pages of *Panache* magazine? The region's newspapers share a preoccupation with crime reporting, with the regional tabloid, *The Gold Coast Bulletin*, using "big" crime to portray the city as having a dark underbelly on par with big cities like Melbourne, while the suburban *Gold Coast Sun* focuses more on "expressions of community concern about the growing incidence of localized crime such as burglary and vandalism" (Griffin, 2002, pp. 113–114).

Beyond the "news from your neighborhood"

Mediated representations of a "neighborhood," such as those in *The Strip*, those produced by the marketing of high-rise buildings, or suggested by the sophisticated consumerism, the expensively promoted plastic surgery makeovers as well as the parochially "glitzy" social pages elements of *Panache* magazine, have the potential to overwhelm the lived community of residents. As a way to explore how people negotiate the mediated representations of the Gold Coast we now turn to two local newspapers through which those who live in its neighborhood(s) have an opportunity to publicly voice their concerns in the "Letters to the Editor" pages. Though regional and suburban newspapers are often maligned in the literature, it has also been argued that the local press plays an important role in constructing and reflecting a sense of community. For Ewart (2000), regional media underpins "the identity and culture of communities and their publics" (p. 1). It is through the representations of the "local" in this media that "a community comes to recognize and hence know itself" with regional newspapers, for example, indicating "what it means to be a member of that region's public" (Ewart, 2000, pp. 1–2). By creating "consensus narratives" around the "values and meaning" a community can or should embody, suburban and regional newspapers, along with other forms of local media, "bind [...] individuals into a social collective or *media public*" (Ewart, 2000, pp. 2–3). However, very little has been written about how the letters pages in these publications, rather than journalist-led stories, contribute to collective community imaginings or media publics.

The "community" newspapers in question here are *The Gold Coast Bulletin*, a regional daily (circulation 40,649, average) with a weekend edition (circulation 70,348), and the *Gold Coast Sun* (circulation 166,401), a free weekly suburban with four geographically targeted editions. Griffin (2002) provides a useful review of both papers – drawing on their similarities and contrasts. He describes the *Bulletin* as gaining considerable revenue from real estate advertising; as having a front page that "presents a flamboyant mix of big photograph and banner headline;" its hard news and investigative reporting often tinged with editorial opinion; human interest stories concentrating on local and international celebrities and "returning hometown heroes;" a personality-centered approach to local government reporting; a geographical focus on the beach, high-rise, tourist and commercial areas of the coastal strip; promotion of annual big-ticket events; and a mix of "banal localism" focused on the area's image renewal (boosterism) and nostalgia (Griffin, 2002, pp. 111–115). On the other hand, the *Sun* is viewed by Griffin as containing a significant proportion of advertising from used car dealers and liquor outlets rather than real estate; as conventional in its lead story reporting, rejecting editorializing, trivializing, and sensationalizing and showing a preference for human interest reports featuring local individuals and community groups;

factual reporting of local government matters; geographical focus on the suburbs with less news about the "spectacular" Gold Coast events; and an overall concern for residents' "immediate material concerns, interests and well being" (ibid.). What both newspapers share is their preoccupation with crime reporting.

This overview of the two papers provides an early indication, perhaps, of what might find its way into their respective letters pages. The *Sun*, for example, promotes itself as being "Australia's largest community newspaper" with "News from YOUR neighborhood!" and talks about giving its readers a "voice": "People can't solve the world's problems but they can voice their opinions on issues close to home" (*Gold Coast Sun*, 2008a, p. 6). "Letters to the Editor" certainly have the potential to be an outlet for the airing of community concerns. One might imagine that it would be in these, even more so than the news stories, that the local would come to the fore. Even if not necessarily providing the voice of a cohesive community, the letters pages of a paper that positions itself as the *Sun* does might be expected to begin to throw light on residents' understandings of the meanings of neighborhood or the image and identity of the local. Similarly, following threads during October and November 2008 in the *Bulletin's* "Chatroom" page, where readers send comments by SMS, one could conclude that a core concern for many residents is dangerous driving by "hoons" in Gold Coast neighborhoods. Many texts described young people's driving habits – young people being the hoons – as disruptive and dangerous and so applauded the launch of a neighborhood "hoon" watch, a collaboration between police and community to tackle this "menace." Some messages then made a link between hoons and the Gold Coast's premiere motor-racing event, the Nikon Indy 300, which was held at the end of October on the streets of Surfers Paradise and Main Beach. As D. Hayson (2008) from Mudgeeraba wrote: "Hoon watch is a great initiative by the people to help the understaffed police catch these clowns who r [*sic*] using our once quiet suburb for their own Indy track" (61). The nature of the texts linking hoons with Indy do hint at a sense of community: "Hopefully the last Indy. The Gold Coast will do fine without it and the worthless drunks and rednecks it attracts" (Phil, 2008, p. 61). However, communities are always multiple and there were as many texts supporting young drivers and the continuation of the Indy race as there were messages opposing them. The "Chatroom" gave no clear indication of a generalizable community attitude to the issue. Nevertheless, it demonstrates citizens' engagement with a topical issue of local concern.

Contrary to expectations, rather than having a local focus on neighborhood concerns close to home, the letters pages of both the *Sun* and the *Bulletin* more often reflect state, national, and global issues. This suggests that while the local identities of communities might be fostered in suburban and regional newspapers, a sense of local identity cannot be separated from national or global concerns – concerns which prove just as meaningful in a neighborhood context. The letters in the Gold Coast newspapers were about the effects of the global "credit crunch," all levels of politics from local government to US elections, and environmental issues including Queensland water restrictions – the latter having significant meaning for what the Gold Coast defines itself against, for example: "Got to look after ourselves some time to prove to Brisbane we are a big city and not just a tourist destination" (GC Born, 2008, p. 32) and "Am I missing something here or do residents of the Gold Coast take another back seat to the residents of Brisbane?" (Hill, 2008, p. 21). The idea that this community has to go outside its borders to understand its own identity, values, and meaning is confirmed by 62-year-old Dallas Fraser, a Gold Coast resident of six years who has written in excess of 100 letters to the *Sun* during that time (*Gold Coast Sun*, 2008b). Fraser, who is "interested in what goes on in the community and [his] local area," and is an equally prolific letter writer to the *Sydney Morning Herald* (a major metropolitan broadsheet) and *The Australian* (the national broadsheet), also believes it is "important for people to be informed on world affairs." His letters to the *Sun* certainly reflect a desire to tackle issues beyond a local community level (*Gold Coast Sun*, 2008b, p. 18).

Without a comparative study of other suburban and regional newspapers we cannot comment on how common it is for letters to the editor in these contexts to have such an outward focus, but we suspect these letters in the *Sun* and the *Bulletin* may well confirm the extent to which the Gold Coast is unconventional in its understanding of community (Wise, 2006). It is perhaps because the community "knows itself" so well (Griffin, 1998), through the multi-mediations of its postmodern, desired and desiring frontier self, that a sense of community now tends to come from a deeper understanding of the region's place in the world. Or maybe this is reflective of the Gold Coast being "outside community" in the same way Wise and Breen (2004) describe the region as "outside history" (164). Whatever the case, the letters pages in these suburban and regional papers do provide residents with a forum in which a sense of "glocal" spatialized belonging can be reflexively negotiated.

Becoming-city: community and nature

The City Council has responded to its dispersed, volatile, multi-community city by undertaking various strategies promoting a Gold Coast community with "shared community values." Despite this, citizens commonly observe an absence of community at a broader level. A desire for a settled sense of identification is a phase a young city can be expected to reach but for the Gold Coast this is just as likely to be impelled by how the city is typically represented in Australian popular culture as "glitter/glitz city," "sleazy," "tacky," "bizarre," "a great place to visit but you wouldn't want to live there," a "cultural desert," and "Surface Paradise." From time to time serious media provide more sophisticated readings in which the Gold Coast becomes a booming conurbation, an emergent economic hub in the globally significant "Pacific Rim" and a paradigmatically postmodern city characterized by the play of surfaces across an implied cultural depthlessness.

People have tried to engender connections with "the real" by seeking out representations of local history, of permanence. But the spaces and discourses of leisure and "lifestyle" tend to override, dominate, and dissolve all others, including those of the daily lives of ordinary residents. In any case, the pace of growth is such that it is unusual to meet a person over 30 who grew up on the Coast. The majority of the adult population arrived in the last fifteen or twenty years, attracted by the same representations that make it difficult to invoke continuity and heritage. Despite frequent observations that wholesale development destroys any chance of community, development tends to be accepted by many residents as a necessary part of their city's economic well-being and its identity. There will be opposition to projects that threaten the environment, which is seen as a precious amenity. However, most locals have a realistic grasp of the fact that high environmental values equate high real-estate values. The city sells nature alongside glamour, leisure, and high-rise living, and the ideas of "nature" and "natural" are deeply implicated in regional cultures, politics, and identities.

For example, "nature" has been incorporated as part of "lifestyle" so that, in a multiple set of dynamics, which we will suggest constitute a distinctive aspect of the Gold Coast urban and regional experience, residents accept extreme and everyday kinds of development up-to-a-point. "A point" can be reached when treasured local beaches, wave breaks, coastal heath, or hinterland forest are at stake. Yet the built environment has looped back into the natural environment as amenity through ubiquitous sales discourses of "panorama," "sweeping views," and "water aspects" that accompany the marketing of apartments, resorts, and houses.

Most strikingly, the environment as panorama is consumed from the high-rises but the high-rises have become and are always becoming part of the panorama. This recalls Deleuze and Guattari's (1987) well-known discussion of the rhizomatics and exchange of signifiers involved in the relationship between the wasp and the orchid. What happens with the Gold Coast's tourism *and* development *and* natural *and* residential amenity *and* marketing *and* lifestyle assemblage is just such a rhizomatics, involving not only complex movements in-between that make multiplicities, but a "capture of code." Just as Deleuze and Guattari stress in their description of the wasp/orchid assemblage that there is more than mimicry involved, the assemblages that have emerged on the Gold Coast entail nothing as simple as locals (who need employment) and tourist operators and developers (who need access to local nature in order to make profits) reaching compromise for mutually beneficial ends. Nor is it only a matter of postmodern contingency whereby aspects of the natural world and nostalgic ideas of community are attached as floating signifiers to real estate discourses that operate as simulacra. As Deleuze and Guattari explain:

> At the same time something else entirely is going on: not imitation at all but a capture of code, surplus value of code, an increase in the valence, a veritable becoming, a becoming-wasp of the orchid and becoming-orchid of the wasp. Each of these becomings brings about the deterritorialization of one term and the reterritorialization of the other; the two becomings interlink and form relays in a circulation of intensities pushing the deterritorialization even further.
>
> (p. 10)

The sets of relationships and interactions we are concerned with on the Gold Coast are productive of public amenity and public imaginaries that for an increasing proportion of the residents entail a local identification with – indeed pride in – the beauty of the environment, the excellence of the surf, the cleanliness of the beaches, the greenness of the hinterland, the excesses of the canal and island residences, the noncommunity ironies of the gated communities, the size of the shopping malls, and the uniqueness of the high-rise-by-the-sea Strip with its associated stylistics and aesthetics (even as those same high rises deal in elite private spaces for a regional, national, and international flow of tourists, knowledge economy professionals, and corporate executives). In such a context, conventional urban analytics will not suffice. It has become essential to attend to the rhizomatics; to understand that "any point of a rhizome can be connected to anything other, and must be" (Deleuze & Guattari, 1987, p. 7); to consider what the effects and challenges of this might be; and to map the various captures of code involved in the becoming-city of the Gold Coast. There is a great deal of analysis to be done of shared and distinctive discourses and movements involved in the mix of local representations and conversations, governmentality and corporate activity, notions of social and cultural life, and marketing of real estate and tourism. In the present discussion, we are especially interested in the development and redevelopment, the deterritorialization and reterritorialization, of the city as a space in which the urban, the global, the local, the high life, simple pleasures, and the natural have become inextricably mingled with real effects and affects for local experiences of identities and belongings.

Even as the Gold Coast strives toward a new identity as a cosmopolitan city by the ocean, however, a new struggle is welling up between new and old residents; between those who invest in the type of vision for the Gold Coast outlined above and those who envisage a very different kind of Gold Coast. A critical social demographic here is the region's youth. A point made repeatedly is that little time, space, and resources are invested in cultural and leisure provision for young people. Those spaces that do exist, typically bars and dance clubs, are heavily regulated by security staff and police. All around the Gold Coast the notion of youth as a "problem" looms large. Random acts of violence, including stabbings, have merely reinforced this stereotype of youth. "Schoolies Week" when thousands of final-year high-school students descend on the Gold Coast at the beginning of their summer vacation has been transformed by the local press and authorities into a security management exercise.

Even outside such critically intense periods of youth activity on the Gold Coast, however, there is an overwhelming sense of youth as a social group with nowhere to go and nothing to do. Corrigan's (1976) essay "Doing Nothing," about bored working-class teenagers in provincial England has a keen resonance with youth on the Gold Coast who are frequently to be seen hanging around outside shopping malls and at childrens' playgrounds during the evening. The City Council, recognizing the need to respond to the demands of youth, have installed a number of facilities, such as skateparks. However, given the scale of distance between neighborhoods in the region and the poor public transport system, many young people are unable to take advantage of such resources and remain confined to their immediate locality during the evening.

Predictably, this has produced a series of strategies among young people through which to counter the boredom and frustration they often experience. One of the more spectacular –

and illegal – examples of this is "hooning" (a localized term for dangerous driving) by young males. In their instructive work on the local night-time economy in the United Kingdom, Chatterton and Hollands (2002) describe the way in which young people transform city center spaces into what the authors refer to as urban playscapes. In the same way, hoons transform the quiet, often sleepy streets of neighborhoods on the Gold Coast into playscapes of their own. There are two elements to hoon culture on the Gold Coast. The first are young people who seek to push the limits of their modified performance vehicles (such as the Subaru Impreza WRX) but also who cruise, driving slowly, if noisily, in heavily populated areas like the Surfers Paradise esplanade. These young people are heavily invested in their cars both culturally and economically (see for example Thomas & Butcher, 2003). But there is also a darker side to Gold Coast hoon culture with young people, often from poorer neighborhoods, joy-riding – that is combining risk-taking and the fetishization of desirable, and often highly expensive, stolen cars. Le Breton (2004) has argued that, in late modern, risk-centered societies, the risk-taking games engaged in by young people give them back some control over their bodies and their lives. The risk-taking games that characterize this second group of hoons is multi-layered – the theft of the car, the danger of the speeds attained, and the threat of being apprehended by the police.

Equally salient in the context of the present discussion is the random night-time appropriation by hoons of particular streets and neighborhoods on the Gold Coast in which to enact the collective rituals that give the hoon culture both internal cohesion and local notoriety. The sudden, spontaneous, and often deeply disturbing emergence of hoon behavior in any given neighborhood on the Gold Coast is a telling reminder of the hood politics that continue to feature in the region even as dramatic urban transformation continues. In the case of hooning, the omnipresent threat of the hood is made all the more powerful; empowered with the speed, and noise, of the car the hood loses its fixity in a given space and place. It becomes instead a fully mobile and highly obtrusive threat to the sanctity of those new and upwardly mobile communities that would rather not be forced to reckon with the ever-present possibility of riotous invasion and disquiet.

Style, milieu, and regional identities

A recognition that citizens do not have "*a* version" of the Gold Coast, however valuable in framing approaches to community-based cultural interventions, needs to be considered in relation to other senses in which people may be actively involved in the production of shared notions of regional identities. As we have noted, residents can appropriate, manipulate, and enjoy the complex processes of deterritorialization and reterritorialization implicit in the experience of living in a city whose core business is to sell itself as a dream city that provides experiences for citizens of other cities. Residents and tourists become actors in the performance of the city as an interactive exhibition space *and* exhibit. At the same time, the city is always already selling images of itself to itself and an emphasis on image construction becomes deeply implicated in community and individual identity construction. The Gold Coast is obviously not alone in the aspects of city marketing whereby cities begin to believe their own public relations – but most citizens affected by such processes also remain aware of well-established historical and demographic continuities within their own city's spin. For Gold Coast residents, what they are currently telling others about themselves becomes apparently naturalized as what they tell themselves about themselves. Codes and traces slide and trail between resort advertising; tourism promotion; real-estate marketing; regional, social, and cultural representations, but also between the material world and questions of identity.

A sense of the interimplication of longer-term personal or group identity with current urban identity can become largely a play of fragments of popular cultural memory and current expressions across striking contemporary surfaces – real and representational – that never settle. Residents, though, assemble their own notions of what it means to be "a Gold Coaster" out of their experience of the city's representations. To expect that they might do otherwise would be to have recourse to a nostalgia for ideas of identity based in a "local" understood as a "locale" with a continuous – and somehow more authentic – population, civic identity, built environment and cultural heritage which, as noted earlier, is not the experience of a Gold Coast resident.

The city is currently in the business of inventing itself as smoothly interimplicated in an international space of flows and to explore this it is helpful to draw on Deleuze and Guattari (1997) again:

> We will call an *assemblage* every constellation of singularities and traits deducted from the flow – selected, organized, stratified – in such a way as to converge (consistency) artificially and naturally; an assemblage, in this sense, is a veritable invention.
>
> (p. 406)

Through processes involving all sorts of capture of code, it has become a feature of Gold Coast living to invent and reinvent one's own ways of living and sense of the available milieus for daily life to reflect a range of ideas about what living-as-a-Gold-Coaster might entail. These processes draw strongly on the marketing materials for high-rise real estate. Across almost the full range of socioeconomic groups, the choice to move to the Gold Coast usually also involves a choice to take up a particular "lifestyle" that, broadly, makes a sense of sub-tropical leisure part of everyday life. "Gold Coasters" can be seen to be choosing certain desirable aspects of life as they might choose desirable aspects of real estate: "a stunning environment," "sweeping views," "many kilometers of clean beaches," "the glorious hinterland with its access to fresh farm food," a "booming regional economy with ready links to global markets," and "excellent educational facilities" – all in conjunction with "a leisurely lifestyle combined with the pace, excitement, and convenience of a global city that is on 24/7." Not only for those with the capacity to actually purchase high-rise apartments but for most who have made a choice to live in the region, there is an impression of at least having access to the best of both worlds – of living and working in a place where everyone else takes holidays.

The milieu that is taken to be uniquely Gold Coast (even if it is not) captures international resort tourism values and aesthetics, and a collection of other components of Gold Coast lifestyle such as certain architectural, landscaping, and decorating preferences, ways of dressing, foods, and leisure activities. To express these traits, in varying ways and to different degrees depending on income and cultural/social capital, the "Gold Coaster" must draw on an awareness of how a resident might be expected to live as seen through the eyes of tourists *and* how a resident might be expected to live as represented in the promotional material for real estate developments. The aspirational habitus is spacious, safe, light, and leisurely with a relaxed air of community while simultaneously (and paradoxically) cosmopolitan, edgy, sophisticated, and glamorous (although at the level of individuals and families, life may be as mundanely cluttered and over-stretched, or as insecure and unhappy, as it can be in any contemporary city).

The expensive and extensive marketing for Gold Coast high-rise real estate appears in focused materials such as brochures and websites for real estate companies but also for particular (and often spectacular) developments. It is an entrenched advertising and advertorial feature in national and regional glossy magazines, the lifestyle and real estate pages of national and regional newspapers, and in television advertising. In addition to these sites, and well before the development actually arrives, its visual placement in the existing environment and its story are unavoidably introduced to the regional imaginary through large-scale billboards along the motorways into the Gold Coast.

The marketing for Circle on Cavill in Surfers Paradise – a mixed-use residential and resort complex consisting of two high-rise towers, a piazza, retail precinct, and subtropical landscaping – exemplifies the style we are describing. The developer, Sunland Group, launched presales marketing by folding the public and the private into each other with "Circle on Cavill. Pulse point of the City, yet a seductively private sanctuary." The built form was in turn folded into the city and into a narrative of city formation: "The smooth fluidity characteristic of modern architecture visually references the progress and pace of a dynamic 24-hour city" (Sunland Group, *Circle on Cavill*, print brochure). Web-based sales materials drew almost seamlessly on a double movement between globalizing and localizing language:

Circle on Cavill. Two stunning residential towers, integrated with a fabulous retail precinct, fulfill every ultra-modern lifestyle need creating a rare convergence of inner-city energy, beach proximity and luxury resort facilities.

(Sunland Group, *Circle on Cavill* pdf brochure, p. 3)

The whole way of life made familiar by this style of marketing has come to be carried in the inclusive disjunction urban beach village, apparently coined on the Gold Coast by Sunland but now used by several major developers:

At the forefront of the exciting revival of the historic heart of Surfers Paradise, Circle on Cavill sets new parameters for contemporary liveability – striking architecture in tune with spacious design, in an urban beach village showcasing the exceptional pleasures of living the high life.

(Sunland Group, *Circle on Cavill* pdf brochure, p. 3)

"Historic" is obviously a decidedly fluid term: Circle involved the demolition of two city blocks in which few of the buildings were more than 40 years old, and many much less than that. Very few of the demolished buildings were residential. The area was a retail and leisure precinct with a small proportion of tourist accommodation. That is, unlike more familiar processes of gentrification, there was not a pre-existing neighborhood from which residents were displaced. The Circle neighbors would arrive when the development was complete.

Deleuze and Guattari (1987) ask: "How could the movements of deterritorialization and processes of reterritorialization not be relative, always connected, caught up in one another?" (p. 10). The Sunland Group's *2006–7 Annual Report* stressed its "commitment to design and creating space for the community" (p. 22) and also observed that "like the communities we create, Sunland's landmark achievements in the past year have been the product of transforming a vision into a reality" (p. 25). So Sunland positions itself as actualizing not only spaces and their community uses, but also communities and even in some way the people who constitute them. Just as marketing produces "community," residents can produce themselves through captures of the real estate codes.

High-rise buildings, even those at the luxury or near-luxury end of the market, provide a sophisticated façade that renders the spaces behind them invisible, including aspects of life that would elsewhere be experienced on the streets of neighborhoods. But these spaces are not so invisible to those who inhabit the buildings or to long-term residents of the region, social and health workers, charities, and police. A minority of the Gold Coast's luxury high-rise buildings are what locals call "owner-occupied one-unit-per-floor" buildings. These are typically secure, gated, swipe-carded, and very private. Their residents have invested large sums in their apartment purchase; are probably (but not necessarily) very well off; and, as one resident put it, are frequently "living in a bubble" in which, ironically, the illusion of Gold Coast life *is* the reality. The residents' body corporate that manages issues like maintenance in strata title buildings can also act as an aesthetic and social watchdog, so that the residents can be assured that other residents will be just like them. The extent to which such a way of living can in any way be taken to constitute neighborhood or community is questionable. But there is much more to the Gold Coast's high-rises than this.

There are, for example, older high-rise buildings with no such guarantees of privacy, security, and shared bourgeois lifestyle. Even when these are owner-occupied, there will be a proportion of residents struggling to maintain the appearance of a lifestyle they cannot fully afford. Elderly people increasingly find that their fixed income has become inadequate, but they continue to *appear* comfortable, living a tanned and slightly glitzy equivalent of "genteel poor." Divorced people have often downsized and bought a radical change in living circumstances that they may not be able comfortably to sustain but are determined to *perform*. There will be young couples who have stretched their finances in order to buy into the Gold Coast dream at the lower end of the high-rise market, believing that 70s and 80s blocks are inevitably "slated for development" and are thus a good investment, if you can hold out long enough to get a good deal from a developer keen to demolish your building and another three in your city block. So it is that familiar Gold Coast buildings, which tourists or incomers encounter as exotic towers gleaming in the sunshine, may in fact contain a considerable proportion of people living less glamorous lives than their architectural surroundings suggest.

On the other hand, as one resident quipped, "it can take a lot of money to look seedy on the Gold Coast." That is, to walk the line between glamour and excess-as-poor-taste that marks the not insubstantial proportion of residents whose interactions with the law and with each other lead the media to describe them as colorful identities. The same people might be players in the flow of illegal and barely legal commodities and activities essential for their lifestyle – drugs, escort agencies, strip clubs, gambling, political corruption, and any number of dubious business dealings. The facilities in luxury mixed-use buildings can be used to entertain clients. Prostitutes who rent can offer building facilities as extra luxuries to their "guests." There are even businesses that organize luxury apartments in five-star buildings for private parties – catered, security provided, and other services (legal or not) provided somewhere in the building.

On the Gold Coast, then, and especially in the high-rise Strip, very little is ever as it seems. Among the excesses of the architecture and the extremes of consumption, there is also loneliness, despair, crime, exploitation, optional hardship, and creeping poverty. Further, the illusion of wealth attracts the very people that many residents of these buildings were trying to avoid by fleeing the suburbs and/or conventional cities. The hoons cruise the Strip; the petty criminals, muggers, and so on cruise the high-rise precincts. It is not their hood, but they bring to it layers of fear and insecurity that accompany an idea like "the hood." This recognition can be made in many cities: for the bourgeoisie and those performing-bourgeois in city "centers" – whether their residences are newly gentrified or simply newly *there* – you can never really leave the hood, or lock it out, because it will come to you by one means or another.

However, we find it interesting to take our investigation further and to ask, how does a high-rise mixed-use building become *in itself* a neighborhood? And if it does, are there aspects of an idea of the "hood" that can be discerned in these settings?

Given the eclectic mix of people, types of tenancy, age groups, income brackets, and ways of life in the Gold Coast's mixed-use buildings, many ordinary and extraordinary encounters take place within their public spaces. Here we refer not only to the foyers, pools, club bars, and barbecues associated with "resort-style living," but also to the underground carparks, the lifts and lift foyers, corridors and stairwells, where more intimate aspects of private life are more likely to take place in public. They are spaces marked by their unpredictability. In these more "private" public spaces, the heterogeneous range of residents is daily revealed, and it can bear little resemblance to the image that such buildings usually project or the image that nonresidents tend to have of them. A resident of an iconic Main Beach high-rise commented to Wise that, "when the lift doors open in the M–, you have absolutely no idea what might greet you – it could be anything: a sad old lady struggling back to her apartment, a noisy family of six with three trolleys of groceries, the nice couple from down the hall, a deal, a fist fight, or a party."

Gold Coast futures

To work effectively with this burgeoning city we need to come to terms with its proliferating material and imaginary manifestations. It shows few signs of any significant slowing of growth despite the world economic crisis. Only one major developer has failed and myriad working cranes still punctuate the skyline of the strip. Huge images continue to invite freeway travelers to buy the peaceful-safe-slow or exciting-glamorous-fast way of life provided by any number of new Gold Coast "communities" "only 20 kilometers" or, like McDonalds, "only 10 minutes" from the billboard. You can "picture yourself in" and "imagine waking up to" a "new" life by becoming part of the "Gold Coast's next community."

Thinking about neighborhood on the Gold Coast requires alertness to these rapidly shifting parameters of locale as well as the multiple aesthetics and lifestyles made available by changing sites in each locale. We need to recognize how frequently entire neighborhoods are produced and that each of them is "a veritable invention" (Deleuze & Guattari 1987, p. 406) which provides the people within it with an opportunity to reinvent themselves, often in terms of the discourses of the developers. It is equally important to remember that the rate of growth and the extraordinary degree of intra-urban residential mobility means that inevitably a high proportion of neighbors in any neighborhood will be relatively new to the neighborhood. By contrast, in the vestiges of older neighborhoods referred to earlier, continuity of residence in that locale is taken to signify "real" locals as well as enabling group identification against the very processes of development that otherwise characterize the city. Residual pockets of a slightly older city nevertheless become part of an overall impression of constant, almost rhythmic, movements of deterritorializing and reterritorializing transformations in the built and natural environments: development and redevelopment, demolition and construction, clearing and regeneration, even renovation and preservation. What emerges is variety of communities, opportunities for choice of living and housing arrangements multiplying in heterotopic settings along the 75-kilometer strip between the mountains and the sea – except that the ubiquitous billboards and real-estate advertisements represent particular demographics in each kind of development, enabling purchasers and residents to self-suggest that "people like you" buy in the kind of community you feel drawn to. Despite extraordinary heterogeneity there is thus an illusion of social as well as architectural homogeneity about each development. People satirizing the Gold Coast tend to ascribe homogeneity most strongly to gated communities and yet, apart from the obvious social discriminator of affordability, there appears to be no less difference behind swipe carded gates than in any Gold Coast suburb or high-rise apartment building catering to the middle class. Similarly, the city is frequently critiqued as more ethnically homogenous than the general Australian community, however in the most recent census 24.7 percent of Gold Coast residents were born overseas, compared to a national proportion of 22.2 percent. The distribution of countries of origin and languages spoken at home largely reflects national patterns, apart from a higher proportion of New Zealanders (7.1% c.f. 2% nationally) and Japanese (0.7% c.f. 0.2%), and a lower proportion of Chinese and Italian (0.4% c.f. 1.0% for both) (Gold Coast City Council/ABS 2006).

An illusion of absence of cultural diversity is a consequence of rapid development. In other Australian cities, problems the media describe as "ethnic tension" tend to arise when marginalized and disaffected people, especially young men, become concentrated in particular racial, ethnic, and/or national groups in neighborhoods abutting those of other disaffected groups. In such settings, a North American idea of the hood has been readily appropriated into Australian youth culture in the form of music subcultures but also in discourses of gang violence. On the Gold Coast, however, few locales remain intact long enough to become associated with waves of ethnic groups reflecting migration and refugee intake patterns. As a consequence, there is a diverse representation of people across a broader spectrum of residential settings precisely because so many Gold Coast neighborhoods are creations of real estate development *produced* as "communities." This effect, which is likely to intensify in the future, can ironically make communities as inventions more "naturally" diverse in relation to notions of multiculturalism, or of social and cultural "thickness," than so-called normal communities. The disadvantages of this are commonly remarked upon only in terms of bourgeois consumption: without ethnic neighborhoods, food, music and design cultures do not acquire the same "vitality" experienced in Australian capital cities. One challenge for Gold Coast futures is how to cultivate an experience of cultural production and consumption more representative of the region's "ethnic communities" – thus providing more accessible contact for recent arrivals identifying with those communities as well as catering for consumers – but to do this without working against dispersal of diversity across locales.

Given a tendency to access feelings of belonging and establish markers of participation through often idiosyncratic, fragmented adoptions of the discourses, stylistics, milieux and practices of the Gold Coast "lifestyle" as represented in real estate sales and tourism promotion, residents of different cultural backgrounds, ages, living arrangements, levels of income, and social needs and networks, can find themselves comfortable with an experience of difference in their neighborhood. This characteristic of the city, that it simultaneously specializes in the construction and promotion of highly varied choices of where and how to live but provides representations that make those feel as if they are choices to join like-minded communities and adopt a shared aesthetic and way of life, is clearly worth maintaining even though it is largely a by-product of a marketing machine. Within the limits of purchase or rental costs, people's communities of choice frequently contain considerable diversity simply because the aesthetics and values appealed to in the sales discourses need to be broad enough to invite multiple identifications in order to maximize real estate consumption.

The Gold Coast is a small-to-medium city, which might be expected to enhance potentials for residents to achieve a relatively homogenous idea of being part of a *whole* community but there is actually more value for citizens in maintaining a sense of heterogeneity. Residents' material and emotional connections with their own bits of the available lifestyle, tourism values, and natural assets provide them with a counter-narrative to national representations of their city as shallow, a "cultural desert," and "not a real city." Residents expect the Gold Coast to behave as if it is a big city, which frequently it does and doubtless will do in future. It is thus promising that, as far as we can glean from regional media discourses and resident conversations, most residents and even the City Council no longer naïvely assume that a "shared sense of community" across the geographic and demographic extent of the city is a necessity for citizens to participate in their city. That this idea has been displaced is probably due to recognition of how effectively several temporary affinity groups have fought spirited campaigns about perceived threats to regional amenity. That is, despite how dispersed the city is, and despite the high proportion of recent arrivals, Gold Coast citizens have increasingly proved as likely as those in more established cities to involve themselves in issues that matter for aspects of the Gold Coast experience to which they feel connected. It has become clear that people frequently view their presence in the city and/or in a particular part of the city very much as a lifestyle choice. A significant lifestyle choice involves a significant investment of one's own subjectivity. People are thus likely to experience strong identifications with the built and natural environments, in whole or in parts, and to become adept at establishing purposeful collectives.

Since the city is likely to go on re-imagining and rebuilding itself, there is a need to ensure that the idiosyncratic and surprising aspects of the Gold Coast, and of becoming a "Coaster," are more fully understood so that they may (somewhat paradoxically) be protected. In an important sense, we are describing the Gold Coast's intangible heritage, which is what will be played out in future manifestations of the city and the future values of its citizens. These intangible assets and the insights that can arise from them are crucial to the management of the tangible assets of infrastructural provision and the natural setting in which the city takes place. If it is to continue becoming a city for residents as well as visitors, terms such as community and neighborhood must be understood as multidimensional ideas to be deployed contiguously with the potentials of citizens to have transient, partial, and multiple involvements. Taking such discourses as essential in relation to planning and community conversation will encourage the kinds of novel and plurivocal engagements between groups of people-as-residents, as well as between residents and government, development, tourism, and media, as are already in evidence. And while it may suit politicians, bureaucrats, the corporate sector and mainstream media to deal with stable, formally constituted community organizations – even, perhaps especially, when they are oppositional organizations – there are many ways in which the very instability and mobility of people in and between sites of community engagement can provide opportunities for maximizing effective use of available skills, networks of influence, strategic thinking, care of the self and of others, and imaginative responses to change such that the Gold Coast can thrive as a creative community as well as a city creating and recreating itself.

Note

1. We gratefully acknowledge the insights provided by colleague Kathy Mackey regarding life in a mixed-use Gold Coast high-rise.

References

Appadurai, A. (1990). Disjuncture and Difference in the Global Cultural Economy. In M. Featherstone (Ed.), *Global Culture: Nationalism, Globalization and Modernity*. London: Sage.

Austen (2008). "Chatroom." *Gold Coast Bulletin*, October 15, p. 26.

Bennett, A. (1999). Subcultures or Neo-Tribes?: Rethinking the Relationship Between Youth, Style and Musical Taste. *Sociology, 33*(3): 599–617.

Bennett, A. (2000). *Popular Music and Youth Culture: Music, Identity and Place*. Basingstoke: Macmillan.

Blundell, G. (2008). Paradise Vice. *The Australian*, September 6. Retrieved from: http://www. australiantelevision.net/the_strip/articles/paradise_vice.html

Braithwaite, A. (2008). Channel Nine Drama The Strip – New Underbelly on Gold Coast. *The Daily Telegraph*, September 1. Retrieved from: http://www.news.com.au/dailytelegraph/ story/0,22049,24275058-5006014,00.html

Chaney, D. (1993). *Fictions of Collective Life: Public Drama in Late Modern Culture*. London: Routledge.

Chatterton, P. & Hollands, R. (2002). Theorising Urban Playscapes: Producing, Regulating and Consuming Youthful Nightlife City Spaces. *Urban Studies, 39*(1), 153–173.

Chef_24 (2008). "Post #87," *Media Spy-The Strip-Forums*, September 4. Retrieved from http://www. mediaspy.org/forum/index.php?showtopic=14726&st=75

Clarke, G. (1981). Defending Ski-Jumpers: A Critique of Theories of Youth Subcultures. In S. Frith and A. Goodwin (Eds) (1990), *On Record: Rock, Pop and the Written Word*. London: Routledge.

Clarke, J, (1976). The Skinheads and the Magical Recovery of Community. In S. Hall and T. Jefferson (Eds), *Resistance through Rituals: Youth Subcultures in Post-War Britain*. London: Hutchinson.

Cohen, P. (1972). *Subcultural Conflict and Working Class Community*, Working Papers in Cultural Studies 2. Birmingham: University of Birmingham.

Corrigan, P. (1976). Doing Nothing. In S. Hall and T. Jefferson (Eds), *Resistance Through Rituals: Youth Subcultures in Post-War Britain*. London: Hutchinson.

Deleuze, G. and Guattari, F. (1987). *A Thousand Plateaus: Capitalism and Schizophrenia*, Minneapolis: University of Minnesota Press.

Doneman, P. (2008). Crime Show The Strip is Close to Real Gold Coast Policing: Officer. *The Sunday Mail*, August 31. Retrieved from: http://www.australiantelevision.net/the_strip/articles/closetoreal. html

Evers, C. (2004). Men Who Surf. *Cultural Studies Review, 10*(1), pp. 27–41.

Ewart, J. (2000). Capturing the Heart of the Region – How Regional Media Define a Community. *Transformations*, No.1, September, pp. 1–13. Retrieved from http://www.cqu.edu.au/transformations.

Ford, N. J. & Brown, D. (2005). *Surfing and Social Theory: Experience, Embodiment and Narrative of the Dream Glide*. New York: Routledge.

GC Born. (2008). Chatroom. *Gold Coast Bulletin*, October 17, p. 32.

Gold Coast City Council. (2006). Community Profile, sourced from: Australian Bureau of Statistics *Census of Population and Housing 2006*. Retrieved from: http://www.goldcoast.qld.gov.au/t_standard.aspx?pid=250.

"Gold Coast Stars in its Own *Underbelly*, "*The Strip*" (2008). *Australian TV Shows*, July 12. Retrieved from http://thestrip.austtvshows.com/articles/gold-coast-stars-in-its-own-underbelly-the-strip/

Gold Coast Sun. (2008a). Your Local Paper Keeps on Shining. *Gold Coast Sun*, Wednesday, November 19, p. 9.

Gold Coast Sun. (2008b). Meet the Faces Behind the Letters to the Editor. *Gold Coast Sun*, Wednesday, November 19, p. 18.

Griffin, G. (1998). The Good, the Bad and the Peculiar: Cultures and Policies of Urban Planning and Development on the Gold Coast. *Urban Policy and Research*, 16(4), 285–292.

Griffin, G. (2002). The City, the Suburb, the Community and the Local Press: A Gold Coast Case Study. *Media International Australia incorporating Culture and Policy*, No. 105, November, pp. 105–118.

Hayson, D. (2008). Chatroom. *Weekend Bulletin*, October 18–19, p. 61.

Hill, W. (2008). Letters. *Gold Coast Bulletin*, October 15, p. 21.

Idato, M. (2008). All that Glitters: Nine's New Drama The Strip Explores the Underbelly of the Gold Coast. *The Age*, September 3. Retrieved from http://www.theage.com.au/news/tv--radio/all-that-glitters/2008/09/03/1220121249923

Jefferson, T. (1976). Cultural Responses of the Teds: The Defence of Space and Status. In S. Hall and T. Jefferson (Eds), *Resistance Through Rituals: Youth Subcultures in Post-War Britain*. London: Hutchinson.

Jensen, T. (2008). "TV Show The Strip Seen as Positive for Coast Tourism." *The Courier Mail*, September 6. Retrieved from http://www.news.com.au/couriermail/story/0,23739,24299300-17102,00.html

Keith, M. & Pile, S. (1993). The Politics of Place. In M. Keith and S. Pile (Eds), *Place and the Politics of Identity*. London: Routledge.

Le Breton, D. (2004). The Anthropology of Adolescent Risk-taking Behaviours. *Body & Society*, 10(1), 1–15.

Lull, J. (1995). *Media, Communication, Culture: A Global Approach*. Cambridge: Polity Press.

Maffesoli, M. (1996). *The Time of the Tribes: The Decline of Individualism in Mass Society* (Trans. D. Smith). London: Sage.

Massey, D. (1993). Power-Geometry and a Progressive Sense of Place, in J. Bird, B. Curtis, T. Putnam, G. Robertson, & L. Tickner (Eds), *Mapping the Futures: Local Cultures, Global Change*. London: Routledge.

Muggleton, D. (2000). *Inside Subculture: The Postmodern Meaning of Style*. Oxford: Berg.

Nine Network. (2008). New Australian Crime Drama Series: The Strip," *Nine Network*, May 5. Retrieved from http://www.ebroadcast.com.au/enews/nine/NEW-AUSTRALIAN-DRAMA---THE-ST.

Phil. (2008). Chatroom. *Weekend Bulletin*, October 18–19, p. 61.

Thomas, M. & Butcher, M. (2003). Cruising. In M. Butcher and M. Thomas (Eds), *Ingenious: Emerging Youth Cultures in Urban Australia*. North Melbourne: Pluto Press.

Thornton, S. (1995). *Club Cultures: Music, Media and Subcultural Capital*. Cambridge: Polity Press.

"TV Drama Hits Town." (2008). *Tweed Daily News*, August 7. Retrieved from http://www.tweednews.com.au/storydisplay.cfm?storyid=3780972.

Urry, J. (1990). *The Tourist Gaze: Leisure and Travel in Contemporary Societies*. London: Sage.

Wise, P. (2006). Australia's Gold Coast: A City Producing Itself, in C. Lindner (Ed.), *Urban Space and City Scapes: Perspectives from Modern and Contemporary Culture*. London: Routledge.

Wise, P. and Breen, S. (2004). The Concrete Corridor: Strategising Impermanence in a Frontier City. *Media International Australia incorporating Culture and Policy*, No. 112, August, pp. 162–173.

Chapter 6

Habitus and Rethinking the Discourse of Youth Gangs, Crime, Violence, and Ghetto Communities

Tamari Kitossa

When the very existence of the poor is deemed the essence of the problem, then the ultimate logic is genocide.

(Ford, 2010)

Youth gangs, crime, violence, and ghetto communities have become synonyms in the discourse of crime, drugs, and urban terror (Hayden, 2004). This convergence is presumed to be natural, inevitable, and an exclusive phenomenon of poor, economically isolated and racially segregated communities. As a way of managing this perceived threat, repression rather than care, public health, and social justice are deemed appropriate measures to the problems of poverty and the economic uselessness of huge swaths of the poor in postindustrial societies. For their part, the media dutifully report on those "known to police" and their last "known address" all the while sensationalizing the deaths of bystanders. Politicians, when not passing legislation in reaction to morality dramas and occasional moral panic about youth gangs, aim to allay the fears of the voting public for whom social control and punishment affirm the rules of fair play. The public, in a mood to punish, clamor for more law and more order while receiving more of the former and less of the latter. They grant their political leadership ever more latitude to reduce individual and group civil liberties, entrench systemic bias, and fritter tax dollars fortifying the albatross that is the criminal legal system.

Given the well-worn use of military metaphors to frame state and societal responses to social problems (e.g., war on poverty/war on crime) (Matza, 1969, p. 145), it is not surprising that as one definition of society's problems falls out of favor its muscular response has not. The discourse of terrorism, at home and abroad, has become the new designation of social problems. It comes as little surprise then that before G. W. Bush's war on terror, Abu Ghraib and Guantanamo, and the creation of "enemy combatants," boot camps, and toughening youth laws animated the response of the state and society to those deemed a menace to it: young men 'of color,' the poor, and the 'unemployed' *inter alia*. These, internal enemies, were the enemy combatants long before Al Qaeda. But, as the war on terror matures, it merges ineluctably, seamlessly, with the war on crime, youth gangs, and drugs. Mass detention and the effective suspension of civil liberties are part of this merging. Similarly, the anti-guerilla tactics of urban, house to house warfare in Falujah and Basra mirror police operations/sweeps in US ghettos and poor Canadian communities. Literally, ghettos and poor communities in North America have become battle zones, where police are armies of occupation and poor and ghetto youth the enemy combatants. If reducing fear of crime, drugs sold and used, and the body count from drug deals gone awry are the measures of success there is little else to show for it. In part this is because militarized police operations both amplify crime and become themselves a major part of the equation of danger. If Stanley Cohen (2007a) is correct in arguing that crime control has failed because this was never its intention, we must confront the view that the war on youth and the ghetto is a dystopian reality in which the development of a police state is disguised by moral panic about poor and ghetto youth and gangs.

This essay concerns a historical and contemporary sketch of how this war on our society's young people has come to be and suggests a way out of the quagmire. Along with reconceptualizing the stereotype of youth gangs as predators rather than victims of structural violence (Farmer, 2004; Galtung, 1969), the ghetto must also be re-imagined. Cut off from the rest of society, the ghetto is framed in nineteenth-century colonial discourse as a far off place, dangerous, hopelessly mired in savagery but brimming with dangerously uncontrolled vitality. But, inasmuch as the ghetto is objectively characterized by a visual architecture that *can* connote civil decay, it is subjectively experienced as home, territory to be defended, a place to be made vital by agents with the will to transform it. It is here that Bourdieu's appreciation of the dynamic interaction between objectivity and subjectivity and structure and agency, compels us to see the potential of the ghetto and the reality of youth responses to structural violence as forces for social transformation.

Habitus

I began this essay by pointing out that youth gangs, violence, and ghetto communities converge in the discourse of urban terrorism in which law and order is the presumed solution. Antipathy toward radical interpretations of these elements of mainstream discourse leads to a preferred reading of youth gangs, violence, and ghetto communities that is in accord with racism and extant capitalist social relations of production. This preference is sustained by a variety of cultural and social institutions (e.g., news media, the state, and its repressive apparatus) that are in accord with the criminal laws' codification of interpersonal harm as a greater threat than the conduct of corporations and the state (Glasbeek, 2002;Kappeler & Potter, 2005; Reiman, 2007; Tombs & Hillyard, 2004). That corporations account for a vast array of harms by externalization (see Gorelick, 1998, p. 46; Young, 2009) and that the state and its repressive apparatus do harm by violating rights, amplifying social problems, and making war, demands rethinking the demonization of ghetto communities as gang-filled and violence prone. Bourdieu's concept of habitus can help to break this preferred reading, but with some qualifications to the 'latent' neoChicagoism existing in its initial conception. It is not clear whether it is his intent but Bourdieu's "Social space and the genesis of groups" might be taken as a clarification, if not barring, of the common-sense 'bourgeois' morality that can be read into the habitus of groups with low cultural and socioeconomic 'capital' (Bourdieu, 1985).

A crass and simplistic way of misunderstanding Bourdieu's concept of habitus is encapsulated in the phrase "you can take the man out of the ghetto but not the ghetto out of the man." Bourdieu can be taken to suggest just such an interpretation, in a one-to-one correlation, that people are the product of their objective social conditions. Hence,

> One of the fundamental effects of orchestration of habitus is the production of a common sense world endowed with the *objectivity* secured by consensus on meaning ... of practices and the world, in other words the harmonization of agents' experiences and the continuous reinforcement that each of them receives from the expression, individual or collective ... improvised or programmed ... of similar or identical experiences [original emphasis].
>
> (Bourdieu, 1977, p. 80)

If one were to assume a narrow interpretation of this quotation, as implied by the Chicago School's 'social disorganization' thesis and its subsidiary claims of social deficit and moral pathology (Agozino, 2003; Matza, 1969), the ghetto, by virtue of its subordinate locus in the capitalist political economy, habituates/disposes/condemns its denizens to a dehistoricized present in which they actively reproduce traditions and modes of thought that perpetuate a history of negative habituating practices (Gilroy, 1987; Wacquant, 2008).

This argument follows a circular logic. It obviates the role of capitalism and government policies designed to maintain and reinforce negative habituations for which the victims of structural violence are blamed (see Ryan, 1971). Much like a colony and those who inhabit it, the sum total of the ghetto is presumed to be compendium of reproduced traditions and modes of thought that are anti-social. The Chicago School's social disorganization theory and the crass readings of Bourdieu are careful, however, not to dismiss *agency* as the interlocutor between the subjective as a force in dynamic interaction with objective social structures. Rather, they contend the agency of the poor is a negative one, as though this is an inherent condition of the poor and being poor. The flaw of blaming the victim, however, is that it does not appreciate that the capitalist mode of production is not *only* the triumph of the owners of production but also that of what John Mepham (1979) calls "bourgeois society"[1] (p. 149; see also Miliband, 1987, pp. 23–45). This is to say that even those who are exploited and excluded from the gains of capitalism, their consciousness and actions, too, are shaped by the capitalist mode of production. Thus, to assume the ghetto has a habitus that is inherently negative is to remain unaware of the limits of this view. For, as Bourdieu argues, in maintaining this view, one is

> condemned to adopt unwittingly for his own use the representation of action which is forced on agents or groups when they lack practical mastery of a highly valued competence and have to provide themselves with an explicit and at least semi-formalized substitute for it in the form of a repertoire of rules, or of what sociologists consider, at best, as a 'role'.
>
> (Bourdieu, 1977, p. 2)

If the residents of the ghetto lack a preferred habitus or have one that is not preferred, this is a matter of judgment by a bourgeois society that ignores the adaptive consequences of imposing privations on ghetto communities. More than this, though, to assume the composition of the ghetto's habitus is the absence of cultural and social capital, is also a failure to see that resistance to oppression is a positive and generative (human) characteristic, even if bourgeois society retards the development of a revolutionary consciousness. Would it be preferred that ghetto youth simply march themselves to prison? No struggle? No resistance to oppressive social conditions?

Habitus, as conceived by Bourdieu, is thus much more dynamic and supple than "social disorganization" or narrow readings allow. The theory insists on objectivity and as such rejects the parochial moral pejoratives in such heavy phrases as "social disorganization." As Bourdieu (1977) notes, "when we speak of class habitus, we are insisting ... that interpersonal relations are never ... *individual to individual* relationships and that the truth of the interaction is never entirely contained in the interaction" (p. 81). This transcendence is not only because individuals act and relate with the urgency of self-interest, but because their actions take place against and within a definite class structure whose idioms, world-views, and practices are to the advantage of bourgeois society's beneficiaries. Hence, individuals pursue their individual interests while representing, unbeknownst to them, forms of class orientation in which they have been socially reproduced (Bourdieu, 1977, pp. 82).[2] The class habitus (a constellation of class-specific, generalized tendencies, traditions, practices, idioms etc. among a group) is thus a product of conditioning relative to a definite class position. In this there is no normative preference for the habitus of one class over another, though the fact of apprehending the existence of habitus is revolutionary for revealing the relationship between the capitalist mode of production and its social relations of production. The habitus then has a specific shape-shifting morphology. In interactions between individuals from different and competing social class positions, the habitus becomes evident by contradistinction, while in intra-class intercourse it is elusive, taken for granted, unseen and presumably non-existent (Bourdieu, 1977).

Given social classes have a habitus, not in an absolute but a general way, the social reproduction of this process and dynamic state of being, as a fact of social distance, is contingent also on spatial distance. For example, linguistic codes, denoting social distance, connote geographical class approximations. "I ain't" versus "I am not" are symbolic codes as solid as the side of tracks denoting what part of town one comes from. A derivative of habitus then is that in a competitive system in which social classes engage in offensive and defensive postures of social closure and usurpation, so-called cultural and social capital[3] are emblems of belonging or acquisitions that enable, as much as possible, transit into a different habitus. Vital to the legitimacy of the capitalist system is the notion, based on the practical evidence of rags to riches, that upward transit into "higher" social strata is possible. The Horatio Alger trope, however, reaffirms there is in fact spatial difference in accord with social difference. Our concern here is *that* place, *that* other side of town, *that* other side of the tracks in which language constitutes an objective structure of difference, is the ghetto. The principle assumption here is that the "non-ghetto" is neither in question nor problematic. It is the universal norm against which the life world of the ghetto is defined (Wacquant, 2008), not in the first instance to stigmatize the ghetto, since this is an ancillary by-product, but rather to demarcate by way of Manichean economy the proprieties that are its dominant and dominating norms.

The ghetto

If the habitus of ghetto residents is other than the compendium of negative traits imagined by bourgeois society, is the ghetto itself not also a state of mind? In terms of urban geography, the ghetto is an ancient institution (Bauman, 2004). Rome, of the Late Republic, for instance had them aplenty and the frequent collapse of shoddy tenements along with their tendency to be engulfed in great waves of fire is legion (Parenti, 2003). Around the world more recently, they go by different names *banlieue* in France, *favela* in Brazil, *degradati* in Italy, *problemomrade* in Sweden, *barrios* in Venezuela (Davis, 2007; Wacquant, 2008). A space of residential segregation, ghettos are involuntary and voluntary; but only the former goes by the name (Bauman, 2008). If then people are forced to live in a geographically-bounded space such as the ghetto, relative to the rest of society in which they are institutionalized, its general characteristics are: dilapidated housing, high population density, mass poverty and limited government services. Yet, as Wacquant (2008) reminds us, urban marginality around the world, the precondition for involuntary ghettos, is not everywhere of the same cloth. Despite their ubiquity, ghettos are institutionalized in ways that are unique to the development of the state and society in which they exist.[4] As a consequence, direct comparisons run short of apprehending the distinctiveness of each of them.

Indeed, comparisons between first-world and third-world ghettos without due care may serve in some instances to compare apples to oranges.[5] For example, the US has nothing comparable to the shanty towns of South Africa or the *favelas* of Brazil. At the same time, these colonies or reserves for bourgeois society's rejects do not compare to refugee camps and slums which defy the neat geographically bounded concept of the ghetto. Bauman (2008) and Davis (2007), for example, show that slums often double as garbage dumps and vice versa. In such places where the inhabitants subsist on less than $1 per day even one protein rich meal a day is a luxury. Evidence of this are Haitian slum dwellers, who just one year prior to the 2010 earthquake were eating cakes of mud (Carroll, 2008). At the same time it is important to maintain some sense of rough equivalency between these places of concentrated poverty and dispossessed human beings. To push the absolute distinction between slums and ghettos too far might accord a sense of privilege to the ghetto where this is not deserved. For example, rates of infant mortality are higher in some US ghettos than in some poor third world countries (Wacquant, 2008; Washington, 2006). But, inasmuch as they are reservations of exclusion, ghettos are dynamic and have a fractal complexity given their locus on the descending scale of relegated uselessness. In some instances, ghettos contain within them slums in which the poorest of the poor live or they may serve as a buffer between slums and the well-to-do (Davis, 2007). Yet, for all the qualitative and quantitative differences between ghettos, slums, shanties, or refugee camps, what we are dealing with are differential and relative geographies of human disposability and uselessness (Bauman, 2004; Rifkin, 2004; Willhelm, 1983). The prospect of their residents "'biodegradation'" (Bauman, 2007, p. 86), by benign or malignant means haunts the lifeworld of the ghetto (see Ford, 2010; Willhelm, 1983; 1970).

A product of media, record companies, and the dominance of US social studies, the image of the ghetto with which we are most familiar tends to be that of the US inner city (Wacquant, 2008, p. 1) – known euphemistically by its young residents as the *hood*. Referred to as a *hyperghetto* by Loic Wacquant (2008, pp. 3, 46), the contemporary US ghetto differs in space from the *banlieue* or the *favela* as much as the ghetto of the 1950's. Wacquant characterizes the modern US ghetto, in view of neoliberalism, urban renewal (expelling the poor) and racial segregation, as a form of social hypertrophy. Wacquant characterizes the US ghetto of the first half of the twentieth century as a *communal ghetto*. Racially segregated for sure, it was largely heterogeneous in class, had a unifying collective consciousness, a thriving service economy, a sophisticated division of labor and vibrant agencies for aesthetic representation and political mobilization (Wacquant, 2008). That said, the *communal ghetto* of yore is not to be sentimentalized. There, confined to a Bantustan, treated with disdain by whites, and an economy at the early stages of being tipped over the precipice of technological uselessness, drugs, gangs, and violence were also a part of social existence. Yet, significantly, only after the leadership and momentum of the civil and human rights movements were decapitated by a range of means.

The *hyperghetto* by contrast is a geographical space of advanced social decomposition under advanced corporate/oligarchic capitalism. In it, social relations are severely distorted by the strains of exclusion, exploitation, police harassment, and the revolving doors of prisons. A product of the intensification of capitalism and technologically-induced uselessness (Willhelm, 1970), as much as state and white vengeance for the uprisings of the 60's, the *communal ghetto* suffered from revitalization schemes, proletarianization, and the retreat of the caring state.[6] These forces lead to communal breakup and instability from which the ghetto has yet to recover (Skott-Myhre, Chapter 2; Willhelm, 1983). The intensification of these processes, compounded by the retrenchment of the caring state and an "intrusive and omnipresent police and penal apparatus" (Wacquant, 2008, p. 3), amplify the scale of social decomposition. Key to *hyperghettoization* is that ghetto inhabitants must confront deproletarianization by technological advances even as the collapse of industrial manufacturing pushes those already on the margins into the nether realm of absolute redundancy (Munford, 1996; Willhelm, 1983). Those pushed out of the class system are not entirely useless though; they serve as economic fodder for the criminal-industrial complex which sustains fragments of the white suburban working class and even whole communities in the far-flung exurbs throughout Canada and the United States (Munford, 1996).

The ghetto cannot, of course, be strictly analyzed as a function of capitalist geospatial distribution and social relations of production. Like the slum, defined in Victorian epidemiology as a "room in which low goings-on occurred" (Davis, 2007, p. 21), the involuntary ghetto is subjected to the externally-imposed stain of moral condemnation – both of its stigmatized/useless residents and the frontier-like informalization of its economy. As an eroticized locus, the ghetto is constituted in the mainstream imaginary as the civic body's *id* force. Like a magnet, in much the same way Vancouver's downtown east side draws adrenaline-filled ghetto voyeurs, the ghetto has an ambivalent attraction: a world away and its residents a people apart. Stripped of their capacity to define both their humanity and their complex adaptations to the structural condition in which they find themselves, the everyday/night reality of ordinary people coping with extraordinarily oppressive conditions is lost (Wacquant, 2008). Stripped of self-definition and human value, ghetto residents, especially young men, are made acutely aware they do not count for anything in society. Ghetto residents are cognizant of the judgments that consign them to the abuses of the criminal-industrial complex and the economic dustbin and most will no doubt take on the psychology the system imposes on them.

Constructed by white supremacist and bourgeois society as "dark skinned animals" living in a "jungle" (Wacquant, 2008), the central ghetto image most conducive to moral panics is that of the gang banger. As suggested by Daniel P. Moynihan (1965) and Frederic Thrasher (1963), fatherless homes and fecund, unwed mothers, combined with blight, high unemployment and the failure of other socializing institutions is assumed to be the causative ingredients leading to criminality, violence, and gang membership. The assumption that the habitus of the ghetto *is* the sum total of the negative objective conditions imposed by its peripheralization is a middle-class bias consistent with the Victorian era's anxiety about the underclasses. To be sure, there is 'criminality,' violence, and gangs in the ghetto, but social studies research has made of such goings on a problem *of* the ghetto rather than manifestations of ongoing violence done *to* the ghetto. In other words, the dialectical is ignored and the concept of 'prime mover' within that dynamism is rejected. What is preferred, by way of explanation, is the transposition of effect for cause and with that stands the hegemony of what David Matza calls correctionalism and the presuppositions of etiology and social pathology (1969).

The gang: insects, "super predators," and "operation ghetto storm"

The fundamental question for those who assume the habitus of the ghetto is a self-authoring compendium of negative idioms, traditions, practices, and worldviews is "what is to be done?"[7] The sense that the youth of the ghetto are vermin and their place of residence befitting such fauna is communicated in a vocabulary familiar to the study of entomology. The legitimation of mistrust of young people conceals the violence of this construction (see Kelly, 2003). Frederic Thrasher (1963), for example, in what is the foundational research on youth gangs, though his conclusions were far more progressive than his language suggested, referred to "gangland" as "'no man's land,' lawless, godless, wild" (p. 6). Rightly alluding to the territorial nature of gangs, which mirrored the feudal character of early twentieth-century capitalistic behavior, he demarcated the ghetto into fiefs: "North Side jungles," "West Side wilderness," "South Side badlands," "Grand Canyon." In such nurseries, like fireflies on a warm night "children fairly swarm over areaways and sidewalks;" there "the buzzing chatter and constant motion remind one of insects which hover in a swarm, yet ceaselessly dart hither and thither within the animated mass;" and "in this ubiquitous crowd of children, spontaneous play-groups are formed everywhere – gangs in embryo" (p. 23). Where Thrasher does attribute human characteristics to the poorest of the poor – "a distinct type bordering on degeneracy" (p. 9) – the specter of eugenics rather than outright extermination is conjured as a just policy.

Thrasher's near-turn-of-the-century Dickensian vocabulary was no doubt a product of its time. More recently, though, the vocabulary used to suggest the youth are a pestilence combines the language of genetics with the imagery of carnivorous predator. Reagan's Secretary of Education cum Bush Sr.'s Drug Czar, Bill Bennett, who mused aborting African-American male children is a sound method of crime control, set alarms ringing with the notion that the first decade of the twenty-first century will be that of the juvenile "super predator." Others before Bennett not only mused about the "purifying" benefits of abortion, it must be understood that eugenics is so much a time-honored policy of US 'crime' control, its insinuation into social services hardly raises a scintilla of condemnation except among the victims (Roberts, 1993). These little monsters, Bennett and his co-authors of *Body Count* asserted, were immune to the "stigma of arrest, the pains of imprisonment, or the pangs of conscience" (cited in Kappeler & Potter, 2005, p. 217). If compassionate understanding and support are not options and punishment does not work, what is left? The imagery of barbarians *within* the gates reflects a deeply held bourgeois bias that justifies waging a war of purification on the ghetto and poor youth. The head of the Los Angeles homicide bureau commented, "Everyone says: 'What are we going to do about the gang problem?' It's the same thing you do about cockroaches or insects; you get someone in there to do whatever they can to get rid of those creatures" (Garvey & McGreevy, 2007, p. 1). In this he is not alone; though serious law enforcers admit they cannot arrest their way out of the crime problem (Crank, 2004; RCMP, 2006). Whatever the reason for such candor, with continually expanding budgets and gadgetry at their disposal, the police are not likely to complain too loudly. Where the news media and political elites such as George W. Bush's former Attorney General Roberto Gonzalez hyped the gang "problem," the legitimacy of directing resources to wage a genocidal war against "insects" and "super predators" is assured. But destruction need not come about by repressive means alone: one can also, Nuremberg style, geneticize and so experiment on the "predators" (Washington, 2006; see also Randall, 1996).

By its name alone the United States's Joint Urban Operations Training Working Group leaves little to be imagined. And, indeed, the increased blurring between the tactics of urban policing and urban anti-guerilla warfare and the easy transit of personnel and training between these organizations[8] is ominous for the future of those imagined as cockroaches, rats, and "super predators." As one army personnel put it:

> The future of warfare … lies in the streets, sewers, highrise buildings, and sprawl of houses that form the broken cities of the world … Our recent military history is punctuated with city names – Tuzla, Mogadishu, Los Angeles, Beirut, Panama City, Hue, Saigon, Santo Domingo – but these encounters have been but a prologue, with the real drama to come.
>
> (Peters cited in Davis, 2007, p. 203)

Planning for urban warfare, however, began as early as the Vietnam War and the explosion of ghetto rebellions in the late 1960's. As early as 1961, Robert McNamara commissioned Pentagon and Rand counterinsurgency research. The centerpiece of this research, "Project Agile," moved easily from its preoccupation with counter-guerilla strategies designed for Vietnamese jungles and cities to "urban disequilibrium" in US ghettos (Klare, 1974, pp. 99–100). The policy initiatives of such research aimed to neutralize radicalized political leadership; infiltrate, provoke, and disrupt urban social movements; and reinforce and expand personnel, weaponry, institutions, and tactics for repression. With SWAT[9] and Rapid Deployment Units (Chambliss, 1994) at the ready, the United States is well prepared for looming internal conflagrations (Meeks, 2006). The United States is not alone in the militarized containment of the ghetto. Around the world, the criminalization of youth gangs in ghettos, slums, refugee camps, and occupied lands is the justification the modern neoliberal state needs for paramilitary incursions whose chief aims are to dispossess and neutralize political opposition, speed up the biodegradation of its residents, and to document the residents who too frequently are beyond the pale of government surveillance (Bauman, 2004; Davis, 2007; Wacquant, 2008).

The habitus of youth culture, gangs, and "crime"

The war on ghetto and poor youth is predicated on reifying crime, gangs, and violence as objective facts of the ghetto's habitus. Can this be empirically demonstrated? By some statistical wizardry, Frederic Thrasher chronicled 1,313 gangs in Chicago's poorest neighborhoods back in the mid-1920s but offered no human tally. Today the number of gangs is no less a matter of conjecture but it is estimated there are 24,000 gangs with some 760,000 members (Greene & Pranis, 2007, p. 34). Whatever the impreciseness of the numbers and debate about the definition of a gang (Brotherton, 2008; Greene & Pranis, 2007), Thrasher taught us that gangs were a normal and natural part of youth culture. In fact, Thrasher's definition of youth gangs was so all encompassing his central distinction was whether the activities of the gang in question was structured by adult society versus those that had to create their own activities. In the case of the latter, Thrasher attributes gang formation to misdirected masculine exuberance. He is, however, quick to note that this is not an inherent flaw in the habitus of youth from ghettos but rather a failure of social policy to provide means and opportunity for youth to have a stake in their society.

Contemporary youth culture owes its existence to developments in nineteenth-century capitalist urbanized society and more recently to a consumer culture that actively targets youth as a niche market – even as young as four years old (Barber, 2007). But then, as now, preoccupation with the youth of the dangerous classes channels analysis away from how the capitalist mode of production under industrial and postindustrial capitalism places youth in a holding pattern before they can meaningfully enter the world of work and full participation in society. Because at a crucial stage of their life marginalized youth are alienated from institutions, roles, and opportunities to engage society in meaningful and productive ways, gangs provide an opportunity to belong and to self-define. One consequence of their exclusion from adult society is that youth become feared. The preoccupation with youth 'crime' has led to commonsensical myths about the dangers posed by poor youth and youth gangs and the myth that youth gangs are "criminal organizations" (Hayden, 2004, p. 115). In the early twentieth century this preoccupation led to the social engineering philanthropy of the Rockefeller's and Ford's, *inter alia*, sponsorship of the YMCA, Boy's and Girl's Clubs, and Scouts. The aim was not primarily to enrich the lives of the poor children so that they could fulfill their human potential rather to socialize them into the habitus of subordination and compliance that philanthropists expected of their parents who were their employees. The consequences of this preoccupation are that the actual dangers posed by youths and gangs are amplified rather than diminished, mystified rather than made clear while the structural sources for interpersonal violence in society – ageism/ableism, capitalism, heterosexism, militarism, patriarchy, and racism – are obfuscated.

As noted by Thrasher (1963), despite his preference for pathologizing ghetto youth, and subsequent research of a critical nature, youth gangs, crews, or street organizations are a societal – rather than a class or racial – phenomenon (Adamson, 1998; Brotherton, 2008; Greene & Pranis, 2007; Padilla, 1996). If gangs in the ghetto take on unique characteristics, practices, and traditions, this is a function of coping with the political economy of uselessness and because powerful groups have the capacity to make of their existence a social problem (see Blumer, 1971). Stanley Cohen (2007b) is here instructive:

> Our society will continue to generate problems for some segments within it, for example, working-class adolescents, and then condemn whatever solution these groups find to their problems. We must recognize that some of our most cherished social values – individualism, masculinity, competitiveness – are the same ones that generate crime.
>
> (p. 47)

Indeed, as early as 1967, remarking on the differential but comparative rates of juvenile delinquency between middle-class and working-class boys, Vaz comments that "Our guess is that all boys who commit themselves to youth culture activities sooner or later break the law" (p. 4). While there is much debate on whether lower-class youth commit more crime, the preciseness of this claim is undermined by survey studies which show white and middle-class teens committing equal if not higher rates of delinquency (Reiman, 2007) and drug use (Wellman, 1993) than African- and Latino-American youth. Youth delinquency is generally a group activity and, as such, a constituency of at least three, in Canada, qualifies for the definition of a gang. Poor African- and Latino-American youth are likely to turn up more frequently in official statistics and to be over counted as gang members because law enforcement agencies benefit from the very impression they create (Greene & Pranis, 2007). In addition, law enforcers falsely assume white kids 'age-out' earlier than African- and Latino-American youth and white society tends to have a higher level of tolerance for the misconduct of white youth, all of which leads to a gross underestimation of white youth gang activity and participation rates (Greene & Pranis, 2007).[10] White citizens of the US are not likely to long ignore the primary violent structural factors that are sources of secondary youth violence. The end of work increasingly augers the uselessness of their young also:

> Teenage gangs have begun to proliferate in the nation's suburbs, and so too has the incidence of violent crimes. Once-safe communities are now becoming war zones, with reports of rapes, drive-by shootings, drug trafficking, and robberies. In generally affluent Westchester County, just outside New York City, police report the emergence of more than seventy rival middle-class gangs in just the past few years.
>
> (Rifkin, 2004, p. 211)

Correlating violence with youth gangs, as implied by Rifkin, however, is a misdiagnosis of the structure of violence in society. Rarely are youth gangs predisposed to violence or are they as indiscriminate as suggested by the "super predator" thesis. Much of their violence directed toward each other and other gangs occurs on the periphery of gang territories and is amplified when gang members (not the same as *the* gang) fight to claim vacuums in drug distribution networks created by police drug sweeps or when police gang sweeps destabilize the gang's internal dynamics of moderately well-organized and powerful gangs. In general, violence within and between gangs is ontologically, psychosocially, and logically consistent with the social and institutional context in which they are constituted.

By any measure, the United States is a violent society and so homicide is a *national* problem *not* a gang one. Using the FBI definition for a gang homicide, some 7–8 percent of the 15, 980 homicides committed in 2001 were ascribed to gang violence (Greene & Pranis, 2007, p. 56). Though gang homicides tend to be more serious in some cities and states than others, it is telling that gang violence tends to be worse in states and cities with aggressive repression programs and harsh sentencing laws (Clear, 2007; Greene & Pranis, 2007; Reiman, 2007). Indeed, left to their own devices youth "age-out" of gangs without help from law enforcement (Greene & Pranis, 2007) and where their ties to the community are deep, despite the problematic nature of the relationship, gangs negotiate treaties and truces that reduce the incidence of gang-related violence (Greene & Pranis, 2007). It is easily forgotten that most of the early African- and Latino-American gangs in Detroit, New

York, Chicago, and Los Angeles emerged as politicized communal self-defense enterprises arising out of the attacks of white citizens and police alike (Adamson, 1998). It is only with the explicit intervention of the FBI's COINTELPRO (Counter Intelligence Program) which destroyed revolutionary groups such as the Black Panther Party that the gangs of the 'Boyz in the Hood' fame truly come into being (see Churchill & Vander Wall, 2002). Indeed, it stands to reason that parasitic "criminal" gangs were preferred by the state when repressive agencies such as the FBI operationalized the idea that "[t]he Negro youth and moderates must be made to understand that if they succumb to revolutionary teaching, they will be dead revolutionaries" (ibid; Mueller and Ellis, 1990). The state is quite comfortable with these groups, so long as they do not make truces or feed the poor but instead contribute to moral panic, chaos, and facilitate the state's destructive program of "law and order" (see Chambliss, 1995; Hayden, 2004; Williams, 2005).

The habitus of capitalism and the primacy of structural violence

Far from youth gangs reflecting the habitus of the ghetto, they are expressive of youth culture more generally. Rather than a phenomenon that typifies the life experiences of poor/out-classed African-, Asian-, Latino- and Native American youth they have been and are very much a part of white adolescent sub-culture. While individual gang members may be involved in crime, few youth gangs fit the activities and name of organized crime or terrorist. Subject to the disruption/infiltration of law enforcement, "aging out," inability to transit illicit profits into licit enterprise, no support from mainstream institutions in the resolution of conflicts, youth gangs are generally highly disorganized outfits (Paoli, 2002). Hence, street organizations that become like the archetypal so-called "criminal organizations" – such as La Cosa Nostra, Yakuza, Triads or any of the biker gangs – can hardly be considered youth gangs any longer. Whatever the form they take or how long they endure, the key point that justifies waging war on the ghetto is that ghetto youth gangs are violent and criminal enterprises. Such youth are presumed "to live in an aimless and violent present; have no sense of the past and no hope for the future … they are the ultimate urban nightmare, and their numbers are growing" (Safe Streets Coalition cited in Kappeler & Potter, 2005, p. 218). This belief misses the central point that if youth live in a violent present and have no hope for the future this is because all of these acts reflect the structural violence of a capitalist society that generates the social conditions in which secondary or micro-violence flourish.

Stanley Cohen (2007b) observes that, "[n]either in rich nor poor countries is death by lung cancer just an unfortunate side effect of industrialization; it is a product of traceable political and economic priorities" (p. 183). As such, it is of vital consequence to theorize violence as constitutive of two general forms: primary or structural and secondary or micro. Primary or structural violence arises where (a) it is known or can be reasonably inferred that maintaining particular forms of social policy actually and potentially will cause a range of harms that are (b) not prevented despite this knowledge (in criminal law this at the least qualifies for negligence) imposed by the state and a given social order (Farmer, 2004; Galtung, 1969; Reiman, 2007; Ward, 2004). These harms include physical, economic, psychological, and cultural injuries, directly or indirectly caused by state agencies and policies (Salmi, 2004) and those of capitalism and corporations (Glasbeek, 2002). Secondary or micro-violence is the expression of those forms of the micro and meso-sociological forms of violence that are influenced by structural violence.

Let us take homicide and violence as examples. The United States has the highest homicide rate of any Western industrialized country and, as I have shown, youth gangs do not figure substantially in these homicides. Youth homicide and violence dipped in the 1990s and into the twenty-first century but, even then, Elliot Currie (1999) suggests this drop is not to be celebrated because it is only a decline from rates that were already exceedingly high relative to other countries. There are various ways to account for the United States's high rate of violence and homicide but systemic or structural factors are the most influential. Beginning at the level of the state, for example, Dane Archer and Rosemary Gartner (1976) have found that since 1900 societies with high levels of homicide tend to be societies that have been at war and in which citizens were aware of high casualty rates. If war is connected to post-war homicide what does this auger for the United States which has to date spent tens of trillions fighting wars in Afghanistan and Iraq, clandestine wars…wars by proxy, sustaining military bases in over 100 countries and "securitizing" society? (see Herszenhorn, 2008; Lutz, 2009; Stiglitz & Bilmes, 2011). What are homicide and violence rates to look like given that 20 percent of US war veterans between 18 and 24 are unemployed (Maze, 2009), while others are drug addicted (Rice, 2009), suicidal (Big News Network, 2009; Kennedy, 2009) and mentally and physically impaired (Daily Mail Reporter, 2009; Seal et al., 2007)? This question is all the more profound as economists Merva and Fowles have argued in their longitudinal study of 30 US cities that a one per cent rise in unemployment results in 6.7 percent increase in homicide and a 2.4 percent increase in violent offenses (cited in Rifkin, 2004, p. 208; see also McNulty, 2000). As the US began to face the front edge of its financial crisis in 2006, homicide and violence were stable but the percentage of homicides involving a gun for African-American juveniles had risen by 85 percent (Fox & Swatt, 2008). African-Americans do not manufacture guns and the rate of poverty and joblessness should make such expensive and lethal death-making equipment out of reach. Corporate greed along with a healthy dose of enabling genocide might well account for corrupt gun dealers (overwhelmingly white) along with a complicit gun industry (all white in ownership) that have colluded to evade gun laws in the illegal supply of more and more lethal weapons that find their way into the ghetto (Woodiwiss, 2005; see also Kappeler & Potter, 2005; Reiman, 2007).

If it can be established that homicide and interpersonal violence are correlated with unemployment, wealth inequality, and lack of gun control, what are we to make of a society such as the United States where the richest 1 percent of the population owns 70 percent of all financial assets and where the combined wealth of 400 of the wealthiest citizens, $1.57 trillion dollars, is equivalent to the net worth of 175 million other citizens (DeGraw, 2010). Elliot Currie (1999) and Jeffrey Reiman (2007) have argued that the relative decline in homicide and violent offences over the mid- to late-stages of the 1990s owed much to higher job participation rates. Interestingly, the bail-out of banks, the crisis of workers disgorged from the economy, millions of Americans losing their homes and millions more "under water" combined with regressive taxation and redundancy of poor youth indicate the ruling class's war on the working class and dispossessed is likely to reap dividends in secondary violence.

Conclusion

The aim of this essay has been to reframe the demonizing discourse on youth gangs, crime, violence, and ghetto communities. I have aimed to show there are primary structuring factors and institutions (capitalism, corporations, and the state) that are relational to subsequent violence expressed by the poor, the marginal, and in the ghetto. Without exonerating youth gangs of the implications of secondary violence, I have, in the tradition of Bourdieu, placed emphasis on the dynamic interaction between social structure and the subjective facts of human action, thought, and feeling. Here, it is tempting to take a liberal approach to strain theory by assuming social inclusion is the best method of social control. But a more fundamental question – one which moves away from the implied correctionalism of the foregoing approach is that if the roots of "crime" are too deep to touch and if expanding social justice has been demonstrated to reduce the "crimes" we are socialized to fear, can "crime" prevention be the basis for social justice? Do we need "the excuse of 'vandalism prevention,'" Stanley Cohen (2007a) asks "to build adventure playgrounds for kids living in high-rise apartments" (p. 264) or do we do so because we believe they contribute to the development of children and are vital community projects? As suggested by Hagan and Coleman (2001), the wars on the abstract nouns crime and drugs must be abolished and in its place put a Marshall Plan to heal poor communities that have fallen prey to destructive social policies and moral indifference.

As the populations of megacities defy imagination, so too do the proliferation and scale of ghettos and slums (Davis, 2007). Consigned to the status of material effluence, having been expelled by technology and deemed a worthless consumer market, despair will mire millions in its grip along with the attendant mental and physical epidemiological consequences. However the ruling class and assorted number of elites will aim to perpetuate the material conditions that deaden the human will to throw off the shackles of oppression and enforced uselessness, the habitus of the ghetto is not solely the binary opposite of the preferred bourgeois standard. The ghetto is a place where people live and experience community and a sense of belonging. Exclusion and marginalization will no doubt be a steady companion, a veritable part of the banality of life as Richardson and Skott-Myhre remind us in their introduction. Despair, especially among the youth, will no doubt transition into secondary forms of predation that will be mistaken as primary violence.

Despair, however, is not of itself the terminus of the habitus of the ghetto. Sidney Willhelm (1983) argued of the ghetto revolts of the 1960's, "The discarded Black rises to challenge the status quo not out of hope but out of despair" (p. 252). There is little romance here and most certainly none to be captured by the heroic language of phoenix rising as ghettos once burned and certainly will again. The future looks to be catastrophic environmentally and socially. But as youth who have no meaning in their lives bourgeois society is prepared to tolerate, the reality is that they do have and make meaning that defines their humanity and reality. Some will accept their fate and sink into addictions, commit suicide, or gain negative power at the expense of others around them. Others will rebel in inchoate fashion, mirroring the social irresponsibility of society's economic and political elite. Others will yet reconcile their experience of injustice and demand the fulfillment of their and our collective humanity through a comprehensive politics of social transformation. Here, "The fundamental revolutionary motive is not to construct a Paradise but to destroy an inferno" (Oglesby & Shaull, cited in Willhelm, 1983, p. 253).

Notes

1. As Raymond Williams (1983) points out capitalism and bourgeois society are not to be confused because "[i]n a strict Marxist usage capitalist [*sic*, capitalism] is a description of a mode of production and bourgeois a description of a type society" (p. 52).
2. Habitus is a complex process of socialization. In his biography of Nelson A. Rockefeller (Governor of New York State, 1959–1973), Joseph E. Persico (1982) recounts, comparatively, how the imperious Rockefeller socialized his son, Mark, in contradistinction to how Persico himself socialized his children.

> Nelson strode in with the casual force that marked all his entrances. He exuded an exuberant self-assurance so unshakable that it must have been instilled from birth ... we quickly settled into reviewing the latest draft of a budget message from the Governor to be delivered to the state legislature ... when a towheaded child bounded into the room ... Nelson swept three year-old Mark, his youngest son, onto his knee ... [W]e plodded on, halting whenever Mark had something to say ... Nelson patiently instructed his son. Everyone grinned on cue. I thought of how I was raising my own children. I did not like them to interrupt when I was talking to friends, and I did not enjoy other people's howling Indians intrude on good conversation. But little Mark went on happily having his say, while his father responded and we waited. Nelson Rockefeller was passing along an unspoken lesson absorbed from his own father – "These people work for us. Never mind their age, their position, they defer to you." Thus are young princes bred. I was doing it all wrong.
>
> (pp. 2–3)

Less monied but middle-class parents have their way too of enculturating their children into the entitlements and institutional skills befitting their social status. Working-class parents, on the other hand, care equally but in a different way: "They see as their responsibility to care for their children but let them grow and develop on their own (Gladwell, 2008, p.104). There are clearly limits to this approach but it is ironic the middle and upper classes should preach rugged individualism while availing their children of every opportunity for emotional, cultural, and intellectual enrichment.

3. These terms and their uses have provoked serious and well-founded criticism. Cultural, human, and social capital is occasionally granted the status of material property. These critiques suggest these are achieved statuses and are not potable objects that can be owned and infused into the capitalist mode of production, but are rather capacities or competencies relative to habitus (Bezanson, 2006; Bowles and Gintis, 1975; Smith & Kulynych, 2002). To be logically consistent with the procedural and dynamic qualities of habitus, Bourdieu likely intended cultural and social capital to denote capacities or competencies. Apart from my sympathy for the critique against cultural, human, and social capital, my concern is that the terms can imply the moral superiority of elite habitus.

4. Referring to racism and the institutionalization of the ghetto, the Kerner (1967) report noted: "What white Americans have never fully understood but what the Negro can never forget – is that white society is deeply implicated in the ghetto. White institutions created it, white institutions maintain it, and white society condones it" (p. 2).

5. Recognizing the value of dialectics but guarding against the First World arrogance that presumes that it does not have the equivalent of colonies such as ghettos, Elliot Currie (1999) notes:

> I was in Brazil recently, and I spent some time in the *favelas* of Rio de Janeiro. It was among the most sobering experiences of my life. Not just because of the extraordinary level of deprivation there and the almost total absence of a public commitment to even the most minimal social protection for the poor. Not just because of the terribly glaring gap between large numbers of affluent people and even larger numbers of desperately poor people. But also because I kept having this chilling sense of *recognition*. Rio's problems, of poverty and violence and drugs, are extreme. But to an American, they are not, unfortunately, altogether unfamiliar (p. 6).

6. Anticipating Wacquant's observation of concatenating caste and class factors in the emergence of the *hyperghetto*, Willhelm (1983) explicitly cites forms of State and white civil society collusion that are given short shrift in Wacquant's (2008) account:

> The ghetto developed not purely in relation to class but also in caste terms as the state sided with whites who actively or passively benefited from the forced racial concentration of the ghetto and the forced non-competitiveness of its inhabitants.
>
> (p. 244)

7. I point out in my first note that physical genocide of African-American males has been casually bandied about in the United States, while in every respect the history of medical experimentation on African-Americans qualify for Raphael Lemkins multipoint definition of genocide. The discourse of ghetto male superpredators has recently been applied to the Palestinian resistance to Israeli occupation. In February 2010, Harvard professor Martin Kramer called for the curbing of Palestinian birthrates leading to the future elimination of those he referred to as "superfluous young men" (Israel Lobby Watch, 2010; Luban, 2010). In much the same way US neoconservatives argue that the welfare state undermines survival of the fittest, Kramer suggests cutting all aid to Israeli's illegally blockaded Palestinian authorities. Kramer has, however, admitted that he borrowed the idea from the University of Bremen's head of the Raphael Lemkin Institute, Gunnar Heinsohn (Luban, 2010).

8. Cynthia Enloe (1980) shows that around the world, particularly in countries where the state is involved in colonialism or was itself a product of colonialism, police and the military have a fluid and complex relationship especially in racially and ethnically fragmented societies (p. 107).

Again pointing to easy transit from military to police employment, Tom Hayden (2004) shows that in the LAPD's Ramparts Division corruption scandal that broke in 1998 "a high proportion of Marines … and other military veterans [were] recruited to the [Division] (p. 101).

9. Tom Hayden (2004) discusses the explicit militaristic nature of SWAT. As proposed by Daryl Gates in 1968, the acronym was intended to stand for Special Weapons Attack Teams but fearing the obvious public relations debacle the unit was instead named Special Weapons and Tactics (p. 91).

10. ABC's 20/20 exposed the willingness of whites to overlook white youth vandalism while presuming decoy African-American youth asleep in a parked car were likely up to no good (ABC, 2008).

References

ABC 20/20. (2008). What Would You Do / Racism In America. Retrieved Part 1 – http://www.youtube.com/watch?v=eNu-WZdHzaA Part 2 – http://www.youtube.com/watch?v=HIVgMvuCM_k&feature=email

Adamson, C. (1998). Tribute, Turf, Honour and the American Gang: Patterns of Continuity and Change since 1820. *Theoretical Criminology, 2*(1), 57–84.

Agozino, B. (2003). *Counter-Colonial Criminology: A Critique of Imperialist Reason.* London; Sterling, Virginia: Pluto Press.

Archer, D., & Gartner, R. (1976). Violent Acts and Violent Times: A Comparative Approach to Postwar Homicide Rates. *American Sociological Review, 41*(6), pp. 937–963.

Barber, B. (2007). *Consumed: How Markets Corrupt Children, Infantilize Adults, and Swallow Citizens Whole.* New York: W. W. Norton and Company.

Bauman, Z. (2004). *Wasted Lives: Modernity and its Outcasts.* Malden, MA, USA: Polity.

Bezanson, K. (2006). Gender and the Limits of Social Capital. *The Canadian Sociology and Anthropology Association, 43*(4), 427–443.

Blumer, H. (1971). Social Problems as Collective Behavior. *Social Problems, 18*(3), 298–306.

Bowles, S., & Gintis, H. (1975). The Problem with Human Capital Theory – A Marxian Critique. *The American Economic Review, 65*(2), 74–82. Papers and Proceedings of the Eighty-seventh Annual Meeting of the American Economic Association.

Bourdieu, P. (1985). The Social Space and Space and Genesis of Groups. *Social Science Information, 24*(2), 195–220.

—— (1977). *Outline of A Theory of Practice.* R. Nice (Trans.). London: New York; Melbourne: Cambridge University Press.

Brotherton, D. C. (2008). Beyond Social Reproduction: Bringing Resistance Back in Gang Theory. *Theoretical Criminology, 12*(1), 55–77.

Big News Network.com. (2009). Up to 16 US Soldiers Committed Suicide Last Month. Retrieved fromhttp://feeds.bignewsnetwork.com/?sid=565776.

Carroll, R. (2008). Haiti: Mud Cakes Become Staple Diet as Cost of Food Soars Beyond a Family's Reach. *The Guardian.* Retrieved from http://www.guardian.co.uk/world/2008/jul/29/food.international aidanddevelopment/print

Chambliss, W. (1995). Crime Control and Ethnic Minorities: Legitimizing Racial Oppression by Creating Moral Panics. In D. Hawkins (Ed.), *Ethnicity, Race, and Crime: Perspectives across Time and Place* (pp. 235–258). New York: State University of New York Press.

Chambliss, W. (1994). "Policing the Ghetto Underclass: The Politics of Law and Law Enforcement. *Social Problems, 41*(2), 177–194.

Churchill, W., & Vander Wall. (2002). *Agents of Repression: The FBI's secret wars against the Black Panther Party and the American Indian Movement.* Cambridge, MA: South End Press.

Clear, T. R. (2007). *Imprisoning Communities: How Mass Incarceration Makes Disadvantaged Neighborhoods Worse.* New York: Oxford University Press.

Cohen, S. (2007a). *Visions of Social Control: Crime, Punishment and Classification.* Cambridge, UK: Polity.

Cohen, S. (2007b). *Against Criminology.* New Brunswick, N.N.: Transaction.

Crank, J. (2004). *Understanding Police Culture,* 2nd ed. USA: Anderson Publishing/Lexis Nexis.

Currie, E. (1999). Reflections on Crime and Criminology at the Millennium. *Western Criminology Review, 2*(1). Retrieved from http://wcr.sonoma.edu/v2n1/currie.html.

Enloe, C. (1980). *Police, Military, and Ethnicity: Foundations of state power.* New Brunswick, N.J: Transaction Books.

Daily Mail Reporter. (2009). 20,000 Neglected Ex-Servicemen are either in Jail or on Probation. Retrieved from http://www.dailymail.co.uk/news/article-1216015/More-British-soldiers-prisonserving-Afghanistan-shock-study-finds.html

Davis, M. (2007). *Planet of Slums.* New York: Verso.

Degraw, D. (2010). The Richest 1% Have Captured America's Wealth – What's it going to Take to Get it Nack? *Alternet.org.* Retrieved from http://www.alternet.org/module/printversion/145705.

Enloe, C. (1980). *Police, Military and Ethnicity.* New Brunswick, NJ: Transaction Books.

Farmer, P. (2004). An Anthropology of Structural Violence. *Current Anthropology, 45*(3), 305–317.

Ford, G. (2010). Obama Sec'y of Education Says Katrina "the Best Thing to Happen" to Education in New Orleans. Black Agenda Report. Retrieved from http://tns1.blackagendareport.com/?q=content/obama-secy-education-says-katrina-best-thing-happen-education-new-orleans.

Galtung, J. (1969). Violence, Peace, and Peace Research. *Journal of Peace Research, 6*(3), 167–191.

Garvey, M., & McGreevy, P. (2007). L.A. Mayor Seeks Federal Aid to Combat Gangs. *Los Angeles Times,* January 4.

Gladwell, Malcolm. (2008). *Outliers: The story of success.* New York: Little, Brown and Company.

Glasbeek, H. (2002). *Wealth By Stealth: Corporate crime, corporate law, and the perversion of democracy.* Toronto: Between the Lines.

Gorelick, S. (1998). *Small is Beautiful, Big is Subsidized.* International Society for Ecology and Culture. Devonshire, UK: The Devonshire Press.

Greene, J. and Pranis, K. (2007). *Gang Wars: The Failure of Enforcement Tactics and the Need for Effective Public Safety Strategies.* Washington, D.C.: Justice Policy Institute.

Fox, J. A., & Swatt, M. L. (2008). *The Recent Surge in Homicides involving Young Black Males and Guns: Time to Reinvest in Prevention and Crime Control.* Retrieved from http://www.jfox.neu.edu/Documents/Fox%20Swatt%20Homicide%20Report%20Dec%2029%202008.pdf

Gilroy, P. (1987). The Myth of Black Criminality. In P. Scraton (Ed.), *Law, Order and the Authoritarian State* (pp. 107–120). Milton Keynes: Open University Press.

Hagan, J., & J. P. Coleman. (2001). Returning Captives of the American War on Drugs: Issues of Community and family reentry. *Crime and Delinquency, 47*(3), 352–367.

Hayden, T. (2004). *Street Wars: Gangs and the Future of Violence.* New York: New Press.

Herszenhorn, D. (2008). Estimates of Iraq War Cost Were Not Close to Ballpark. Retrieved from http://www.nytimes.com/2008/03/19/washington/19cost.html

Israel Lobby Watch. (2010). Harvard Fellow calls for Genocidal Measure to Curb Palestinian Births. *Electronic Intifada.* Retrieved from http://electronicintifada.net/v2/article11091.shtml.

Kappeler, V. E & Potter, G. W. (2005). *The Mythology of Crime and Criminal Justice,* 4th edn. Long Grove, Ill: Waveland Press.

Kelly, Peter. (2003). Growing Up as Risky Business? Risks, Surveillance and the Institutionalized Mistrust of Youth. *Journal of Youth Studies* 6(2): 165–180(16).

Kennedy, K. (2009). Navy Attempted Suicide Rate Nearly 3 Percent. *Navy Times*. Retrieved from http://www.navytimes.com/news/2009/12/navy_health_report_122309w/

Kerner Report (National Advisory Commission on Civil Disorders). (1967). Retrieved from http://www.blackpast.org/?q=primary/national-advisory-commission-civil-disorders-kernerreport-1967

Klare, M. T. (1974). Policing the Empire. In T. Platt and L. Cooper (Eds), *Policing America* (pp. 56–65). Englewood Cliffs, NJ: Prentice Hall, Inc.

Luban, D. (2010). The World's Nastiest Genocide Scholar. Lobelog.com. Retrieved from http://www.lobelog.com/the-worlds-nastiest-genocide-scholar/

Lutz, C. (2009). Obama's Empire. *Newstatesman.com*. Retrieved from http://www.newstatesman.com/asia/2009/07/military-bases-world-war-iraq

Matza, D. (1969). *Becoming Deviant*. Englewood Cliffs, NJ: Prentice-Hall, Inc.

Maze, R. (2009). Unemployment for Young Vets Surpasses 20%. Retrieved from http://www.armytimes.com/news/2009/12/military_veterans_unemployment_121109w/

McNulty, T. (2000). More on the Costs of Racial Exclusion: Race and Violent Crime in New York City, 1980–1990. *Race and Society*, 2(1), 51–68.

Meeks, D. (2006). "Police Militarization in Urban Areas: The Obscure War against the Underclass. *The Black Scholar*, 35(4), 33–41.

Mepham, J. (1979). The Theory of Ideology in Capital. In J. Mepham and D-H Ruben (Eds), *Issues in Marxist Philosophy*, Volume III: Epistemology, Science, Ideology (pp. 141–173). Sussex: The Harvester Press.

Merva, M., & Fowles, R. (1992). *Effects of diminished economic opportunities on social stress: Heart attacks, strokes, and crime*. Washington, D.C.: Economic Policy Institute.

Milliband, Ralph. (1973). *The State in Capitalist Society: The analysis of the Western system of power*. New York: Quartet.

Moynihan, P. (1965). *The Negro Family: The Case For National Action*. Blackpast.org. Retrieved from http://www.blackpast.org/?q=primary/moynihan-report-1965

Mueller, D & Ellis, D. (1990). *The FBI's War on Black America* (DVD).

Munford, C. (1996). *Race and Reparations: A Black perspective for the 21st Century*. Trenton, NJ:Africa World Press.

Oglesby, C., & Shaull, R. (1967). *Containment and Change*. New York: Macmillan.

Paoli, L. (2002). The Paradoxes of Organized Crime. *Crime. Law & Social Change*, 37, 51–97.

Parenti, M. (2003). *The Assassination of Julius Caesar: A People's History of Ancient Rome*. New York: The New Press.

Persico, J. E. (1982). *The Imperial Rockefeller: A Biography of Nelson Rockefeller*. New York: Washington Square Press/Pocket books.

Peters, R. (1996). Our Soldiers, Their cities. *Parameters*, Spring: 43–50.

Randall, Vernellia R (1996). Slavery, segregation and racism: trusting the health care system ain't always easy! An African American perspective on bioethics. *Saint Louis University Public Law Review*, 15 (2), 191–235.

RCMP. (2006). Youth Gangs & Guns: Canada. *Environmental Scan*. Retrieved from http://www.rcmpgrc.gc.ca/focus/youth_gun/canada19_e.htm

Reiman, J. H. (2007). *The Rich Get Richer and the Poor Get Prison: Ideology, Class and Criminal Justice* (8th edn). Boston: Allyn and Bacon.

Rice, J. (2009). Taliban Getting US Soldiers hooked on Drugs. Retrieved from http://airamerica.com/liveinwashingtonwithjackrice/blog/10-20-2009/taliban-using-heroin-weapon-video-audio/#

Rifkin, J. (2004). *The End of Work: The Decline of Global Labor Force and the Dawn of the Post-Market Era*. New York: Jeremy P. Tarcher/Penguin.

Roberts, D. (1993). Crime, Race and Reproduction. *Tulane Law Review* 67: 1945–1977.

Ryan, W. (1971). *Blaming the Victim*. New York: Vintage Books.

Seal, K. H., D. Bertenthal, C. R. Miner, S. Sen, & C. Marmar (2007). Bringing the War Back Home: Mental Health Disorders Among 103 788 US Veterans Returning From Iraq and Afghanistan Seen at Department of Veterans Affairs Facilities. *Archives of Internal Medicine* 167, 476–482.

Salmi, J. (2004). Violence in Democratic Societies: Towards an Analytic Framework. In P. Hillyard, C. Pantazis, S. Tombs, & D. Gordon (Eds), *Beyond Criminology: Taking Harm Seriously* (pp. 55–66). London, Pluto Press; Black Point, Nova Scotia: Fernwood Publishing.

Smith, S. S., & Kulynych, J. (2002). It May Be Social, but Why is it Capital? The Social Construction of Social Capital and the Politics of Language. *Politics and Society*, *30*(1), 149–186.

Stiglitz, S., & Bilmes, L. (2011). Estimating the Costs of War: Methodological Issues, with Applications to Iraq and Afghanistan.

Retrieved from: http://www.socsci.uci.edu/~mrgarfin/OUP/papers/Bilmes.pdf

Thrasher, M. (1963). *The Gang: A Study of 1,313 gangs in Chicago*. Chicago: University of Chicago Press.

Tombs, S., & Hillyard, P. (2004). Towards a Political Economy of Harm: States, Corporations and the Production of Inequality. In P. Hillyard, C. Pantazis, S. Tombs, and Dave Gordon (Eds), *Beyond Criminology: Taking Harm Seriously*. London; Ann Arbor, MI: Pluto, Black Point, Nova Scotia: Fernwood Publishing.

Padilla, F. (1996). *The Gang as an American Enterprise*. New Brunswick, NJ: Rutgers University Press.

Vaz, E. W. (1967). Introduction. In E. W. Vaz (Ed.), *Middle-Class Juvenile Deliquency* (pp. 1–4). New York: Harper and Row.

Ward, T. (2004). State Harms. In P. Hillyard, C. Pantazis, S. Tombs and D. Gordon (Eds), *Beyond Criminology: Taking Harm Seriously* (pp. 84–100). London, Pluto Press; Black Point, Nova Scotia: Fernwood Publishing.

Washington, H. (2006). Medical Apartheid: The dark history of medical experimentation on Black Americans from colonial times to the present. New York: Doubleday.

Willhelm, S. (1983). *Black in a White America*. Cambridge, Mass: Schenckman Publishing Company, Inc.

Willhelm, S. (1970). *Who Needs the Negro?* Cambridge, Mass: Schenckman Publishing Company, Inc.

Wilkins, L. (1965). Some Sociological Factors in Drug Addiction Control. In D. Wilner and G. Kassenbaum (Eds), *Narcotics*. New York: McGraw Hill.

Williams, C. J. (2005). To Unnerve and Detect: Policing Black activists in Toronto. In L. Visano (Ed.), *Law and Criminal Justice: A Critical Inquiry* (pp. 95–114). Toronto: APF.

Williams, R. (1983). *Keywords: A Vocabulary of Culture and Society*. Revised edition. New York: Oxford University Press.

Wacquant, L. (2008). *Urban Outcasts: A Comparative Sociology of Advanced Marginality*. Cambridge, UK: Polity Press.

Wellman, D. (1993). *Portraits of White Racism*. Cambridge [England]; New York: Cambridge University Press.

Woodiwiss, M. (2005). *Gangster Capitalism: The United States and the Global Rise of Organized Crime*. New York: Carroll and Graf Publishers.

Young, T. (2009). Corporations Cause $2.2T in Environmental Damage Every Year. *Greenbiz.com*. Retrieved from http://www.greenbiz.com/print/32758.

Chapter 7

Activist Literacy in the Hood: Lessons for Youth and Urban Education

Pamela Hollander and Justin Hollander

Developed, modern cities throughout the world are facing population decline at an unprecedented scale. Over the last 50 years, 370 cities throughout the world with populations over 100,000 have shrunk by at least 10 percent (Oswalt & Rieniets, 2007). Wide swaths of the United States are projecting double-digit declines in population in the coming decades. Present-day notions of the hood will change as more and more of the urban American landscape is decimated by population loss. In this chapter, we describe these changing neighborhoods through the lens of community activists and the literacy artifacts they produce.[1]

Activists working in community-based organizations have responded to the depopulation crisis by writing about population decline in a positive or neutral way, as opposed to the negative perspective most often associated with decline.[2] This movement has rallied around the word *shrinkage* to better articulate the changes that occur in cities when they depopulate. This new language has allowed activists and planners to begin exploring creative and innovative ways for cities to successfully shrink. One site of this reconceptualization process has been at the community level where activists have embraced some or parts of this new shrinkage discourse. These activists use a variety of literacy artifacts, from neighborhood association newsletters and letters to the editor to reports, to engage with the shrinkage discourse and fight for change in their communities (Beauregard, 2003).

For children growing up in the hood, the challenges of crime, unemployment, and poverty can have harsh effects on hope, optimism, and sense of self-worth. The sociologist William Julius Wilson (1987) has documented how crime, unemployment, and poverty are commonplace in shrinking cities and can weigh heavily on children's confidence and world outlook. The discourse of decline and negativity can be injurious to children and even turn them off literacy. In contrast, the shrinkage discourse provides an entrée for many of these children into a world of reading and writing that gives them confidence and pride in their community beyond the typical stereotypes of what the hood might mean.

Content Area Literacy (CAL) has received much attention in recent years. No longer is generic reading and writing considered enough for success in the content areas from elementary school on up. Drawing on existing approaches to literacy and ideas from writing across the curriculum (WAC) findings from the eighties and nineties about discipline-specific values concerning writing, content-area literacy has become the current approach to literacy K-12. Science, math, history, and English teachers are being asked to see themselves as teachers of science literacy, math literacy etc. (Fynders & Hynds, 2002; Vacca & Vacca,

2008). Those of us who teach content area literacy for pre-service teachers are working to help teacher candidates build "literacy teacher" into their content area from the beginning.

In this research we ask: what are the discourses and values embedded in the work of activists working in the hood and how can that work be used in classrooms to help empower youth? We begin by looking at the literacy artifacts of community-based organizations in three US cities with persistent population decline: Pittsburgh (PA), Youngstown (OH), and Richmond (VA). We asked pre-service content area teachers to aid us in exploring how these documents could be used in a content area classroom in ways that both connect students to their communities and involve them in appropriate content area learning. Our analysis reveals that the literacy artifacts can be used in the classroom to engage students in the challenges their cities face. Examining these artifacts, which show the flexibility of the city to reinvent itself, can be an empowering, authentic activity for youth, and portends a brighter future for even the most distressed city. Here an opportunity exists to enhance students' understandings of content area literacy while attending to the challenges that they face in their own communities.

Brief review of the literature

Before reporting on the empirical findings of our research, we turn first to a conceptual review of the literature to frame our study. We begin with an introduction to the topic of activist literacy and then explain the relationships between activist literacy and content-area literacy in classrooms. Next, we describe the theoretical basis for examining discourses with an overview of relevant discourse theory. Last, we frame the challenge of the shrinking city as a setting for this study.

What is activist literacy?

Literacy and activism have had a longstanding relationship. Community activists get their messages out, ask for help, and build name recognition through written materials. Causes associated with change have had written materials representing their desires since antiquity. In modern times, activists produce written materials and disseminate these materials widely, enjoying accessible and inexpensive production methods. These brochures, announcements, posters, invitations and the like become part of the fabric of community life, a ubiquitous part of visits to stores, doctors, libraries and walks down the street (Fisher, 2009).

In the realm of education, activism and literacy have been connected at theoretical and practical levels, often through the term "critical literacy." Shor (1992) talks about critical literacy in the classroom as those practices that enable people to see beyond accepted dominant discourses and ideologies and imagine "how to act on the meaning to change the conditions it reflects" (p. 129).

In his well-known teaching and advocacy projects with Brazilian peasants, Paulo Freire (1970) showed the reflexive nature of this relationship, helping his students to become activists and literate at the same time. Freire's method involved literacy instruction focused around issues close to the peasants, such as labor exploitation, poverty, food, work, building materials, so that "learning to read and write, the students would also be gaining the power to critique and act on their conditions" (Shor, 1992, p. 47). In this same way, children in school who study new forms of language that reject the negativity of decline may be better prepared to address the changes at work in their neighborhoods.

In the worlds of higher education and public education, attention has been paid to activist literacy in several ways. Community service learning courses, especially in composition, have made it possible for students to get involved in writing materials for non-profit or charitable organizations (Deans & Meyer-Goncalves, 1998; Deans, 2003). Within this community service movement there has been some theorizing about the value of offering students the opportunity to actualize their roles as "citizens" through such activity (Deans, 2003). At the secondary and elementary levels students get involved in community improvement events through nonprofit organizations, using reading and writing skills. For example, hundreds of elementary school students read and wrote as part of a New York Department of Environmental Conservation water sampling event along the Hudson River (Bowser, 2007). Activist literacy also encompasses the applied critical work students do in school. For example, students in writer-educator Linda Christensen's (2000) classroom have written letters to editors about general problems of racism and sexism in the media.

In her dissertation studying critical literacy in a composition classroom and an activist organization (Greenpeace), Virginia Crisco (2005) builds on the idea of critical literacy to define "literacy activism." Crisco writes, "Activist literacy augments critical literacy through the *enactment* of critical literacy in democratic contexts, and it is *not only* sponsored by educational contexts but also in community contexts" (p. 24). Our study brings together educational and community contexts in the way that Crisco describes and focuses on an area which has taken center stage in importance in recent years: content area literacy.

Activist literacy as content area literacy

A common set of principles and skills for all disciplines has emerged from Content Area Literacy as well as discipline specific requirements (Fynders & Hynds, 2002; Vacca & Vacca, 2008). Some of the common methods to be used and skills to be taught in all subject areas are graphic representation, vocabulary, reading strategies, general ideas about the writing process, critical reading and writing, and using real life applications (Vacca & Vacca, 2008). Examples of other, more subject-specific literacy preparation includes writing of labs and specialized knowledge of relationships and vocabulary in science, reading primary documents and reading maps in social studies/history, differences between everyday word meanings and the meanings of those words in math, writing explanations of solutions to problems, and understanding figurative language and character development in English (Fynders & Hynds, 2002).

Literature disseminated by neighborhood groups asks its readers to interact with it in similar ways to those expected in CAL. Readers are asked to interact with excerpts from primary sources, read maps of neighborhood landmarks and proposed improvements, make critical judgments, learn about historical and current events and people, understand new vocabulary, understand relationships such as cause and effect, follow and apply mathematical calculations, and read all kinds of graphic representations (Fynders & Hynds, 2002).

The overlap between skills required to read activist literacy and those stressed by CAL teachers, along with the benefits suggested by our earlier discussion of community service learning, makes bringing activist literacy into the classroom an exciting opportunity for engaged learning of core research-based CAL skills.

Discourse theory

In the fields of urban planning and education the relationship between reality and language is central. Our understanding of literacy draws on the theories of discourse that address the reflexive nature of language and reality. These theories, often referred to as New Literacy Studies, talk about language as being composed of discourses, ways of seeing the world, which position the language user as well as the receiver, and influence the individual and collective understanding of self and reality (Ivanic, 1997). Discourses vie for power in the open market of culture (Ivanic, 1997). These discourses wield different amounts of power and influence, depending on their cultural dominance at any one moment in time.

We argue that the notion of discourses is particularly exciting for urban planners and educators for two reasons: (1) discourses reveal the values of an individual or culture when analyzed, and (2) discourses can influence peoples' thinking and identities. Discourse theory, which posits that discourse helps to (re)produce identities (often called subjectivities or subject positions) to be taken up (Ivanic, 1997), gives urban planners and educators the ability to raise consciousness and the potential to generate positive change through a person's adoption of these identities. An example of this process would be the Global Warming/Save the Planet Discourse, which has spread, perhaps most notably with Al Gore's documentary *An Inconvenient Truth* (2006) and the media coverage of that film, which appeared to offer subjective positions for people, young and old, to take up as "someone informed about Global Warming and trying to do something to help." In some cases, these identities may not have existed before in quite the same way.

Data and methods

Building on the research of one of the authors (Hollander, 2009) into policy and planning challenges faced by distressed cities, we examined three shrinking US cities: Pittsburgh, Youngstown, and Richmond. We selected these cities because they are each host to community-based organizations that employ a wide-range of literacy practices in their activism. For each city, we collected at least three literacy artifacts from community organizations; these artifacts included newsletters, brochures, historical notes, and a webpage.

We employed critical discourse analysis in order to explore the key values, themes, and subject positions made available by each literacy artifact. In the analysis, we looked particularly for examples of smart decline ideology introduced earlier in this paper. The goal of critical discourse analysis, outlined in work done by Fairclough (1995) and extended by Ivanic (1997) and other New Literacy Studies theorists, was to elucidate aspects of language that are generally invisible to people because they seem "natural." These aspects include at least one of the following: (1) the way language positions those who read and write it, so that they take on available identities, referred to as subject positions; (2) the way language draws on particular discourses – worldviews associated with institutions or groups having different amounts of power are expressed through language; (3) the way that language in a text may refer to other texts – referred to as intertextuality; and (4) the way that language is constitutive – shapes the user's identity and what subject positions are available generally.

The goals of critical discourse analysis illustrated above will be enacted in this study through the methodology of microanalysis. As characterized in work done by Bloome and Egan-Robertson (1993) and Willett, Solsken, & Wilson Keenan (1998), microanalysis allows the researcher to study a piece of text at the micro-level without losing sight of the macro-level. The researcher gains insight into the micro-level through categorizing small units of text, while at the same time, because the categories are inherently tied to larger "big-picture" ideas, the researcher can gain insight into the macro-level. Next, we needed an approach to take the findings from the discourse analysis and translate that into avenues for introducing activist literacy into the classroom. We accomplished that through two brainstorming sessions with content area secondary undergraduates. We met with two sets of undergraduates (34 students in the first, 32 students in the second), presented them with the literacy artifacts and the results of the discourse analysis, and then had them work in teams with their fellow content area students.

Results

While the smart decline ideology introduced earlier in the paper was not obliquely evident in the literacy artifacts, the discourses, values, and subject positions made available were largely sympathetic to smart decline and provides a useful insight into the workings of activist literacy practices. Table 1 summarizes the discourses and values for three literacy artifacts, one from each city. As the table illustrates, the community organizations used the literacy artifacts to express a range of discourses but leaned heavily on Working Collaboratively and Community Empowerment Discourses. In the Hazelwood Initiative, Inc. Brochure, there was evidence of the use of the Quality of Life Discourse, which is highly compatible with smart decline and suggests to its readers that quality of life, rather than growth, should be the aim of activists.

Table 1: Discourses and values from literacy artifacts[3]

Literacy artifact	City	Discourses present	Excerpts	Values
The Gillies Creek Park Foundation Brochure	Richmond	Working Collaboratively Discourse	"The … Foundation is working with the City of Richmond to connect a series of new and existing parks."	Teamwork, working within the system, cooperation
		Community Empowerment Discourse	"The story of Gillies Creek Park began with just a few people asking how they could help improve the area."	Change is possible, agency matters, individuals count
		Cultural & Historic Preservation Discourse	"This effort faithfully maintains existing properties, with each retaining its current identity and features … The proposed park system encompasses areas that are rich in local and national historical significance."	Celebrate the past, capitalize on history and culture
"Waiting for the Future" Report	Youngstown	Community Empowerment Discourse	"the people of Youngstown can find hope for the future when they look to the small signs of progress around them" (p. 3) "people can start to share ideas and hear about some of the positive things that are happening" (p. 38).	Change is possible, agency matters, individuals count

		Hopelessness Discourse	"the community is waiting for someone or something to move it ahead" (p. 2) "People wonder aloud how, and if, the city could survive another blow" (p. 7)	Positive change is unlikely, structural forces matter, individuals can do little
		Working Collaboratively Discourse	"they need to find a way to come together to define their priorities and set a common direction for moving ahead."	Positive change is possible through coming together
Hazelwood Initiative Inc. Brochure	Pittsburgh	Working Collaboratively Discourse	"the Hazelwood Initiative can solve neighborhood problems and get people in the neighborhood to work together."	Positive change is possible through coming together
		Community Empowerment Discourse	"The Hazelwood Initiative is guided not by outside forces, but by the collective vision and participation of our community members."	Outsiders do not control residents destiny, agency matters, individuals can make a difference
		Quality of Life Discourse	"Founded in 1994 to improve the quality of life in our neighborhood … With your knowledge, abilities, and commitment, the Hazelwood Initiative can do even more to enhance the community."	Quality of life in the community can be enhanced.

As Table 1 indicates, the values embedded in the literacy artifacts are largely positive, laying out the possibilities for agency in affecting change. The exception to this is the example in the Waiting for the Future Report where a Hopelessness Discourse is employed for dramatic effect. Overall, in all the artifacts examined, throughout the three cities, the discourses used by the activists were intended to position their readers as agents for change and in doing so empowers them. As the Gillies Creek Park Foundation Brochure reads "The story of Gillies Park began with just a few people asking how they could help improve the area." Margaret Mead has oft been quoted as saying that one should never doubt that a small group of thoughtful, committed citizens can change the world. Indeed, it is the only thing that ever has. People can be empowered to fight for change in their communities and in their neighborhoods when success stories are told and retold both orally and in print. The values of fighting the status quo and building a better future (together) are somewhat evident throughout these artifacts and form the basis for the second phase of the research.

The brainstorming sessions with undergraduate pre-service teachers revealed that the values and discourses embraced by the community organizations had potential for supporting urban education curriculum in the content areas. In Table 2 we present a summary of the results of the brainstorming session, with ideas for incorporating the literacy artifacts into secondary education classrooms in shrinking cities. For each content area, Math, History/Social Studies, English, and Science, the brainstorming sessions resulted in at least two ideas for utilizing the literacy artifacts. While some of the ideas were narrow and connected to specific curriculum, for example the idea of juxtaposing the Waiting for the Future report for Youngstown with *To Kill a Mockingbird*, other ideas were more general and less tied to a particular curriculum, like connecting generic history lessons to literacy artifacts' recounting of local history.

Table 2: Results from brainstorming session with undergraduate pre-service secondary teachers

Math

Collect data on population and demographic change over time and make mathematical calculations. Examine what was happening historically at the time of population loss (in the neighborhood, the city, or the country).

Analyze things done with numbers and statistics, students could create own idea-fundraiser and what they would do with funds (figure out how much $ they would have to work with, what would you do with the vacant land-calculate acreage.

Social studies/History

Creative writing looking at neighborhood's history, what was there and is not there today. Write about why historic properties should be protected as part of funding proposals to state and federal government agencies. A class lesson on that funding process.

Have students brainstorm their own ideas for small projects that compliment local organizations small-scale efforts.

Connect generic history lessons to literacy artifacts recounting of local history.

Teach about industrialization and how it relates to Hazelwood, look at family history to see if it fits in with history of industrialization as written in pamphlet, have students work on timelines for area, talk about preserving history-what purpose that could serve-visit old rehabbed historic site.

English

Juxtapose Youngstown community report with *To Kill a Mockingbird*.

Pull out literary themes (racial tensions, economic conditions) and see how they play out in a real neighborhood.

Collaborate with Science for planting to contribute. Inform with press release – cover non fiction writing, pick out metaphors and why pamphlets use metaphors

Science

Environmental/Earth science class, field trip to park location – tree identification. Test water quality. Examine landfill, study erosion.

Study the effects of new building (i.e., Ball fields, park facilities) on environmental conditions.

Talk about water quality, erosion; Field Trips: wildlife, trees, talk about process of capping pollution

Create brochure showing all services and resources and events focusing on Hispanic population. Incorporate vocabulary.

Discussion

The results of the discourse analysis and the brainstorming session with pre-service teachers yielded promising results. The sorts of discourses revealed in the literacy activist artifacts are mainly empowering discourses. These discourses, which value collaboration, ties to history and the community, have stature in their own right, but can be seen to be overshadowed by the more dominant discourses associated with capitalism and individualism. Their appearance in these artifacts means that readers will have a chance to take up these discourses and the identities associated with them, perhaps for the first time for some. For the reasons scholars and educators associated with New Literacy Studies have cited, it promises to be an empowering experience for students to interact with these empowering discourses, particularly as teachers and community organizers offer them opportunities and show them how to engage and contribute to the discourses. By reading these texts and studying them in the classroom, students will have available to them the values and identities associated with working for positive change in their own hood. In the cases where there might be conflicting discourses, like when Hopelessness Discourses show up in contrast with Community Empowerment Discourses, students can be asked to critically examine the problems and possible solutions these discourses describe.

In addition to the benefits in terms of access to new discourses and identities, activist literacy artifacts also suggest to teachers activities which are literacy work of any content area class. The pre-service teachers, very familiar with literacy teaching methods for their content areas, found many ways that they could use the artifacts in their subject area classes. They imagined projects which involved using the artifacts to give students experience interacting with primary documents, maps, scientific findings, historical secondary sources, and figurative language. They also thought of ways to actively engage students in their own brainstorming of ways to extend what the community group was doing. As a result of such lessons, students would write, collect data, interview people and analyze written, mathematical, and scientific information and data.

Conclusions

This paper set out to examine the potential for literacy artifacts in the hood to be used in content-area teaching. We found that there is some potential for such a pedagogical approach and recommend further research that could test the effectiveness and utility of using these artifacts in classrooms. Activist literacy exposes students to potentially empowering discourses they might not otherwise be exposed to if the students are not directly engaged with local agencies. In addition, activist literacy can provide the opportunity for teachers to engage students in activities well-suited to the goals of the content area classroom.

We recommend that teachers working in North America attempt to link literacy artifacts with content-area lessons and find ways to track and measure the impact those innovations have on students' identities and attitudes toward the spaces and communities in which they live and interact. The research reported here suggests that the use of literacy artifacts may have greater potential for connecting students with their own hoods.

Notes

1. This chapter was adapted from: Hollander, Pamela W. and Justin B. Hollander. 2008. Activist literacy in shrinking cities: Lessons for urban education. *Language Arts Journal of Michigan*. 23, 3.
2. In August 2008, *Forbes Magazine* described US cities with the greatest population loss rates as "dying cities." Beauregard (2003) documented how widespread this type of labeling has been in recent decades in the popular and academic literature in his book *Voices of Decline*.
3. These literacy artifacts drew on discourses that avoided the conventional growth-oriented economic development discourse commonly present in official government documents and media stories.

References

Beauregard, R. A. (2003). *Voices of Decline: The Postwar Fate of U.S. Cities*. 2nd edn. New York: Routledge.

Bloome, D. and Egan-Robertson, A. (1993). The social construction of intertextuality and classroom reading and writing. *Reading Research Quarterly*, 28(4), 303–333.

Bowser, C. (2007). Class Assignment. Marist College. December.

Crisco, V. (2005) Activist literacy: Engaging democracy in the classroom and the community. Ph.D. diss. University of Nebraska - Lincoln.

Deans, T. (2003). *Writing and Community Action: A Service-Learning Rhetoric and Reader.* NY: Longman.

Deans, T., & Meyer-Goncalves, Z. (1998). Writing Out of Bounds: Service-Learning Projects in Composition and Beyond. *College Teaching*, 46.1 (Winter), 12–15.

Fairclough, N. (1995). *Critical Discourse Analysis.* London: Longman.

Finders, M. and Hynds, S. (2003). *Literacy Lessons: Teaching and Learning in the Middle School.* Columbus, OH: Merrill, Prentice Hall.

Fisher, M. T. (2009). *Black Literate Lives: Historical and Contemporary Perspectives, Critical Social Thought.* New York: Taylor & Francis.

Freire, P. (1970). *Pedagogy of the Oppressed.* New York: Continuum Publishing.

Ivanic, R. (1997). *Writing and Identity: The Discoursal Construction of Identity in Academic Writing.* Philadelphia: John Benjamins Publishing Company.

Hollander, J. B. (2009). *Polluted, and Dangerous: America's worst abandoned properties and what can be done about them.* Burlington, VT: University of Vermont Press.

Oswalt, B. P and Rieniets, T. (2007). Global Context. Shrinking Cities. Retrieved from http://www.shrinkingcities.com/globaler_kontext.0.html?&L=1.

Shor, Ira. (1992). *Empowering Education: Critical Teaching for Social Change.* Chicago: University of Chicago Press.

Vacca, R.T., Vacca, J.L. (2008). *Content Area Reading: Literacy and learning across the curriculum,* 9th ed. Boston, MA: Allyn & Bacon.

Wilson, W. J. (1987). *The Truly Disadvantaged: The Inner City, the Underclass, and Public Policy.* Chicago: The University of Chicago Press.

Willett, J., Slosken, J., & Wilson Keenan, J. (1996). Linking Texts, Linking Cultures: An Intertextual Analysis of Interaction and Ideology in a Multicultural Classroom. Paper presented at the meeting of the American Educational Research Association, New York, NY, 1996.

Chapter 8

The Girls from Compton Go to College

Donna J. Nicol and Jennifer A. Yee

Some people say their paths cross for a reason. Often, those reasons manifest in mysterious ways. Even though our lives are unique, we have found that our journeys mirror each other's and that our life paths have converged in a Women's Studies Program suite at California State University, Fullerton (CSUF).[1]

We are faculty neighbors in the Humanities Building. Donna, who had been teaching as a lecturer in Women's Studies since 2002, was appointed as a tenure-track faculty member in Fall 2007. That semester, Jennifer moved into the office next door to Donna's because the Ethnic Studies suite upstairs was already full. The location seemed a good fit, as Jennifer, also a new tenure-track faculty member, was scheduled to teach the "Asian-American Women" course, which is cross-listed in both Asian-American Studies and Women's Studies.

One day, in the common area of the Women's Studies suite, Donna was telling stories (about working at a private, sectarian college for women in Los Angeles) to her incredulous colleagues. Jennifer heard Donna, came out of her office, and confirmed that the stories were true. We discovered that both of us had worked at the same college at different times. We had been attracted to working at the college because of its explicit social justice mission. With our similar perceptions of its culture, leadership, and management with regard to women and people of color after a year of working there each of us decided to leave. Through a quick exchange of narratives, we realized that we shared much more than a history of working at the same institution in Los Angeles. With our shared histories as "girls from Compton," our friendship and professional relationship clicked.

This office space is an intersection of multiple, continually shifting dimensions – race, gender, class, geography, and time – that echo across the span of our personal and professional journeys. Through our autoethnographic conversations about growing up in Compton, California, we realize that the worldview developed as a result of our origins is a common theme in our life journeys. Reflecting on our childhoods and subsequent directions, we have come to realize that Compton – also as an intersection of race, gender, class, geography, and time – has figured deeply into our senses of selves, tied to the history and legacy of place. We are *from* Compton and *of* Compton, but not necessarily *straight outta* Compton. Being *from* and *of* has conferred a cultural and social capital on each of us that has affected our life choices and our orientation towards our work as social justice educators.

Previewing the chapter

The purpose of this chapter is to explore how the experience of growing up in Compton, California has shaped our worldviews and life trajectories. This worldview manifests itself in remarkably similar motivations underlying our choices in terms of study and work. We seek to understand the origins of our approaches to teaching and research by focusing on our unique childhood experiences through this shared experiential lens. Therefore, we have relied on Pierre Bourdieu's conceptualization of cultural capital and habitus as the theoretical framework for our work. As Bourdieu explains, cultural capital relates to the habits and dispositions that comprise resources for individuals who can use these dispositions to generate a profit. Generally, these forms of capital are present in bodily knowledges and attitudes that are (re)produced within social circles as well as perpetuated in representations of certain groups (Bourdieu, 1984; Bourdieu & Passeron, 2000 [1970]). Media representations of Compton, for example, have led many outsiders to associate the city with black-on-black crime, juvenile delinquency, welfare mothers, and gangsta rap. These attitudes and practices work as negative cultural capital for all who are associated with them. And thus, we would like to explore, in part, just how two "girls" from Compton could earn doctoral degrees and become faculty at the largest campus in the CSU amidst this cultural and social backdrop.

This chapter describes how Compton influences our attitudes about education, our sense of community, and our politics. When we say that we are from this "hood," we destabilize fixed notions about race, class, gender, and geographic space, particularly the stereotypical notions reified through popular media. In our courses, we use our personal stories to create "teachable moments" that challenge our students' assumptions about people's lives in the hood and the people who come from the hood. As a result, students develop multilayered perspectives that contribute to their critical understanding of larger social issues (i.e., racism, welfare reform, sexism, poorly performing schools, transnational migration, and unemployment). This chapter is part of the story of our journeys – from Compton to college as students, as administrators, and now, as professors.

Methodology and conceptual framework: understanding how and why we conducted our study

Our choice of methodology is political and activist-oriented. Autoethnography and the use of narratives from interviews reflect the values we bring to our work. In this section, we describe how we conducted our study while weaving in theoretical strands to identify the lenses with which we will analyze the data.

Our narrative has resulted from months of conversation about our personal, educational, and career paths. We conducted autoethnography[2] by interviewing each other and eliciting narratives that serve as our data, which we have coded, analyzed, and now organized into a coherent piece. This method allowed us to write from the "outsider-within" perspective that we bring to our work as faculty. Our methodological approach draws heavily from the "counterstories" of Critical Race Theory and academic "race women" such as Patricia Hill Collins (1990), Maxine Hong Kingston (1989), Gloria Anzaldúa (2007) and Chela Sandoval (2000).

Collins' (1990) term, "outsider-within" (pp. 11–12) can be used to describe the perspectives of people of color or ethnic minority groups working in institutions of higher education created historically and primarily by white men. Briefly, this term sets forth how people of color may have a "distinct view of the contradictions between the dominant group's actions and ideologies" at the institutions in which they work.[3] Examining the "power of the dominant group to suppress knowledge created by subordinate groups" from an outsider-within perspective allows us to see and cast light on contradictions between institutions' explicitly stated values and institutional members' behaviors. This outsider-within perspective connected us as we recalled our former jobs at the same college. Denise Taliaferro Baszile (2006) describes a critical race feminist way of approaching her work as "a way of teaching and doing scholarship that embraces duality, subjectivity, and narrative in our attempts to authorize our voices" (p. 200). She describes "counter-stories" as "not only a form of resistance and recognition, which disrupt the culture of power; they also depict a kind of complexity that is unattainable through traditional academic discourse" (ibid.).

In this chapter, we present counterstories as reflections of our outsider-within status as professional academic women. To organize our conversations, we wanted to find out more about who we are, where we come from (and how we have constructed where we are from), and what effect our origins have had on our current professional lives. So, we asked ourselves: How did we get to Compton and how did Compton shape us? How did the experience of growing up in Compton shape our decisions for our education and careers? How do we use "Compton" in our scholarship, teaching, and social justice work/activism?

We started with these questions and allowed for more to emerge based on the individual's experience. Each of us has extensive experience with interviewing and felt comfortable without a set protocol. In addition, the interviewer also transcribed the interviewee's responses during the conversations.

Our choice for employing autoethnography comes from our intellectual commitment to give voice to the experiences of the oppressed, particularly women of color, long denied in academe. Further, autoethnography has allowed for us to reflect more thoughtfully on how our origins in Compton have made it possible for us to navigate highly contested social spaces which have traditionally excluded the "Other" (Said, 2003).

Bourdieu (2007) describes habitus as "the product of history, produc[ing] individual and collective practices" (p. 82). He calls it "a past which survives in the present and tends to perpetuate itself into the future by making itself present in the practices structured according to its principles" (ibid.). Third-world feminism, as posited by cultural theorist Chela Sandoval (2000), has enriched our analysis of the concept of habitus. Sandoval states that individual and collective experiences with racial, gender, and class discrimination and oppression force women of color to learn how to navigate a hostile society in order to survive. Specifically, Sandoval maintains that citizen-subjects of colonization, poverty, racism, and gender or sexual subordination resist subordination by developing skills

> to self-consciously navigate modes of dominant consciousness, learning to interrupt the "turnstile" that alternately reveals history, as against the dominant forms of masquerade that history can take, "focusing on each separately," applying a "formal method of reading," cynically but also un-cynically, and not only with the hope of surviving, but with a desire to create a better world.
>
> (p. 104)

Sandoval (2000) characterizes the experiences of women of color in the United States as one of being considered different from the dominant racial/cultural and gender norms and, as a result, being outcast or treated as deviant of this perceived difference. She describes women of color as being colonized into a third world within a first-world nation. Thus, women academics of color may interrogate the language used to dominate them and may view deconstruction as an inherently necessary part of their work to address social injustice and power inequities.

As "citizen-subjects" from the hood, we have learned how to become "bi-cultural" in our personal and professional pursuits – particularly in our work as educators – so as to "disrupt" narrow conceptualizations of the hood which emanate from both popular culture and society-at-large. We contend that Compton enriched our cultural and social capital by fostering our ability to "code-switch" – allowing us to enter and operate in various social spaces and to communicate in the language of respective audiences (see Gardner-Chloros, 2009; Isurin, Winford, De Bot, 2009; Wheeler & Swords, 2006). This is especially important to our teaching, given that our students are primarily first-generation ethnic minorities who are unfamiliar with the term, "code-switching," which they may already be practicing. In addition, because each of us could see how language and informal/formal power structures oppressed people of color in Compton, we employ pedagogical practices that deconstruct language and power relations.

Chicana feminist theorist Gloria Anzaldúa's (2007) description of the "Borderlands" mirrors the intersections we witnessed while growing up in Compton. We refer to her work to further our analysis and discussion of what it means to be "bi-cultural."

> The U.S.-Mexican border es una herida abierta where the Third World grates against the first and bleeds. And before a scab forms it hemorrhages again, the lifeblood of two worlds merging to form a third country – a border culture. Borders are set up to define the places that are safe and unsafe, to distinguish us from them. A border is a dividing line, a narrow strip along a steep edge. A borderland is a vague and undetermined place created by the emotional residue of an unnatural boundary. It is in a constant state of transition. The prohibited and forbidden are its inhabitants. Los atravesados live here:

the squint-eyed, the perverse, the queer, the troublesome, the mongrel, the mulatto, the half-breed, the half dead; in short, those who cross over, pass over, or go through the confines of the "normal." Gringos in the U.S. Southwest consider the inhabitants of the borderlands transgressors, aliens – whether they possess documents or not, whether they're Chicanos, Indians or Blacks.

(p. 25)

While Anzaldúa talks about people moving through Borderlands, we are also talking about people moving by both choice and necessity. Jennifer's family moved to Compton in the white flight period of the late 1950s because her father's job had just been transferred there from Chinatown and because the residents of Compton had recently voted to desegregate the city's schools. Housing had also become more readily available and affordable, and her parents bought the house in a "For Sale by Owner" transaction. Due to restrictive covenants, there were few places where families of color could live in Los Angeles with the exception of a few over-crowded ethnic enclaves such as Watts and Chinatown. Donna's maternal and paternal grandparents moved to Compton immediately following the end of World War II where both her maternal great-grandfather and paternal grandfather served in the US Army. Due to the growth and popularity of the war industry in neighboring Watts, African-Americans began to move to Compton en masse starting in the 1950s and Compton would complete its transition to a "Chocolate City" by the early 1970s.

We expand on Anzaldúa's (2007) conceptualization of the "Borderlands" to include borders which we *choose* in addition to borders imposed on a person because of gender, race, religion, language, or social class. Anzaldúa's "Borderlands" gives us a construct to explain how figurative and actual borders affect one's cultural capital. Thus, Anzaldúa's work informs our understanding of Bourdieu's concepts of habitus and cultural capital. To us, Compton is not only a city where residents live, but also an intersection of race, gender, class, geography and time. Our stories describe how people can *choose* to move to this "intersection" and to take the intersection with them through the rest of their lives. Our families chose to settle in Compton long before the rise of the infamous Piru (Blood) street gang in the 1970s or gangster rappers such as N.W.A. in the late 1980s and, more recently, The Game which gave the city a dubious distinction as one of the most dangerous inner city/suburban areas in the United States. Before developing this notorious reputation, Compton was home to large tracts of agricultural land, the first African-American male and female mayors of a metropolitan city, and the one-time home of former president George H. W. Bush (Bush, 2000). For these reasons, our recollection of Compton is far more complex, nuanced, and varied than the limited media representations of the city would leave a naïve outsider to believe. While the outside world simply sees Compton as another hood, we call it "home."

How the girls from Compton got to college: counter-stories of origin: our families' journeys to Compton

Being raised in Compton, we have derived a particular habitus informed by our personal and familial experiences with poverty, racism, sexism, war, immigration, educational achievement, and drug addiction. Race and class concerns figured prominently in our families' choice of Compton as a place to live and raise their children. Nevertheless, our stories are neither identical, nor common.

Donna

In 1945, Donna's maternal and paternal family moved to Compton at the end of World War II following the honorable discharge of her paternal grandfather and maternal great-grandfather from the US Army.

Donna's maternal great-grandfather, Robert, was a "colored" medical doctor from Shelton, South Carolina. After completing his medical training at Lincoln University in Pennsylvania, Robert established a medical practice in Columbia, South Carolina. Robert's parents were former slaves who were fathered by white slave owners and their black female slaves. Due to his pale complexion and blue eyes, Robert was able to enter into social spaces that were closed off to his darker African-American brethren. In fact, upon the death of his Irish grandfather, Andrew, Robert's mother, uncle, and grandmother were freed from slavery and given several acres of land in Shelton, South Carolina. They rented plots of land to black families who went into share-cropping and they established a family cemetery. The privilege afforded to Robert due to his bi-racial heritage and lighter skin would influence how successive generations of Robert's family would confront issues of class and racial privilege when the family settled in Compton.

Robert entered the US Army in the 1880s after he was unable to turn a profit from his medical practice. His first assignment was to serve as a medical doctor in the Philippines during World War I. There, Robert met his wife, Rosario, a young Filipina from Cebu province. The couple married in Manila. While in the Philippines, Rosario gave birth to the first four of their seven children. At the end of the The Great War, Robert was promoted to the rank of tech sergeant and sent to the army base in Ft. Huachuca, Arizona to command a group of black nurse orderlies. While in Ft. Huachuca, Rosario gave birth to three more children. The family experienced a level of class privilege that was elusive for most African-Americans in the early 1900s. Donna's grandmother often spoke about growing up with nannies, cooks, and even a housekeeper. She said the family was not necessarily wealthy. Yet, due to her father's rank and educational level, the wives of the black nurse orderlies readily offered their services, especially as Donna's great-grandmother, Rosario, was still adjusting to American culture and learning English. Donna's maternal family remained at Ft. Huachuca until the end of World War II when her great-grandfather retired from the military.

The family chose to move to Compton largely because of racial concerns for Donna's Filipina great-grandmother. Filipino immigrant farm workers who came to California under a contract labor or peninsado system in the 1920s were often victims of violent racist attacks and insults by white nativist groups opposed to immigration for non-whites. This anti-Filipino hatred remained strong throughout the United States until the end of the Second World War when Filipino soldiers who served in the armed forces were finally given the opportunity to become US citizens. Donna's great-grandfather made a calculated decision to move his family to California – as opposed to his native South – to avoid the more overt racism that was pervasive in the American South at the time.

Historian Rayford Logan (1954) coined the phrase "the nadir period in American race relations" to describe the rise in lynchings, segregation, and anti-black violence by groups such as the Ku Klux Klan (KKK), which swelled to historic highs from the end of Reconstruction through the early twentieth century. This rise in anti-black violence became one of the major influences in African-Americans' decisions to move to the North during the First Great Migration (from roughly 1915 to 1930) and to the West during the Second Great Migration (from roughly 1940 to 1970). Sensing that his Filipina wife and multiracial children (African-American, Filipino, and Scottish-Irish) would be a special target of white supremacist racism and violence, Robert took his family to California in hopes that race relations would be less openly hostile and violent toward African-Americans and other ethnic minorities.

In 1944, the family moved to Willowbrook, an area of Los Angeles immediately north of Compton, which was part of an African-American ethnic enclave known as Watts. According to Gerald Horne (1997), Watts was annexed in 1926 by the City of Los Angeles as a place to contain and house African-Americans, although the Los Angeles City Council claims that the purchase of Watts was to broaden the tax base to pay for water brought by the Owens Valley Aqueduct. The narrowness of the land lots for homes and the poor quality of the housing guaranteed that only African-Americans would ever become lifelong residents of the area and not of their own choosing. Restrictive covenants in housing and denial of bank loans to African-Americans wishing to purchase homes in white areas was commonplace in Los Angeles as it was in the rest of the country. Watts was the only area of the city open to African-Americans. The two immediate adjacent cities, Compton and Lynwood, remained almost exclusively white until the late 1950s. In fact, Lynwood described itself up until 1960 as the "friendly Caucasian city" (Horne, 1997, p. 27). Segregation of African-Americans was reinforced in Los Angeles Superior Court decisions in which the courts heard more than one hundred lawsuits concerning restrictive covenants from 1937 to 1948 and upheld and enforced this discriminatory legislation in spite of a growing number of lawsuits (Horne, 1997).

Because the Los Angeles City Council provided few public services to Watts beyond building three large housing projects – Nickerson Gardens, Jordan Downs, and Imperial Courts – Willowbrook residents depended on Compton for public services (i.e., schools and police) and paid a portion of their property tax to Compton. Donna's maternal grandmother, great aunt, and uncle attended public school in Compton, and all three of the youngest children attended Compton Community College. As white flight from Compton to the suburbs began in earnest in the early 1950s, African-Americans living in Watts who could afford to buy a home would eventually settle in Compton. Additionally, an unintended consequence of anti-Filipino discrimination in California and across the country, as well as white flight from Compton was the establishment of Filipino ethnic enclaves known as "Historic Filipino Towns" or areas with a relatively large concentration of Filipino residents. Compton served as one of these unofficial "Filipino Towns" from some time in the 1950s until the annexation of neighboring Carson, California in 1968. Filipina wives of African-American servicemen, including Donna's great-grandmother, Rosario, formed a close-knit community who assisted each other with their adjustment to American life. They took English language courses together, took the rail car to the pier at San Pedro to purchase seafood, played *po-keno* and *sunka* games together, and became godparents to one another's children.

Donna's paternal grandfather, Arthur, used to tell her stories of the racial indignity and injustice he and his wife endured while living in their native Alabama. Upon his return from serving in World War II, he had no desire to remain in the South and be treated like less than a human being, especially after having risked his life fighting the Germans. When the Chrysler Corporation began advertising car-painting jobs for colored workers who were willing to relocate to the West Coast, Arthur and Maggie, Donna's paternal grandparents, jumped at the opportunity to leave the segregated Jim Crow South. In 1950, the family moved to Watts, similar to her maternal great-grandparents. Like other African-American families, Donna's paternal grandparents migrated to Los Angeles during the late 1940s when the prospect of getting jobs in the war industry enticed many African-Americans living in the South to head West. Unfortunately, however, the African-Americans' hopes of securing war-industry jobs were dashed by persistent racial discrimination. Los Angeles, like the rest of the country, was not isolated from this phenomenon.

Initially, Donna's paternal grandparents lived in Watts. When her grandfather was promoted to head car-painter at Chrysler, he was able to purchase a modest home for his wife and four small children in Willowbrook, an area of Los Angeles immediately north of Compton. Nearly a decade after first relocating to Southern California, Donna's paternal grandfather became the first "colored" member of the United Auto Workers union in California and was promoted to international trade negotiation representative. Following his promotion, the family moved into a larger home on the west end of Compton.

Donna's parents, Paul and Wanda, are second- and third-generation residents of Compton, respectively. Donna was born in the early 1970s, and her sister and brother followed.

Jennifer

Jennifer's historical line draws from her parents' immigration to the United States in the 1950s. Both of Jennifer's parents were born in the early 1930s in the Toi-San region of Guangdong (also known as Canton), in southern China.

When the Japanese Imperial Army invaded China during World War II and began its occupation, Jennifer's maternal grandparents decided to emigrate and take Jennifer's mother, then a two-year-old toddler, to live in Baguio, a city in the northern part of the Philippines. There, they established a small bakery and restaurant, and raised Jennifer's mother, plus four other children. As the eldest and a girl, Jennifer's mother was expected not only to help care for her siblings, but also to set an example with her educational achievements and to assist her father with business correspondence. Though her parents were Buddhist, Jennifer's mother converted to Catholicism when she was fifteen, and she took the English name of Agnes. Agnes attended schools where the curriculum was taught in English, graduated as valedictorian of her high school class, and earned a scholarship to attend Immaculate Heart College in Los Angeles, California. In the mid-1950s, she sailed 21 days across the Pacific Ocean and arrived in Los Angeles. As a college student, she lived with her maternal aunt and their family, while also working as a hostess in a Chinese restaurant.

Prior to Japanese-occupied China, Jennifer's father recalls a playful boyhood in the countryside. After the invasion of the Japanese Imperial Army, Jennifer's father had to leave home at the age of eleven to work in the city. He described the Japanese occupation as the city looking normal, except that all of the homes formerly owned and lived in by Chinese were now occupied by Japanese soldiers. Yet, because it was a city, all of the businesses and services still needed to run, and the Chinese were expected to run the businesses and provide the services needed by the Japanese soldiers. Jennifer's father would send money through a messenger to his mother. Following the occupation, he returned to his family's home in the countryside.

As the second son in a Chinese family, Jennifer's father's position might normally call for him to follow the lead of the first son. However, because of her father's physical stamina, he was chosen by his father to leave China and to immigrate to the United States so that he could work and send money back home to his family. So, in 1952, Jennifer's father flew to the United States and stepped off the plane with literally $10 in his pocket. In Los Angeles, he took the English name Paul, and went to work in Chinatown. He worked any job he could find: first in sanitation and then as a dishwasher in a restaurant. Eventually, he became a cook. He met Jennifer's mother when he was a cook in the restaurant where Jennifer's mother worked as a hostess. One of their first dates was to a concert required by Jennifer's mother's music class.

Jennifer's parents married and had a son in 1958. A daughter was born the following year. With their family growing, they began to search for a larger home. Paul now had a job working for Chun Wong, a company that produced frozen Chinese foods. Chun Wong built a manufacturing facility in Compton, and Jennifer's father was assigned to work there.

Jennifer's father said that he would go to Coles' Market in Compton to shop for groceries, particularly cuts of meat. One day, after shopping, he drove around the neighborhood to look for possible housing for his growing family. He saw a sign, "For Sale By Owner," down the street from Coles. At this time in the late 1950s, Compton was home to mostly white residents on a certain side of the railroad tracks. Yet, when Paul approached the owner to buy the home, the owner agreed because he had an urgent family situation, and the first Chinese-American family moved in on the block of Mayo Avenue. There, the family welcomed two more sons and three more daughters. The youngest child, born in the late 1960s, was Jennifer. In a little over a decade since buying the home, white flight hit Compton. Jennifer's mother said that Compton residents had voted to desegregate the schools. By the time Jennifer started kindergarten in 1973, all of their neighbors were African-American. While our journeys to Compton are unique, our experiences as native daughters affected us in similar ways. In the next section, we focus on three ways in which Compton shaped who we are.

Counter-stories of being and becoming: how Compton shaped us

In this section, we describe how the experience of growing up in Compton shaped our educational and career decisions, as well as how we use "Compton" in our activist-oriented scholarship, teaching, and work for social justice. Looking back over our interview transcripts, we see a number of themes emerging: (1) learning how to be "real;" (2) addressing the suffering of others as "outsider-within" activists, due to our "outsider-within" status in Compton, in our education, and in our careers; and (3) navigating/negotiating various cultural, social, and educational terrains by living in and apart from Compton.

We have chosen to organize these narratives by theme because they represent an intersecting, multi-layered understanding of how Compton's habitus, or "sociocultural milieu," has certainly shaped our "actions, tastes and judgments" relative to our multiple identities, including ethnicity/race, gender, social class, and sexuality. Yet, what our autoethnography shows is that we have engaged in agency to transform this concept of habitus from an act of social reproduction into a mechanism for transforming our own and others' lives through our work as educator-activists.

Being real

We begin with the concept that Compton provided us with a way to be "real." By "real," we mean that being from and of Compton gives us a lens through which we can see that multiple groups exercise power and privilege depending upon context and standpoint. Our experiences growing up in Compton taught us to be authentically ourselves, to speak truth to power (i.e., to speak plainly, honestly, directly, and if necessary, forcefully about what we perceive to be true and just), and to appreciate the privilege of earning a living wage, living in a safe neighborhood, and being treated with dignity and respect regardless of one's race, gender, or socioeconomic status. Being "real" also means being able to "see" how Compton can be a place of oppression as well as a place of hope.

For Donna, Compton taught her how to be "real" in the sense that she says, "it [Compton] fostered this brutal honesty that I take with me into my teaching." When asked to be more specific, she says,

> Because I allow students to ask thorny questions that they wouldn't feel comfortable asking another black person. And even though I'm in a women's studies department, I am critical when women participate in their own enslavement. Women participate in sexism or perpetuating sexism without realizing they're doing it half the time. And I have decided that if I am going to be the bridge between people of color or people from Compton or the poor or women … If I am going to be a bridge between students of all different backgrounds, I am going to be real with them. If I come across as politically incorrect, I don't care. For a lot of people, this is about life and death.

Donna explains that being a child of a drug addict, a survivor of sexual assault, and being forced to assume the role of parent for her younger brother and sister taught her how to speak her mind and be brutally honest because survival was a natural instinct even for a young child. She recalls that in being raised by her maternal grandmother and great-grandmother,

> I remember being or acting like an adult. I hung around adults and I was smart enough to keep my mouth shut so adults would talk around me. And I think because of that I developed a strong sense of responsibility toward my family very early.

The downside of missing out on her childhood was that

> there was no insistence by the adults in my family for me to be a child so the expectation from about the time I was five years old was to warm up my sister's bottles, tell my mom when she needed to be changed or do it myself. No adults in my family stepped in and insisted that I be a little kid.

When Jennifer asked Donna how she knew what to do at such a young age, she responded,

> I guess I'd have to say it was innate. I just knew my mom and my grandmother were in their own little world. I think it was hard for them being so bright and being women and living in Compton.

This last statement opened up a later conversation on gender expectations for both women's families and what role, if any, geography played in shaping gender norms and roles.

The societal expectation that women during the 1950s get married and have children proved to be "a living hell" for Donna's grandmother who suppressed her desire for more education and a love for learning to take on the role of the dutiful wife until her children got a little older. Once her three children were all in high school, Donna's grandmother enrolled in Compton College but she had not anticipated her husband's reaction. Says Donna, recalling a conversation about her grandmother's decision to attend college,

> My grandfather enrolled [at Compton College] just to compete with her and prove she wasn't as smart as she thought. It backfired on him though because her professors would ask him if he was married to her [because of the same distinct last name] and suggest that he let her be his tutor. This was a direct affront to his manhood. He dropped out and his drinking and eventually cheating intensified. My grandmother coped with books. She survived the divorce by becoming an avid reader.

Donna went on to explain how being a middle-aged, divorced woman of color did not deter her grandmother from her goal of earning her bachelor's degree, which she completed in History from the University of Southern California in 1969. Donna's grandmother subsequently earned a master's degree in Chinese history and became a proficient speaker of Mandarin. Donna explains in this exchange (below) that both her grandmother and being from Compton played a role in her decision to become an educator.

D: She really encouraged my love of learning. Even when we didn't go to summer school, it came to us in the form of my grandmother. She would handwrite tests and quizzes, reading assignments, and activities for us to do over the summer. She exposed me to theater, classical music. She really encouraged me to learn more about my Asian identity, but she was militantly black. And all of the activism that I do now can be traced back to the activism she had me do as a kid. In so many ways, she had a tremendous impact on who I am as an educator.

J: How so?

D: Because she always taught me to keep being curious. And to question stuff. It didn't matter what the subject was. And she would say, you can believe in God, but you also need to believe in the power of questioning. So, from her, I developed this model that faith and reason are not mutually exclusive.

J: Would you say that being in Compton had anything to do with this impact as well?

D: Definitely. Because although we grew up with this privilege of being educated, we could have simply left Compton and lived a very middle-class life. But by living in Compton, living with and among working-class and poor people, Latinos and blacks and the few Filipinos in the neighborhood, it gave me an ability to speak in the language of my audience. Compton taught me about the inequities in society, particularly when I left it. Because people made a lot of assumptions about what life was like in Compton, or made the assumption that people in Compton were lazy, instead of looking at the structural inequities that caused Compton to be a place where you have a large population of poor people. So it [Compton] made me really sensitive to class issues, even when I didn't have the language by which to address those issues. Race was there, but class was ever-present.

Just as Donna contends that being from Compton made her acutely aware of race and class distinctions, Jennifer also developed this worldview. In addition, Jennifer's growing up as a Chinese-American in Compton while it was a predominantly black community affirmed her sense of self and gave her the ability to socialize and work professionally with multiple groups of people of varying race and class backgrounds. She is able to facilitate complex, emotional classroom discussions on the ways people are marginalized in our society because of the cultural and social capital Compton conferred. Of this ability, Jennifer says,

Compton provided me with a sense of place where I could be "real," to a certain extent, because although we were Chinese-Americans, we could be real with our neighbors who were black.

Jennifer further says that she got the chance to be part of the black community in a way that other non-blacks would likely never have the chance to experience. She explains,

As an adult, I can look back at it [living in Compton] and can see how I can "code-switch" (i.e., understanding cadence of language, jokes, slang, racism, and racial hierarchy) and understand inter-group and intra-group racism and display my understanding by changing my "look."

When asked to elaborate on what she means by the "look," she explains that some people of color and African-Americans, in particular, display their thoughts and feelings through what she calls "cultural and racial body language transmission" which means that the other person (usually a person of color) will respond with the same "look" as if to say, "Can you believe how racist and ignorant this person is acting?" During the course of this particular interview, Donna mentions how other African-American colleagues of theirs have noted how Jennifer seems much more comfortable (compared to her Asian-American and other non-African-American peers) with black people,

We were talking about you (Jennifer) the other day and both of us remarked on how you have the ability to enter and exit spaces that most Asian-Americans would not venture into. And part of why we came to this conclusion is by the way in which you recognize where there is a time and place to really fight and really pull back. The "stereotypical" Asian-American might just say "yes" to every demand made by white supervisors and colleagues whereas black folks would set boundaries and just say "no." I think because there is a recognition that self-preservation is the first rule of law. You do the exact same thing [as black folks] but you finesse better. You may not initially come off as abrupt but you still make your point.

Jennifer, hearing this assessment, nodded in agreement. She also commented on how being an outsider in Compton also taught her how to be "real" in another way. She says of being one of the few Chinese-American families in the neighborhood, "I also knew that while Compton was my home, there were also aspects when it didn't feel like home because I wasn't black." In analyzing how Compton shaped her personal sense of self, Jennifer said,

My mother was a great role model for speaking up in the sense that she would speak out on our behalf (and by "our," I mean her children). So I could see how it was already done. In terms of the neighborhood, I think the effect wasn't just on my individual sense of what was normal. There was a collective effect on my siblings and me that we weren't white and everybody around us weren't white except in Catholic schools because we went to Catholic schools where my classmates were white and Latino and we were the only Asians. So, as a child, making sense of this racialized existence wasn't really explicit. It came more in the form of television shows we chose to watch [*Sanford and Son, Good Times*], the music we chose to listen to [Motown, Diana Ross and the Supremes, Jackson 5], and just knowing that we're not white. But we also knew very well that we weren't black either because there was a certain emphasis at home about being proud of being Chinese.

While teaching, Jennifer also mentions that even if she gains entry to some African-American "in-group" discussions, she cannot claim membership because society views her phenotypically as Asian. But because of what she has seen and knows from growing up in Compton, she can actively bear witness to the racism that African-Americans endure daily and deeply, as well as how many other groups are discriminated against due to their race, gender, class, sexuality, religion, abilities, and more.

When asked if being one of the few Asian families in the area had any explicitly negative repercussions, Jennifer replied,

We were targets of violence and back then that meant rocks through your windows, eggs on your doors, breaking and entering burglary. And so we were reminded of not belonging in the neighborhood. I think we assumed because we were Chinese.

But this racially motivated violence did not seem to alter Jennifer's feeling that Compton provided a sense of home and belonging. Her memories from the 1970s show Compton as a city where working-class families raise children.

As a young child, I loved our home in Compton. I loved our home because it was small – only three bedrooms plus an add-on room, a big backyard with cemented area for riding bikes, playing with mud, and a large grassy area where we had a tether ball pole, played croquet, rode on a teeter-totter, hung laundry, had an orange, avocado, and two types of guava trees – the red and the white. We all had to share rooms, and there was a certain neatness to our home because we didn't have much. With so many kids, everything had to have some kind of order, and my mom was great at helping us to learn how to organize ourselves, our stuff, our clothes, our books. We had a lot of security, in the sense that we had schedules and order in our lives. We went to school, came home, did our homework and played on the weekdays. On the weekends, we helped to clean up outside when my dad mowed the lawn. We went to church on Sundays. I have another friend who also grew up in Compton, and we talk about how people outside of the city don't understand that there can be a very "family" middle-class feel to Compton.

There were so many things I remembered about Compton that I loved, and I think that I've romanticized it in my head. Part of it is because we moved when I was 10. At that time, I had no say in the matter. My parents started to look for a new home, and found one and said we were moving in the middle of the school year. I still went to the same school because it was a Catholic school and we didn't have zoning restrictions. But after we moved, I had such a bout of "homesickness" for the *place*, the quiet, the colors, the weather, the sounds, the light, the architecture of our home, that I didn't know was possible.

Upon leaving Compton, we began to construct meaning of what it meant to live there. We developed the ability to see ourselves by stepping outside of ourselves. We also began to see contradictions between how we perceived Compton as native daughters and how those outside the city perceived it. This ability to identify standpoint gave us a flexibility of heart and mind, particularly as described in the next section.

Addressing others' suffering as outsider-within activists

The second theme that emerged from our interview data is "addressing the suffering of others" through our "outsider-within" status. This theme is based on Patricia Hill Collins' (1990) work, *Black Feminist Thought,* in which she describes the type of knowledge that women of color (African-American women, in particular) bring to bear on their work as teachers and scholars. Hill Collins contends that one's lived experience is a criterion for making meaning and generating theory among African-American women. This very personal type of knowledge is often generated by women of color in the Academy. Yet, because of the positivist over-reliance on objectivity and the scientific method as the privileged means of arriving at "truth" in the academy, Hill Collins points out that this type of knowledge generated by women of color is often delegitimized and subjugated within the Academy.

As women of color in a university system created and led primarily by white people, we are expected to be familiar with and behave according to the social norms and values of whiteness.[4] James Scheurich and Michelle Young (1997) describe *societal racism* as the notion that non-whites should behave in accordance with the "prevailing social or cultural assumptions, norms, concepts, habits, expectations [that] favor one race over one or more other races" (p. 6). Societal racism, unlike individual or institutional racism, does not necessarily call for exclusion of non-whites from major social institutions such as the Academy. Instead, societal racism tells academics of color how they must conduct themselves once they are *included* in institutions of higher learning. From expectations of appropriate dress and speech to the values which guide one's research and writing priorities to the criteria by which one earns tenure, Scheurich and Young (1997) maintain that even our research epistemologies are racially biased:

> Epistemologies, along with their related ontologies and epistemologies, arise out of the social history of a particular social group. All of the epistemologies currently legitimated in education arise exclusively out of the social history of the dominant White race.
>
> (p. 8)

Societal racism thus forces academics of color to become "bi-cultural" if they want to advance in their careers and be successful in the Academy. In other words, we have learned to speak and act in ways that are "normalized" by the dominant racial group of a particular socioeconomic status, while validating our experiences as women of color from Compton. As scholars and educators, we acknowledge our "outsider-within" status: the contradiction of simultaneously being members of a faculty elite while holding onto our stories of origin that clearly place us outside of this elite. We do this because we view occupying the margins as a source of power that gives us a lens by which we can view and critique the world. As "outsiders-within," we understand the suffering of others as we have either experienced or witnessed suffering in our own lives while growing up in Compton and even as we left Compton to pursue our educational and professional goals. Taking this stance allows us to acknowledge that our social and cultural capital–influenced by our race, gender, class, and location-frames our worldview and shapes our ability to be bi-cultural.

Experiencing oppression and being exposed to the suffering of others can create a sense of hopelessness or a desire to change a situation for the better. Here, we describe how our outsider-within status in various locations influenced the caring, activist approach to our work.

Donna recalled in her early childhood years how her grandmother exposed her to social justice activism in Compton and how these experiences shaped her understanding of systemic poverty, political disenfranchisement through graft, and the need for local grassroots organizations to address pressing community needs. She says,

The reason why Compton played such a pivotal role shaping who we are as academics and activists is being able to have a family life. It felt safe, not in "I'm empowered" but I was given the opportunity to learn how to be an activist as a small child. Through doing activist work in Compton and in Watts. I have an affinity because as early as 6 years old, my Grandma was involved in Compton politics. That gave me a sense that I could be involved in shaping and changing not just politics but people's daily lives.

When asked for her impressions of attending Compton political events with her grandmother and how people reacted to her presence, Donna says,

From what I can remember as a kid … I took an instant like or dislike to a candidate based on how they treated kids or poor people. I thought that some of the politicians were just as corrupt and crooked as they wanted to be. But there were so many who really cared about trying to make Compton a better place. We also had a connection to Watts. My grandmother was one of the founding members of the Office for Black Community Development. This office was given a $1.16 million grant by the Governor Jerry Brown to develop community-owned and operated grocery stores in the Willowbrook area in the late 1970s. So, I think the impression I got early about Compton was that it might not be the best place in the world, but there were people trying to make it better. Because I was being raised by my grandmother, I learned to be quiet enough so that adults could talk and I could take in all of this information. I think that a lot of them were pretty shocked by how much I knew about the intricacies of the politics. And they would ask my opinions, if they wanted a brutally honest opinion about a politician or a policy, they would ask me first.

Donna's introduction to activism through her grandmother allowed her to develop an outsider-within lens at a very early age. While her grandmother's involvement allowed her entrée to city politics, her age and status placed her on the margins of the center of power. Likewise, Jennifer was also introduced to the notion of speaking up and speaking out through another strong female figure: her mother. Jennifer recalls how she became aware of gender oppression due in part to traditional expectations of behavior for Chinese/Chinese-American women, though she did not develop language for her understanding until she began to teach. Speaking of her mother's experiences with sexism while growing up in the Philippines, she says,

I want to say sexism was complex in my family because two things were happening in my perspective. One, my mom had been terribly punished for not fitting the social construction of gender while she was growing up. Which meant in her case, complete obedience to whatever her parents said. So for example, and this happened to all the children in the family. She was born in China and they moved to the Philippines because of World War II. And she was telling me at 5, she was changing diapers and getting food for her mom while her mom recovered from delivery and pregnancy. She also went to an English school instead of a Chinese school (I don't know how this decision was made). I think part of it was to learn English to help her family business. I think it was a bakery. But my grandparents were so ethnocentric that they always put her down for being in that school because it wasn't Chinese. And there is another story that my mom tells, she's around 7 or 8 and her father is berating her for not writing a business letter that sounds like a business letter. Completely inappropriate for a child that age and then the expectations on her as a first daughter [were extraordinary and involved abusive physical punishment].

Jennifer describes her own mother as an activist-oriented person in the sense that her mother consciously changed the ways she parented so that her children would have a happier, more liberated childhood. Yet, Jennifer also experienced a different type of silencing and shame, and consequently, low self-esteem about her evolving womanhood during adolescence due to cultural values of modesty.

J: In my generation, on one hand, my mom was really interested in making sure that we could be children without these horrendous pressures to have adult responsibility. But on the other hand, some of the attitudes toward children being expected to comply and obey carried forward. So as a child, I felt that there were certain ways that I was supposed to be 'cause that was what was expected of me.

D: So were there any gender-specific expectations for how you were to behave that were different from your brothers?

J: I have three brothers and three sisters. A lot of the expectations were gender neutral when I was growing up. But in hindsight, I can see that the tone of voice I was supposed to use, the way that I was supposed to dress, the level of modesty I was supposed to have, the attitudes toward my body as a woman, I was taught to be ashamed of my developing body because it wasn't modest [to wear fitted clothes]. Maybe I should unpack what modesty is because it's BIG. So like, that's why when you ask me if it was gender specific, I realize now that I grew up with a confluence of expectations because my mom wanted us to be able to speak up for ourselves, and she did that really well for us.

Jennifer resisted these gendered, cultural expectations, though at times the resistance created conflict and a feeling of not fitting in her family. She also experienced being an outsider in the community due to being Chinese-American in a predominantly African-American neighborhood. All of these experiences caused Jennifer to find her voice and speak out against injustice at an early age. From first through fourth grades, Jennifer recalled speaking out against bullies who picked on her friend, Ruby, a Mexican-American girl:

I think I knew what it felt like to be kind of an outsider in my own family. My family being an outsider in my neighborhood. And knowing that you can either try to fit in or you can do it your own way. So, if no one wanted to play with Ruby for whatever reason, I didn't have to be part of that group that said "I'm not going to play with her." I played with her and no one would dare pick on me because I had the privilege of being the "smart" kid. Does that make sense? I felt like I knew what it was like to feel the pain of ostracism and I didn't want to be part of that; inflicting pain through ostracism. That's how I feel my being in the neighborhood affected my sense of self.

But Jennifer says that although she sometimes heard that Compton was not a safe place, she loved her home and neighborhood and even experienced a long, painful bout of "homesickness" when her family moved to Cerritos (a suburb of Los Angeles about 10 miles east of Compton). In becoming aware of people's negative perceptions of Compton, Jennifer began to see the difference between how outsiders viewed the city, while being aware of how various racial groups saw one another within the city. This intra-group racism gave her insight into how power and privilege operated, depending on the context and situation. She came to see that the effect of white-on-black racism could translate into racism among and between racial groups seeking dominance and power. She says,

J: I heard while I was growing up and living in Compton that where I lived wasn't safe. That most people would not necessarily come to visit but we could visit them. And it had something to do with what Compton *was*. I also (sigh) knew we didn't have a lot of money. And while I thought we had a really nice home, I also saw that my friends that I visited had their own rooms and a lot of really nice toys, while we were three to a room and pretty sparse in terms of toys. I think people gave me the impression that Compton was not a safe place to be. I think as we had incidents of violence directed towards us, like, back then, they didn't have guns, but eggs on our door at night, rocks through our front window, our house burglarized while we were at school. That feeling of safety was compromised.

D: Do you think it was racially motivated violence?

J: We thought so at the time but we never really talked about it. I'm sure my brothers and sisters who are older than me would have more to say.

D: Were there ever explicit racially-motivated incidents?

J: Maybe at school. I only went to kindergarten [public school] across the street from our house. So I was pretty young. And I was in a combination K-3 class. I think the kids in my class were pretty nice and I had friends that I played with. But the kids on the playground from other classes would come up in my face and say things. They would literally come up in my face and say things and they were bigger than me but I didn't know what they were doing. Also the year before my sister was in that kindergarten class I remember that my mom and the teacher had a hard time getting my sister to go to school until they finally found out that some big kids were bothering her.

D: Do you know the race of these kids?

J: No. But from my recollection, almost everybody at the school was black except for us. And then when I got older and went to Catholic school in Long Beach, I would tell people that I lived in Compton, some people would say "oooohhh." Like "Wow, you live in Compton."

D: So it was more pejorative?

J: Oh yeah. It was more like "how can you live in Compton?" because it was an unsafe place to live.

D: Did this make you defensive?

J: I was proud of living in Compton. It was my home. It made me think that a lot of people can have ideas about things they don't know anything about.

D: Were you perceived as being different or treated differently because you lived in Compton?

J: No and Yes.

D: Elaborate.

J: So no when I was a child. Yes, when I got older and I'd be among a group of African-Americans and for people who were friends with me, we'd be cool. But for people who didn't know, and then they found out and then I was okay (accepted). When I was among a group of Asian-Americans and getting the feeling or the implication that I wasn't "Asian" enough, when I said that I'm from Compton, they would say "Oh" like that's why you don't act "Asian." When I'd be in a multi-racial group, talking about issues of race, I'd have to explain my context. And when I said I was from Compton, I could see that they were surprised and also giving me more credibility than if I was "just Asian."

For Jennifer, the question of her racial and cultural authenticity as a Chinese-American can be directly linked to her geographic location. In other words, Jennifer's family's choice to live in Compton as opposed to Chinatown resulted in a particular habitus in Jennifer and her siblings. From the outside, others perceived that she lacked an "authentic" Chinese or stereotypically Asian essence because she and her siblings were not raised around other Chinese. As Jennifer has progressed in her career on both West and East Coasts and attended graduate school at Stanford and UCLA, many people assumed that she grew up in an upper-middle-class white community until she would describe her hometown as a working-class black community. Among some Asian-Americans who did not know her, she was not "Asian" enough. While engaging in work with people of color, she was considered not white by whites, and not having the experience as a person of color by other people of color. This being "in-between" or in the "borderlands" has given her a unique perspective as an educator and researcher.

In many ways, Jennifer has been affected by essentialist notions of race. Derived in philosophy, essentialism is the idea that to be part of a group (i.e., a racial or religious group), one must possess certain universal characteristics that are not dependent on context (see Spivak, 2009). For example, in Jennifer's case, her inability to speak Chinese may be viewed with skepticism by other Chinese/Chinese-Americans who believe that speaking the language is essential for membership into the Chinese/Chinese-American community. Essentialist positions are often reductionist in that they reduce a person's identity down to a few "essential" characteristics and often ignore both the context and complexity of cultural and social identity.

In many of the same ways in which Jennifer's racial allegiance was called into question because of where she resided, Donna experienced similar marginalization due to her family's class and skin color privilege. As evidence of her "outsider-within" status in the black community, Donna recalls being singled out for having lighter skin and longer hair than her darker-skinned counterparts in school. She says,

D: We also faced a backlash for being light-skinned and educated. People simultaneously admired and hated us. I had a girl throw a big wad of gum in my hair.

J: At school?

D: Yeah. I think because my hair was long and hers wasn't; so it was almost her way of evening the score so to speak. For first and second grade, I went to public school in Compton and was harassed daily about my complexion. I was always called the "high-yella heifa" [heifer] and I was the only girl in the gifted group so I was targeted because I was thought to be a nerd. And most of it was from other girls. I was called the "first-lick chick." That meant I was always the first girl to get hit in a fight. This was the assumption based on my skin color and because I was smart until I had a fight with a boy, Caleb Jones (laughs), and I beat the hell out of him. So the "first-lick chick" thing went away. But the teasing about being smart never left. And I attribute this nowadays to a "crabs in a barrel" mentality. Fortunately for me, I was prepared by my grandmother to – not so much defend myself – but to ignore people's comments.

Donna's early experiences with harassment for having lighter skin and longer hair gave her insight into the phenomenon of "crabs in a barrel," that is, the idea that when one is perceived to be better, getting ahead, or "getting out of the barrel," the others grab them and pull them back in. She could see how internalized negativity about skin color affects individual psyches, and she addressed these defensive-offensive attacks from girls with darker skin by deflecting them. But Donna also recalls that the negative comments seemed to have hurt her mother much more deeply, which she believes led to her mother's drug addiction. She described her mother's experience of being sent to an all-white school where she had no friends or anything in common with the other students.

D: Remember me telling you about her [Donna's mother] going to an all-white school – that rejection from that all-white school made her cling to Compton even more. But at the same time, there were people in Compton who made her feel guilty for being smart, for being mixed-race.

J: You also talked about your grandma's choice to remain in Compton.

D: My grandma's choice was twofold: (1) it was familiar and safe for her and (2) she was really cognizant of how she was perceived by other black people because of her skin color and mixed-race heritage. She did not want to perpetuate the stereotype that light-skinned blacks thought they were better than dark-skinned blacks. So I think she chose to stay in Compton to prove her racial allegiance to other black people. Ironically, though, in our home, we were both black and Filipino. Outside the home, we were just black.

J: What does that mean?

D: At home, with family members and close friends, we would participate in Filipino cultural traditions. Outside the home, however, we knew we were being looked upon as being black only and so if someone asked if we were mixed with something, we would tell them. But we didn't volunteer the information.

The experiences of Donna, her mother, and her grandmother taught her how complex, cruel, and confusing intragroup and intergroup race relations can be. In particular, Donna learned how she should manifest aspects of her identity as she grew up. Inside her home, she could be all of who she was. Yet, publicly, she was taught to identify herself as black because of how she looks phenotypically. Her experience in Compton shaped her by creating a strong resistance to the negativity that could have led to an internalized urge toward self-destruction. She sees Compton also as the home of her role models who are her source of strength:

D: That Cornel West piece really helped me.[5] He talks about how people see the "hood" as a place of rampant nihilism. [By contrast,] he talks about growing up in a "neighborhood," where he felt supported … I have a "both-and experience" with Compton. I experienced the nihilism directly and indirectly with my mother's drug addiction, the times we had to go on welfare, and being singled out because of perceived light-skin privilege. But on the other hand, when people accepted me, I was fully accepted, brought into the "community," encouraged to do well because I could inspire other people.

I guess what I experienced was both that "crabs in a barrel" mentality from people who were very depressed and didn't feel like they could do anything about their situation and wanted to bring other people down. But those people who had a strong sense of self didn't feel the need to tear me down, but instead build me up. So, for me, Compton gave me both positive and negative reinforcement. But it gave me enough strength, I think, having enough of those negative experiences to deal with the challenges I would face later on in my life.

I think that folks who live outside of the hood assume that seeing negative or bad things is always bad – you should avoid that at all costs – whereas my perspective is that you need to learn how to adapt to different types of situations and experiencing poverty, experiencing racism, experiencing abuse, you know – I was sexually assaulted when I was a kid, but I fought back. You know, I turned it around and it helped me later on to clarify my goals and to make a family.

For both of us, being raised in Compton gave us an outsider-within perspective. That is, it taught us about how people construct race based on broad sweeping generalizations, which often ignore context and the ways in which race interacts with other forms of identity. Historian Evelyn Higginbotham says that literary critics such as Henry Louis Gates "present race 'as the ultimate trope of difference' – as artificially and arbitrarily contrived to produce and maintain relations of power and subordination" (in Clark Hine, King, Reed, 1995, p. 4). Not only is race socially constructed to maintain power and subordination from the dominant/majority group, but it is also reinforced by members of minority groups who internalize these narrow constructions of what it means to be part of an ethnic or racial group. By deconstructing and then redefining what it means to be Chinese-American or a mixed-race black person on a meso (or community) level, we can challenge the stereotypes and generalizations attached to these groups in general. More specifically, because we are aware that this subconscious acceptance of stereotypical and/or negative constructions of race or ethnicity can create conflict and suffering, we view our experiences of growing up in Compton not only as a source of pride and personal power, but also as a source of cultural and social capital that we use as academics. We have become educator-activists who seek to transform our students' consciousnesses and understandings about multiple forms of oppression, particularly as they intersect with race.

Navigating and negotiating cultural, social, and educational spaces

The final theme that emerged from our conversations addresses how Compton has impacted our teaching styles and research commitments. For this section, we rely heavily on Pierre Bourdieu's concept of cultural capital as his articulation of these ideas best describes how our upbringings in Compton shaped our educational goals and career paths as educators. Bourdieu and Passeron (2000) argue that cultural habits and dispositions from the family were critical to a French student's educational achievement in the 1960s; an idea which contrasted sharply with traditional sociological notions of culture. For Bourdieu and Passeron, economic obstacles are not sufficient to explain differences in educational attainment among children from different social classes. Instead, one's cultural habits and dispositions must also be considered when examining how students from poor or low-income backgrounds perform in school and in their careers.

Yet, family influence only explains part of what makes up one's cultural and social capital. We argue that geographic location – as an intersection of space, time, and a convergence of people in a particular historical moment – can play a critical role in helping a person develop cultural and social capital. Contrary to what is presented in popular media about the hood, and Compton in particular, being from a place like this does not preclude anyone from excelling in school or becoming a leader. In fact, our shared experiences of learning how to navigate various cultural, social, and educational terrains in order to be successful in pursuit of our educational and professional goals has helped us to be highly effective in the classroom. Donna acknowledges how critical a role her grandmother, who so closely identified with Compton, played in terms of being a model and guide for navigating her education. She seeks to do the same for others:

> Honestly, the reason why I teach is so I can reach poor students, minority students because I know what that credential means in terms of empowering students, giving them social mobility, and helping them become critical thinkers. I know that I probably would be a statistic, teenage mother or drug addict or any number of other things if it hadn't been for education. I wouldn't have a Ph.D. right now if it wasn't for my grandmother creating lesson plans for us over the summer or sacrificing for us to go to private school. So, I teach because I just know how much education means, not just in terms of getting a job, but in terms of something that people can't take away from you.

In this section, we describe how we have used Compton as a way to navigate and negotiate our classrooms as cultural, social, and educational spaces. Both of us view our work as educators as having an explicit social justice mission not only to broaden a student's understanding of the world but also to make students aware of how they can positively impact society. One way in which we bring social justice activism into the classroom is to use our personal experiences of being raised in Compton as a teachable moment to expose students to the complex ways in which identity is influenced by class, race, gender, and geographic location. Jennifer explains how she uses Compton in teaching Asian-American Studies courses:

> I think having the perspective that I've had helps me to explain the black-white binary paradigm in a way that a lot of other people who haven't been immersed in it can't really understand. My professional background is in higher education but I teach in Asian-American Studies. And a lot of students will assume that I grew up in a Chinese ethnic enclave. Then when I tell them I grew up in Compton, they start to conceive of me as someone from the hood. Someone who shouldn't be messed with, someone who is tougher than I look. But I can also explain the model minority stereotype. I feel like I have this visceral understanding of how oppressed black folks are/have been. So my lens is not from an [insular] Asian-American community, which I think, in some ways, can be very

protectionist – by that, I mean that "you help your own" and sometimes anybody else is suspect. So, one, I don't act that way because I've seen the inequity and injustice and, two, it's really important to me that contemporary Asian-American students understand the history of oppression in this country based on sanctioned racism and racist institutions.

Jennifer's ability to discuss the "model minority stereotype" from the perspective of a Chinese-American having been raised in a black community allows her to use her marginality as a teaching tool for students who have never taken the time to even question some of the racist implications of being labeled as the "model minority" (see Bascara, 2006; Li & Wang, 2008). The term, "model minority" comes from the 1960s, when an anthropologist's description of Japanese Americans in *Time* magazine called for comparing this group to other ethnic and racial groups that were rallying against the continued race-based inequities in American society. Having been stripped of their civil rights and imprisoned in camps during World War II, many Japanese-Americans left the camps in 1945 with the determination to show that they were "good" Americans. Two decades later, their resistance to society's hostility had resulted in their higher levels of education, income, and the perception that they would not "make waves." This perception that Japanese Americans – and by extension – all Asian-Americans were "better" than other minority groups leads to dissension and resentment among the groups being compared, with Asian-Americans being cast as "superior" and other racial minority groups being labeled "inferior." It is a classic "divide-and-conquer" strategy that maintains power in the dominant group. Jennifer further says:

> My concern with what I'm seeing now is that students have internalized this "model minority" [stereotype] and believe in this superiority because they have lived a middle- to upper-class existence. Because their history education does not include the incredible systematic and institutionalized racism against people of Asian descent in the US. So they don't even know of this terrible history and I have to frame it first within the black-white binary paradigm before I can introduce them to the depth of the racism against Asian-Americans. Some have been so inoculated that they can't believe this has happened to people like them in history.

Donna added that in disclosing her Filipina ancestry in the classroom, she believes she has been able to discuss specific issues of race and racism with her Asian students that she might otherwise have been unsuccessful in doing had she chosen to remain silent. Donna says:

> When I talk about the model minority stereotype, I feel very protective of Asians because I'm Asian too. Asians have been discriminated against like other people of color. When we discuss waves of feminism, I ask the Asian-American students, where were you? Because from 1882–1965, you couldn't come here unless you were already here (with the passage of the Chinese Exclusion Act). You are people of color too!

Just as Jennifer speaks about the intricacies of racial group dynamics, Donna also brings this to her interactions, both as an academic and as a friend:

> And I think, by growing up in Compton, it really helps me teach about the interplay of race, class, and gender in some of the ways that maybe some of my colleagues might not be able to do … And being mixed-race allows me to build coalitions with other minorities in ways that – because I understand being Asian, I don't feel the need to compete with Asians (both laugh). So instead of looking at other minorities as enemies, I look at them as friends.
>
> I've taken this – all of these things into my teaching and into my research. And most importantly in how I interact with people inside and outside the Academy. Friends can ask me questions about race and class and gender that they probably wouldn't feel comfortable asking another black person, because … I'm brutally honest.

By utilizing personal experience in the classroom, we believe we can create an atmosphere where dialogue about sensitive issues about gender, race, and social class can occur more openly. We establish trust by talking about our personal experiences, and we provide students with a first-hand look at the complex nature of identity and social location that is impacted by one's cultural capital. Donna talks about how Compton taught her to survive in a seemingly cold and hostile world, and Jennifer talks about how Compton allows her to address the complexity of racism. Specifically, Donna says that her teaching is influenced by being raised in Compton, witnessing self-destructive behaviors from her own family members, and seeing violence on a frequent basis:

> It [being from Compton] allows me to be brutally honest. I don't even know what else to say. I don't beat around the bush. When I'm talking in class, I'm very real with the students. I'm very much a pragmatist. Some might say fatalistic, but I don't think so. Having seen all that I've seen with my family and my neighbors – seeing people getting killed in the street – I don't have any interest in coddling students. So if I have to be provocative in order to get their attention, that's what I do.

Jennifer says that being from Compton allows her to discuss race in her classes in ways that are far more complicated than simply saying either "racism doesn't exist" or "Asians have always been victims of racism." Again, living on the margins as a minority within a minority has afforded Jennifer the opportunity to see racism as a multi-layered phenomenon in which minority racial groups are: (1) simultaneously discriminated against and (2) participate in discriminating against others.

> D: You mentioned identity as being as much as a function of being able to discuss where you come from and to make sense of all of that. How receptive are your students,

specifically Asian/Pacific Islander Americans (APIA) students, when you relay your personal story?

J: I think depending on where my students grew up, they will either register shock or surprise or this happy kind of relief that I'll understand what their experience is like. So for example, my students who may have grown up in predominantly Asian communities, have a harder time understanding where I've come from but I think they have respect for what my lived experience has been. For my Asian students who have grown up in communities that are predominantly white, they seem shocked because there is a sense that most other Asians have experiences like them. And for my students who grew up in communities that are predominantly an ethnic minority, such as Latino or black, they get kind of excited because they feel that I'll be able to understand them. And then for my students who are not APIA, I think I'm a little bit of a conundrum because I don't fit into a little box. But what I've found is that they are more likely to understand why I talk about race in the way that I do.

D: Why do you think that is?

J: I think it's because I talk about different groups being inclusive or marginalizing and how various groups have privilege or can be discriminatory. And over-arching all of that is a sense of understanding the history and experience of white-on-black racism. So for example, I can call out Asians for being racist against blacks and see lots of heads nodding in the room. I can call out white privilege and explain how it is an excuse for color-blind racism. I can say that in a group of all people of color, African-Americans and Latinos will say Asians can't possibly experience racism because they're like whites. So this is what I mean when I can talk about the fluidity of privilege, power, racial dynamics, and students will react to me in a certain way. I think because they know I'm from Compton.

Being from Compton has not only influenced our pedagogical approaches, it has also affected our curricular content and design. As a historian, Donna infuses her curriculum with references to laws and social customs that have codified racial inequity in America. Jennifer facilitates discussions with a compassion that acknowledges the deep emotions that "race work" elicits.

Donna says how she brings race into the classroom is dependent on which specific course she is teaching but often she brings up issues of class and gender to help her students better understand racism:

D: In Introduction to Women's Studies where the majority of the students are white, race is infused into the readings such that I don't have to bring it up explicitly. It comes out in the topics. So, this way, students feel like they're learning about gender socialization, even when they're examining gender socialization for a specific or particular racial or ethnic group. For my upper-division courses, there's a much more candid in-your-face approach to race because the students expect to be challenged about issues of difference as Women's Studies majors. In Black Women in America, there's absolutely no way to get around it. But instead, I frame race historically so that the students can then talk about macro-social instances of racism. I give them a historical framework for understanding race in the United States, by examining laws and social customs, and then we can talk about what this looks like in a more global sense.

I'd say that my approach to race, however, for my more beginning students, is to use my "self" as a way for them to examine race. I talk about experiences with racism and sexism that I encountered as a student that I encounter in the workplace, and everyday interactions with people. And also because I am sensitive to issues of class, as well, I really try to make a connection between the students – I can get students to understand race through class. By that, I mean most of the students at Cal State Fullerton come from lower-income or middle-income families. And when we talk about how they were disadvantaged by their class, it helps them to understand race a bit better.

J: Do you ever encounter people saying that racism is just about classism?

D: No, they're not that complex in terms of thinking yet. I get more "racism doesn't exist" or "just get over it." As soon as they say that, I ask them to get over not going to Harvard, not getting a particular job because they went to Cal State Fullerton, or get over being a woman. I really talk a lot about the "bootstraps" theory and always end up asking the students, "What if you don't have any boots?" So, it forces them to think about what it's like to not have the basics, you know, food, shelter, etc.

Donna tailors her inclusion of issues of race, class, and gender to the experiences and level of critical thought that her students exhibit. When Jennifer brings race into the classroom, she also considers where her students are developmentally. She tries to create an atmosphere of trust so that students will discuss difficult, emotionally draining topics that foster deep learning, and even healing.

I don't start out talking about race [directly] because my understanding of doing race work is that it involves a lot of anger and hurt and sadness and frustration. So I try to structure my classes first just to get comfortable and trust one another. And then as we progress through the semester and talk about progressively more controversial topics, the students trust we can "go there" and they can get upset and no one is going to laugh at them. And people (their classmates), are going to try at least to understand where they are coming from, even if they say something that is not politically correct. I've had conversations with students after class, and even after the semester, where they tell me we talk about things in this class that they never talk about anywhere else … they also say that it's some of the most satisfying conversations they've ever had. And it helps them to understand and put a name on the racism and sexism they've experienced because up to this point most people have told them they should just get over it or that it doesn't exist or matter.

Here, we have made explicit the cultural and social capital that being *of* and *from* Compton has conferred on us. More specifically, we have explained that doing "race work" in the classroom not only involves our choice of curricular content, but also our approach and teaching styles.

Concluding this counter-story

As educator-activists, we bring who we are and where we are from into the work we do. This chapter conveys not only how we came to Compton, but also how Compton shaped us, helped us to develop outsider-within standpoints, and conferred on us cultural and social capital that influences our professional missions, pedagogical approaches, and scholarly directions. Our work challenges simplistic and stereotypical notions of how a hood like Compton and its residents are portrayed in popular media and perceived from the outside. Additionally, our work challenges whose knowledges are valued in the academy, how they should be created, and what purposes they should serve. Above all, this chapter tells the counter-story of how two women from Compton enter the classroom every day and ask their students to question what they take for granted.

Notes

1. CSUF is a comprehensive public university serving approximately 33,000 students at its main campus in north Orange County and a satellite campus in south Orange County. As of Fall 2010, its student population is 58 percent female. The ethnic distribution of its student body is: American Indian: 1 percent, Asian/Pacific Islander: 21 percent, Black: 3 percent, Hispanic: 29 percent, White: 31 percent, Unknown: 10 percent, and International Students; 5 percent. (Total exceeds 100% due to rounding.). (CSUF Fact Sheet, 2010).
2. "Authoethnography ... is an autobiographical genre of writing and research that displays multiple layers of consciousness ... Autoethnographers ... first look through an ethnographic wide angle lens, focusing outward on social and cultural aspects of their personal experience; then, they look inward, exposing a vulnerable self that is moved by and may move through, refract, and resist cultural interpretations" (Ellis, 2004, p. 37).
3. See also Bourdieu's (1999) concept of "Outcasts on the Inside" in which he interrogates how marginalized students in academe are forced into a sort of double-bind in which they appear to have "made it" while simultaneously "don't belong" in the institutions that they have entered.
4. Whiteness is a class and cultural identity in which a certain type of speech, dress, and conduct is utilized to distinguish oneself as an insider as a means of securing the best educational and job opportunities, housing and other sources of asset/wealth accumulation for one's self and racial group. George Lipsitz (1998) contends that because whiteness carries with it a "cash value" and considerable material benefits, "white Americans are encouraged to invest in whiteness, to remain true to an identity that provides them with resources, power and opportunity" (p. vii). This "possessive investment in whiteness," Lipsitz (1998) contends, is responsible for creating and maintaining the racialized hierarchies in American society through various public policy and private prejudice (p. vii).
5. See West (2008).

References

Anzaldúa, G. (2007). *Borderlands: The New Mestiza* (3rd edn). San Francisco: Aunt Lute Books.

Bascara, V. (2006). *Model-Minority Imperialism.* Minnesota: University of Minnesota Press.

Baszile, D. T. (2006). In This Place Where I Don't Quite Belong: Claiming the Ontoepistemological In-Between. In T. R. Berry, & N. Mizelle (Eds), *From Oppression to Grace: Women of Color and their Dilemmas within the Academy* (pp. 195–208). Sterling, VA: Stylus.

Bourdieu, P. (1984). *Distinction: A Social Critique of the Judgement of Taste.* (R. Nice, Trans.) Cambridge, MA: Harvard University Press.

Bourdieu, P. (2007 [1977]). *Outline of a Theory of Practice.* (R. Nice, Trans.) Cambridge: Cambridge University Press.

Bourdieu, P., & Passeron, J-C (2000 [1977]). *Reproduction in Education, Society and Culture* (2nd edn.). (R. Nice, Trans.) London: Sage Publications.

Bush, G. (2000). *All the Best, George Bush: My Life in Letters and Other Writings.* New York: Simon and Schuster.

California State University Fullerton. (2010). *2010 Fact Sheet.* Retrieved from California State University Fullerton: http://www.fullerton.edu/aboutcsuf.htm.

Collins, P. H. (1990). *Black Feminist Thought: Knowledge, Consciousness, and the Politics of Empowerment.* New York: Routledge.

Ellis, C. (2004). *The Ethnographic I: A Methodological Novel about Autoethnography.* Walnut Creek, CA: AltaMira Press.

Gardner-Chloros, P. (2009). *Code-Switching.* Cambridge: Cambridge University Press.

Hine, D. C., King, W., & Reed, L. (1995). *"We Specialize in the Wholly Impossible": A Reader in Black Women's History.* New York: Carlson Publications.

Horne, G. (1997). *Fire this Time: The Watts Uprising and the 1960s.* New York: Da Capo Press.

Isurin, L., Winford, D., & Bot, K. D. (2009). *Multidisciplinary Approaches to Code Switching.* Philadelphia: John Benjamins Publishing.

Kingston, M. H. (1989). *The Woman Warrior: Memoirs of a Girlhood among Ghosts.* New York: Random House.

Li, G., & Wang, L. (Eds). (2008). Model Minority Myth Revisited: An Interdisciplinary Approach to Demystifying Asian American Educational Experiences. New York: Information Age Publishing.

Lipsitz, G. (1998). *The Possessive Investment in Whiteness: How White People Profit from Identity Politics.* Philadelphia: Temple University Press.

Logan, R. W. (1954). *The Negro in American Life and Thought: The Nadir, 1877–1940.* New York: Dial Press.

Said, E. W. (2003 [1978]). *Orientalism* (25th anniversary edn). New York: Vintage Books.

Sandoval, C. (2000). *Methodology of the Opppressed.* Minnesota: University of Minnesota Press.

Scheurich, J., & Young, M. (1997). Coloring Epistemologies: Are Our Research Epistemologies Racially Biased? *Educational Research, 27*(4), 4–16.

Spivak, G. C. (2009). *Outside in the Teaching Machine.* London: Routledge.

West, C. (2008). *Hope on a Tightrope: Words and Wisdom.* Carlsbad, CA: Smiley Books.

Wheeler, R. S., & Swords, R. (2006). *Code-Switching: Teaching Standard English in Urban Classrooms.* Urbana, IL: National Council of Teachers of English.

Part II

Representing the Hood in Music, Film, and Art

Chris Richardson and Hans A. Skott-Myhre

We have argued above that the line separating representations of the hood and lived practices within the hood will be arbitrary at best. A film such as *Boyz N the Hood* (1991) depicts the lives of young black men through images moving at 24 frames per second accompanied by music, sound effects, professional lighting, and a number of other cinematographic techniques. This is clearly a *representation* as opposed to an *experience* of the hood itself. The plot, the characters, and the environment in which the film takes place, however, are based on the lived experiences of many young people in California. As deWaard points out, the film begins with the statistic that "One out of every twenty-one Black American males will be murdered in their lifetime. Most will die at the hands of another Black male." Though this statistic frames the film, it is not a diegetic fact but a real-life problem that living and breathing African-American males face. Evidently, the link between "reality" and "fiction" is an elusive – and in all likelihood imaginary – one.

In his biography of the late Tupac Shakur, Dyson (2001) quotes French philosopher Michel Foucault, who asks "couldn't everyone's life become a work of art? Why should the lamp or the house be an art object but not our life?" (p. 153). Dyson adds, "The interesting questions of Tupac's art – whether it furthered the artistic ideals he claimed to represent, whether it musically or lyrically measured up to the best of what the genre had to offer, or whether it suffocated in a miasma of rhetorical posturing – are hardly asked" (ibid.). This neglect, Dyson argues, is due to a heavy focus on morality. And while morality should not be absent from a critical judgment of representations of the hood and its residents, it must not overshadow the ways in which representations of the hood do something else – inform artistic practices. These works are pieces of art that also teach viewers about marginalized spaces in their societies as well as help to construct those spaces within a collective imagination. Films like *Boyz N the Hood* and music produced by artists like Tupac may represent a fictional universe; however, the implications of these representations within the societies from which they are created are a part of actual and material politics.

In his chapter, Richardson argues that politics are an important element within representations of the hood. He quotes Decker (1993), who argues that "in the absence of a black CNN, rap records are an invisible network that can inform and mobilize" (p. 103). Artists in this genre, though not politicians, "are involved in the production of cultural politics – its creation, its circulation and its interpretation – which is tied to the everyday struggles of working-class blacks and the urban poor" (p. 101). There is much debate about the value of hip-hop artists – and to this one could add the vast array of cultural producers of the hood from graffiti artists and painters to filmmakers, videographers, and journalists. Do they bask in the subversive glory of negative representations as many gangsta rappers stand accused of doing? Are they working to expose the wretched living conditions and imbalanced power structures to a broader public? Is the sum of their creative work larger than the contribution of their individual endeavors? Many of these questions remain open for the authors that follow as they interrogate cultural productions from a number of perspectives.

Britt engages with the field of hip hop through the work of the rapper who calls himself Game. Born Jayceon Terrell Taylor, the artist has developed a unique brand of "realness" that acknowledges the hood as both an evolving mobile entity and a space for multiple temperaments, argues Britt. Sciurba takes hip-hop scholarship in a different direction by examining the popular claim that incorporating hip-hop culture into the school curricula of "urban" or "disenfranchised" students will allow teachers to get through to their pupils. She suggests that because most young people – particularly, young people of color – are presumably consumed with hip hop, the art form is seen as a means of bridging the gap between their outside-of-school and inside-of-school lives. However, she questions the suppositions behind bringing artists like Kanye West into classrooms and interrogates what such methods actually offer students and teachers. Mann encourages viewers of popular culture productions not to believe the hype – in this case as it relates to public housing and its residents. She examines the discourses of two films with competing narratives about the hood, one which presents it as a space deserving to be demolished and abandoned and the other questioning the mythology of the inner city. Drissel expands this collection's global scope by examining neighborhoods in Berlin that have adapted graffiti and other hip-hop elements derived from New York's subcultures and made them their own. These low-income areas have changed drastically since the fall of the Berlin wall and are negotiating the identity politics of their environments through a number of cultural/political activities.

Of the many claims that can be made about the hood and its representations, the only one that seems uncontroversial is the assertion that creative works produced within the hood and outside of it (re)present a cultural politics. These creative moments are infused into the debates about the lived hood, its residents' experiences, and the dominant power structures that surround it. None of the following authors would claim that representations of the hood are neutral. And through methodologies falling into the broad categories of textual analysis, critical discourse analysis, and ethnography, the authors interrogate how meanings circulate in relation to the hood through its representations and the political implications of these creations.

References

Decker, J. L. (1993). The State of Rap: Time and Place in Hip Hop Nationalism. *Social Text* (34), 53–84.
Dyson, M. E. (2001). *Holler if You Hear Me: Searching for Tupac Shakur*. New York: Basic Civitas Books.

Chapter 9

Making "Changes": 2Pac, Nas, and the Habitus of the Hood

Chris Richardson

Better learn about the dress code, Bs and Cs
All them other niggas copycats, these is Gs [...]
We might fight amongst each other but I promise you this
We'll burn this bitch down get us pissed

2Pac, "To Live and Die in L.A." (1998a)

Manner, by definition, only exists for others, and the recognized holders of the legitimate manner and of the power to define the value of manners – dress, bearing, pronunciation – have the privilege of indifference to their own manner (so they never have to *put on* a manner).

Bourdieu (1986, p. 95).

In this chapter, I examine a place Tupac Shakur (1998a) calls the "city of angels and constant danger." It is a place where Tupac is known to have lived, written, cruised, and fought. Whether "real" or "fictional," it is a place from which certain groups reflect upon a country that fellow rapper Nas (2008a) calls "the home of the thieves" and Cornel West (1999) argues has undergone "gangsterization from the White House all the way down" (p. 94). By analyzing the lyrics of one of Tupac's most popular singles, "Changes" (1998b), I explore the habitus vocalized by the rapper using Bourdieu's concept as my central theoretical framework. Tupac's self-reflexive recognition and vocalization of a group habitus is an important step, I argue, in the process of making positive changes in the communities he represents. Nas's "Black President" (2008b), which samples "Changes," demonstrates how the habitus that existed in the 1990s (when Tupac recorded "Changes") continues to adapt to new circumstances and shifting social conditions. Ultimately, I argue that the habitus that is described over a ten-year period through popular hip-hop lyrics can help scholars and casual listeners better understand the way practices are established and outlooks are formed both inside and outside of the hood. This framework also leads to an appreciation of how such patterns can be altered and reconstituted. As the quotations at the beginning of this chapter demonstrate, one's articulation, dress, habits, manners, etc. are products of histories and the social groups and spaces through which history takes place. Though these dispositions appear inevitable to those who hold them, a great danger lies in forgetting that they are not natural but the learned product of particular power relations.

On habitus and vicious cycles

The concept of habitus takes into account an objective and subjective approach to studying society and its representations. My purpose for deploying habitus in this chapter is twofold: first, it leads to an understanding of how a vicious cycle is able to operate and shape the future of the hood; second, it points to a way out of such a seemingly unalterable situation. Both of these movements are reflected in Tupac's work, which highlights the intersection of structural forces and individual choices. In his life, Tupac was born into poverty, a racist power structure, and a macho street mentality rampant within his neighborhoods. He also chose to pursue acting and the performing arts, to speak up about the world he witnessed, and to become a leader among his peers. In short, he worked within certain social structures while making personal choices that affected his future relationships to these structures.

As one of the editors of this book, I clearly believe that habitus is an important concept. It allows us to better understand the subjective choices people make and the objective structures within which they make them. Bourdieu suggests that to argue the world is solely comprised of structures and objective facts denies individual agency and the capacity to think critically. We are not automatons. In contrast, Bourdieu warns against romanticizing agency and subjectivity to the point where everyone is presumed to be free and autonomous. As Marx famously wrote:

> men [sic] make their own history, but they do not make it just as they please; they do not make it under circumstances chosen by themselves, but under circumstances existing already, given and transmitted from the past. The tradition of all dead generations weighs like a nightmare on the brains of the living.
>
> (Marx, 1962, p. 247)

Bourdieu continually builds on this notion by introducing terms like cultural capital, field, and symbolic violence to interrogate how and why individuals pursue the avenues they do and why they so frequently perpetuate dominant power structures. He argues that the economic sphere is an important variable but definitely not the only one to contribute to the situation. To help explain the social and psychological aspects he finds in addition to economic ones, Bourdieu(1990a) turns to the concept of habitus, which he defines as "systems of durable, transposable dispositions, structured structures predisposed to function as structuring structures, that is, as principles which generate and organize practices and representations" (p. 53).

To better understand the definition Bourdieu provides, it may help to break it down. To begin, there are "systems of durable, transposable dispositions." It is important to note that Bourdieu (2002) uses the term disposition to "give a more concrete intuition of what habitus is" but not, however, to define habitus as a disposition or as a habit (pp. 27–8). The latter terms would imply a more conscious and logical thought process akin to the Cartesian philosophy of action to which Bourdieu is clearly opposed.[1] Another important point is the contrast between "durable" and "transposable." These "structures" are not real in an objective or physical sense, meaning there is no fixed structure dictating how individuals operate. At the same time, these malleable structures do not exist entirely in the mind of the individual, which is why Bourdieu speaks of durable structures that impose themselves on individual agency to guide and shape it – *the nightmare on the brains of the living* – but not to determine it. Such structures may be altered by individuals. The "structuring structures," therefore, work to exclude certain improbable practices by "a kind of immediate submission to order that inclines agents to make a virtue of necessity, that is, to refuse what is already denied and to will the inevitable" (Bourdieu, 1990a, p. 54). They do not dictate what is, in actuality, possible for the individual.

Habitus concerns not only physical or mental practices but also representations. Representations of society influence beliefs, customs, and interactions. They become "the active presence of the whole past of which [they are] the product" (Bourdieu, 1990a, p. 56). As Bourdieu notes in *The Weight of the World* (1999), residents of low-income communities are particularly weary of the representations that objectify their bodies and their environments. One must take seriously, argues Bourdieu, "the fear of patronizing class attitudes which, when the sociologist is perceived as socially superior, is often added to the very general, if not universal, fear of being turned into an object" (p. 612). Objectification is often a negative, dehumanizing experience. This process, however, also forces one to become more self-reflexive as Tupac and a number of other hip-hop artists demonstrate. A conscious recognition of habitus, rather than living it without reflection, may allow residents to interrupt or subvert the vicious cycles that often occur when left unchecked. The interpretation of an objectified habitus can therefore have very real, and hopefully very positive, implications for residents of marginalized communities.[2]

Bourdieu (2007) notes that "habitus is an endless capacity to engender products – thoughts, perceptions, expressions, actions – whose limits are set by the historical and socially situated conditions of its production" (p. 95). He argues that each production "is as remote from a creation of unpredictable novelty as it is from a simple mechanical reproduction of the initial conditionings" (ibid.). In other words, habitus is malleable, not mechanical. It cannot necessarily predict the future. Nor does it generate completely random actions. If one recognizes the factors that are conditioning detrimental practices in the hood, then it follows that one could change these conditions. This is where Tupac's "Changes" becomes a rich source for investigation.

Tupac Shakur: the life of a ghetto saint

Tupac Amaru Shakur remains one of the most influential and prolific hip-hop personalities in global popular culture. Even after succumbing to gunshot wounds on September 13, 1996, Tupac's voice continues to resonate from car stereos, nightclub speakers, and television screens around the world. Considering the unrelenting popularity of his music, Tupac continues to inform the way many North Americans negotiate concepts of black culture and "the hood." In *Holler If You Hear Me: Searching for Tupac Shakur*, Dyson (2001) writes that "Tupac is perhaps the representative figure of his generation. In his haunting voice can be heard the buoyant hopefulness and the desperate hopelessness that mark the outer perimeters of the hip-hop culture he eagerly embraced" (p. 13). Dyson adds that "Tupac's ascent to ghetto sainthood is both a reflection of the desperation of the youth who proclaim him and a society that has had too few saints" (p. 17). Thus, Tupac is one of the few people who can embody and vocalize what we have in this collection referred to as the *habitus of the hood*.

An important aspect to consider is the genre in which Tupac operated (and in which he continues to operate after his death). Decker (1993) writes that "in the absence of a black CNN, rap records are an invisible network that can inform and mobilize" (p. 103). He argues that artists in this genre, though not politicians, "are involved in the production of cultural politics – its creation, its circulation and its interpretation – which is tied to the everyday struggles of working-class blacks and the urban poor" (p. 101). Hip hop, as Tricia Rose (1994a) writes, "replicates and reimagines the experiences of urban life" (p. 71). Within this subculture, artists attempt to "negotiate the experiences of marginalization, brutally truncated opportunity and oppression" (ibid.). More recently, hip hop has been called political "tap water" (p. 10) by authors such as McWhorter (2008) who argues that "we are infected with an idea that snapping our necks to black men chanting cynical potshots about the Powers That Be in surly voices over a beat is a form of political engagement" (p. 12). Furthermore, Rose (2008) has questioned the direction of hip hop's political engagement in contemporary culture. "Over the last three decades, the public conversation has decidedly moved toward an easy acceptance of black ghetto existence and the belief that black people themselves are responsible for creating ghettos and for choosing to live in them" (p. 9). She argues that the split between commercial rap and conscious rap has increased dramatically in recent years, the former being politically hegemonic while the latter is relegated to mainstream obscurity. Hip-hop culture remains, however, built on a subversive terrain and I would argue that it still holds a potential for counterhegemonic reflection on the circumstances of the hood. As Dyson (2007) argues, "Critics, including McWhorter, don't account for the complex ways that some artists in hip hop play with stereotypes to either subvert or reverse them" (p. xvii). While there are numerous ways to interpret hip hop – lyrically, stylistically, symbolically and economically – one thing remains relatively clear: hip hop comes from, and helps to construct, the predominantly young, working-class, minority groups that embrace it.

Rap is an inherently confrontational and political style within hip-hop culture. As Martinez (1997) writes:

[T]he political and gangsta rap of the late 1980s and early 1990s was an ardent form of resistance and a definite expression of oppositional culture, bringing to light long perceived problems in [American] inner cities, and effectively heralding the 1992 Los Angeles riots that shocked a nation and a globe.[3]

(p. 268)

She argues that rap has brought controversial messages to the public that can be summarized thematically as "distrust of the police," "fear of a corporate system that plans genocide," "disillusionment with the health care system," and "anger at racism and lost opportunities." Furthermore, rap frequently advocates for action in the face of oppression and pleads for recognition of these problems from the general public. This genre of music is anything but passive.

Tupac represents a substantial influence in what is already a significant mode of expression. He was "the ghetto's everyman," argues Dyson (2001), "embodying in his art the horrors and pleasures that came to millions of others who were in many ways just like him" (p. 107). The major difference is that Tupac had a "protean genius" to write the variety of lyrics that he performed and "a microphone to amplify tragedy and triumph" (ibid.). Tupac represented residents of the hood, their struggles, their passions, and their dreams. Simultaneously, he was a unique resident with a distinct personality and, from about the age of 20, a crowd of paparazzi recording his every move. While Tupac's experiential lyrics are not necessarily representative of all others in the community, it is important to consider that Tupac's popularity is in large part attributed to the fact that he spoke for the hood, reflecting insiders' experiences back to them ("now I'm back with the facts giving it back to you") and making outsiders curious about a world they had never seen before ("Sellin' crack to the kid ... well that's the way it is"). Tupac became a sort of bridge for these two groups, bringing them together through his music.

People who have not seen South-Central Los Angeles in person likely form their understanding of such a place from popular representations by Tupac and other highly visible artists. Thus, whether songs like "Changes" represent reality or construct a highly stylized notion of reality, people nevertheless incorporate these objects of discourse into their individual habitus. As Forman (2000) argues, "the issue of whether or not [rap] tracks refer back to a consistently verifiable reality is rendered moot by the possibilities they present as textual spaces of representation" (p. 83). One learns what people of the hood look like, talk like, and act like from such depictions. These representations have very real consequences for both residents of this space and those outside it. The hood is simultaneously real and unreal. In a sense, this is Los Angeles – the streets and neighborhoods to which Tupac alludes all exist on maps – but, in another sense, this is an interpretation of these spaces by Tupac that has been further mediated as the song passed through the production process. By the time the track reaches listeners' ears, this is a hood that has been worked on and smoothed over to the point where it becomes both fiction and non-fiction. In the end, however, the purpose of this undertaking is not to understand Los Angeles as a "reality" or even as a social construct. I am less concerned with "realistic" representations than with how any significant representation ingrains itself in the cultural imaginations of listeners and shapes the practices they consider appropriate or inappropriate within such spaces.

"Changes"

"Changes" remains one of Tupac's most popular singles. Released posthumously and later nominated for a Grammy in 2000 (four years after Tupac's death), the song begins with a piano arrangement from Bruce Hornsby and The Range's 1986 hit "The Way It Is." The keys are soon accompanied by a heavy bass guitar and drum arrangement that sounds both fresh and reminiscent of the early 1990's West Coast rap scene. Tupac enters the track with the line: "I see no changes" and quickly paints a vivid picture of depressing circumstances, poverty, racism, black on black violence, drug and alcohol abuse, and the trauma of growing up too quickly. In the third verse, the lyrics that I believe underline the main premise of the song are as follows:

> As long as I stay black
> I gotta stay strapped
> And I never get to lay back
> 'Cause I always gotta worry 'bout the pay backs
> Comin' back after all these years
> Rat-tat-tat-tat-tat
> That's the way it is

This verse best illustrates a habitus formation by presenting what Bourdieu (1999) would call a "practical hypothesis based on past experiences" (p. 109). To examine how the lyrics demonstrate the formation of a habitus, I would like to rephrase the first two lines. Here, Tupac presents an implied syllogism that is exemplary of the gangsta rap habitus he personifies, which roughly translates as:

> Black men have to protect themselves (with weapons).
> Tupac will always be a black man.
> Therefore, Tupac will always have to protect himself (with a weapon).

Here, Tupac vocalizes a habitus literally by retelling experiences, which then demonstrates that similar experiences are inevitable. Tupac is a black man and as authors such as Fanon (2008) have demonstrated one has very little control over how others see and react to this fact. This reality makes the artist vulnerable to external structural forces such as racism, discrimination, and a set of expectations which pre-exist Tupac as an individual. Though his actions can reinforce or call into question the preconceived notions of what it means to be a black man, Tupac is situated within a discourse that is always-already present. Mercer (1994) elaborates on how cyclical patterns of behavior have occurred in Britain, where other young black men have acted out the stereotypical characteristics that have been ascribed to them, furthering the stereotypes and creating a vicious cycle from which it becomes extremely difficult to escape.

The prevailing stereotype projects an image of black male youth as "mugger" or "rioter;" either way he constitutes a violent and dangerous threat to white society ... This regime of representation is reproduced and maintained in hegemony because black men have had to resort to "toughness" as a defensive response to the prior aggression and violence that characterizes the way black communities are policed ... This cycle between reality and representation makes the ideological fictions of racism empirically "true" – or rather, there is a struggle over the definition, understanding and construction of meanings around black masculinity within the dominant regime of truth.

(Mercer, 1994, pp. 137–8)

In addition to personal experiences, Tupac refers to others whom he has seen personally (or via news media) hurt or killed by the current social arrangement. "It's time to fight back, that's what Huey said / Two shots in the dark, now Huey's dead." It is fair to assume Tupac is referring to the co-founder and leader of the Black Panthers Party, Huey Newton, who was shot in Oakland in 1989. No doubt, Tupac saw the sad irony of this murder occurring in a hood that Newton attempted to improve through social outreach programs decades earlier. These experiences, both personal and mediated, work to form Tupac's sense of what the hood holds for him and his peers. This understanding of what is to be expected then informs his future decisions. In other words, Tupac's personal experience with systemic violence in his neighborhood registers internally as a personal history. It is also externalized as the characteristic dangers of the outside world. These factors influence Tupac to carry a gun and present a tough image. But by reacting to such experiences in this way Tupac perpetuates the situation and adds to the stereotypical image of the violent black man.

When he says, "I gotta stay strapped," he illustrates perfectly how his actions contribute to his current state of mind, and thus, the formation of a habitus that extends beyond himself as an individual and becomes embodied in social relations. Bourdieu (1999) refers to habitus as a dialectic, an "embodied history, internalized as a second nature and so forgotten as history" (p. 111). It is completely understandable that living in a dangerous neighborhood would lead one to carry a gun. The risk, however, is that one will misrecognize this reality as a natural occurrence rather than a reflection of a social power dynamic. This misrecognition can lead to what Bourdieu calls symbolic violence, which refers to imposing a certain meaning as legitimate "by concealing the power relations which are the basis of its force" (Bourdieu & Passeron, 1990, p. 4).

Bourdieu (1990b) writes that symbolic power is most evident in the ability to produce scapegoats, stereotypes, and subordinate groups. To best accomplish this task, those exercising symbolic power need two things: first, they need to possess symbolic capital (the power to impose social divisions on the minds of others), and second, they need the groups that are created to be found, to some degree, in reality (i.e., there must be some resemblance of truth to any claims). The stereotype of black on black violence is so prominent in North America because, as we see here, it can be self-perpetuating.[4] Tupac reacts to his experiences in the hood by staying "strapped." In doing so, however, he creates enemies from whom he must protect himself, which further necessitates gun use and aggression toward others. Tupac acknowledges this, though he seems to place more emphasis on structural factors when he says "Give 'em dope and let 'em deal the brothers / Give 'em guns, step back and watch 'em kill each other." In lines like this, it is unclear who is giving these things to the community. Nevertheless, whether it is a specific group of individuals or a disembodied white power structure, as James Baldwin might say,[5] the perpetrator is clearly external in Tupac's view. At the same time, Tupac acknowledges internal sources of conflict, as reflected in lines like "the only time we chill is when we kill each other," illustrating the interplay of external forces influencing personal agency. This brings us to a common critique of Bourdieu's work: if it is so easy to perpetuate vicious cycles of violence and poverty, is there any hope of altering such a habitus? Does the concept of habitus refute the possibility of change?

Rethinking reproduction

Habitus remains a contentious concept. Bridge (2004) writes that the term has "come under fire for being too 1960s, too limited to the French social structure and too static" (p. 62). Lipietz (1997) writes that Bourdieu has been "systematically criticized on two fronts: as a structuralist and also as a methodological individualist" (p. 255). Bourdieu (2002) recognizes his critics and responds by asking "is habitus a definitely static concept, intrinsically doomed to express continuities and to repetition?" (p. 27). This, he says, "is difficult to attempt to answer in a completely satisfactory manner." Elsewhere, he writes that "I do not see where my readers could have found the model of circular reproduction which they attribute to me (structure→ habitus→ structure)" (Bourdieu, 1990b, p. 118). He points to *Homo Academicus* (1988) as one of many examples where changes not only occur but are produced by the very social arrangement in which they are formed.[6]

Readers must pay careful attention to Bourdieu's language. Bourdieu (2007) describes habitus as a past that "survives in the present and tends to perpetuate itself into the future" (p. 82). Habitus represents a past that does not necessarily *repeat*, rather it *survives* – as memory, as residue, as trace. It influences, but does not determine, the present and the future. It tends to perpetuate itself but it is not condemned to do this. Habitus is ultimately a concept that allows us to understand practices which "neither the extrinsic and instantaneous determinisms of a mechanistic sociologism nor the purely internal but equally punctual determination of voluntarist or spontaneist subjectivism are capable of accounting for" (p. 82). This concept is not static.

What Bourdieu seems to offer in response to critics is that habitus is always changing. As Deleuze and Guattari (2007) might posit, habitus is in a constant state of becoming, perpetually being reinforced or altered. Change is greatly dependent upon the circumstances in which things take place and the confluence of individuals and environments. The problem is, however, that situations one experiences are often reliant upon the same factors and therefore often reinforce the same beliefs and practices. Furthermore, an important counterpoint is to acknowledge that vicious cycles are not unique to Bourdieu's theory. They exist in many peoples' lived experiences. It seems, at least as far as Tupac illustrates, habitus may reflect social realities too well. In fact, the criticisms as they relate to continuities and repetitions may not be targeting a theoretical misstep by Bourdieu but more so the dissatisfaction of the bleak-looking future the concept implies. Yes, change is possible. But there are reasons marginalized neighborhoods, populations, and individuals continue to be in the disadvantaged circumstances in which they have existed for decades if not centuries. As Althusser (2008) has argued, seemingly disparate parts of society often work alongside one another to reproduce a "teeth-gritting" harmony that perpetuates dominant social arrangements.

For all the changes Americans have seen in the recent past – the desegregation of the 1950s; the increase in post-secondary-educated visible minorities; the election of an African-American president – a disproportionate number of African-American inmates remain in US prisons and a skewed representation of minorities continues in the media (see Baker, 2008; Dyson, 1993, 1996, 2004; West, 1999). As West (2008) writes, "we have to recognize that there is a radical continuity between the killing fields of the plantations, the bodies hanging from the trees, police brutality, the prison-industrial complex, and the Superdome in New Orleans after Hurricane Katrina" (p. 45). Though it is seldom acknowledged, racism and brutality are not historical relics. They continue to operate in America today. Lynching has occurred in the United States as recently as the late 1990s, even in "cosmopolitan" cities like New York (Thompson, 2007). Change is possible. But every future retains traces of the past practices from which it attempts to escape. Tupac so vividly illustrates this continuity with his lyrics.

Fortunately, both Tupac and Bourdieu reveal in their work ways of recognizing and altering destructive patterns. Bourdieu (2002) argues that dispositions may be "changed by history, that is by new experiences, education or training" (p. 29). He also notes in parenthesis that this "implies that aspects of what remains unconscious in habitus be made at least partially conscious and explicit." Webb, Schirato, and Danaher (2002) echo this statement, writing that "categories of meaning and perception can only function effectively as habitus if we do not think about the specific sociocultural conditions or contexts of their production and existence" (p. 39). Bringing unconscious beliefs and practices to the surface is a precondition for creating meaningful changes in the way societies operate.

To examine this idea of change, I return to Tupac's most explicit attempt to challenge the social order: his aptly titled "Changes." After the first two verses, Tupac's voice becomes more conversational. Earlier in the track, he raps while telling stories of the social conditions and practices that seemed to be second nature. There are lines like "my stomach hurts so I'm looking for a purse to snatch" and "Sellin' crack to the kid 'I gotta get paid' / Well hey, well that's the way it is." But after this line, Tupac stops rapping. During the bridge, he speaks in a mode Dyson (2001) terms the "pastoral letter" (p. 107). Tupac explicitly breaks with the idea that the aforementioned conditions are natural or inevitable – that it's just "the way it is." He challenges these practices by saying:

> Let's change the way we eat
> Let's change the way we live
> And let's change the way we treat each other
> You see the old way wasn't working
> So it's on us to do what we gotta do to survive

Dyson (2001) argues that Tupac's ability to speak "directly to the heart" is what "gave him an intimacy and immediacy of communication that are virtually unrivalled in hip hop" (p. 107). We hear this charismatic voice most clearly in the bridge after the second verse. In great detail, the song relates the structural conditions and personal histories that contribute to the problems of the hood. Then, in Tupac's often-contradictive style, the rapper says "that's the way it is" and "it's time … to start making some changes." In bringing history back from the realm of unquestioned reality, of unconscious behaviors, Tupac forces the listener to recognize a habitus that has thus far been lingering unexamined in the background of everyday practices and representations of the hood. This recognition of one's habitus is a crucial step in undoing the symbolic violence that Tupac may himself be guilty of perpetuating in lines like "I gotta stay strapped" and "You gotta learn to hold your own."

Tupac acknowledges the un-naturalness of the situation. He "recognizes" the symbolic violence by questioning assumptions. In terms of the stereotype that crack is a black problem, Tupac raps "both black and white is smokin' crack tonight." In terms of constructing African-Americans as a naturally violent people, Tupac questions where this notion comes from. He raps "all I see is racist faces / misplaced hate makes disgrace to races." Finally, Tupac questions public policy and why the legal system disproportionately affects low-income, African-American citizens. He says "It ain't a secret, don't conceal the fact / The penitentiary's packed and it's filled with blacks … Instead of war on poverty they got a war on drugs / So the police can bother me."[7] Through these observations, the rapper confronts what Bourdieu terms misrecognition, that is, "the process whereby power relations are perceived not for what they objectively are but in a form which renders them legitimate in the eyes of the beholder" (Bourdieu & Passeron, 1990, p. xxii). In this case, black men who partake in violence because it is naturalized as "the way it is," would be guilty of misrecognition. They would be guilty of a form of forgetting that makes these practices seem natural. This misrecognition leads to a symbolic violence. In the streets of Los Angeles, it often leads to actual physical violence as well. By recognizing these conditions on a conscious level Tupac does just what Bourdieu argues is necessary to create change.

"Black President"

Listening to Tupac more than a decade after his death, two things resonate for me. The first is Tupac's incredible skills to envision the future. In an interview with actor Larenz Tate of *Menace II Society* (1993) and *Dead Presidents* (1995), the rapper's friend calls Tupac a prophet. "Everything he had talked about before he died actually happened" (as quoted in Dyson, 2001, p. 4).[8] The second thing that "Changes" highlights is the dated circumstances in which Tupac wrote his lyrics. In the mid-1990s, few would argue with these lines from the second verse: "And though it seems heaven sent / We ain't ready to see a black president." While calling for changes, Tupac's habitus – and, by extrapolation, the habitus of many residents of the hood – *weighs like a nightmare* on what he saw as possible in the future. Even within his optimism, as he urged residents to start making changes and to heal one another, Tupac did not think an Africa-American president was a possibility. This was one thing Tupac failed to predict.[9] A decade after "Changes," an African-American president would become not only a possibility but a reality in the United States. While Tupac's views had not disappeared in 2008, they were beginning to change within the black community and within America in general.

Nas's 2008 album provides the most interesting illustration of this changing habitus.[10] On November 24, 1998, Tupac's *Greatest Hits* was released, which featured the line "We ain't ready to see a black president." On July 15, 2008, Nas's album, featuring the track "Black President" hit store shelves, sampling Tupac's "Changes." On November 4, 2008 – a decade after "Changes" – Barack Hussein Obama II was elected America's 44th president. Clearly, change had taken place. Listening to "Black President," we can hear Bourdieu's notion of habitus formation at play.

As Rose (2008) argues, the trend toward commercialization in hip hop "is so significant that if the late Tupac Shakur were a newly signed artist today, I believe he'd likely be considered a socially conscious rapper and thus relegated to the margins of the commercial hip hop field" (p. 3). Ironically, Nas, who once existed in the field alongside Tupac, now seems to occupy this position today. Dyson (2006) writes that "Nas, arguably, has best carried forth Tupac's restless quest for broad literacy" (p. 16). Unfortunately, he has also earned himself the moniker of conscious rapper and suffered the commercial tribulations that tend to accompany this title. Regardless of Nas's relative position in the hip-hop field, however, he remains one of the most admired and revered rappers in the game and therefore provides an important contribution to the collective understanding of a changing habitus within hip-hop culture. "Black President" literally picks up where Tupac left off. The song begins and ends with an address by President Obama juxtaposed to a sample of Tupac's "Changes" – specifically, the lines "And though it seems heaven sent / We ain't ready to see a black president." In addition, the hook adds a line reminiscent of Obama's campaign slogan after the Tupac sample: "Yes we can … change the world." The song's up-tempo arrangement, the militaresque drum beat, and the uplifting synthesized melody present not only a reflection of what has come before, but also a call to action for real change (which was still to come at the time of the song's release). It builds upon Tupac's words, his thoughts, and his outlook, and carries this frequently bleak-looking past into a brighter, more hopeful-looking future. I would caution, however, that this analysis does not espouse the idea of "progress" or a teleological notion that Americans are somehow getting closer to freedom and equality; the celebrations of a postrace society have been dutifully challenged by authors like Dyson

(2010) who writes that "The race to get to the White House may be over … but race itself can't be disposed of that easily" (p. 43). What this song suggests is that a clear change in outlooks, in habitus, has occurred.

Nas begins the song by highlighting the similarities between the hood of the mid-1990s and the early twentieth century. He relates the history of struggle and continuing plight of African-Americans living in poverty. In short, he evokes all the problems Tupac highlighted a decade earlier – the prison-industrial complex, police brutality, affordable housing, drug addiction, etc. But then Nas says something that was not part of Tupac's repertoire: "America surprise us, and let a black man guide us." While Nas acknowledges that this is no ordinary event, it is nevertheless a *possibility* in 2008. Thanks to President Obama's message of hope and change – whether one agrees with its rhetoric or not – the possibility of a black president no longer seems far-fetched or wishful thinking for Nas. In fact, as Nielson (2009) points out, though not all rappers have moved away from the misogyny, violence, and crime for which gangsta rap is famous, Obama's ascent into American politics has led to a great influx in rap songs that explore new and uplifting themes.

I would argue that no hip-hop fan in the twenty-first century could hear Nas's "Black President" without recalling Tupac's "Changes" and identifying the whole web of connotations it holds. Though little has arguably changed in the hood between 1998 and 2008, this hopefulness personified in President Obama's early successes translates into a slightly altered message in Nas's "Black President," which can be seen as a considerable step toward creating real political change. The conservative – many have argued racist – politics of Bush Sr. during Tupac's era and Bush Jr. during Nas's were being replaced by an African-American presidential candidate who quotes Sam Cooke just as easily as he quotes Congressional statutes. Tupac's words and visions reverberate in all of hip-hop listeners' histories, influencing and reflecting, to varying degrees, their ideas about what was and was not possible in America and continue to represent "a past which survives in the present" (Bourdieu, 2007, p. 82). It is a past upon which Nas builds his vision of the future.

Habitus is like a building that is continually reconstructed. It is built on a foundation, it is resurrected, storey by storey, and usually we can predict what it will look like. But this is not to say it is predetermined. No blueprint is final. It is easier to make small alterations than large-scale structural changes. But it is not impossible. In time, whole sections can be demolished and reconstructed. Although the remnants and the traces of the past will survive, the building can change drastically. This is what Nas's song demonstrates. As Bourdieu (1990b) notes, a crucial step toward making changes is envisioning an improved society. Of course, merely thinking differently will not change social structures or political practices. But without the ability to imagine a better future, without hope and optimism, change is impossible. No one would have gone to vote for the next president if they did not think he could deliver, to some degree, the changes he evoked in the imaginations of voters. "Changes" reflects a part of the past that guides the future and perceptions of what is and is not possible. But these guiding structures can be modified through new and different experiences. In "Black President," Nas refers to American history, saying "Every other president was nothing less than white … But on a positive side / I think Obama provides hope / And challenges minds." He reflects a history that would indicate another white, male president is virtually inevitable. Then, à la Cornel West, Nas inserts a message of hope into the equation and reminds listeners that nothing is predetermined. If Obama could make it this far, who is to say he couldn't make it all the way? "Black president" represents a new chapter in the psychosocial drama of America that hip hop has been documenting for decades.

Organic gangsta intellectuals

This chapter explores the work of Tupac, with a brief look at how Nas takes him up a decade later, for very specific reasons. As outlined above, Tupac is not just a rapper. He was average – the "ghetto's everyman" – because many people could identify with him. At the same time, Tupac was able to speak for, and represent, a large group of people and interests through his talent, his unique style, and his position within popular culture. In this way, Tupac was unique. Though it has become popular – even to the point of cliché – to view hip-hop artists through the lens of the Gramscian organic intellectual, I would like to briefly explore why such an outlook remains a valuable way to understand Tupac and his role in society. Rodman (2006), arguing in relation to another popular rapper, writes "I don't want to simply romanticize Eminem as some sort of organic intellectual or working-class hero – that would be precisely the sort of patronizing elitism that I'm trying to guard against here" (p. 113). Instead, he writes, "I do want to suggest that, as cultural critics, we could stand to be more self-reflective about our own class position and biases, and about how readily we dismiss potentially valuable cultural criticism simply because it comes from someone who says 'motherfucker' in public without flinching" (ibid.). Similarly, I have argued that those of us in academe who seek to understand how societies work can – and should – look to certain popular artists for the sharp social criticisms and practical theoretical descriptions they provide (Richardson, 2011). Artists like Nas and Tupac may reveal more about society than "pure theory" (if there is such a thing) could ever have the capacity to relate. Regardless of the medium and dialect – or possibly because of these things – hip-hop artists provide glimpses of the world and reflections of attitudes that cannot be found in quantitative or qualitative academic research.

In *Hope on a Tightrope*, West (2008) writes that "hip hop music is the most important popular musical development in the last thirty years" (p. 122). Like many other scholars, West believes that, at their best, hip-hop artists "respond to their sense of being rejected by society at large, or being invisible in the society at large, with a subversive critique of that society" (p. 123).[11] These perspectives provide a definite value that I do not suggest should replace traditional research but can be used to augment it and work as distinct counterpoints to the dominant academic discourses in circulation. As Jay-Z writes in an introduction to one of Dyson's (2007) recent books:

The folks from the suburbs and the private schools so concerned with putting warning labels on my records missed the point. They never stopped to worry about the realities in this country that spread poverty and racism and gun violence and hatred of women and drug use and unemployment. People can act like rappers spread these things, but that is not true. Our lives are not rotten or worthless just because that's what people say about the real estate that we were raised on. In fact, our lives may be even more worthy of study because we succeeded despite the promises of failure seeping out from behind the peeling paint on the walls of every apartment in every project.

(p. xi)

In "Antonio's B-Boys: Rap, Rappers, and Gramsci's Intellectuals," Abrams (1995) points to four major conditions in which rappers can work as organic intellectuals: (1) if they are members of aggrieved communities; (2) if they reflect the needs of those communities; (3) if they disseminate subversive ideas that challenge taken-for-granted social orders; and (4) if they attempt to construct a coalition united around similar ideas (p. 3). These attributes are easy to see in Tupac and a number of other high-profile rap icons that came before and after him.[12] In terms of Abrams's characteristics, (1) Tupac is known for his upbringing in low-income, predominantly black neighborhoods across America; (2) he articulates the needs and desires of these communities; (3) he is critical of the social order as "Changes" demonstrates; and finally, (4) Tupac, though known for his aggressiveness and "gangsta" attitude, was attempting to unite the community in "Changes" ("It's time for us as a people to start makin' some changes"). Thus, Tupac works as an organic intellectual very clearly in these ways. I would also add an important point to these qualifications. By exposing the habitus of his community in songs like "Changes," Tupac laid the groundwork for what was needed to break with destructive cyclical patterns in the hood. This must become one of the tasks of anyone who considers himself or herself to be an OG [Original Gangsta]. In fact, maybe instead of privileging OGs, listeners can start seeking OGIs [Organic Gangsta Intellectuals].

As an intellectual, Tupac was often contradictory. This was apparent in "Changes" but is even more apparent when listening to his entire body of work. Dyson (2001) claims that it was the rapper's ability to easily switch from what he calls "conscious rap" to "political hip hop" to "party music" to "hedonism rap" to "thug rap" to "ghettocentric rap" that gave Tupac the status and influence that he continues to hold. In a 2003 symposium co-sponsored by Harvard University, Mark Anthony Neal presented a paper entitled "Thug Nigga Intellectual: Tupac as Celebrity Gramscian." While Neal claims that Tupac was a "walking contradiction," he argues this characteristic made "the process of being an intellectual accessible to ordinary people" (Gewertz, 2003). Tupac's vivid depictions of his lived experiences may not necessarily represent the rest of his community, but the rapper no doubt brings an important point of reference to the forefront that represents the communal landscape.

Geographical space is one of the major sites where people become united through similar cultural experiences. Bourdieu (1999) writes that while it is impossible for any two people to have the exact same experiences it is more likely that members of the same group would be confronted with similar situations more often than those within different settings. He notes that "individuals who move into a new space must fulfill the conditions that that space tacitly requires of its occupants" (p. 128). In short, social structures can quickly become spatial structures. Bourdieu adds that "the imperceptible incorporation of structures of the social order undoubtedly happens, in large part, through a prolonged and indefinitely repeated experience of the spatial distance that affirms social distance" (p. 126). The distance traveled to work each day, the proximity of desirable stores, businesses, and schools, access to meaningful social groups, all of these things shape the shared practices of the community and distinguish it from other communities. "Capital makes it possible to keep undesirable persons and things at a distance at the same time that it brings closer desirable persons and things ... thereby minimizing the necessary expense (notably in time) in appropriating them" (Bourdieu, 1999, p. 127). This is another case in which it would be inappropriate for dominant social groups to say that they want to isolate and remove undesirables – but somehow the legitimate forces of society (government, private business, the judicial system) allow for this segregation to happen. Anyone is free to buy a home in Beverly Hills, for example, but for some reason the majority of residents all look the same.

Tupac shared enough similar experiences with those he related to – and those who related to him – that he may very well be indicative of a group habitus that is very different from the mainstream habitus that is presented as natural or normal within popular discourses. Tupac's popularity speaks to his distinct ability to voice the concerns of his community, to raise delicate issues without batting an eye, and connect them with larger groups of people or, in Gramscian terms, *historical blocs*. In this way, he was able to present the group's habitus in a subversive style that popularized such debates and paved the way for real and significant change. While the incorporation of his work into the mainstream and its appropriation by privileged young white men in particular raise other issues about the transformation of his message, there is no doubt that Tupac, like Nas today, was an OGI.

The old school and contemporary institutions

In both "Changes" and "Black President," the artists do not use statistics or quantitative data to get their points across but they very much act as social scientists (or at least astute cultural critics). As Dyson argues:

At their best these rappers are like ethnographers ... searching anthropologists trying to figure out the folk ways and the mores of the culture that they emerge from ... Nas is one of the greatest ever to do so and has written such a powerful music that has been balanced between high cerebral art and the kind of street vitality that it takes to make that music viable.

("Professor and Preacher," 2007)

Tupac and Nas, however, direct their words not to academe or the white suburbs – though they reach them. Instead, they speak to the communities from which they came.[13] In "Changes," notice the pronouns in lines like "*We* can never go nowhere / Unless *we* share with each other / *We* gotta start makin' changes." There is little debating to whom Tupac is speaking and where he situates himself in relation to that group. Ten years later, Nas situates himself in a similar position: "*They* forgot *us* on the block / Got *us* in the box / Solitary confinement / How violent are these cops?" Listening to "Black President" in contrast to "Changes" allows listeners to mark the transformations, however slight, that have taken place in the habitus of the hood. I do not claim that these songs themselves altered the habitus of the people who listened to them. In fact, I believe that McWhorter (2008) has a point in arguing that too much focus may be given to hip hop which, in and of itself, "cannot *do* anything" (p. 179). However, I differ greatly with his suggestion to just "move on" (ibid.). Rather, scholars must look to these social texts to better understand the power dynamics and the habitus formations that are present within North American social relations. As Bourdieu (1992) argues, "social reality exists, so to speak, twice, in things and in minds, in fields and in habitus, outside and inside of agents" (p. 127). One may never be able to grasp fully why people act the way they do; however, one can look to examples in music, texts, and other artistic productions that elaborate the perceptions, strategies, and ways of life of various groups. This understanding may allow for better comprehensions of what certain groups feel is possible and impossible and therefore how social power dynamics are reproduced and challenged.

As Chicago hip-hop artist Lupe Fiasco (2006) says, "I ain't Cornel West / I am Cornel Westside." In this turn of phrase, Fiasco gestures toward the similarities between academics and hip-hop artists. He also points to the sense of place and struggle that tends to be muted when echoed through Princeton corridors. Perhaps not in the traditional vernacular, "Changes" helps to illustrate the idea that external structural factors and internal subjective interpretations work in conjunction to form habits, opinions, dispositions, and representations of the world and the possibilities it holds. I would not contend that "Changes" was the catalyst that led to President Obama's election victory. I do argue, however, that the habitus of Americans, both inside and outside of "the hoods," had to change before the election of an African-American president could take place. The way "Black President" evokes Tupac's vision in "Changes" ten years later provides a valuable example of how such change has manifested in popular music, which can be used to interrogate the minds of listeners who hear their own views reflected in Nas's subtle revision.

Hip hop continues to play a vital role in forming strong communal bonds and negotiating the past, present, and future of marginalized spaces. A future project, which will take place in academe, in street corners, and be disseminated through the headphones of countless music devices, will be to understand and articulate the further changes that must be made both inside and outside the hood. These changes can only happen with an awareness of the habitus that must be beaten, broken, and burned down in order to make way for a distinctly new one to take its place. Tupac and Nas provide material evidence that can be harnessed within the arts and social sciences to examine what the habitus of the hood sounds like at certain points in time. The differences in songs such as "Changes" and "Black President" are precisely those elements of hip-hop culture to which listeners must attend.

Notes

1. Bourdieu argues that habitus "collides head on with the illusion of (intellectual) mastery of oneself that is so deeply ingrained in intellectuals" (Bourdieu & Wacquant, 1992, p. 132). See also Bourdieu (1990b, 2007).
2. This project, however, does not fall solely on residents. Habitus must also be reconsidered in the minds of outsiders whose practices help to perpetuate the dominant social order. Bourdieu is clear in virtually all of his work that any community movement must reach broader social structures in order to make real change. Similarly, in "Never B Peace" from *Better Dayz* (2002) Tupac raps "We can't never have peace 'til you motherfuckers clean up this mess you made / 'Til you fucking clean up the dirt you dropped / 'Til we get a piece."
3. See also Mitchell and Feagin (1995), Stuckey (1987), Scott (1990) and Rose (1994b), from whom Martinez builds her argument.
4. It can also, of course, be perpetuated through popular culture, public discourses, news media, and numerous other sources. All of which can work together to reinforce such representations.
5. See Boyd, 2008.
6. In this case, the swelling ranks of university departments and the lowering prestige of higher education degrees due to oversaturation in the intellectual marketplace led to a number of academics protesting against the very system they had entered and within which they formed their habitus.
7. Houston Baker Jr. (2008) argues that "what was once a war on poverty has become a war on the impoverished" (p. 205). After prison, "those who are released are sent back to the crumbling streets, disrupting even further possibilities for orderly civil life in their black and Hispanic majority 'hoods" (207).
8. This prophetic legacy has led many to argue that Tupac is not dead but hiding away in an undisclosed location (which would explain why he is able to come out with a new CD roughly every year after his death).
9. In all fairness, Tupac says we "ain't ready" for an African-American president – not that we will never *be* ready for one. I am convinced, however, this was an event that Tupac would not likely have anticipated in the near future.
10. This controversial album was originally entitled *Nigger*, and explores the history and mythology of this very powerful noun. The title was changed last-minute, however, because of alleged studio interference. In the first single, *Hero*, Nas raps "First L.A. and Doug Morris was riding with it / But a *Newsweek* article startled big wigs / They said, Nas, why is he trying it? / My lawyers only see the Billboard charts as winning [...] So untitled it is."
11. See also Todd Boyd (1997, 2008), Michael Eric Dyson (1993, 1996, 2003, 2007), Murray Forman (2002), Mark Anthony Neal (2003, 2006), Imani Perry (2004), and Tricia Rose (1994a, 1994b).
12. In "Old School," from Tupac's *Me Against The World* (1995), he details his influences name by name. The chorus repeats "What more can I say? I wouldn't be here today if the old school didn't pave the way."
13. As Dyson (2007) writes, "the metaphorical root of hip hop is connected to the ghetto whether or not many of its artists grew up there" (p. 11).

References

2Pac. (1998a). To Live and Die in L.A. *Greatest Hits*. Death Row Records.

——. (1998b). Changes. *Greatest Hits*. Death Row Records.

——. (2002). Never B Peace. *Better Dayz*. Amaru/Death Row Records.

Althusser, L. (2008). *On Ideology*. London: Verso.

Baker, H. A. (2008). *Betrayal: How Black Intellectuals Have Abandoned the Ideals of the Civil Rights Era*. New York: Columbia University Press.

Bourdieu, P. (1986). *Distinction: A Social Critique of the Judgement of Taste*. (R. Nice, Trans.). Cambridge, MA: Harvard University Press.

——. (1988). *Homo Academicus*. (P. Collier, Trans.). Cambridge: Polity Press.

——. (1990a). *The Logic of Practice*. (R. Nice, Trans.). Stanford, CA: Stanford University Press.

——. (1990b). *In Other Words: Essays Towards a Reflexive Sociology*. Stanford, CA: Stanford University Press.

——. (2002).Habitus. In J. Hillier and E. Rooksby (Eds), *Habitus: A Sense of Place* (pp. 27–34). Aldershot: Ashgate.

——. (2007). *Outline of a Theory of Practice*. (R. Nice, Trans.). Cambridge: Cambridge University Press.

Bourdieu, P. and Passeron, J.-C. (1990). *Reproduction in Education, Society, and Culture*. (R. Nice, Trans.). London: Sage Publications.

Bourdieu, P., & Wacquant, L. (1992). *An Invitation to Reflexive Sociology*. Chicago: The University of Chicago Press.

Bourdieu, P., Accardo, A., & Ferguson, P. P. (1999). *The Weight of the World: Social Suffering in Contemporary Society*. (P. P. Ferguson, Trans.). Palo Alto, CA: Stanford University Press.

Boyd, H. (2008). *Baldwin's Harlem: A Biography of James Baldwin*. New York: Atria Books.

Bridge, G. (2004). "Pierre Bourdieu." In P. Hubbard, R. Kitchin, & G. Valentine (Eds), *Key Thinkers on Space and Place* (pp. 59–64). London: Sage Publications.

Decker, J. L. (1993). The State of Rap: Time and Place in Hip Hop Nationalism. *Social Text, 34*, 53–84.

Deleuze, G., & Guattari, F. (2007). *A Thousand Plateaus: Capitalism and Schizophrenia*. (B. Massumi, Trans.). Minneapolis: University of Minnesota Press.

Dyson, M. E. (1993). *Reflecting Black: African-American Cultural Criticism*. Minneapolis: University of Minnesota Press.

——. (1996). *Between God and Gangsta Rap: Bearing Witness to Black Culture*. Oxford: Oxford University Press.

——. (2001) *Holler If You Hear Me: Searching for Tupac Shakur*. New York: Basic Civitas Books.

——. (2004). *The Michael Eric Dyson Reader*. New York: Basic Civitas Books.

——. (2006). Tupac: Life Goes On. *Black Issues Book Review*. September/October, 14–18.

——. (2007). *Know What I Mean? Reflections on Hip Hop*. New York: Basic Civitas Books.

——. (2010). Intellectuals and their America. *Dissent*. Spring, 41–43.

Fanon, F. (2008). *Black Skin, White Masks*. (R. Philcox, Trans.). New York: Grove Press.

Forman, M. (2000). "Represent": Race, Space and Place in Rap Music. *Popular Music, 19*(1), 65–90.

Lipietz, A. (1997). Warp, Woof and Regulation: A Tool for Social Science. In G. Benko and U. Strohmayer (Eds), *Space and Social Theory: Interpreting Modernity and Postmodernity* (pp. 250–284). Oxford: Blackwell Publishers.

Lupe Fiasco. (2006). Just Might Be OK. *Food and Liquor*. 1st and 15th/Atlantic Records.

Martinez, T. A. (1997). Popular Culture as Oppositional Culture: Rap as Resistance. *Sociological Perspectives, 40*(2), 265–286.

Marx, K. and Engels, F. (1962). *Karl Marx and Frederick Engels: Selected Works.* London: Lawrence and Wishart.

McWhorter. (2008). *All About the Beat: Why Hip-Hop Can't Save Black America.* New York: Gotham Books.

Mercer, K. (1994). *Welcome to the Jungle: New Positions in Black Cultural Studies.* London: Routledge.

Mitchell, B. L., & Feagin, J. R. (1995). America's Racial-Ethnic Cultures: Opposition within a Mythical Melting Pot. In B. Bowser, T. Jones, & G. A. Young (Eds), *Toward the Multiculural University* (pp. 65–86.). Westport, CT: Praeger.

Nas. (2008a). Black President. *Untitled.* Island Def Jam/Columbia Records.

——. (2008b). Hero. *Untitled.* Island Def Jam/Columbia Records.

Professor and Preacher Michael Eric Dyson on Hip Hop & Politics, Don Imus, The "N"-Word, and Bill Cosby. *Democracy Now.* (2007). July 18. Retrieved from http://www.democracynow.org/2007/7/18/professor_and_preacher_michael_eric_dyson.

Nielson, E. (2009). "My President is Black, My Lambo's Blue": The Obamafication of Rap?" *Journal of Popular Music Studies, 21*(4), 344–363.

Richardson, C. (2011). "Can't Tell Me Nothing": Symbolic Violence, Education, and Kanye West. *Popular Music & Society, 34*(2), 97–112.

Rose, T. (1994a). A Style Nobody Can Deal With: Politics, Style and the Postindustrial City in Hip hop. In A. Ross & T. Rose (Eds), *Microphone Fiends* (pp. 71–88). New York: Routledge.

——. (1994b). *Black Noise: Rap Music and Black Culture in Contemporary America.* Hanover, NH: Wesleyan University Press.

——. (2008). *The Hip Hop Wars: What We Talk About When We Talk About Hip Hop – and Why It Matters.* New York: Basic Civitas Books.

Scott, J. C. (1990). *Domination and the Arts of Resistance.* New Haven, CT: Yale University Press.

Stuckey, S. (1987). *Slave Culture.* New York: Oxford University Press.

Thompson, K. M. (2007). *Apocalyptic Dread: American Film at the Turn of the Millennium.* Albandy: SUNY Press.

Webb, J., Schirato, T., & Danaher, G. (2002). *Understanding Bourdieu.* London: Sage Publications.

West, Cornel. (1999). *The Cornel West Reader.* New York: Basic Civitas Books.

——. (2008). *Hope on a Tightrope: Words and Wisdom.* New York: Smiley Books.

Chapter 10

The Mobile Hood: Realness and the Rules of the Game

Thomas R. Britt

One of the foremost virtues of the rap genre is a unique capacity to connect lived experiences with various lyrical inventions and extrapolations. This dual focus on the real and fantasy generates myths and heroes more readily than the kind of storytelling and world building found in other popular music genres. As a result, the narrative and visual flair that exists throughout mainstream rap music is frequently cinematic. One could surmise from countless rappers' back-stories that the desire to escape from a dangerous or difficult physical environment is a significant motivator for this virtual enhancement of actuality. Curiously, however, the means of escape for many rappers involve a label-assisted highlighting of that very harshness of their former hoods. As a narrative form, rap is disproportionately concerned with exposition.

The nexus of a hardened past with a bright promised future leaves story-enhanced rappers in an uncertain present. Their rhymes might be laced with imagined adventures and their videos might be decorated with rented homes, cars, jewelry, and models, but there is a certain everyman – or everywoman – vulnerability to the rapper who is stuck in the daily hustle. The drawback to this reality is that, by and large, the rap industry does not reward the tales of an average person. Its cinematic style demands heroes and villains.

Whereas the record label still determines, in a sense, the worth of the characters on its roster, modern decisions about the value of artists and their work now also fall to Web 2.0 companies and tools. Monetization quandaries surround all forms of digital assets and intellectual property. For rappers, this is another new environment in which to sell their stories. Yet if there was already a kind of socioeconomic limbo that preserved artists between their hood hustle and the promise of major label riches, then this new digital hood adds a third, nonphysical space to the network of intersections that connect real life with fantasy. Musician, author, and computer scientist Jaron Lanier, an expert and quasiprophet of virtual reality, compares the nontactile anonymity of Web 2.0 with the strong personalities of Hip-Hop. In the Frequently Asked Questions section of his website, Lanier (2010) writes:

I wish Web 2.0 was more like Hip Hop. Imagine if you usually didn't get to know who was rapping, or if you could only know a name, but not the person's story? Would that be culture? Hip Hop is about people – some vastly more talented or ethical than others – but the actors are humans with character and history, not information fragments.

In his writing, Lanier often points out the "antihuman quality" of the Internet in its current form, and it is not difficult to trace a similar antihuman impulse within the music industry.

Although Lanier finds a useful point of contrast between rappers and the "information fragments" that stand in as humans on the Internet, it is important to note that artists of every musical genre, and many who contribute to the visual arts and other fields, are threatened with the neutralization of identity that modern technology encourages.

Some rappers lyrically push back against the downturn of their worth. Veteran Ghostface Killah used a couple of his bars on Raekwon's "Cold Outside" to advocate for rappers to "go on strike so we can get more cash." Relative newcomer Young Jeezy has made a couple of albums that directly confront the comparative economies of drug dealing and making music, going so far as to title his 2008 LP *The Recession*. Most fascinating, however, are those rappers who actively combat the surrender of their human, physical identity to the realm of virtual and replaceable commodities. More than any other figure, Compton rapper Game personifies the self-aware, postmodern "real" rapper. In the second half of this chapter, I will examine his radical career trajectory and the way in which he has cannily manipulated the convergence of a social field comprising street, corporate, and digital hoods. Game's music and documentaries, though frequently laced with anarchic humor and unrestrained speech, illustrate what Wacquant (1992) sees as the moral message within Pierre Bourdieu's reflexive sociology: "The more aware [subjects] become of the social within them by reflexively mastering their categories of thought and action, the less likely they are to be actuated by the externality which inhabits them" (Bourdieu & Wacquant, 2002, p. 49). His example provides guideposts for artists hoping to wrest their identities from those who would turn them into negotiable assets in the age of expendability.

Identity and independence

Long before the Internet put the music industry on edge by becoming an unregulated field of play, often speciously compared to the Wild West, slavery and free agency were already convenient but idealized analogies for artists' relationships to industry. Modern debates about net neutrality and the monetization of digital assets carry a veneer of technosophistication and promise that a solution is on its way. An optimist would say that the sheer number of proposals, panels, and models would have to eventually reveal something fair and sustainable for all parties (companies, labels, distributors, songwriters, performers, and consumers). However, historical comparisons to the staking and settling of physical space suggest a more complicated set of consequences. If as immense a cultural force as Manifest Destiny transformed from end to means over time, then claiming the Internet under any fixed terms will likely prove to be a stopgap. Demand for new roads and new rules will likely arise. Artists, the unsettled journeymen, face choices today that seem fresh yet still fall within familiar basic poles: Either play by the establishment's rules or establish one's own game.

The Internet's nonphysical space seems to complicate the choice in the sense that it is in many ways harder to see what lies ahead. However, pop musicians trade in metaphor, and what they have done on record has always been an imaginary statement of actual potential. A heartfelt love song might lead to romance or heartbreak and a hardcore rap beef might lead to supremacy or defeat. These are the risks an artist takes (within the song and beyond the song) in the attempt to claim and navigate spaces both invented and concrete, as well as to establish an identity within those fields:

> By virtue of the fact that he states things with authority, that is, publicly and officially, he saves them from their arbitrary nature, he sanctions them, sanctifies them, consecrates them, making them worthy of existing, in conformity with the nature of things.
>
> (Bourdieu, 1991, p. 222)

These acts of naming and claiming intersect with the ambitions of artists and their propensity to learn and follow rules and/or regularities within a changing commercial environment. Karl Maton (2008) interprets Bourdieu's "habitus" as bringing "together the existence of social regularities with the experience of agency" (p. 55). One possible playing field for the artist could be referred to as a mainstream hood – that field of music distribution which exists in FM radio, VH1 television, or exclusive release at a store like Target. There is also an alternative field that consists of self-distribution and street channels. This is the field of an artist that ignores or antagonizes the major labels and retains control over publishing. Both these fields and the games played on them might be understood in part through the value they place on independence: "Even though a field is profoundly hierarchized, with dominant social agents and institutions having considerable power to determine what happens within it, there is still agency and change" (Thomson, 2008, p. 73). Independence could therefore be understood as a form of capital that shares a relationship and/or has effects on the other "economic ... cultural ... social ... and symbolic" forms of capital therein (p. 69).

Alex Grange (2008), Chief Executive Officer of Pure Play Music, figures the new age of artist independence has already begun. He writes in "A New Era of Monetizing Music: The Artists' Model":

> Cracking the code to online monetization of music, while retaining the artist's publishing rights, seemed as fruitless as the effort to untie the Gordian knot. But the rogue and rebellious spirit of the independent music distributors – a.k.a. the artists – welcomed this paradigm shift. The opportunity finally emerged for artists to chart their own course, and steer the direction of their own careers. It appeared as a breath of fresh air to the talent of the industry.
>
> (p. 1)

Grange describes this opportunity with such optimism – and tellingly, in the past tense as if the new model were already settled and operating successfully – that it is tempting to believe that such independence is available to anyone and everyone. In his vision, Musician X now has the means to carve out a unique space within the digital hood. Yet he uses this heightened language about "artists [tasting] freedom from the shackles of the music industry monoliths" toward the ultimate end of promoting his own online music portal (Pure Play Music), which "shops indie and unsigned artists for commercial play and major label pickup" (Grange, 2008, p. 1). Grange's efforts to support and empower artists might come from the best intentions, but for an artist navigating the new system, he is just another option – another chance for them to take. Therefore, artists hoping to distinguish themselves within this virtual space have a couple of broad options: join its network of supported, collective identities or embrace its equalizing reduction of physical boundaries in pursuit of individual enterprise.

Genre distinction, playing fields, and pathways to the "real"

Putting aside the potential of the Internet to offer allegiance and autonomy, it is worthwhile to investigate the ways in which a couple of current hot genres have reflexively wrestled with these issues. To very broadly define the parallel developments: Rock music has elevated "independence" from a commercial (nonmajor label) status to a stylistic subgenre ("indie rock") that carries a tag of legitimacy. As if bound to a vow of poverty, the indie rockers' punishment for transgression – in many cases, simply the act of being called up to the majors – is to lose that legitimacy as an artist. This is changing slowly, with more "indie" artists licensing their work to high-profile films, television shows, or commercials, but the integrity standards for many fans of such music remain rigid, and as a result, cries of "sellout" lie just around the corner for the enterprising independent. Conversely, hardcore rap, seduced by the major labels' gold rush-like appropriation of East Coast versus West Coast drama in the 1990s, remains proudly capitalist. In rap, the effect of not being on the paper chase is to not be taken seriously as a future business leader/chart topper. Julius Hudson (1977) predicted rappers' prioritization of "the hustling ethic," which combines "an obsessive drive to become wealthy and to display such wealth in an ostentatious manner" with "an extreme sense of contempt and disdain for work, particularly those manual-labor and service jobs traditionally available to lower-class blacks" (p. 415). Generally speaking, independent rock musicians are expected to "keep it real" by accumulating a community-based cultural capital, whereas rappers "keep it real" by building individualized economic capital.

If rock bands get too much press or money in exchange for their antics, then the fans inevitably lash back, and a race for who liked them first becomes a competition for who dumped them earliest. Therefore the middle ground for such artists is to get just enough attention to appear on a tastemaker's radar, but to step back before appearing to care too much about popular opinion or, Heaven forbid, avenues to mainstream success. The rules of realness in rap, on the other hand, come from a completely different matrix of concerns. As the late Proof raps in a D12 song appropriately titled "Rap Game":

> We finally could "Say Goodbye to Hollywood"
> Cause Proof and Shyne man shit nothin' in common
> The nastiest band with gas in each hand
> We never bow down to be a flash in the pan

Proof's verse sets up a stubborn duel between men fully committed to winning the rap game. Later, he articulates the stakes of that game: "So we can battle with raps, we can battle with gats. Matter of fact, we can battle for plaques." By word or by gun, the goal is to produce a profit and stay in the game. These lyrics recall Dr. Dre's own defense of his post-*Chronic* (1992) inactivity in "Forgot about Dre":

> Now all I get is hate mail all day saying, "Dre fell off"
> What, 'cause I been in the lab wit a pen and a pad
> Trying to get this damn label off?
> I ain't having that; this is the millennium of Aftermath
> It ain't going be nothing after that
> So give me one more platinum plaque
> And fuck rap, you can have it back

If as unparalleled a genre innovator as Dr. Dre felt compelled to excuse his stepping back from the spotlight, then any lower-level rapper with his eye on the number one spot would have to also prove his hunger. Distinct playing fields emerge among rock and rap: Whereas to be "real" in indie rock is to prove one's lack of concern for popular standards of success, to be "real" in rap is to prove oneself hardnosed in the pursuit of money and power – to always be gunning for that number one spot.

Perhaps this difference goes some ways toward explaining indie rock tastemakers' fascination with hardcore rap. On some level, the rock field that expects its artists to starve wants to vacation in a rap field that depends on its artists' hunger. While there are some artists – Dizzee Rascal, The Streets, Mos Def, and The Roots, to name a few – who fit more or less comfortably into both rock and rap fields, there are others, such as Lil Wayne and especially the members of the Wu Tang Clan, that seem to occupy an inordinate amount of attention and admiration among suburban middle-class consumers and critics whose life experiences almost certainly fail to intersect with the street narratives that fuel the music. Pitchfork Media, for example, is a publication that covers many rappers in a style that could be described as naked fawning. In a review of Lil Wayne's *Tha Carter III*, Ryan Dombal writes, "Just as the record's cover playfully skews the *Ready to Die/Illmatic* baby-picture formula with Photoshopped tattoos, Wayne updates what it means to be the best rapper alive here. Gangster dandy. Fender-slinging sex god. Intergalactic prankster. It's all in him"(1). In fairness, such subjective, evaluative opinions are what a publication like Pitchfork is expected to provide. Yet too frequently, the impression Pitchfork's rap reviews creates is a desperation to align with the urban and/or ghetto lifestyle, and a compulsory approval that has less to do with the quality of music than an insecure attraction to the lifestyle. Although the digital hood (in which Pitchfork is an esteemed publication) creates the opportunity to express and define oneself in relation to any number of ephemeral styles and trends, cracks begin to appear when that manufactured relationship assumes a connection to an actual urban physical space. Perhaps these writers seek legitimacy through associating with a perceived "realness," the stakes of which are higher than a loss of artistic integrity. One wonders, though, if these critics would want to vacation in the ghetto, "for real"?

Convolution and adaptation

In the past couple of decades, as emerging technologies have opened up a new world of opportunities for exposure and distribution, countless artists have found themselves caught in the maelstrom of harsh commercial realities, social and cultural expectations, and demands of creativity and originality. Especially for hardcore rappers, those necessary assertions of strength, independence, and authenticity have too often relied on the creation of an immutable, undefeatable distance between artist and audience, adherence to a narrow subgenre or geographical space, and/or a disavowal of other forms that ultimately undermined the attempt to self-define. This boxed-in effect is nothing new for rappers, and some degree of constraint is almost always necessary in the beginning stages of one's career. Indeed, the history of rap and hip hop is largely a story of artists seeking conditional or associative distinction as a launching pad for individual stardom. Several worthy volumes have been written on the fascinating development of rap's constituent elements, artistic merits, economic power, and social effects: David Toop's *Rap Attack 3* (1999), Jeff Chang's *Can't Stop Won't Stop: A History of the Hip-Hop Generation* (2005), and Ronin Ro's *Gangsta: Merchandizing the Rhymes of Violence* (1996), among others. For my study it is useful to consider a relationship central to the rap field – the tricky intersection between hood loyalty and individual agency that has generated untold riches for some and damned others to obscurity.

If there is a paramount rule for playing the rap game, it is to be aware of the need for, and power of, convolution. Distinct from duality, convolution should be understood here as it is in the mathematical context: "an integral that expresses the amount of overlap of one function as it is shifted over another function. It therefore 'blends' one function with another" (Weisstein, 2009, p. 1). Marcus Reeves' (2008) extended anecdote about a 1994 press day with a new-to-the-rap-game Biggie Smalls at the Bad Boy Records office perfectly illustrates this process of overlap:

What he's wearing is a T-shirt, shorts, and a pair of Timberland construction boots … the six-foot-three, almost-three-hundred-pound MC continues on into the office, garment bag and box in tow. "Big'll be right out," a publicist informs us. "He's just going to get changed" … And sure 'nuff, forty-five minutes later Big resurfaces looking no longer like a hood fresh off a Brooklyn corner but like a dapper, somewhat sophisticated hustler whose clothes say he's a tad higher on the illegal food chain.

(pp. 177–178)

Reeves asserts, and popular memory maintains, that Puff Daddy and Bad Boy Records had found in Christopher Wallace a rapper with the skills and persona to answer Death Row Records' West Coast "realness." Wallace, a former drug dealer, could transform from "hood" to "sophisticated hustler" in a way that preserved both modes. This blending of functions within the individual was part of a greater blending of functions within a re-emergent East Coast rap identity. If a figure like Puffy could construct an answer to the West Coast and its legendary street credibility (secured once and for all by N.W.A. and its acolytes), then part of that design was to cast *from* the street and to highlight the hustle. Yet even as Puffy was elevating images within black popular culture to something increasingly sophisticated and dapper, he was – more actively than those rock critics who now vacation in the Lil Wayne narratives – slumming in a territory where risks remained dire and real. Worse was Puffy's (and other label bosses') willingness to expose stars to those risks through "a cynical exploitation of conflicts running deep under life that much, though not all, hip hop purports to document" (Toop, 2000, p. xiii).

In the figure of Tupac Shakur, whose star moved from East to West over the course of his career, there was already a cautionary tale developing that should have given Puff Daddy pause. Returning a final time to Reeves: "the blurring of Tupac's art with his reality … what he rapped about was becoming his life, and … his turbulent life was feeding the authenticity of his music. The music and the mayhem served Tupac's wish to be perceived as a supreme outlaw" (p. 165). Eventually, all of these factors contributed to the tragic deaths of both Tupac and Biggie. After a series of escalating altercations, in real life and on wax, each man came to define his chosen hood to such a degree that he could not escape it alive.

Although the substance of the East Coast versus West Coast feud has probably been overstated, providing as it does a convenient frame for the battle (as if applying such a narrative device could make sense of the senseless events), some responsibility should fall to record labels that branded and pushed the dispute. Very wealthy men, who had no practical reason to live by the desperate rules of the streets, were still doing so. In part, the drive of desperation had become part of the "realness" capital. This is also an insight into the role of habitus within the rap game: "Ways of adapting to difficult conditions may outlive those conditions, such that social groups may continue to act as if poverty stricken even after escaping poverty" (Crossley, 2008, p. 94). One could argue that the message this sent the consumer was directly counter to the legitimate success tales of young men like Biggie who had escaped the drug game. Death Row and Bad Boy would have aspiring rappers believe that the drug game was the true route to the rap game, and in turn the rappers' habitus resulted in a reproduction of the drug game's disposition. Although specific causes and perpetrators for the deaths of Biggie and Tupac have never been identified, the corporate culture that created and supported their star trajectories likewise incited their paths toward violent death.

These deaths, still the two highest-profile reminders of rap beef's real consequences, resulted in the elevation of both men to hero status beyond any living rappers. They moved from the street to the club to the stuff of myth, as merchandising continues and recordings are relentlessly remixed, repackaged, and resold. Such exploitation is nothing new, as evidenced by the continuing economic capital of the deceased Elvis and Michael Jackson. Though the uniquely disturbing aspect of the cardboard cutout versions of Tupac and Biggie that popular culture has preserved in time is that they are victims of a system that convinced these two otherwise shrewd businessmen that they could indeed "take it with them" to the grave.

If the story stopped at this point, then there would be little hope of finding redeeming qualities within the rap game. After all, social transcendence is unlikely when a high-stakes economic force like major label rap subsumes and distorts codes and conditions of individual experience. In short, the game of rap is riddled with traps. Those who compare a career in major label rap to slavery, express some approval of rappers' symbolic capital despite their limited agency. Scott Wilson (2008) asserts that, "Images of the freed African slave make a profit because they resonate throughout the years with the promise of liberation from the order of production that haunts the slavish consciousness of the white American *homo economicus*" (p. 70).

Yet Wilson does not deny that similar orders of production continue to bind the rap game's players: "This unbinding from the order of production is prohibited by the universal homogeneous state that constrains the 'last man' to an animal existence of pure consumption" (p. 70). Few industries advocate for the 'last man' as openly as hardcore rap, which, as previously described, thrives off of a culture of contention, battle, and beef. What distinguishes the rap game's "last man" from Friedrich Nietzsche's apathetic "last man," however, is that persistent desire for distinction and supremacy within a hierarchized order. As part of the October 1999 international symposium "Slave Routes: The Long Memory," professor Tricia Rose addressed the slavery/industry connection by defining slavery as "the control and exchange of black bodies in a capitalist system," before going on to say that "now, the physical domination isn't as obviously severe. We are free, we are full citizens, but the psychological as well as the economic domination seems to still be of concern" (quoted In Meadows-Ingram, 1999, p. 1). Even as they disavow the notion of modern rap as a new form of slavery, Wilson and Rose both find outgrowths of slavery within the socioeconomic field of corporate rap.

Emergence of a new game

Game (née Jayceon Terrell Taylor) is a figure that embodies the best-case scenario for rap's 'freed man.' Game developed a unique brand of "realness" that acknowledges the hood as both an evolving mobile entity and as a space for multiple temperaments. Through his ability to take his uniquely interpreted hood wherever he pleases, as well as the specificity with which he deconstructs the industry before consumers' ears and eyes, Game seems to solve the conundrum of convolution that plagued Biggie and Tupac.

While it was clear from almost the very beginning that Taylor wanted to *be* Game rather than learn the rules of the rap game, his method of navigating the system and eventual success owes much to the players that came before him. Wilson's (2008) explanation of soldiers and warriors could be used here to describe what sets Game apart: "Warriors (rather than mere soldiers, the equivalent of the industrial workforce) bear no allegiance to anyone other than themselves and their own code of honor" (p. 35). Even prior to the release of his first album, it is possible to spot evidence of that warrior spirit within Game.

As rap's free man, Game is keenly aware of "social performatives, ritualized and sedimented through time, that are central to the very process of self-formation as well as the embodied, participatory *habitus*" (Butler, 1999, p. 120). Game constructs his claims of independence with several illustrative measures of "realness" that feature his bona fide street virtues while self-reflexively exposing the commercial context and consequences of that character. With the documentary *Stop Snitchin' Stop Lyin'* (2006) and on mixtape tracks such as "300 Bars N Runnin'" he has emerged as one of the rap game's most intriguing characters by devoting attention to both the actual and the constructed, as well as shrewdly vacillating between the two. Doing so has allowed him to resolve the contradiction of a corporate cog operating at street level.

At the beginning of his career, however, Game was captive to a major label that tightly controlled his persona, and to review that label's domination is to observe a young man being presented with manufactured "realness" that clearly does not conform to his spirit. *The Game: The Documentary* DVD (2005) reached audiences courtesy of Aftermath, G-Unit, and Interscope, among other companies. In a large typeset on the back of the DVD case, credits shout "Executive Producers: Dr. Dre & 50 Cent." The effect of all of these visible brands on the package and throughout the DVD is to offer up Game as the newest product of an industry that has the power to create and shape cultural tastes, as well as to testify to sociopolitical "realities" that the content reflects. Yet the crude force of the entire work undermines the stated documentary reality of the program on the disk (a long form video that promotes a companion debut album, also called *The Documentary*), and in doing so, throws the integrity of all involved parties into question.

Game is presented to the viewer as a nihilistic gangster, a Blood son of a Crip mamma, who has shot and been shot at, learned how to hustle at a young age, and lives in a hood constantly under the threat of violence. The location of this portrait could be called rap's Everyhood, as its signifiers are so predictable and bereft of power when considered within the parameters of Bourdieu's reflexive sociology. The film proceeds with a fetishistic focus on certain images and concepts, such as the intersection of Brazil St. and Wilmington Ave., the NWA/Compton credentials, and the visual thrill of sneering young men. Clearly, the filmmakers are under the impression that they are reinforcing an image of Game's hood that links the rapper to a long history of similar gangsters-turned-rappers who have captured the imaginations of tens of millions of listeners. The aesthetic reasoning of the film seems to go something like this: If these images of the Game's hood are the stuff of those legends' hoods, then simply placing Game in the same environment and letting him stew will make him credible. In doing so, the film is unconcerned with its central character's habitus.

Try as it might to be a generic, legacy-fueled product, *The Game: The Documentary* ultimately fails at its own game. Yes, the signifiers of street culture are in place, but as Bourdieu (1990) writes, "the objects of the social world ... can be perceived and expressed in different ways ... even combinations of the most constant properties ... are submitted to variations in time so that their meaning, in so far as they depend on the future, is itself held in suspense and relatively indeterminate" (p. 133). Hence, Game's levity and humor occasionally emerge from the film's passively presented objects of the hood. The presence of these qualities predicts a much more significant display in later releases. In scenes with Busta Rhymes, Game cannot hold back his enthusiastic expression. It is clearly a thrill for him to be meeting and recording with one of rap's icons. But the strictures of an Aftermath, G-Unit, and Interscope co-production demand that he spend most of his time grimacing. This is unfortunate, since Game's supercapitalist warrior persona would later prove to be an infinitely more interesting character.

Also, the physical environment said to be so dangerous and tragic does not seem threatening. Large groups of Bloods and Crips feel comfortable enough to assemble in front of cameras and sound recorders in order to join the rising rap superstar as he hosts a travelogue of their mean streets. In one interview shot, a family with a child strolls in the background as Game discusses the unwelcoming environment, and the camera cuts away before the pleasant family becomes so visible that it destroys the hostile impression the film tries to create.

Perhaps most telling is a sequence in which Game and his friends recreate a classic NWA photo shoot with none other than Dr. Dre. As with the Busta Rhymes scenes, Game has every reason to be thrilled to be in the presence of an icon, but instead of pursuing that positive feeling, the film captures Dr. Dre, Game, and Game's posse putting on "serious" expressions for the cameras. The stagecraft of this whole sequence makes Compton seem like Gangster Fantasy Camp. Even the occasional appeals to emotion – the death and funeral of William C. Lusk, Jr. aka Billboard aka 4 Cent and shots of Game with his baby son – are shot in a way that tries to capture the melodramatic strains of John Singleton's *Boyz N the Hood* (1991) (see De Waard, Chapter 11), but their dissonance with the unconvincing nihilistic stance that runs through the rest of the film renders such moments ineffective.

The DVD's most substantial clue about Game's already-burgeoning transition away from the G-Unit crew is the way in which Game subverts his own music videos. Two videos appear as special features on the DVD, and both of them are for songs that feature 50 Cent, the G-Unit leader and an important figure in Game's career. In the video for "How We Do," Game wears an unconvincing snarl and looks none too happy to have made it to the top. In the clip for "Hate it or Love It," directed by the Saline Project, Game provides sly glances towards the camera during the lines, "Envy me, I'm rap's MVP, and I ain't going nowhere so you can get to know me." His unique engagement with the camera/spectator in this moment invites us to pay closer attention to a related element of the video, which is the way in which he and 50 Cent share the physical space on the screen. Although they effortlessly trade lines on the song, creating a propulsive contrast of their voices, no one would mistake the relationship reflected in the video as an easy friendship. This tension adds another degree of meaning for Game's lines in the chorus – if he truly is rap's MVP, then where does that leave 50?

The mobile hood

These small revelatory moments of *The Game: The Documentary*, during which the rapper asserts his ambition and independence, paved the way for Game's unprecedented level of hood mobility in the year following his debut album's release. *The Documentary* CD arrived in January 2005 with classic Dr. Dre/West Coast production style, a bevy of recognizable guest contributors, and (in Game) an exciting new label-styled gangsta emcee. *The Documentary* DVD followed in May 2005. But the intervening months had seen fissures and disagreements within the G-Unit crew develop into a beef with massive potential – namely, a mutinous Game vs. everyone who remained. Most significantly, a February 2005 incident outside of Hot 97, during which an offended Game attempted to confront 50 Cent for dismissing him on air, resulted in one of Game's friends being shot and 50 Cent fleeing the building. With that catalytic event still fresh, June 2005 would prove to be the point of no return in the now-legendary beef, as Game publicly renounced 50 Cent and G-Unit at Hot 97's Summer Jam and dropped the *You Know What it Is, vol. 3* mixtape.

As a mixtape, *You Know What it Is, vol. 3* both continues an underground tradition of releasing exclusive material on the street level, as well as textually asserts Game's problems with 50 Cent and G-Unit. "300 Bars N Runnin" has become the standout track of the album. Influenced in part by "100 Miles and Runnin," the 1990 NWA release that signaled that group's beef with estranged member Ice Cube, "300 Bars N Runnin" shifts to the perspective of the defector rather than of the abandoned crew. Revealing Game's keen sense of hip-hop history, the track also reworks samples from classic songs from other hip-hop/rap forerunners. That active historical foundation supports Game's intense contribution to the track: a diss that runs 300 bars spanning nearly fifteen minutes.

Though the whole of the mixtape is concerned with taking down 50 Cent and G-Unit members Tony Yayo, Lloyd Banks, and Olivia, "300 Bars N Runnin" synthesizes within one song everything else that is expressed on the album, and is therefore the anthem of the G-Unot movement. Ever adept at clever wordplay, Game's Hot 97 set had introduced the "G-Unot" phrase to the audience in an attempt to de-legitimize and disarm 50 Cent's gangsta credibility. Game, by this point no stranger to the impact of branding, used the phrase to deny the "realness" of the Gangster Unit/Guerrilla Unit.

In addition to the audacity of going fully rogue after only a few months since his G-Unit sponsored debut, as well as the sheer spectacle of an unprecedented epic length diss, perhaps the most striking aspect of "300 Bars N Runnin" is the fearlessness with which Game attacks his opponents on any number of levels that have arguably proved dangerous or even deadly for other rappers in the past. Conflating separate commentaries on street codes, masculinity, industry, and mortality, Game disputes 50 Cent's gangsta credentials, minimizes 50's contributions to songs from *The Documentary*, accuses 50 of collaborating with the police, questions G-Unit rappers' sexuality (and in Olivia's case, her gender), and threatens to kill a number of people. This lyrical assassination of 50, while violent and off-putting, is not without creative verve:

> I kill a gorilla quick
> beating on your chest, I see to your death, yep
> Tell Ecko to make him a suit
> Tell Reebok to make him some boots
> get him a headband to cover the holes in his head
> He a dead man …

Calling out a code name for 50 Cent (gorilla), Game uses the threat of violence to comment on what he perceives as the rapper's greed, elsewhere questioning "Who's this fake … on pictures with the Jake … Got his crew starving cause he ate the whole cake." Because 50 Cent appeared to profit from a G-Unit clothing line and G-Unit shoes, yet did not share that money with his crew, Game imagines an ironic scenario wherein 50's own funeral will be decorated by the brands of his corporate manufacturer collaborators. This criticism, borne from Game's desire for free agency, calls attention to how 50 is conversely not a free man. The cumulative message of "300 Bars N Runnin" is that 50's allegiance to the cops and to commerce restricts him to being, at best, someone else's soldier. By extension, the rest of the G-Unit crew under 50 is even less respectable – Game uses the phrase "G-Unit toy soldier." In contrast, Game gains independence through the illocutionary act of the song itself and becomes a sort of self-reliant fearless warrior who (in his mind) will rise to the levels of legends:

> Feel me? If not then I guess you gotta kill me
> But you ain't going do that so motherfucker move back
> while I do B.I.G. and Pac impersonations on two tracks […]
> If Eazy ever decides to return, I remain Jayceon
> a king in the making, and the throne is for the taking.
> So I climb the mountaintop and put my stake in.

Externalizing the social within

The final stage of Game's lightning fast movement from protégé to master arrived just short of one year after his debut album was released. The *Stop Snitchin', Stop Lyin'* DVD presents an entirely different version of the gangsta/rapper who appeared in *The Game: The Documentary* DVD, as well as a radically different view of the various hoods he moves through. Unlike the first DVD, which basked perversely in the hopelessness of a stereotypical Compton experience, *Stop Snitchin', Stop Lyin'* actively "distinguish[es] zones of necessity and of freedom" (Bourdieu & Wacquant, 1992, p. 49). Although the physical spaces Game traverses within the documentary are diverse (from Beverly Hills to Harlem to Times Square to the Bronx to Farmington, Connecticut), it is his internal, mobile hood – "the social within" – that unifies the documented events and experiences.

Game's renunciation of the corporate rap game is evident in sequences such as the tour of his apartment – an undecorated, largely unfurnished space – that he says is "nothing like" MTV Cribs, but rather "Hood Cribs." His closet floor is covered with clothes. Magazine covers and hit record plaques demonstrating his hot career lean in stacks against the wall instead of being on full display. At one point, Game picks up a bulletproof vest that carries the logo of his company, Black Wall Street. If he has consciously calculated this scene to create the appearance of rebelling against the culture of MTV Cribs, then even that pose is an act of upheaval within an industry where appearance often creates reality. His entertaining move is to steal the posturing power from his opponents (most squarely targeting G-Unit and 50 Cent) by frankly confronting the issue of multiplicity and positioning himself as the champion of that particular performative game. Game embraces "regularities which have as part of their essence a certain amount of variability, plasticity, indetermination, and imply all sorts of adaptations, innovations and exceptions" (Bouveresse, 1999, p. 62). Throughout *Stop Snitchin', Stop Lyin'*, Game directly addresses the camera and spectator, providing inside information about the players in the greater rap game. Nearly everything he shows us within this travelogue approach is designed to deftly exploit the business that would exploit him, and to assert his dominance as a free agent. Within the same sequence, he pledges his allegiance to both Beverly Hills and Compton – an honest sentiment from an upwardly mobile artist unconcerned with the limiting disposition of "keeping it real."

Mostly rejecting the Interscope gangsta archetype that appeared in *The Game: The Documentary, Stop Snitchin', Stop Lyin'* much more convincingly (and compellingly) documents Game's attempts to blaze his own path. There are short selections from a night exterior interview, in which Game is dressed in black and wearing a vitriolic expression. This interview stands at odds with the rest of the footage. Only here does the spectator identify any semblance of that other, grimmer character. The inclusion of this interview is puzzling, but ultimately motivated by the functional contrast it provides to the otherwise more authentic journey being documented. A humorless version of Game, even in small doses, reminds the viewer of how confining the major label hood can be.

Freed and mobile, Game is still a man of means, and the independent Black Wall Street logo appears on a fleet of expensive cars, repurposing these signifiers of the corporate ghetto fabulousness into a testament to self-determination. In an extended interview that makes up a large percentage of the total running time, a dressed-in-Blood-red Game sits by a window and extemporaneously narrates the story of his career. Within this interview, he talks openly about playing the major label system for "free promotion:"

> A lot of people think I got kicked out, but I quit before I was even inducted. The whole "Game being part of G-Unit" was a marketing tool that was coincided by myself, 50 Cent, Dr. Dre, Jimmy Iovine, and my management.

Lest the spectator think that Game is just an upstart radically biting the hand that fed him, he seems genuinely more invested in both the art and commerce as an independent artist than he did when he was at the mercy of all of those potential bosses outlined in the above quotation. Instead of reporting up to someone or even delegating responsibilities to those below, Game of *Stop Snitchin', Stop Lyin'* takes matters into his own hands. His simultaneous musical output also supports this impression, as Game continues to release multiple mixtapes, one of which (the *Ghost Unit Mixtape*) plays a key role in one of *Stop Snitchin', Stop Lyin's* most effective scenes. In another room of the sparse apartment, Game stands above stacks of envelopes and explains that he encouraged fans to purchase *The Documentary* CD for a second time in order to upset Tony Yayo's CD release sales, and then to mail that "re-copped" CD to Game. Fans' reward for their efforts would be a signed copy of the *Ghost Unit Mixtape* that Game would put in the CD case and return to them. This is no hype mechanism either: Cameras capture Game reading fan letters, signing disks, and preparing packages to mail back to fans. Such a scheme might seem like a waste of time to label heads and their hungry hustlers, but it is perfectly in keeping with Game's desire to navigate the system creatively and independently. The benefits of the scheme are quite utilitarian: Tony Yayo still sells some disks, Interscope and Aftermath see a rise in sales of *The Documentary,* and Game fans receive a personalized copy of his new music, which in turn promotes him on the street.

Game's relationship to his fans is evident not only in his envelope-stuffing idea, but in the often rousing street footage shot during his travels. One young male New York fan simply states, "50 wack. I stay reppin' Game. That's what's good. We need to leave that in the hood." That spontaneous lyricism explains the reactions we see elsewhere. A female fan in the same segment says, "What I like about the Game is, he says what's real." Her statement is itself an assessment of Game's multiplicity/supremacy: Not only do his rhymes reflect the real, but also his authority is capable of determining the real. That is the kind of continuum of perception that no amount of high-profile contracted rappers could generate for 50 Cent, who by contrast appears less real as a result of physically steering clear of the fans' hood. In fact, even as "300 Bars N Runnin" "solidified" the end of G-Unit, to use Game's phrase, 50 Cent was casting again from the street in order to re-up his credibility. This time, his reach extended to legendary street crews like Mobb Deep and M.O.P., but the diminishing G-Unit image backfired. Game – by now all too aware of the perils of wearing a brand one doesn't support ideologically – claims that Mobb Deep's reported G-Unit tattoos (a corporeal branding) "soured whatever street credibility they had left."

By contrast, Game spends much of *Stop Snitchin', Stop Lyin'* amongst fans, enjoying their company rather than trying to foist a created "reality" on them. Across boroughs, Game is greeted and celebrated with the watchword he publicly inaugurated at the infamous Summer Jam: "G-G-G-G-G-G-G-U NOT"! Fans' rhetorical takedown of G-Unit, including the introductory stutter 50 used to promote his group, is a sign that the competition is over. Murals and T-shirts with the slogan are on the market, independently of Game's sanction. The enthusiasm of the public is clear throughout the film's street scenes, but never is it more euphoric than when a parade forms around Game in the Bronx. His expression, echoing and expanding that earlier telling moment with Busta Rhymes, is that of a man who has now become a popular culture icon.

As the rapper joins a game of basketball and the crowd continues to grow, one young man sums up the moment thus: "You don't see 50 coming to the hood." The implication of this footage is that Game, not 50, has succeeded in winning the territory of "the streets," defined by Cheryl Keyes (2002) as "a subculture of the urban milieu that operates by its own rules, economics, lifestyle, language, and aesthetics" (p. 6). Despite acquiring the sorts of capital that allow him to practically leave "the streets" behind, Game constructs his realness by embracing adaptability and linking his habitus to each of those components. The adaptable, mobile hood within allows him to "really" return.

Beyond the law

The last characteristic of Game that suggests his mastery of the mobile hood is the way in which he relates to the law. He reserves his harshest condemnation, on wax and on video, for 50 Cent's role in snitching on Kenneth "Supreme" McGriff and Murder Inc.'s Irv Gotti. As this topic is obviously a key concern in a documentary called *Stop Snitchin', Stop Lyin'*, the film illustrates this section singularly, superimposing text from affidavits and "NYPD Documents." Although Game's beef with 50 Cent and G-Unit is a scattershot collection of personal and professional disagreements, the snitching issue – a rare unifier of street, corporate, and digital hoods – runs deep, and its consequences are universally known. Most street codes frown on snitching, because it necessarily involves collaborating with the law, and for many people it is both easier and morally preferable to look the other way rather than jeopardizing one's own community by joining forces with those who have the power to police the hood. So while Game (and the spectator) can have a good-natured laugh at a beef with Tony Yayo over being too old to rap and lying about his incarceration, the real stakes of the snitch debate are much more complicated and serious. The impact of Supreme's life sentence is not lost on Game, who marvels at 50's conscience (or lack thereof) about having any role in putting Supreme away "forever. Forever-ever?"

Yet 50's status as a law enforcement collaborator further denudes his credibility, and Game definitely relishes the chance to tell the spectator about 50 holding meetings at the Federal Building. According to Game, 50 gained (in exchange for collaboration) "three feds to walk around with for free." This allegation completes Curtis Jackson's movement from "50 Cent," king of a self-styled street crew, to "5-0," the protected center of a gaggle of federal agents. Although Game comically warns the audience not to jump 50 because the feds will "kill your ass," he does set up a possible conflict with 50 Cent strictly for the benefit of the cameras. Throughout the travelogue, Game has mentioned that he's searching for 50 Cent. Yet at every step, he's also careful to point out the "hip-hop cops" who stay on his trail. The search for a snitch is juxtaposed with scenes of peaceful co-existence with the law. Game's non-collaborative relationship with the law is not antagonistic, and the stakes of that relationship are far less than they would be if he had become entwined with the law as closely as 50 Cent has. This even-handedness is important to Game's own independent code, which allows him to interact with cops and lose none of his hood credibility. In fact, Game greets the cops who tail him at airports, the streets of New York, and at convenience stores. Offering them donuts and coffee, Game plays with the police officer of mainstream popular imagination rather than the "ghetto bird" police helicopters that keep a watchful eye on citizens of Compton or the brutal cop portrayed so often in rap culture.

When *Stop Snitchin', Stop Lyin'* approaches its promised climax – a showdown with 50 Cent – Game says goodbye to the friendly hip-hop cops. Technically, Game and the Black Wall Street crew outrun the cops by crossing into Connecticut and out of jurisdiction. Yet the transparency, humor, and independence of Game in the preceding footage reflect libertarian ethics rather than a commitment to lawlessness. Freed from his major label persona, Game would not likely risk fulfilling that nihilistic image by trying to actually murder 50 Cent – and he does no such thing. In fact, the conclusion to *Stop Snitchin', Stop Lyin'* is (apart from the impromptu parade in the Bronx) the film's most celebratory sequence. Game, his friends, and the camera document the Xanadu-like mansion that 50 Cent's business sense and police protection have wrought. The doors are barely visible from the street, and the surrounding gates are impenetrable. So instead of knocking on 50's door to give him a pair of sneakers from Game's Hurricane brand, they throw the shoes over a power line, bringing a little of the hood to Farmington. Before the visit is over, the guys steal 50's basketball rim, taunt the guard at the gatehouse, and spray-paint G-Unot graffiti on surrounding street signs. There's no real danger in any of this, and the closing gunshot sound effect punctuates their playful visit but also works against the nonviolent game they play.

Aftermath

In late 2009, 50 Cent promoted his album – the now Gold-certified *Before I Self Destruct* – to ABC News' *Nightline* from the lonely confines of Mike Tyson's former mansion in Farmington, Connecticut. Meanwhile, Game had experienced the lasting effects of multiple beefs and some scrapes with the law. The North Carolina cops who appeared briefly in *Stop Snitchin', Stop Lyin'*s single contentious police scene lost their case against Game, whom they had accused of illegally documenting the moment they arrested him for causing a disturbance at a mall (footage mostly relegated to a DVD special feature). *The R.E.D. Album*, Game's latest Interscope release, suffered through years of delays, and his beef with 50 Cent continued on-again, off-again, with recent apologies and recantations in flux.

Despite their diss war, both men are still alive, and both are still pushing product. 50 Cent's combined music and Vitamin Water fortunes assure that he never has to participate in the music game ever again, and while his 2009 album title hinted at a farewell, he too has new music on the horizon. Although Game hasn't maintained the visibility of his 2005–2006 glory days, he has bounced back with a vengeance in 2011, both as a rapper (with lauded mixtape *Purp & Patron*) and as a powerful figure in South Central's Drew League basketball circuit. Game and 50 are now being paid to act in films. Hoods are converging so quickly and confusingly that players will be forgiven for false moves. Especially in the digital hood, seemingly no one knows anything, and multiple rappers' presences in peripheral markets create an opening for both great innovation and gross misstep. The rules of the rap field continue to change.

The value of Game's vanquishing of 50 Cent in the middle of the decade does not diminish if Game falls off with future releases or if 50 someday recaptures hood credibility. Instead, the lesson of that struggle for artistic, commercial and street supremacy is that independence and cross-cultural fluidity have the potential to emerge victorious – to successfully buck the expectations and demands of partisanship by pressuring crews. Game showed that the habitus and knowledge of oneself ("hood within") is the foremost position from which all other relationships ("hoods without") could flow. His self-reflexive documentation of the embodiment of that character was a sort of rap game epistemological experiment that upended many of the collective codes through which other rappers have avoided a firm statement of self. If more high-profile artists possessed the opportunity and self-determination to rebuff the manufactured "reality" and instead explore a dynamic space borne from boundless self-awareness, then performativity itself – "this is how we do" – would become more accepted as a pathway to the real. Each contender for rap's "last man" status could instead become a free man.

References

Bourdieu, P. (1990). *In Other Words: Essays Towards a Reflexive Sociology*. Stanford: Stanford University Press.

Bourdieu, P. (1991). *Language & Symbolic Power*. Cambridge: Harvard University Press.

Bourdieu, P., & Wacquant, J. D. (1992). *An Invitation to Reflexive Sociology*. Chicago: University of Chicago Press.

Bouveresse, J. (1999). Rules, Dispositions, and the *Habitus*. In R. Shusterman (Ed.), *Bourdieu: A Critical Reader* (pp. 45–63). Malden: Blackwell.

Bradford, M., Mathers, M., & Young, A. (1999). Forgot About Dre. [Recorded by Dr. Dre]. On *2001* [CD]. Santa Monica: Aftermath.

Butler, J. (1999). Performativity's Social Magic. In R. Shusterman (Ed.), *Bourdieu: A Critical Reader* (pp. 113–128). Malden: Blackwell.

Carlisle, V., Holton, D., Johnson, R., Mathers, M., Moor, O., Porter, D., & Resto, L. (2002). Rap Game. [Recorded by D12]. On *8 Mile* [CD]. Santa Monica: Interscope.

Chang, J. (2005). *Can't Stop Won't Stop: A History of the Hip-Hop Generation.* New York: St. Martin's Press.

Dombal, R. (2008). Lil Wayne: Tha Carter III. *Pitchfork Media.* Retrieved from http://pitchfork.com/reviews/albums/11608-tha-carter-iii/

Grange, A. (2008). A New Era of Monetizing Music: The Artists' Model. *Indie-Music.com.* Retrieved from http://www.indie-music.com/modules.php?name=News&file=article&sid=7773

Hudson, J. (1977). The Hustling Ethic. In T. Kochman (Ed.), *Rappin' and Stylin' Out.* (pp. 410–424). Chicago: University of Illinois Press.

Jackson, C., Lyon, A., Taylor, J., & Valenzano, M. (2005). Hate It or Love It. [Recorded by Game featuring 50 Cent]. On *The Documentary* [CD]. Santa Monica: Aftermath/G-Unit/Interscope.

Johnson, D.(Producer & Director). (2005). *The Game: The Documentary* [DVD]. United States: Aftermath.

Keyes, C. (2002). *Rap Music and Street Consciousness.* Chicago: University of Illinois Press.

Kimbrew, M. & Skee, D. J. (Producers), & Thedford, E. (Director). (2006). *Stop Snitchin', Stop Lyin'* [DVD]. United States: Bungalo Records.

Maton, K. (2008). Habitus. In M. Grenfell (Ed.), *Pierre Bourdieu: Key Concepts.* (pp. 49–65). Stocksfield: Acumen.

Meadows-Ingram, B. (1999). *Rappers Rock a Different Chain: Hip-Hop and Slavery in the 1990s.* Retrieved from http://journalism.nyu.edu/pubzone/slave_routes/7_rap.htm

Reeves, M. (2008). *Somebody Scream! Rap Music's Rise to Prominence in the Aftershock of Black Power.* New York: Faber and Faber.

Ro, R. (1996). *Gangsta: Merchandizing the Rhymes of Violence.* New York: St. Martin's Press.

Taylor, J. (2005). 300 Bars N Runnin. [Recorded by Game]. On *You Know What it Is, vol. 3* [CD]. United States: Black Wall Street Records.

Thomson, P. (2008). Field. In M. Grenfell (Ed.), *Pierre Bourdieu: Key Concepts.* (pp. 67–81). Stocksfield: Acumen.

Toop, D. (2000) *Rap Attack 3.* London: Serpent's Tail.

Weisstein, E. W. Convolution. (2009). MathWorld – A Wolfram Web Resource. Retrieved from http://mathworld.wolfram.com/Convolution.html

Wilson, S. (2008). *Great Satan's Rage: American Negativity and Rap/Metal in the Age of Supercapitalism.* New York: Manchester University Press.

Chapter 11

Hip Hop's Cultural Relevancy in the Hood: Examining the "Subversive" in Urban School Curricula

Katie Sciurba

The irrefutable public education crisis in the United States, particularly in urban areas, has left educators grappling with any and all possibilities for reaching students who face the greatest risk of academic failure. As funds dwindle further below their insufficient levels, school dropout and community unemployment rates escalate, and poverty, crime, and violence continue to be standard elements of city life, urban schools are struggling more than ever to keep students interested in their education and to provide them with equal opportunities to thrive amongst their peers. Given the difficulties endemic to urban spaces, urban schools are not even expected to be successful in their attempts. As Noguera (1999) writes, urban schools are "the backwater of public education, and their continued failure blends in easily with the panorama of pathologies afflicting the inner-city and its residents." In an effort to reconfigure the landscape of urban neighborhood education, educators have infused curricula with what they perceive as a transformative, resistant, capital-producing aspect of urban students' sociopolitical environment – hip hop.

Arguments for incorporating hip hop into school curricula center on the notion that students, especially "urban" or "disenfranchised" students, will identify with the "youth cultural interest" (Morell, 2004) material that is taught and, consequently, become more deeply invested in their educations (Au, 2005; Duncan-Andrade, 2004; Morrell, 2004). Though youth "interest" can encompass a variety of music, art, film, sports, and other recreation or entertainment activities, hip-hop music has come to dominate educators' and scholars' understandings of what it means to identify with urban youth culture. Because most young people – particularly, young people of color – are presumably consumed with hip hop, the art form is seen as a means of bridging the gap between their outside-of-school and inside-of-school lives (Dimitriadis, 2009; Morell & Duncan-Andrade, 2002; Stovall, 2006). As such, Hip-Hop-Based Education (HHBE), as Hill (2009) terms it, has emerged as a means of making learning "relevant" to urban students, especially black youth who would otherwise feel disconnected from school spaces. This type of instruction falls under the "culturally responsive" (Ladson-Billings, 1994) or "multicultural" (Cortés, 1995) umbrella, by which teachers are encouraged to tap into children's cultures – in this case, their *popular* culture – in order to better meet their educational needs.

"Culture" is a complex term, broadly defined as falling under one of "three inflections": "intellectual, spiritual, and aesthetic development; the way of life of a people, group, or humanity in general; and the works and practices of intellectual and artistic activity (music, literature, painting, theater, and film, among many others)" (Yúdice, 2007, p. 71). In other words, it is an action, something to be *performed* or *enacted* (Heath, Street & Mills,

2008). Within HHBE discourse, youth "culture" is limited narrowly to all that is hip hop, irrespective of students' own relationships to or performances of the art. The urban spaces or "'hoods" they occupy, popularly pathologized as "battle grounds," "war zones," and "jungles", are considered to be realistically depicted in hip-hop music (Ginwright, 2004, p. 29). Hip hop, therefore, becomes a mechanism through which youth can resist "complex systems of control and containment," providing them with a reappropriated sense of "identity" (p. 30). Although hip-hop culture has conveyed a multitude of meanings to its audiences since the 1980s and is presently "in a terrible crisis," according to Rose (2008, p.1), HHBE advocates almost unanimously speak of its "subversive" or counter-hegemonic nature. For instance, in drawing upon Gramsci's concept of hegemony, Morrell (2004) argues that popular culture (understood as hip hop) is a "terrain of ideological struggle between dominant and subordinate classes, or dominant and subordinate cultures" (p. 32). Therefore, hip hop's inclusion in urban classroom settings, where educators are more likely to find "subordinate cultures," is thought to have empowering effects. However, this gravitation toward the subversive may be more closely rooted in educators' "nostalgia" than related to our students' responses (Jenkin, 2007).

While sample lessons (Cooks, 2004; Morrell & Duncan-Andrade, 2002), student perspectives (Dimitriadis, 2009; Duncan-Andrade, 2004; Hill, 2009; Stovall, 2006), and select hip-hop lyrics (considered the "voices of the authors of rap music," Au, 2005) have been examined with respect to education, as well as mis-education, what has not been considered is the degree to which hip hop is resistant and may, in fact, transform once it is utilized in or designed for a classroom context. Though Murray (2004) and Dimitriadis (2009) caution against the overly celebratory stance some HHBE advocates take, scholars have not ventured much into the disconnect between educator and youth perspectives on the appeal of hip hop. Love (2010), like Stovall (2006), revealed that students are not always cognizant of the *meanings* of the hip-hop songs they enjoy; rather, they are drawn to the melodies or the beats. This data suggests that we, as educators, may be misguided in our understandings of hip hop as a form of social critique, resistance, or subversiveness, at least with regard to how the art form is considered "relevant" among urban youth.

Instead of performing the roles of revolutionaries, using their art to upset inequitable systems of hierarchy and power, hip-hop artists frequently portray themselves first and foremost, if not exclusively, as "entertainers" who want to sell albums and reap the benefits of capitalism. In relying upon celebrity hip-hop *entertainers* to engage disenchanted youth, scholars and educators have gravitated to the likes of Kanye West – one of the few contemporaries who falls into the category of being a "conscious" rapper. By celebrating his perceived consciousness or subversiveness without facilitating a form of "dialogue [that] requires critical thinking," pertaining especially to his lyrics and commercial packaging, educators may, in fact, miss opportunities to help their students achieve "true education" (Freire, 1970, p. 81). By examining lesson plans, song lyrics, artist interviews, and a case study related to the music of Kanye West, I will discuss (1) the ways in which these pedagogical practices are conceptualized as "relevant" to urban youth, (2) the degree to which these

HHBE practices can be considered "subversive," and (3) the ways in which educators might expand upon current popular culture (i.e., hip hop) understandings, assumptions, and practices in order to develop students' critical media literacy.

Theoretical framework

Two theoretical frameworks inform the concepts of youth cultural identity and relevancy, subculture/resistance, and consumerism discussed in this chapter:

1. *A Critical Multiculturalist View of Cultural Relevancy.* According to Ladson-Billings (1995), "culturally relevant pedagogy ... not only addresses student achievement, but also helps students to accept and affirm their cultural identity while *developing critical perspectives* that challenge inequities that schools (and other institutions) perpetuate" (p. 469, emphasis added). The elements of this theory are rooted in empowering students of color by increasing their own cultural awareness. Rather than simply incorporate elements of popular culture, such as hip hop, into school curricula to hook students' interests, Ladson-Billings' work calls for the development of skills that will enable children to *critique* what is selected to represent them and their communities.

    Similarly, May (1999) offers critical multiculturalism as a way of viewing "differences" among racial and ethnic groups, especially as they pertain to those that have been historically marginalized, without making blanketed assumptions about what certain groups may or may not have in common. To apply this to hip hop in the urban school classroom, children's cultural backgrounds should be *acknowledged* without placing limitations on what students may or may not connect or relate to. May suggests that critical multiculturalism initiate a "reflexive critique" of cultural practices that "avoids the vacuity of cultural relativism, and allows for criticism (both internal and external to the group), transformation, and change" (pp. 31–33).
2. *The "Subversive" in Youth (Popular) Culture.* In drawing upon the works of Hebdige (1979) and Giroux (1996), I discuss the complexity of youth counterculture, especially in relation to a capitalist market, and discuss the implications of consumerism on seemingly "resistant" movements such as hip hop. Given postmodern concepts of identity, which argue for the plurality and fluidity of children's identities, Giroux argues that "[youth] can no longer be seen as either bearers of counter-hegemonic cultures or as drop outs, sheepishly slacking off into an aimless and dreary accommodation to the status quo" (p. 32). Rather, their relationship to their own identities is complex – sometimes a hybrid of dominant and dominated aspects of culture.

In addition, Storey (2003) argues that youth have a complex relationship with pop music, stemming largely from their needs to establish themselves as distinct from adults (p. 117). Although the music, in this case hip hop, reflects certain realities of their burgeoning adult existences, it is also a type of "fiction" they are able to live through symbolically. In other words, the music is not necessarily the most realistic portrayal of the lives they are actually living in their urban contexts. My research takes into account the complexity of young people's identifications with hip hop, which may be quite distinct from the relationships adults have with the same music.

Method

Over the last year, I conducted an analysis of hip-hop-related lesson plans, many of which were downloaded from "Lesson Planet, The Search Engine for Teachers," which features over 150,000 "Teacher Approved Lesson Plans" (www.lessonplanet.com). Several of the lesson plans on this website consisted of links to external sources, such as VH1's website, PBS. org, *The New York Times*, Oregon Public Broadcasting, and the Rock & Roll Hall of Fame. In addition, I reviewed lessons found in *Hip-Hop Poetry and the Classics* (Sitomer & Cirelli, 2004), *The Hip-Hop Education Guidebook, Volume 1* (Runnell & Diaz, 2007), *Hip Hop Street Curriculum: Keeping it Real* (Kunjufu, 2005), practices described in *California Educator*, the children's picture books *Hip Hop Speaks to Children: A Celebration of Poetry with a Beat* (Giovanni, 2008) and *And the Winner Is…* (LL Cool J, 2002), and field notes collected as part of a national study on single-sex schools for black and Latino males conducted through New York University's Metropolitan Center for Urban Education and led by Dr. Pedro Noguera. These lessons and practices were examined for common themes, which are linked to arguments made for hip-hop cultural "relevancy" in urban schools. For example, to what degree do the lessons reflect Au's (2005) discussion of rappers' resistance to the "Discourse of education," which ostensibly offers African-American youth means of identifying with a distinct form of education? In addition, these lessons were examined for their "subversive" characteristics by asking, in what ways do these lessons reflect the effect of inequities and encourage students to empower themselves? Lastly, I examined the lessons to determine, to what degree do these practices encourage students to engage in "dialogue, which requires critical thinking" (Freire, 1970, p. 81)?

I downloaded song lyrics from Vh1's website and read interviews with hip-hop artists found on MTV.com as well as in Small's (1992) *Break it Down: The Inside Story from the New Leaders of Rap* so as to critically examine the "consciousness" of such artists as Kanye West, who frequently appeared in the lesson plans and books I discovered, and to determine the extent to which such entertainers considered themselves "political," "resistant," and/or "empowering." Given West's prevalence in hip-hop lesson plans, as well as his appearance in a classroom in the national study, I have decided to focus this chapter exclusively on pedagogical practices related to his musical performance. His song lyrics, like the lesson plans and practices mentioned above, were examined with respect to their pedagogical or educational implications.

Field notes and a sample unit plan from one all-male classroom, collected from a school in the Englewood area of Chicago, were examined as a hip-hop pedagogy case study. The materials from this school, related to Kanye West, were collected as part of a national study on single-sex schools, and this particular school is comprised entirely of black male students. Analysis of these materials is provided in order to illustrate the potential of hip hop in the classroom, as well as some of its shortcomings.

"Through the wire": hip-hop cultural relevancy, Kanye style

Although he is now notoriously known for stealing the microphone from Taylor Swift during her MTV Award acceptance speech in 2009 and for proclaiming his own "genius" (as ridiculed in a South Park episode), Kanye West is one of the few contemporary artists to be considered simultaneously mainstream and "conscious." His popularity among youth, as well as his palatable-to-adults lyrics, have made him a very common hip-hop curricular choice. Whether featured in a children's picture book (Giovanni, 2008), online lesson plans (IRA/NCTE, 2002–2009; Vh1, 2008), or in an actual classroom setting (field notes, 2008), West is one of the most common bridges, at least as perceived by adults, between students' outside-of-school and inside-of-school lives. Despite his criticized middle-class upbringing in a "comfortable home" (Lamb, 2009), he is considered relevant to disenfranchised urban students because he allegedly represents the city spaces they occupy. This conclusion is drawn largely because students are familiar with his music, as well as his highly-publicized image. Regardless of the fact that many youth do not "know what the heck they're saying," they are able to recite the lyrics of West's songs verbatim (personal interview, Mr. James, US History Teacher, May 28, 2008). In an effort to tap into students' prior (popular) knowledge, and make learning relevant to them, the lesson plans I examined are "willing to meet students on their 'terms' (i.e., conditions and platforms that the students themselves are comfortable with)" (Kawakita, 2002–2009). This line of thinking is guided by educators' assumptions that students will see their urban lives reflected in the material and become more engaged with the lessons they are being taught. However, meeting students where they are "comfortable" does not necessarily mean such lessons have critical educational value.

According to research by Au (2005), rap or hip hop is generally celebrated pedagogically as doing one of two things: (1) bridging "the cultural divide that exists between schools and students' home and community cultures," and (2) developing "critical consciousness among students" (p. 211). Most lesson plans I examined seemed directed at this first goal, toward ameliorating the "divide" between schools' and students' "cultures." Interestingly, culture in these instances, is limited to students' popular culture(s), which may or may not be successfully coopted by educators, whose adult status is something with which students do not necessarily identify. As Love (2010) pointed out, through a discussion of her work with students in a hip hop after-school program, she realized very quickly that she, as an instructor, was "not cool," in the eyes of teenagers whose interest in hip hop was quite distinct from her own. In their efforts to reach kids or be relevant to them, educators risk missing the "cool" mark by engaging "popular" texts that either are not popular anymore or were never popular among students. Also, in the case of Kanye West, it seems educators place a different value on his music, celebrating a "subversive" relevance with which the students do not identity – especially given that they are not always cognizant of the meanings of the references found in his lyrics (such as Stovall (2006) revealed with the students in his study, regarding other hip-hop music) and/or attach their own complex meanings to the music to which they are drawn (Lipsitz, 1990; Storey, 2003). Ginwright (2004) writes that hip-hop culture "oftentimes validates, legitimizes, and celebrates the experiences of violence, pain, fear, love, and hope that for urban youth are overlooked in mainstream America" (p. 32). While possibly true in many cases, this statement is rooted in a monolithic understanding of the urban space – as a place most students view as subverting a "mainstream" (i.e., white American) lifestyle. It is difficult to give this interpretation credence without knowing more about the associations students make between the music and their own urban home contexts.

In his analysis of artists' lyrics, Au (2005), suggests that hip-hop music is engaged with a figurative battle with the discourse of education, revealing the ways in which it falls short of "meeting the material, social, and cultural needs of African-American youth" (p. 213). He conceptualizes the urban space as a mechanism for producing an alternative education for black youth. He refers to Kanye West, in particular, claiming that the artist "rejects the discourse of all institutionalized education in favor of an individualized education of his own design to meet his own ends – which could be construed as the education with the least amount [of] alienation possible" (pp. 213–214). While this reading is problematic on many levels, it is most notably so for its celebration of an "individualized education" that most African-American youth will not have the privilege of receiving within their outside-of-school spaces, given that West did *not* grow up in a similar urban context. More than a rejection of all "institutionalized education," which employed his very own mother as a professor, West's *The College Dropout* is a mockery of those who *did* decide to go to college: "No, I've never had sex, but you know what? My degree keeps me satisfied" ("School Spirit Skit 1"). Unlike KRS-One, Ice Cube, and other hip-hop predecessors who made pointed efforts to discuss the value of an education relevant to black youth,[1] West dismisses higher learning as economically foolish and socially weak. Instead of celebrating an "individualized *education*," West propagates stereotypes of the nerdy academic, transmitting the message to his young listeners that his success – following his rejection of college – is the sexier, cooler, more acceptable path to take, especially for black males. This is a dangerous message to send to "disenfranchised" students whose best opportunities for success – economic and career-wise – may, in fact, come with a college education. Given such an anti-higher-education stance, it is ironic that his music infiltrates schools like the one in Chicago, which recently boasted sending all of its black male student graduates to college.

In an effort to connect West to relevant black history, three of the lessons I examined – including one from the case study in Chicago – utilized his song, "Through the Wire," for its reference to Emmett Till and/or focus on the artist's personal struggle (following a car accident that left his jaw wired shut). The Vh1 lesson plan, "Vh1 Driven: Kanye West," was written in conjunction with The National Association for Music Education, by organization member and elementary school teacher Bonnie H. Capes from Monmouth Junction, New Jersey. One of the objectives of this lesson, intended for grades 7–12, is for students to "be able to draw connections between their lives and the life of Kanye West" (p. 1), particularly after viewing the Vh1 program on the star's "life story." By encouraging students to make explicit connections with West, the author of this lesson plan "emphasizes the personal at the expense of the social and political," which Lewis (2000) describes as a misguided attempt at reader response.[2] In addition to not asking students to discuss West's mention of Emmett Till, or any other aspects of the lyrics such as the fact that he claims to "[explain] the story about how [B]lacks came from glory," this lesson includes questions related to students' "dreams," "obstacles," and thoughts about proving "the world wrong" (Vh1, 2008, pp. 4, 6). Their concluding activity is to "compose a rap in the style of Kanye West using his song 'Through the Wire' as an example" (p. 1).

Many educators conceptualize cultural relevancy as making similar types of text-to-self connections, as well as producing creative autobiographical work. This type of lesson is a good example of a missed opportunity to engage students in a critical analysis of one of the songs with which they presumably connect. Put another way, such practices, as Share (2009) writes, "can be problematic when they favor individualistic self-expression over socially conscious analysis and alternative media production" (p. 9). He adds, "Many media arts programs unproblematically teach students the technical skills to merely reproduce hegemonic representations with little awareness of ideological implications or any type of social critique" (p. 9). The "hegemonic representation," in this case, could very well be the rap song students are asked to compose in that this assignment celebrates the musical format produced by their "educator," Vh1. The entertainment industry, well-known for exploiting youth culture, cannot afford to critique the artists who appear in their videos and programming at the expense of losing profit. It seems Vh1's intention in providing lesson plans such as this one is to encourage educators, as well as young people, to celebrate West's album, uncritically, in a school-sanctioned context with the potential benefit of selling more of his albums.

While West claims that his songs honor black history, the lyrics of "Through the Wire" are at best a way to familiarize or remind listeners of the *name* Emmett Till. He makes the following reference, in describing his car accident:

> How do you console my mom or give her light support
> When you telling her your son's on life support
> And just imagine how my girl feel
> On the plane scared as hell that her guy look like Emitt [*sic*] Till
>
> (Vh1, 2008, p. 4)

West compares his relative facial disfigurement, which was caused accidentally, to the distortion of 14-year-old Emmett Till's face, which was the result of grotesque beatings by racist whites that left him dead in 1955. Rather than illuminate the atrocities committed against Till, West uses his name solely to conjure up sympathy for himself and his "girl," who feared that her boyfriend's face would be mangled beyond recognition. West's personal link to Till is at once grandiose and decontextualized, giving the impression that his "struggle" after a car accident can by likened in any way to the racialized murder of a young black man in the 1950s. For students unaware of Till's historical importance, West's lyrics do little to help them gain understanding. On the contrary, these lyrics may contribute to the *mis*understanding that Till's name is simply synonymous with facial injury.

Unlike the Vh1 example that gives no credence whatsoever to the Till reference, Kulowiec (Teaching American History, 2008) and Mr. James (field notes, 2008) utilized West's song in an effort to teach students "why the artist chose Till as a point of comparison" (Kulowiec, p. 2). Both lesson plans served as a means of introducing students to the story of Emmett Till, offering them the background necessary to more fully understand West's song. Mr. James did this intentionally with his Chicago students because, as noted earlier, the kids would recite all the lyrics to "Through the Wire" but were unaware of their significance. To begin his series of related lessons, he showed the students a PowerPoint presentation that started with five slides related to West's song, including an excerpt of the line containing the reference to Emmett Till. The question sequence included in his PowerPoint follows:

Table 3

Slide 3	Slide 4	Slide 5
* Kanye West's girl was afraid his face was going to look like Emmett Till. * What happened to Kanye West that made his girl think his face was going to be messed up?	He got into a Car Accident. [image of a car accident]	* So what the heck happened to Emmett Till if when you get into a car accident, your face is compared to him? * Who was Emmett Till? * What happened to Emmett Till?

Extract from Mr. James's 9th-grade History Class PowerPoint Presentation

Note: This table is reflective of PowerPoint slides that were photocopied and given to me by the teacher, Mr. James, during a classroom observation conducted on May 28, 2008.

Similarly, Kulowiec's lesson includes the questions:

What happened to Emmett Till?
Why did Kanye West make a reference to Till in "Through the Wire"?

Both Mr. James and Kulowiec utilized material from students' popular culture in order to help them gain valuable knowledge about Emmett Till, (de)segregation, and the Civil Rights Movement. However, West's lyrics alone cannot be credited with raising students' level of historical consciousness. If anything, his reference was so decontextualized and obtuse that the educators found it necessary to explain it to the students who were singing the line without knowing "what the heck" they were saying. In essence, the lesson plans served as a reintroduction, however brief, to West's lyrics. The song was not the focal point of the lesson, nor was it extensively examined within the classroom setting.

For these two cases, hip hop served as a hook to capture students' interest, and this interest was quickly redirected to other textual material (articles, textbooks, historical documents) and questionnaires related directly to Emmett Till and then to the Civil Rights Movement. In fact, Mr. James did not even play all of "Through the Wire" for his eager students. He turned the music off after West's line about Till and, when they complained, stated jokingly that his classroom was not "a club." Although the song itself may very well help bridge students' inside-of-school and outside-of-school lives, the educators in these instances had to work to develop the kids' "critical consciousness" (Au, 2005), as this critical consciousness was not built into the lyrics. Further, neither Kuloweic nor Mr. James returned to "Through the Wire" after students had learned what happened to Emmett Till in an effort to reexamine the line about how West's "girl" would be "scared as hell that her guy look like Emitt [sic] Till."

Each of these lessons brilliantly exposed students for singing and celebrating lyrics they did not understand; yet, the educators could have taken these lessons the next step and challenged students to turn the reflective lens on themselves as well as on one of the artists that they admire. Just as Giroux (1996) argues with respect to Disney films, it is imperative that we "[interrogate]" hip-hop "as an important site for the production of children's culture" (p. 96). Rather than simply bring texts into the classroom because we view them as relevant to youth or as material they are deeply engaged with, as a means of teaching important lessons the artists barely address, educators and scholars must consider the "boundaries between entertainment, education, and commercialization" inherent in hip-hop culture and begin the critical media work that needs to be done in classrooms. This is especially important for disenfranchised youth who may feel empowered upon learning that the celebrity artists who seem so relevant to them are not as omnipotent as they appear, nor are they necessarily as representative of the urban space as they seem.

Breaking down the "consciousness" of Kanye West

Another one of Kanye West's songs that appeared in the lesson plans I examined was "Diamonds from Sierra Leone." In "A Collaboration of Sites and Sounds: Using Wikis to Catalog Protest Songs," Chris Kawakita of Normal, Illinois lists "Diamonds" as one of the resources teachers will need to complete the two-day lesson he has designed (IRA/NCTE, 2002–2009). As an introduction during session one, Kawakita writes:

> Begin this lesson by playing the chorus of rapper Kanye West's "Diamonds from Sierra Leone." Ideally, students will instantly recognize the track and artist, and even sing along. Before you hand out the materials, ask the class to speculate as to why you played this particular song. Play snippets of other "recognizable" protest songs, including Bob Marley's "Get Up Stand Up," Dave Matthews Band's "Cry Freedom," Christina Aguilera's "Beautiful," and Erwin Starr's "War."
>
> (p. 3)

Like the examples in the previous section, as well as many of the teachers and scholars who advocate hip-hop pedagogy, Kawakita plays upon the students' instant connection with Kanye West. He assumes that they will know the lyrics and, therefore, be able to recognize why this song is a "protest song." Rather than facilitate a critical discussion about the lyrics – or use them to enhance students' knowledge about the diamond trade – this lesson, again, utilizes West as a hook and then maneuvers the students into searching the internet for their own examples of protest music. While this type of lesson, ostensibly designed around the promotion of "conscious" artists, may help bridge the cultural divide between students and schools, it does little to elicit analysis of this particular hip-hop song or to deepen students' understandings about Kanye West as a symbol of subversion or "protest."

While West's "Diamonds From Sierra Leone" video implicated the diamond industry for its role in blood diamonds (by depicting white Europeans as the consumers of the diamonds African children mine), the lyrics to this song do little more than perpetuate the artist's image as a master rapper:

> *[Chorus]*
> Diamonds are forever (forever, forever)
> Throw your diamonds in the sky if you feel the vibe
> Diamonds are forever (forever, forever, forever)
> The Roc is still alive every time I rhyme.
> Forever ever? Forever ever? Ever, ever? Ever, ever? Ever, ever? Ever, ever? …
>
> I was sick about awards
> Couldn't nobody cure me
> Only playa that got robbed but kept all his jewelry

Alicia Keys tried to talk some sense to them
30 minutes later seems there's no convincing them
What more can you ask for?
The international assholes nah
Who complains about what he is owed?
And throw a tantrum like he is 3 years old
You gotta love it though somebody still speaks from his soul
And wouldn't change by the change, or the game, or the fame,
When he came, in the game, he made his own lane
Now all I need is y'all to pronounce my name
Its Kanye – But some of my plastic – they still say Kane
Got family in the D, Kin-folk from Motown
Back in the Chi – them folks ain't from Motown
Life movin' too fast I need to slow down
Girl ain't give me no ass, ya need to go down.

While he states, "Throw your diamonds in the sky if you feel the vibe," throughout the song and utilizes the hook "Diamonds are forever," he never once mentions the atrocities of the diamond trade or states why anyone should throw their diamonds "up like you bulimic." He focuses more on his own fame and success. In fact, this verse refers to the fact that he got "robbed" of an award, but still managed to keep "all his jewelry" – most likely the diamonds and chains he is well-known for wearing. MTV's Sway called him out on this contradiction during an interview in 2007:

Sway: [Y]ou still wear a lot of diamonds yourself. What's the logic behind that?

West: How are you a human being, would be more of the question, like, "How are you still human when you know what's going on? How do you still wear what it took your whole life to get?"

Sway: Someone from the outside might say, "There he goes again," and say that that's borderline hypocritical.

West: Yeah, a whole part about being a human is to be a hypocrite. They say that if you're an artist you have to stand for this, and they try to discredit you (MTV Networks).

Although West dismisses the disconnect between what he sings and the image he projects as simply being hypocritical, as all human beings are, he is celebrated by Kawakita as he is by Au (2005) for being conscious or countercultural. In actuality, West did not even come up with the idea for this song and hardly deserves the credit for raising awareness about blood diamonds. It was the director Mark Romanek and artist Q-Tip who introduced him to the idea of blood diamonds. West admits this in his interview, as well:

And Q-Tip's like, "Sierra Leone," and I'm like, "Where?" And I remember him spelling it out for me and me looking on the Internet and finding out more. I think that was just one of those situations where I just set out to entertain, but every now and then God taps me on the shoulder ... so he'll place angels in my path ... and it's like a treasure hunt or something. And I finally found the gold mine, which was the video "Diamonds."

(MTV Networks, 2007)

Instead of crediting West for the political message he spouts through a song – or, in this case, the video – educators must take into account the marketing machine behind what is produced and what is directed to popular audiences. Here, the rapper acknowledges that he had no knowledge of Sierra Leone and had to search the internet in order to find out more about it. Rather than refer to this process as political, or subversive, he mentions that it was a "gold mine" for him. While he merely "set out to entertain," he was given the opportunity to release a message that increased his notoriety and his record sales. He refers, ironically, to a song highlighting the atrocities of diamond production as "gold" – another precious commodity.

West is not alone in referring to himself first and foremost as an entertainer. While many artists, like him, are viewed as subversive or resistant, many of them state explicitly that they should not serve as role models to children or be considered anything but rappers (Small, 1992). In addition, they admit that young people need to be realistic about the music world and what it takes to become successful. In addition to sending this message indirectly through albums like West's *The College Dropout* (in his rants against all the haters), artists like Ice-T have stated this explicitly in an interview with Small (1992). Small asks, "Most kids can't make money the way you did. What about them?" Ice-T's response is as follows:

First thing, I make sure they know that it took me eleven years. I coulda took those same eleven years and been a brain surgeon, a lawyer, an aircraft scientist.

(p. 20)

In order to use hip-hop to teach children about alternative education, school lessons should incorporate background information such as this to demonstrate that it is not always as easy as it might appear, nor is it always as political or even conceptualized by the artists who are the face of the music. Further, while many artists are critical of education in their lyrics or discuss the impacts of poverty, many of them are educated themselves and/or grew up in comfortable middle-class homes with parents who were educated (like Kanye West). A danger in celebrating hip hop as representing all people who struggle or are disenfranchised is not taking into account the ways in which lyrics are invented, hyperbolized, or adopted by the artists who sing/rap them. It also does not take into consideration the complex relationships students have with their own urban environments nor the ways in which the urban spaces are marketed for capitalist purposes. Students should be encouraged to analyze the music they listen to, even if they enjoy it, as a way of fostering critical thinking and learning.

Conclusions

Within educational scholarship, hip hop has become one of the most salient features of what is considered culturally relevant to urban, especially black, youth. Hip hop is seen as relevant because it highlights some of the problems endemic to urban communities. Bringing the music into the classroom is thought to foster cultural capital, as well as encourage students to become more invested in their educations. While the incorporation of hip hop or other aspects of popular youth culture into the classroom has educational potential, the music and artists are often uncritically celebrated for representing or speaking on behalf of disenfranchised students and their urban communities. This way of thinking ignores both the complexity of youth identities and the entertainment/fictionalized aspects of hip-hop lyrics. In addition, it does not take into consideration the disconnect between the lives students are living and the lives hip-hop artists are currently living – as a result of their album and performance sales. While hip hop is seen as a realistic reflection of the urban environment, it is important to remember that there is already a disconnect between the performer and the performed, by nature of the art's having become popularly accepted (Bourdieu, 1993). In this sense, hip-hop artists' criticisms of education should be analyzed carefully because while certain artists like Kanye West have become successful through other avenues, the children listening to their music may not. The children listening to them may, in fact, benefit from the educations they are receiving in their current school settings in ways that they would not from following the paths of hip-hop artists like West. If educators are to incorporate hip hop into the classroom as a reform effort, in order to combat current inequities, it is imperative that they continue to critique their approach.

The choices of teachers and scholars often reflect their perceptions of what they consider conscious, political, or subversive. With respect to Kanye West, these efforts do not look at his lyrics in their entirety, nor problematize some of the grandiose comparisons he makes between his own life and that of historical black figures like Emmett Till. In addition, his songs like "Diamonds from Sierra Leone" are celebrated for being "protest" songs when they, in fact, do not even make explicit reference to the events they are supposed to be protesting. Artists like Kanye West must be considered in light of their celebrity entertainer statuses. They are awarded certain privileges such as being handed a "gold mine" like ideas they did not come up with that are celebrated as their own. While hip hop may indeed provide the bridge between urban students' inside-of-school and outside-of-school lives and reflect a relevant aspect of their culture, educators must not forget the pedagogical need to critique these texts as they would any other text in a literature- or art-based classroom. Artists like West should be included in classroom contexts; however, it is just as important to teach students to be critical of what ostensibly represents them. It is not enough to simply bring hip hop into the classroom to hook students or meet them on their "terms" so as to keep them engaged, especially if schools are not meeting their academic needs or preparing them to compete with students outside of urban spaces. The entire purpose of HHBE is to assist youth on their path of acquiring new knowledge, and some of that new knowledge may be somewhat uncomfortable – for both the educators and the students. But it is necessary if we want our students to be successful.

Among educators, there seems to be a fear of critiquing what the students are into or what they find relevant. We should not be afraid to go there. This type of discussion, after all, is what Freire (1970) would call "authentic reflection" that ultimately frees human beings from oppression. He writes:

> Only dialogue, which requires critical thinking, is also capable of generating critical thinking. Without dialogue there is no communication, and without communication there can be no true education.

(p. 81)

Rather than assume that the only "relevant" education to our students is that which celebrates their interest in hip hop, we should encourage dialogue that expands their knowledge about what they think they already know.

Notes

1. Ice Cube, for example, is quoted as saying, "This school system is not the right place for a [B]lack boy or girl. They're being taught by [W]hites that never gave a shit about them ... If you don't know what your race of people have done in science and medicine and every other subject, you're going to figure it's all obsolete. So you're not going to be interested in any of it" (Small, 1992).
2. Rosenblatt's (1995) "aesthetic" aspect of reader response theory requires the reader to "experience, live through" a text (p. xvii). Although her theory does not require the reader to make exact matches between his or her own life and the text, many educators encourage students to make this type of connection to literature. As Lewis (2000) points out, this approach limits students' abilities to critically analyze what they are reading.

References

Au, W. (2005). Fresh Out of School: Rap Music's Discursive Battle with Education. *The Journal of Negro Education*, 74(3), 210–220.

Bourdieu, P. (1993). *The Field of Cultural Production*. New York: Columbia University Press.

Cortés, C. E. (1995). Knowledge Construction and Popular Culture: The Media as Multicultural Education. In Banks, J. (Ed.), *The Handbook of Research on Multicultural Education* (1st edn) (pp. 169–183). New York: Jossey-Bass.

Dimitriadis, G. (2009). *Performing Identity/ Performing Culture: Hip Hop as Text, Pedagogy, and Lived Practice*. New York: Peter Lang.

Duncan-Andrade, J. (2004). Your Best Friend or Your Worst Enemy: Youth Popular Culture, Pedagogy, and Curriculum in Urban Classrooms. *The Review of Education, Pedagogy, and Cultural Sudies*, 26, 313–337.

Ginwright, S. (2004). *Black in School: Afrocentric Reform, Urban Youth, and the Promise of Hip-hop Culture*. New York and London: Teachers College Press.

Giroux, H. A. (1996). *Fugitive Cultures: Race, Violence & Youth*. New York: Routledge.

Hebdige, D. (1979). *Subculture: The Meaning of Style*. New York: Methuen.

Hill, M. L. (2009). *Beats Rhymes and Classroom Life: Hip-Hop Pedagogy and the Politics of Identity*. New York: Teachers College Press.

Freire, P. (1970). *Pedagogy of the Oppressed*. New York: The Seabury Press.

Giovanni, N. (2008). *Hip Hop Speaks to Children: A Celebration of Poetry With a Beat*. Naperville: Sourcebooks, Inc.

Heath, S. B., Street, B. V., & Mills, M. (2008). *On Ethnography: Approaches to Language and Literacy Research*. New York: Teachers College Press.

Jenkin, E. (2007). Wayward Souls: Beyond Subcultural Nostalgia Toward a New Hip-Hop Politics. *Words. Beats. Life: The Global Journal of Hip-Hop Culture, 2*(2), 40–43, 64.

LL Cool J. (2002). *And the Winner is …* New York: Scholastic.

Lamb, B. (2009). Kanye West. About.com. http://top40.com.about.com/od/artistsls/p/kanyewest.htm?p=1

Lewis, C. (2000). Critical Issues: Limits of Identification: The Personal, Pleasurable, and Critical in Reader Response. *Journal of Literacy Research, 32*(2), 253–266.

Lipsitz, G. (1990). *Time Passages: Collective Memory and American Popular Texts*. Minneapolis, Oxford: University of Minnesota Press.

Kawakita, C. (2002–2009). A Collaboration of Sites and Sounds: Using Wikis to Catalog Protest Songs. IRA/NCTE – Retrieved from www.readwritethink.org/lessons/lesson_view_printer_friendly.asp?id=979

Kulowiec, G. (2008). From Kanye to Dylan: Understanding the Emmett Till Case through Music and Primary Source Documents. *Teaching American History*. Retrieved from www.Webhostbridgew.edu/tahg.

Kunjufu, J. (2005). *Hip Hop Street Curriculum: Keeping it Real*. Chicago: African-American Images.

Ladson-Billings, G. (1995). Toward a Theory of Culturally Relevant Pedagogy. *American Educational Research Journal, 32*(3), 465–491.

Love, B. (2010). The Beat of Hegemony: Hip-Hop, Critical Pedagogy, and Urban Youth. Presented at the American Educational Research Association conference, 2010.

May (Ed.). (1999). *Critical Multiculturalism: Rethinking Multicultural and Antiracist Education* (pp. 11–41). London and New York: Routledge-Falmer, Taylor & Francis Group.

Morrell, E. & Duncan-Andrade, J. M. R. (2002). Promoting Academic Literacy with Urban Youth through Engaging Hip-Hop Culture. *The English Journal, 91*(6), 88–92.

Morrell, E. (2004). *Linking Literacy and Popular Culture: Finding Connections for Lifelong Learning*. Christopher-Gordon Publishers: Norwood, Massachusettes.

MTV Networks (2007). All Eyes on Kanye West. Retrieved from www.mtv.com/bands/w/west_kanye/news_feature_081805/index2.jhtml.

Murray, D.C. (2004). Hip-Hop vs. High Art: Notes on Race as Spectacle. *Art Journal, 63*(2), 4–19.

Noguera, P. (1999). Transforming Urban Schools through Investments in Social Capital. In *Motion Magazine*. Retrieved from http://www.inmotionmagazine.com/pncap1.html.

Rose, T. (2008). *The Hip Hop Wars: What We Talk about When We Talk about Hip Hop – and Why it Matters*. New York: Basic Civitas Books.

Rosenblatt, L. (1995). *Literature as Exploration*. New York: The Modern Language Association of America.

Runell, M., & Diaz, M. (2007). *The Hip-Hop Education Guidebook, Volume 1.* New York: Hip-Hop Association, Inc.

Share, J. (2009). *Media Literacy is Elementary: Teaching Youth to Critically Read and Create Media.* New York: Peter Lang.

Sitomer, A., & Cirelli, M. (2004). *Hip-Hop Poetry and the Classics.* Beverly Hills: Milk Mug Pulishing.

Small, M. (1992). *Break it Down: The Inside Story from the New Leaders of Rap.* A Citadel Press Book, Carol Publishing Group: New York

Storey, J. (2003). *Cultural Studies and the Study of Popular Culture.* Athens: The University of Georgia Press.

Stovall, D. (2006). We Can Relate: Hip-Hop Culture, Critical Pedagogy, and the Secondary Classroom. *Urban Education, 41*(6), 585–602.

Vh1 Music Studio (2008). Vh1Driven: Kanye West. www.vh1musicstudio.com.

Yúdice, G. (2007). Culture. In B. Burgett, & G. Hendler (Eds.), *Keywords for American Cultural Studies* (pp. 71–76). New York and London: New York University.

Chapter 12

The Hood is Where the Heart is: Melodrama, Habitus, and the Hood Film

Andrew deWaard

A fucked up childhood is why the way I am;
It's got me in the state where I don't give a damn.
Somebody help me, but nah they don't hear me though,
I guess I'll be another victim of the ghetto.

MC Eiht (of Compton's Most Wanted and
Menace II Society), "Streiht Up Menace"

Rarely does such a consistent and self-contained collection of representational material offer itself unto analysis like the short-lived hood film cycle of the early 1990s. Rarer still is the foundational structure of such a symbolic collection completely overlooked by its critics. Quickly gaining notoriety as a result of the vast media attention they garnered from unexpected financial success and headline-grabbing violence at some theatrical exhibitions, not to mention its sociopolitical context,[1] the hood film disappeared almost as quickly as it appeared, marking the first major wave of African-American film production in nearly twenty years. "Production in 1990 and 1991 alone," according to Guerrero (1993), "easily surpassed the total production of all black-focused films released since the retreat of the Blaxploitation wave in the mid-1970s" (p. 155). *Boyz N the Hood* (John Singleton, 1991) and *Menace II Society* (Allen and Albert Hughes, 1993) are the hood film cycle's most renowned and successful films, as well as its most representative. Spike Lee, while often transcending the confines of the hood film genre, is a significant figure in the development of African-American filmmaking at this time, and his classic *Do the Right Thing* (1989) can be seen as the hood film's precursor, while *Clockers* (1995) marks its end by self-consciously examining the genre's conventions.[2] Other examples of the hood film include *New Jack City* (Mario Van Peebles, 1991), *Straight Out of Brooklyn* (Matty Rich, 1991), *Juice* (Ernest Dickerson, 1992), *Just Another Girl on the IRT* (Leslie Harris, 1992), *Deep Cover* (Bill Duke, 1992) and "over twenty similarly packaged feature-length films between 1991 and 1995" (Watkins, 1998, p. 172).

These hood films are all united, for the most part, by largely African-American creative talent, contemporary urban settings (primarily black communities in Los Angeles or New York), a strong intermedial connection to youth rap/hip-hop culture (via soundtrack and "rappers-turned-actors"), particularly the subgenre of "gangsta" rap, and a thematic focus on inner-city social and political issues such as poverty, crime, racism, drugs and violence. Consequently, film critics and scholars were quick to explore and interpret this uniquely confined set of films, collecting them under a variety of labels other than just *the hood film* moniker: "male-focused, 'ghettocentric,' action-crime-adventure" films (Guerrero, 1993,

p. 182), "the new Black realism films" (Diawara, 1993, p. 24), *New Jack Cinema* (Kendall, 1994), "trendy 'gangsta rap' films" (Reid, 1995, p. 457), "black action films" (Chan, 1998, p. 35), and, in what would be the most accurate description had he included the prefix *melo*, Spike Lee himself disparagingly called the cycle "hiphop, urban drama, ghetto film" (as quoted in Setlowe, 1993, p. 12). The gangster, action, and crime genres are continually mentioned as influences, as they clearly are; even film noir is suggested occasionally. However, in all of these considerations of genre and classification, the word *melodrama* rarely appears; if it does, it is in its typical, derogatory usage and does not warrant discussion.[34] This is a detrimental oversight: the hood film's fundamental core, I argue in this chapter, is the melodramatic mode, centered around the experience of being "another victim of the ghetto."

In Bourdieu's (1984) terms, mapping this cycle of films and their hitherto undiscovered melodramatic underpinnings reveals that the hood film cycle not only embodies and expresses a particular class habitus – "the internalized form of class condition and of the conditioning it entails" (p. 101) – but (melo)dramatizes the very production of this habitus, particularly with its primary focus on coming-of-age story lines and a youth audience. The interaction *with* and representation *by* various forms of media is also crucial in this structuring of habitus – what James Baldwin (1968) calls the black artist's unavoidable "burden of representation" – as is the "dialogue" that occurs between the films as the hood genre progresses.[5] Beginning in early childhood, the habitus, according to Bourdieu (1977), is the product of a long process of inculcation, resulting in "systems of durable, transposable *dispositions*" (p. 72) that shape particular lifestyles. For young, black, male residents of the hood – whose life-style is the subject of much debate as well as consumer exploitation – this habitus is conditioned by its existence within a specific urban space rife with crime, poverty, violence, and drugs. In this sense, these hood films are all about habitus, and as we shall see, this habitus is structured *by*, and *through* melodrama.

The realization of such a melodramatic habitus will unfold in two parts: mapping the melodramatic mode onto a previously unconsidered genre – the hood film cycle of the early 1990s, the *melo-ghetto* – and then analyzing the significance of what amounts to be the melodrama of the map. Plotting the melodramatic mode onto such a disparate and seemingly incompatible genre such as the hood film should explicate the geography of the melodramatic mode, showcasing its fundamental characteristics and concerns. Witnessing its application in such a violent and "masculine" genre as the hood film should also demonstrate the versatility of the melodramatic mode. Following this structural task, this new melodramatic incarnation will be explored in terms of its evolution of the melodramatic mode, demonstrating the ways in which melodrama is continuously reinvented and redefined. With the hood film, a key shift occurs: the home – a crucial concern in melodrama – becomes the hood, and it requires abandonment. Intimately connected to this disfigured sense of space is another, often overlooked concern of melodrama: the *melos*. Music in the hood film is of central importance in mediating the spatial and temporal logic of the hood. With the hood film, melodrama is put in the service of a far more serious concern than its traditional domestic or soap-opera utilization: the sociopolitical crisis of the African-American urban community.

The geography of melodrama: pathos n the hood

> Express yourself, from the heart
> Cause if you wanna start to move up the chart,
> Then expression is a big part.
> Dr. Dre (of N.W.A. and *Juice*), "Express Yourself"

Recuperating the term melodrama within the field of film studies has become quite the melodramatic project unto itself. Scorned and disdained, this 'suffering victim' has been the object of much derision, particularly in its latest incarnation in popular American mass culture. Vulgar, naïve, sensational, feminine, sentimental, excessive, overly emotional[6] – these are but a few of the disparaging descriptions that have 'robbed' melodrama of its 'virtue' and prevented any academic consideration of its continuing contemporary significance. However, in true melodramatic form, its virtue has been restored in recent years with 'heightened' and 'sensational' gestures by such 'noble heroes' as Christine Gledhill and Linda Williams. Not content with simply defending its honor, Williams (1998) claims that "Melodrama is the fundamental mode of popular American moving pictures" (p. 42), and "should be viewed … as what most typifies popular American narrative in literature, stage, film and television" (Williams, 2001, p. 11). But like any good melodrama worth its weight in tear-soaked hankies, the melodrama of melodrama's recuperation does not have a clear-cut happy ending – there is still much work to be done.

Drawing heavily from Peter Brooks' seminal 1976 book, *The Melodramatic Imagination: Balzac, Henry James, Melodrama, and the Mode of Excess*, the work of Gledhill and Williams opens up a new avenue for the study of cinematic melodrama. Rather than its typical, albeit contentious configuration as a genre, melodrama can also be viewed as a mode: melodrama's "aesthetic, cultural, and ideological features [have] coalesce[d] into a modality which organizes the disparate sensory phenomena, experiences, and contradictions of a newly emerging secular and atomizing society in visceral, affective and morally explanatory terms" (Gledhill, 2000, p. 228). If melodrama is to be understood as continually evolving, "adaptable across a range of genres, across decades, and across national cultures" (p. 229), then its progress needs to be consistently charted, its latest forms constantly delineated. Unfortunately, much of the scholarship concerning melodrama is still preoccupied with either reclaiming past works, rarely moving beyond the classical Hollywood era, or focused on specific auteurs, from D.W. Griffith to Douglas Sirk to contemporary directors such as Pedro Almodóvar and Todd Haynes. As "a tremendously protean, evolving, and modernizing form that continually uncovers new realistic material for its melodramatic project" (Williams, 2001, p. 297), melodrama's dominance as a fundamental mode will only be widely received and accepted after significant scholarship that considers its various contemporary forms.

Considered by Williams (1998) to be "perhaps the most important single work contributing to the rehabilitation of the term *melodrama* as a cultural form" (p. 51), Brooks'

The Melodramatic Imagination (1976) traces the historical origins of the form, applies his findings to the work of Balzac and Henry James, and establishes melodrama as a significant modern mode in the process. Situated as a response to the post-Enlightenment world that arose out of the French Revolution, "melodrama becomes the principal mode for uncovering, demonstrating, and making operative the essential moral universe in a post-sacred universe" (Brooks, 1976, p. 15). With the traditional imperatives of truth and ethics thrown into question, melodrama was to express what Brooks calls the "'moral occult,' the domain of operative spiritual values which is both indicated within and masked by the surface of reality" (p. 5).

Brooks' isolated concern with the nineteenth-century realist novel, particularly Balzac and James, proves to be both an asset and a hindrance to the theory of melodrama. Brooks is able to earnestly re-evaluate the form without the trappings of ideological condescension, allowing him to highlight its core characteristics, but he does not trace its importance in popular culture, where it has continued to evolve. Considering its modern reinvention, Gledhill and Williams break with Brooks in his view of melodrama as being in opposition to realism and as a mode of 'excess.' In Gledhill's (1987) consideration, contemporary forms of melodrama are firmly grounded in realism: "Taking its stand in the material world of everyday reality and lived experience, and acknowledging the limitations of the conventions of language and representation, it proceeds to force into aesthetic presence identity, value and plenitude of meaning" (p. 33). Williams (1998) goes a step further, suggesting that the term "excess" be eliminated from melodramatic discourse all together: "The supposed excess is much more often the mainstream, though it is often not acknowledged as such because melodrama consistently decks itself out in the trappings of realism and the modern (and now, the postmodern)" (p. 58). As melodrama has developed, it has cloaked itself in "realism" but remained fundamentally concerned with revealing moral legibility.

For all her rhetoric concerning melodrama being the primary mode of contemporary American mass culture, Williams' examples do not quite do her thesis justice. "Melodrama Revised" focuses on D. W. Griffith's *Way Down East* (1920), only briefly contemplating *Schindler's List* (Steven Spielberg, 1993) and *Philadelphia* (Jonathan Demme, 1993), as well as some select Vietnam films, while *Playing the Race Card* only goes as far as the *Roots* miniseries (Alex Haley, 1977), moving to "cultural event" with the Rodney King and O. J. Simpson trials as her most contemporary consideration. The hood film shall prove a convincing illustration of contemporary melodrama that grounds itself in urban 'realism.' Using Williams' five-point systematic breakdown of the melodramatic mode, we can structurally outline the melodramatic hood film:

1. "Melodrama begins, and wants to end," according to Williams (1998), "in a space of innocence" (p. 65), usually represented by the iconic image of the home. Immediately, the hood film puts a spin on this most central of melodramatic concerns, adhering and deviating from the convention. As will be considered in more depth in the second part of this essay, the home has become the community at large – the hood – and it is portrayed

as an area of crisis, not a space of innocence. However, a recurring motif that transpires in all hood films *does* express the innocence and virtue from which melodrama typically originates: the juxtaposition of children against the rough backdrop of the hood. Spike Lee, for example, often celebrates his Brooklyn community with loving tributes to the way children manage to generate fun out of minimal resources and confined spaces, such as the jubilant respite-from-the-heat fire hydrant scene in *Do the Right Thing*, and the opening montage of various street activities – jump rope, hopscotch, foot races, street baseball, etc. – in *Crooklyn*.

Many hood films take the form of coming-of-age tales, charting a path of lost innocence as the corrupting influence of the hood takes its toll on the film's young protagonists. *Clockers* begins with a montage of children witnessing grisly murder scenes in their neighborhood, and a central conflict is the protagonist's relationship with a younger boy from his building, Shorty, who idolizes Strike and is inevitably drawn into the cycle of violence. *Straight Out of Brooklyn* follows three teenagers navigating the treacheries of the hood, to varying degrees of success; *Juice* follows four, and also features a scene of the main protagonist attempting to dissuade his younger brother from venerating violence. Both *Boyz* and *Menace II Society* track children growing up across many years in the hood; in the former, "Singleton explores at least three ideological paths for young black men, as represented in the dispositions and fates of his three principal *Boyz*" (Guerrero, 1993, p. 184). Both films also feature extended introductory scenes of the trauma faced by prepubescent inhabitants of the hood. *Boyz* begins with four schoolchildren walking down a dilapidated, garbage-laden street, discussing their homework in the same breath as the previous night's shooting. Exploring a crime scene, one child is rebuked for not recognizing bullet holes; she responds by proclaiming that at least she knows her "times-tables." The subsequent shot is a slow pan across a classroom wall, displaying the children's endearingly simplistic art depicting police cars, helicopters conducting surveillance, and family members in coffins – a striking juxtaposition of innocence and affliction.

2. "Melodrama focuses on victim-heroes and the recognition of their virtue" (Williams, 1998, p. 66). The hood film's usage of victim-heroes is comparable to Thomas Elsaesser's (1987) position on 1950s family melodrama: these films "present *all* the characters convincingly as victims" (p. 86). Characters in hood films are (nearly) all compelling victims because of the dire depiction of their surroundings. Poverty, crime, drugs, racism, and violence – everyone is a victim. Even disagreeable characters are viewed as victims on account of this situation. *Boyz's* Doughboy (Ice Cube), for instance, is a violent, misogynistic drug dealer, but he attains sympathy on account of the troubled relationship he has with his mother, a single mom struggling to provide for her two sons, privileging the athletically skilled one over the other. Doughboy is also given the film's key piece of dialogue in its concluding scene, both incendiary critique and induction of pathos: "Either they don't know, or don't show, or don't care about what's going on in the hood." As victims of the hood, suffering is felt by one and all.

Emotionalism is key in recognizing the virtue of the victim-hero, and it is highly visible in the hood film, despite its rough exterior of tough language, gritty violence, and unrelenting hostility. In *Boyz*, for instance, following an unjust encounter with the police, Tre (Cuba Gooding Jr.) returns to his girlfriend Brandi's (Nia Long) house and proceeds to have an emotional breakdown. Swinging his fists wildly in the air before falling into Brandi's arms, Tre acts out his frustration and demonstrates his vulnerability, "a pivotal moment" according to Michael Eric Dyson (1992), "in the development of a politics of alternative black masculinity that prizes the strength of surrender and cherishes the embrace of a healing tenderness" (p. 135). *New Jack City*, perhaps the cycle's most simplistically violent and one-dimensional film, still has its gangster villain sharing tears with his brother (even if it ends in his murder), as well as a textbook melodramatic montage portraying the victims of drug addiction – "I have a crack baby. He was born blind" – and the trials of rehabilitation, set to a mournful piano score.

In hood films that primarily revolve around one central protagonist – Tre in *Boyz*, Caine (Tyrin Turner) in *Menace*, Mookie (Spike Lee) in *Do the Right Thing*, Strike (Mekhi Phifer) in *Clockers* – the victim-hero is always torn between allegiances to his fellow victims in the hood and the opportunity for upward mobility. As "the key function of victimization is to orchestrate the moral legibility crucial to the mode" (Williams 1998, p. 66), the victim-hero of the hood film always has his or her virtue recognized in the conclusion of the film as testament to the conditions of the hood. Whether by refusing to participate in the cycle of black-on-black violence and pursuing a college education (*Boyz*), shielding a child from a drive-by shooting (*Menace*), or inciting a riot in response to a savage murder by a police officer (*Do the Right Thing*),[7] the victim-hero makes a moral stand in opposition to the injustice perpetrated against the hood.

3. "Melodrama appears modern by borrowing from realism, but realism serves the melodramatic passion and action" (Williams, 1998, p. 67). While conventional wisdom posits melodrama as a crude, retrograde form out of which a more modern 'realism' developed, upon considering contemporary melodrama it becomes clear that realism is in fact at the service of the traditional melodramatic mode, albeit in a disguised, modernized fashion. The second part of this essay will explore the way the hood film is rooted in a realist portrayal of a specific spatial and temporal existence, but at this point, we can briefly look at the introduction of *Menace* as an example of the way realism is used in the service of melodrama in the hood film.

Explicit in its foregrounding the narrative amidst a history of racial violence, *Menace* uses pixelated archival footage of the 1965 Watts riots immediately following its opening scene. This imagery would most certainly have resonated with audiences at the time, as the Los Angeles riots that occurred in response to the acquittal of Rodney King's assailants happened the previous year. Our introduction to the current state of Watts is perceived in a bird's-eye view long shot, "in an almost ethnographic manner, with an invasive camera looking down on and documenting the neighborhood" (Massood, 2003, p. 165). A testament to the film's tagline, "this is the truth, this is what's real," *Menace* is quick to establish its "realistic" backdrop before delving into its otherwise typically melodramatic portrayal of a victim-hero's eventual recognition of virtue.

4. "Melodrama involves a dialectic of pathos and action – a give and take of 'too late' and 'in the nick of time'" (Williams, 1998, p. 69). Williams makes a key insight into the melodramatic mode when she connects pathos to action, permitting the most seemingly *un*melodramatic of films to be viewed in a new light. In its elucidation of a character's virtue in the climax, melodrama tends to end in one of two ways: "either it can consist of a paroxysm of pathos ... or it can take that paroxysm and channel it into the more virile and action-centered variants of rescue, chase, and fight (as in the western and all the action genres)" (p. 58). *Boyz* provides a tremendous example of this transition between pathos and action, complete with all the requisite ingredients: the virtuous 'good son,' Ricky (Morris Chestnut) is mistakenly caught up in a turf war, and Tre's warning calls are 'too late' to save him from a drive-by shooting, as is Doughboy's rescue attempt. The chase and fight to revenge this innocent's death is triggered, while the pathos is increased by the letter indicating Ricky's successful completion of the SATs – his ticket out of the hood – waiting in the mail all the while.

Paradoxically, Albert and Allen Hughes claim that the impetus for creating *Menace* was being "outraged by the Hollywood sentimentality" (Taubin, 1993, p. 17) of *Boyz*; it was their self-imposed mission to capture what they considered was the 'real' situation in the hood. Upon consideration of its similar use of the melodramatic mode, however, there is very little difference between the 'sentimental' climaxes of each film. True, Caine dies in *Menace*, as opposed to Tre's escape to college in *Boyz*, but the recognition of virtue in a dialectic of pathos and action is equally as strong in the climax of *Menace*, perhaps even more so: by threatening the death of an innocent child, and melodramatically delaying the outcome, the Hughes Brothers are even more 'guilty' of "Hollywood sentimentality." Like Ricky's death in *Boyz*, the climax of *Menace* plays on the qualities of "too late" and "in the nick of time." Crosscutting between the final stages of Caine and Ronnie's (Jada Pinkett) packing up of their lives – mere minutes from escaping the hood – and the oncoming evil in the form of a drive-by shooting, the scene is an example of melodramatic temporal and rhythmic relations: "we are moved in both directions at once in a contradictory hurry-up and slowdown" (Williams, 1998, p. 73). The car approaches in slow motion, its gang members brandishing their weapons, while Caine and his friends unknowingly laugh and fraternize in real-time. The action feels fast, but the duration of the event is actually slowed down and deferred, and the outcome of whether or not the child is killed is also delayed. Evoking the melodramatic motif of tableaux, a final montage of images from Caine's life in the hood – violence, laughter, teaching a child, a police arrest, a tear in prison, a tender kiss – are intercut with quick fades to black, Caine's redemptive voice-over, and the sound of his slowly fading heartbeat. Punctuated by a final jarring gunshot, this scene of intense action and violence is directly in the service of procuring pathos for its virtuous victim-hero.

5. "Melodrama presents characters who embody primary psychic roles organized in Manichaean conflicts between good and evil" (Williams, 1998, p. 77). The most derided characteristic of melodrama, the lack of complex psychological depth common to melodrama is a potentially objectionable quality, but there is no denying its prevalence in mass culture. Reductive vilification of perceived evil is frequent and widespread, often in the service of a separate agenda, and the hood film cycle certainly sets its 'good' victim-heroes in opposition to its one-dimensional 'evil' villains (Bishop in *Juice* and Nino in *New Jack City* are the most overt). But while the narratives of these films may focus on the limited, psychological conflict between these characters, thematically, the hood film again recasts the terms of its employment of melodramatic form. There is a much larger villain wreaking havoc in this cycle of melodrama: crack cocaine. Apart from *Do the Right Thing*, which controversially avoided its depiction, each and every single hood film foregrounds its urban plight directly within the context of the crack epidemic that swept major American cities during the 1980s, and the deepening cycle of poverty, unemployment, political apathy, police repression, and gang activity that arose in its wake. The hood film cycle goes to great lengths to portray this affliction from all angles: dealers, drug lords, addicts, cops, and residents. Suffice it to say, crack cocaine is deserving of its Manichaean vilification, and certainly suits its melodramatic portrayal. With the melodramatic mode of the hood film now adequately mapped, we can turn to the subject of this vilification: the melodrama of the map.

The melodrama of geography: the hood film's spatial pathos

> It ain't nothin like the shit you saw on TV.
> Palm trees and blonde bitches?
> I'd advise to you to pack your shit and get the fuck on;
> punk motherfucker!
>
> Ice Cube (of N.W.A. and *Boyz N the Hood*),
> "How to Survive in South Central"

The hood film certainly operates on the principles of the melodramatic mode, but as a narrowly defined cycle of films with specific concerns, it is of particular interest to note how the hood film adapts melodrama for its own spatial problematic. This reconfiguration entails the modification of two of the most central concerns of melodrama – the home and the *melos* – in a decidedly uncharacteristic manner. The home has typically been the "space of innocence" (Brooks, 1976, p. 29) in melodrama, but as the home is portrayed as just one of the many afflicted and deprived spaces in the hood film, the central place of concern becomes the hood *writ large*. Although there are central characters with which to follow the narrative, a multitude of characters and relationships are presented in order to attempt a full portrait of the community. Private spaces in the home are viewed very rarely; instead, much of the action takes place on the streets, in alleyways and vacant lots, and throughout the hood's urbanscape. "It is the primacy of this spatial logic, locating black urban youth experience within an environment of continual proximate danger that largely defines the hood film" (Forman, 2002, p. 258). The focus of the hood film becomes the power relations inherent in space, where race determines place; this is a story of the melodrama of geography.

Paula J. Massood's *Black City Cinema* (2003) provides a useful approach to analyzing the hood film, as she utilizes Mikhail Bakhtin's concept of the chronotope to explore the way African-American film is often preoccupied with the urban cityscape. A *topos* (place or person) that embodies or is embodied by *chronos* (time), Bakhtin's chronotope is a model for exploring temporal and spatial categories embodied within a text. The chronotope views spatial constructs as "'materialized history,' where temporal relationships are literalized by the objects, spaces, or persons with which they intersect" (Massood, 2003, p. 4). In Massood's judgment, the chronotope is of particular relevance to African-American filmmaking, as its main historical moments are often concerned with the contemporary city, from Oscar Micheaux's connection to the Harlem Renaissance to blaxploitation's use of the sprawling black ghetto in Los Angeles and New York City, resulting in the black ghetto chronotope. In the early 1990s, the hood film would come to redefine black cinematic space with what Massood refers to as the hood chronotope.

A strong sense of 'here and now' pervades the hood chronotope. All of the narratives in the hood film genre take place in confined geographic coordinates – South Central Los Angeles, Watts, Brooklyn, or Harlem – and all are filmed on location. Nearly every narrative is explicitly marked to be diegetically taking place concurrently with the film's theatrical release. Corresponding to the coming-of-age trope, the hood functions as the space where *right now*, young African-Americans are struggling to grow up in bleak conditions. According to Massood (2003), *Boyz* "literally mapped out the terrain of the contemporary black city for white, mainstream audiences" (p. 153). An important impetus for the creation of this hood chronotope is to shed light on a then mostly unseen geographic space in mainstream media.

It is fitting that *Boyz* and *Menace* are both set in Los Angeles, a city that notoriously manufactures its reality through fantasy, primarily via Hollywood's spectacular imagery. Creating a self-image of abundance and sunny paradise, L.A. privileges its prosperous areas – Beverly Hills, Hollywood, Bel-Air, Malibu – while excluding its "other" spaces from representation. *Boyz* and *Menace* construct an image of Los Angeles overrun with poverty, violence, drugs, and racism – "a likeness that stands in contradistinction to the tropical paradise manufactured both by the city's boosters and by the movie industry" (Massood, 2003, p. 148). The films are thus self-reflexive discourses about the dynamics of power inherent in representation and image manufacture. Along with rap music and footage of the Rodney King beating and the subsequent riot, the hood film exposes the 'two-ness' of African-American identification, both inside and outside the 'American' experience.

On the other hand, the hood film is also concerned with remedying an outsider (read: white) examination of the hood. South Central Los Angeles had only received cursory treatment in the American social imagination up until the hood film, and what was represented was crude and sensationalistic. A highly publicized 1988 TV special by Tom Brokaw and the film *Colors* (Dennis Hopper, 1988) both concentrated solely on gang warfare, failing to provide any substantial context for the catastrophic environments presented. "Singleton's task [with *Boyz*] in part," according to Michael Eric Dyson (1992), "is a filmic demythologization of the reigning tropes, images, and metaphors that have expressed the experience of life in South Central Los Angeles" (p. 125). The melodramatic mode is crucial here in presenting a diverse range of sympathetic characters and relationships that complicate this previously unsophisticated and undeveloped view of the hood. Thus, the hood film bears a heavy burden of representation; it must portray the ugly realities of a Los Angeles rarely seen, but not fall into the sensationalistic, one-dimensional depictions that it is attempting to correct.

One of the ways the hood film navigates this tenuous representation is to present the city as a bounded civic space made up of contained communities. The feelings of enclosure and entrapment become palpable in the hood film, and a system of signs is encoded in the terrain to make this atmosphere explicit. The first shot of *Boyz* – following its title card and chilling statistic that "One out of every twenty-one Black American males will be murdered in their lifetime. Most will die at the hands of another Black male" – has the camera dramatically tracking in on a stop sign, filling the screen with the word "STOP" while a plane flies overhead in the distance. Signaling both the desire for mobility and the institutional limits that prevent such movement, this sign is just the first in a series of "One Way" and "Do Not Enter" signs that pervade the urban environment of the film, controlling movement and preventing free passage. *Menace* exhibits a similar system of signs; prior to Caine being shot and his cousin fatally wounded, a sign for Crenshaw Boulevard is shown while a streetlight turns red, again suggesting the limitations of movement within the hood.

On the other side of the country, entrapment and enclosure takes on a different materialization. As opposed to the horizontal hood of South Central Los Angeles, the hood in *Straight Out of Brooklyn*, *Juice*, and *Clockers* is a vertical construction, set among New York's high-rise housing projects and adjacent neighborhoods. Constraint and restricted mobility is evidenced here by visual tightness and spatial compression, fueling the stress and tension of the narrative. Rather than street signs, buildings and brick exteriors become the visual motif of "a world of architectural height and institutional might that by contrast diminishes their own stature as black teenagers in the city" (Forman, 2002, p. 270). Unlike the spatial expanse of South Central Los Angeles, the hood in New York is a maze of constricting and connecting contours, violence and death waiting around every corner. Like the airplane in the opening of *Boyz*, *Clockers* uses the motif of the train to signal the desire for mobility.

Common to hoods on both the East and West coast, however, is the ominous presence of the police. While most characters in the hood are seen as victims of their surroundings, there is one individual that is unanimously disdained in the hood film: the oppressive police officer. In *Boyz*, the recurring appearance of two patrol officers, the more abusive of the two being black, again indicates a strong institutional constraint on mobility. A multitude of aural and visual cues also speaks to this ubiquity of police surveillance, particularly the persistent searchlights and off-screen sounds of police helicopters. Invoking Foucault's panopticon,

Massood (2003) claims "this method of control, dispersed over the urbanscape, facilitates efforts to keep the community in its place through the internalization of surveillance and the consciousness of perceived criminality" (p. 156). Scenes in both *Boyz* and *Menace* show the boys being stopped and harassed by the police for simply driving in the wrong place at the wrong time, reinforcing this idea of perceived criminality based on geography.

From Michael Stewart (see Levine, 1987) to Eleanor Bumpers (see Prial, 1987) to Rodney King (see Mydans, 1992) to Amadou Diallo (see Fritsch, 2000), there is a long history of police brutality against innocent African-Americans with no justice brought upon the perpetrators. *Do the Right Thing* was released in the midst of a series of racially motivated crimes perpetrated by New York City police officers, and a few of these cases are explicitly mentioned in the film, as characters yell out "Michael Stewart," "Eleanor Bumpers," and "Howard Beach" (see McFadden, 1986) during the riot scene. The credit sequence also pays respect and dedicates the film to the families of six recent victims of police brutality. Michael Stewart is of particular importance to this film, as Radio Raheem's (Bill Nunn) death is a direct mirroring of Stewart's attack. In 1983, Michael Stewart, a 25 year-old black man, was arrested for scribbling graffiti and was subsequently choked to death by three officers who were eventually acquitted of any wrongdoing. The scene is re-enacted in *Do the Right Thing*, an example of what is referred to by Spike Lee, in the DVD director's commentary of the film, as the "Michael Stewart Chokehold."

Another integral element in this spatial configuration of the hood is the strong connection to rap and hip-hop culture. In fact, it was the song "Boyz-N-the-Hood" by Easy-E in 1986 that first established 'the hood' as an important term in the spatial discourse of young urban blacks across the country. West Coast 'gangsta rap,' particularly N.W.A.'s *Straight Outta Compton* in 1989, "vividly portrays the hood as a space of violence and confrontation, a zone of indiscriminate aggression where threat and danger are commonplace, even banal" (Forman, 2002, pp. 263–4). Both intimately concerned with spatial logic, sharing narrative and visual imagery, as well as common language and codes of masculinity, gangsta rap and the hood film demonstrate a bond of cross-pollination and reciprocal influence. The casting of popular hip-hop artists as key characters – Ice Cube in *Boyz*, MC Eiht and Pooh Man in *Menace*, Ice T in *New Jack City*, Sticky Fingaz in *Clockers*, and Tupac Shakur in *Juice* – as well as many more in supporting roles contributes to each film's credibility and authenticity among young audiences, while at the same time providing enhanced exposure for the musicians, most of whom contribute to the film's soundtrack. Dyson (1992) partially attributes this coalescence to the problems of the hood, whereby "young black males have responded in the last decade primarily in a rapidly flourishing independent popular culture, dominated by two genres: rap music and black film ... [where they can] visualize and verbalize their perspectives on a range of social, personal, and cultural issues" (p. 124). As a result, the use of rap music is a textual and paratextual modernization of the melodramatic mode.

Not only does the use of rap music contribute to the hood film's specificity of place, but also its specificity of temporality. In *Boyz*, for instance, the scenes of Tre's childhood are accompanied by nondiegetic jazz-based, ambient music, but when the narrative is propelled into the present, to the same year as the film's release, rap music signifies and solidifies this shift. In addition, the hood film's use of urban dialogue and clothing (such as Spike Lee's fixation with basketball sneakers and sports jerseys) complement the sound of urban experience with its look. Placing the narrative in a specific time and place, providing it with cultural currency, rap music – and its accompanying urban referents – is essential to the portrayal of the hood chronotope.

As indicated in its literal meaning, "drama accompanied by melody," melodrama is fundamentally tied to its use of music to emphasize and underscore its pivotal moments. Rap music is used in just such a fashion, but it also incorporates another melodramatic trope: the lower classes. As its historical emergence among the poor in the French Revolution indicates, "melodrama sides with the powerless" (Vicinus, 1981, p. 130). Rap music similarly arose out of lower-class conditions – the Bronx in New York City – and along with its spatial and temporal priorities, provides a perfect complement to the melodrama of the hood film. Public Enemy's "Fight the Power," commissioned specifically for *Do the Right Thing*, acts as a diegetic soundtrack within the film, the physical catalyst for the film's violent conflict, and a rallying call against the injustice faced in the hood. Again cloaking itself with a veneer of realism, in this case hip hop, the hood film puts the melos back in melodrama.

Beyond mere melos, however, the hood film also updates the melodramatic form by including multiple forms of media within its diegetic world, amounting to an explicit engagement with intermediality. Playing news media clips of crime reports is a common trope used in many of the films, and as viewers we are often watching the characters watch, both film and television. A pivotal scene in *New Jack City* has Nino and associates watching *Scarface* (De Palma, 1983), the image of Tony Montana projected on to his body in a not-so-subtle allusion, while *Juice* similarly has Bishop excitedly cheering on his gangster idol when watching *White Heat* (Raoul Walsh, 1949). *Juice* foregrounds DJing both as Q's (Omar Epps) chance at escaping the hood and as the main attraction in a variety of settings, while *Menace* has O-Dog continually replaying a surveillance videotape of himself throughout the film, and Caine summarily dismisses the shiny optimism of *It's a Wonderful Life* (Frank Capra, 1946). *Clockers* contains the most explicit intermedial examples, Lee having created both an egregious music video of exaggerated rap clichés (brandishing guns, scantily clad women, malt liquor), seen on television in the bar, as well as a violent video game called "Gangsta" (which required its own production team), played by young Shorty in the film. Both underscore the media's contribution to urban violence. "The use of media within each film's narrative framework represents," according to Antonio (2002), "a cinematic vaccine, concocted by each director and offered in small yet powerful doses, to stimulate the mind's critical abilities and encourages a different kind of resistance" (p. 117). More than just melo-drama then, we get a kind of media-drama that collages various media to express its spatial pathos.

These multiple elements that build the spatial and temporal logic of the hood lead to the central dilemma of the cycle: should the hood be abandoned? This is a unique twist on the typical melodramatic trajectory; whereas the home is traditionally the space of innocence to be restored in melodrama, the hood – in the place of the home – is seen as beyond rescue in the hood film. *Boyz*, *Menace*, and *Clockers* problematically advocate fleeing the hood as the only means of survival and advancement. Paradoxically, with the privileging of the father in *Boyz* (also problematic), Furious Styles (Laurence Fishburne) instills Tre with the ethical responsibility desperately needed to stop the violence in the hood, but it instead equips him with the mobility to leave the hood for college in Atlanta. Similarly, *Menace* also suggests leaving the hood as the only means of escaping the cycle of violence and crime, although Caine does suggest Atlanta is just another ghetto where they will remain victims of institutional racism. To those who cannot escape the hood, or cannot escape it in time, only death awaits.

On the surface, we can take issue with such a seemingly contradictory resolution. If the hood film works so hard to communicate the problems facing this community, why would it advocate its abandonment? This false dilemma seemingly

reinforces the conservatives' one-sided picture of personal responsibility and choice, conceals the racist underpinnings of spatial containment, and deflects attention from the need of governmental and social agencies to financially and logistically support and assist black inner-city districts in urban renewal and social healing.

(Chan, 1998, p. 46)

While a critique such as Chan's against the hood film's abandonment of its own concern is certainly valid, viewing the dilemma from the perspective of its melodramatic mode presents another story. This logic of "flee the hood or die" is typical of the melodramatic "logic of the excluded middle" (Brooks, 1976, p. 15), in which dilemmas are posed in Manichaean terms. By framing the protagonist's predicament as a do-or-die scenario, the opportunity is created for the pathos-through-action climaxes discussed previously. As a result, the victim-hero earns sympathy and the moral good is revealed, inviting the viewer to be moved by the victim's dire circumstances, in this case, the detrimental conditions of the hood.

Furthermore, as Laura Mulvey (1987) so elegantly states, "the strength of the melodramatic form lies in the amount of dust the story raises along the road, a cloud of over-determined irreconcilables which put up a resistance to being neatly settled in the last five minutes" (p. 76). Even if the conclusion of *Boyz* were a lavish Hollywood wedding between Tre and Brandi, it would not erase the previous 90 minutes of turmoil. In this sense, the contention over the abandonment of the hood, and the difference between the endings of *Boyz* and *Menace*, is rendered moot on account of the melodramatic actualization of the hood. There are certainly other problematic features of the hood film – its paradoxical glorification of the spectacle of violence while advocating against it, its "troubled" gender roles, to put it mildly – but its overarching melodrama is of an ultimately racist spatial construction of the hood, where physical and psychological barriers are erected that confine an underclass to a segregated space. This overarching problem is not lost to whatever narrative or thematic inconsistencies one may find.

Williams (1998) claims that "critics and historians of moving images have often been blind to the forest of melodrama because of their attention to the trees of genre" (p. 60). The first half of this essay aims to have remedied that mistake concerning the hood film cycle and its overlooked foundation of melodrama. With a consideration of its focus on the hood as a whole rather than merely the home, as well as its intermedial update to the mode, the second half of the essay reminds us that whatever problems with the *melo-ghetto* we may find, we would be wise to not be distracted by the trees of its problematizations; instead, we should focus on the forest of the hood's spatial melodrama. "A class is defined," according to Bourdieu (1984), "as much by its *being-perceived* as by its *being*" (p. 483). As evidenced by the hitherto undiscovered melodramatic core to hood habitus, we might add that a class is defined as much by its being-*mis*perceived as well.

Notes

1. The hood film cycle occurred in the midst of a series of high-profile racial injustices, culminating in the 1992 Rodney King verdict and subsequent riot: "the stark videotape, the acquittal of the four white police officers, and the uprising that followed it marked a consciousness-shaping moment for a whole new generation of Americans" (Guerrero, 1993, p. 162).
2. With *Clockers*, Spike Lee intended to create "The hood movie to end all hood movies" (as quoted in Taubin, 1995, p. 76), which it accomplishes, arguably, through its self-conscious genre deconstruction. The release of two successful parodies, *CB4* (Tamra Davis, 1993) and *Don't Be a Menace To South Central While Drinking Your Juice in the Hood* (Paris Barclay, 1996), as well as a mockumentary, *Fear of a Black Hat* (Rusty Cundieff, 1994), further solidified the cycle's expiration date of 1996, at the latest. Distant 'tremors' would include *Belly* (Hype Williams, 1998) and *Slam* (Marc Levin, 1998), while Eminem's quasi-autobiography *8 Mile* (Curtis Hanson, 2002) at least pays homage to Douglas Sirk's classic melodrama *Imitation of Life* (1959), with a clip of it seen on television in his trailer. HBO's universally acclaimed *The Wire* (David Simon, 2002–2008) also exhibits many of the characteristics of the *melo-ghetto*, again cloaking itself in realism, spatial logic, and hip hop.
3. Antonio (2002) traces the utilization of the American gangster formula and style through *New Jack City*, *Boyz*, *Juice*, *Just Another Girl on the I.R.T.*, *Menace II Society*, and *Clockers*; she fails to mention melodrama even once.
4. The *Cineaste* review of *Boyz* is representative: "Behind the streetwise verisimilitude is the soundstage sensibility of a very traditional Hollywood melodrama" (Doherty, p. 16). Guerrero (1993) at least goes beyond mere disparaging one-off comment, accusing *Boyz* of "dominant narrative convention" because of "its melodramatic devotion to the cult of the enterprising individual" which results in it "becoming the raw material of consumer materialism" (p. 186). But not only is this a misreading of melodramatic form, Guerrero misses the manner in which *Boyz* actually utilizes melodrama to achieve what he commends as its "subtle weave of aspirations, frustrations, and violent outburst [that add] complexity and occasional contradiction to the director's antiviolence message" (p. 185). A similarly mistaken conflation of melodrama with "Hollywood formula" occurs with his

consideration of *Juice*; whereas Guerrero locates its weakness in "reduc[ing] pressing collective issues to the drama of individual weaknesses and victimization," (p. 189), I would maintain that it is through this very victimization and melodramatic recognition of innocence and virtue that *Juice*, and the hood film in general, expresses its "pressing collective issues."

5. *Do the Right Thing* was criticized for its lack of drugs in its depiction of Bed-Stuy, to which *Boyz* and other early hood films can be seen as responding to with their ample inclusion of drug use and its detrimental effect on the hood. *Menace* is then an explicit response to what the directors saw as sentimentalism in *Boyz*, followed by Lee's *Clockers*, which self-consciously deconstructs the entire genre.

6. The contempt cinematic melodrama receives is most immediately recognizable in negative reviews of Hollywood's 'serious' dramas intended for Oscar consideration; recent examples include *The Blind Side* (John Lee Hancock, 2009), *The Reader* (Stephen Daldry, 2008), and *Crash* (Paul Haggis, 2005).

7. The implications of this controversial scene have been debated endlessly (Mitchell, 1991; Christensen, 1991; McKelly, 1998; etc.), but to my knowledge, never from the perspective of Mookie as melodramatic victim-hero.

References

Antonio, S. D. (2002). *Contemporary African American Cinema*. New York, NY: Lang.

Baldwin, J. (1968, July 23). Sidney Poitier. *Look, 32*, 50–54.

Bourdieu, P. (1977). *Outline of a Theory of Practice*. Cambridge, England: Cambridge University Press.

Bourdieu, P. (1984). *Distinction: A Social Critique of the Judgement of Taste*. Cambridge, MA: Harvard University Press.

Brooks, P. (1976). *The Melodramatic Imagination: Balzac, Henry James, Melodrama, and the Mode of Excess*. New Haven, CT: Yale University Press.

Chan, K. (1998). The Construction of Black Male Identity in Black Action Films of the Nineties. *Cinema Journal, 37*(2), 35–48.

Christensen, J. (1991). Spike Lee, Corporate Populist. *Critical Inquiry, 17*(3), 582–595.

Doherty, T. (1991). Two Takes on *Boyz N the Hood*. *Cineaste, 18*(4), 16.

Diawara, M. (1993). Black American Cinema: The New Realism. In M. Diawara (Ed.), *Black American Cinema: Aesthetics and Spectatorship* (pp. 3–25). New York, NY: Routledge.

Dyson, M. E. (1992). Between Apocalypse and Redemption: John Singleton's *Boyz N the Hood*. *Cultural Critique, 21*, 121–141.

Elsaesser, T. (1987). Tales of Sound and Fury: Observations on the Family Melodrama. In C. Gledhill (Ed.), *Home Is Where the Heart Is: Studies in Melodrama and the Woman's Film* (pp. 43–69). London, England: BFI Pub.

Forman, M. (2002). *The Hood Comes First: Race, Space, and Place in Rap and Hip-Hop*. Middletown, CT: Wesleyan University Press.

Fritsch, J. (2000, February 26). 4 Officers in Diallo Shooting are Acquitted of all Charges. *New York Times*, p. B6.

Gledhill, C. (1987). The Melodramatic Field: An Investigation. In C. Gledhill (Ed.), *Home Is Where the Heart Is: Studies in Melodrama and the Woman's Film* (pp. 5–39). London, England: BFI Pub.

Gledhill, C. (2000). Rethinking Genre. In C. Gledhill & L. Williams (Eds.), *Reinventing Film Studies* (pp. 221–43). London, England: Arnold.

Guerrero, E. (1993). *Framing Blackness: The African American Image in Film*. Philadelphia, PA: Temple University Press.

Kendall, S. D. (1994). *New Jack Cinema: Hollywood's African American Filmmakers*. Silver Spring, MD: J.L. Denser, Inc.

Levine, R. (1987, March 28). M.T.A. Won't Charge 10 in Michael Stewart Case. *New York Times*, p. 31.

Massood, P. J. (2003). *Black City Cinema: African American Urban Experiences in Film*. Philadelphia, PA: Temple University Press.

McFadden, R. D. (1986, December 21). Black Man Dies after Beating in Queens. *New York Times*, p. A1.

McKelly, J. C. (1998). The Double Truth, Ruth: *Do the Right Thing* and the Culture of Ambiguity. *African American Review, 32*(2), 215–227.

Mitchell, W. J. T. (1991). Seeing *Do the Right Thing*. *Critical Inquiry, 17*(3), 596–608.

Mulvey, L. (1987). Notes on Sirk and Melodrama. In C. Gledhill (Ed.), *Home Is Where the Heart Is: Studies in Melodrama and the Woman's Film* (pp. 75–79). London, England: BFI Pub.

Mydans, S. (1992, April 30). The Police Verdict; Los Angeles Policemen Acquitted in Taped Beating. *The New York Times*, p. A1.

Prial, F. J. (1987, February 27). Judge Acquits Sullivan in Shotgun Slaying of Bumpurs. *New York Times*, p. B1.

Reid, M. (1995). The Black Gangster Film. In B. K. Grant (Ed.), *Film Genre Reader II* (pp. 456–73). Austin, TX: University of Texas Press.

Setlowe, R. (1993, October 8). Shiftin' Gears, Movin' out of the Hood: Black Filmmakers Expanding Horizons – and Expectations. *Daily Variety*, p. 12.

Taubin, A. (1993). Girl n the Hood. *Sight & Sound, 3*(8), 16–17.

Taubin, A. (1995, September 19). Clocking in: Two Critics Rate Spike Lee's Ultimate Hood Movie. *Village Voice*, p. 76.

Vicinus, M. (1981). Helpless and Unfriended: Nineteenth-Century Domestic Melodrama. *New Literary History, 13*(1), 127–43.

Watkins, S. C. (1998). *Representing: Hip hop culture and the production of black cinema*. Chicago, IL: University of Chicago Press.

Williams, L. (1998). Melodrama Revised. In N. Browne (Ed.), *Refiguring American Film Genres: History and Theory* (pp. 42–88). Berkeley, CA: University of California Press.

Williams, L. (2001). *Playing the Race Card: Melodramas of Black and White from Uncle Tom to O. J. Simpson*. Princeton, NJ: Princeton University Press.

Chapter 13

Do Not Believe the Hype: The Death and Resurrection of Public
Housing in the American Visual Imagination

Nicola Mann

Of the 53 high-rise public housing buildings that once marked a gray and red slash across Chicago's inner-city skyline, only sixteen remain standing. Motivated by the racial and socioeconomic inequalities that have alienated the predominantly African-American population from their neighbors since the 1970s, the Chicago Housing Authority (CHA) is razing its projects and replacing them with mixed-income accommodations (see Figure 11). Announced in 2000, the $1.6 billion urban renewal initiative, titled the Plan for Transformation, aims to integrate public housing residents in the same neighborhood as doctors, teachers, and others gainfully employed in the hope that diversity will counteract the projects' association with concentrated poverty, organized crime, and welfare dependency. While various academics, politicians, and journalists have chronicled these problems over the years, there is no greater critic of Chicago's public housing than late twentieth-century popular culture.

From the wailing police sirens in the television show *Cops*, to the gun-toting bad boys in MTV hip-hop videos of the early 1990s, urban public housing has been a stage on which to enact terrifying anxieties about the "ghetto," forever cementing an out-of-control vision in the collective American mind. Mediated through these highly edited and decidedly dramatized channels, the public's understanding of Chicago's projects has been reduced to a bewildering ideological terrain of stereotypes, exaggerations, and moral panics. This visual panic over public housing allegorized the conservative myth-making strategies and ideologically over-determined images central to the late twentieth-century discourse on the "urban crisis." Blaming the urban minority poor for the poverty and social isolation they faced and exaggerating the threat they posed to the rest of society, television shows like *Cops* helped to establish crime as one of the nation's most significant problems. A 1993 article from the Chicago-based newspaper the *Times Mirror* located the source of this panic by asking the public where they obtained their information about crime. 65 percent responded that they learned about it via the news media.[1] Such fears helped to justify social policies such as the 1994 Violent Crime Control Law Enforcement Act, which subjected public housing communities to increased policing as well as to cuts in income support and social services. Yet the terror of the city was greatly exaggerated, as the national rate of violent inner-city crime actually declined slightly between 1973 and 1994.[2] In other words, the danger posed by the urban "underclass" was disproportional to the toxic discourse that surrounded it. The mainstream news media were not alone in their inflation of the menace of the inner-city. Rather, the real ideological damage was committed on the big screen.

Figure 11: Division Street, Cabrini-Green, 2006.

Today, as the Plan for Transformation implodes the last of Chicago's public housing, this chapter considers two different "ghetto-based" dramas that emerged during the early 1990s; one that parallels the conservative political climate of the time in mythologizing public housing as a site that *deserves* to be razed and the other that argues for the permanence of public housing by offering visual modes of tactical resistance to these myths. I focus attention on how public housing space is performed in terms of the represented residents' spatial mobility and access to the social institutions and resources that make up the metropolitan matrix of Chicago. My first film, Stephen Hopkins' *Judgment Night* (1993), constructs public housing as a site of social isolation through textual references to its cartography: space is hierarchical – zoned, segregated, gated – and encodes boundaries. Chronicling the exploits of four suburbanites who, after taking a wrong turn on the highway, find themselves in the projects, *Judgment Night* depicts Chicago's public housing as a truly nightmarish urban landscape of mindless violence and despair. Incarcerated by iron gates, walls, street signs and red lights, the group spends the duration of the film struggling to get "out" of the hood. In this sense, *Judgment Night* allegorizes the discourses of politicians, policymakers, and developers who described Chicago's projects using metaphors of disease and decay, and other adjectives that constructed the community as "socially isolated."[3] The biggest perpetrator of the social isolation argument is American sociologist William Julius Wilson who sees public housing as a "container" of "neighborhood effects," an environment within which residents fester passively and dysfunctionally "separate" from education and employment opportunities.[4] *Judgment Night*'s spatial transgressions between centeredness and marginality correspond with Wilson's attempt to provide "a spatial fix" for "generalized insecurities and complaints" about American society.[5] In framing the projects as the moral inverse of the suburbs – as a deviant urban core populated by a hopelessly pathological "other" – public housing is sentenced to death in the viewer's imagination.

Released just one year before *Judgment Night*, Bernard Rose's horror film *Candyman* (1992) offers a more democratic vision of spatial justice. Based on Clive Barker's short story, "The Forbidden" (1986), *Candyman* features a black ghost who haunts anyone who dares to say his name five times into a mirror.[6] Rose alters the narrative from a white, lower-class British inner-city to Chicago's Cabrini-Green. Smashing through the sociospatial barriers portrayed in *Judgment Night*, *Candyman* reconceptualizes public housing as a site of spatial negotiation and opportunity. For most of the film, white anthropology graduate student Helen Lyle (Virginia Madsen), like her male suburban counterparts in *Judgment Night*, assumes the role of privileged "investigator" of the projects. In pursuit of the Cabrini-Green folk legend, she too *crosses over* to the projects and yet, unlike the characters in *Judgment Night*, there is no escape at the film's conclusion. With her death Helen pays the ultimate price for her mis*judgment* of public housing. Through various observational motifs such as aerial shots, mirrors, and holes in walls, Rose offers a new way of *seeing* public housing. Employing *Candyman*'s central theme of epistemological and mythological resurrection as a framework, this chapter warns against notions of black sociopathy that render public housing residents "socially isolated" from the wider urban metropolis.

The spatial negotiations in *Candyman* are key to understanding the social mobilization of "real" residents of Chicago's public housing. By linking Pierre Bourdieu's place-based concept habitus and Krista Brumley and Kevin Fox Gotham's conceptual tool "using space" to the lived experiences of public housing dwellers, I draw attention to the attempts of some residents to contest their perceived marginality.[7] Bourdieu has described habitus as a "sense of one's place ... a sense of the other's place" in the world of one's surrounding environment and is concerned with how these "senses" affect our ability to maneuver within different fields.[8] "Using space" builds on the "navigative" possibilities inherent in Bourdieu's concept by focusing specifically on the transitional link between socioeconomic constraints and survival tactics employed by tenants in order to go about their daily lives. I apply Brumley and Gotham's tool to the work of Chicago's only public housing newspaper, *Residents' Journal*. This bi-monthly newspaper is written, produced, and distributed entirely by public housing residents and is free to all of the city's remaining public housing households, health care facilities, community centers, and religious institutions. It is also available at a subscription rate to others outside of public housing. *Residents' Journal* was introduced in 1996, a year and a half after the U.S. Department of Housing and Urban Development (HUD) provisionally took control of the CHA, as a response to executive director Vincent Lane's failure to address infamous housing conditions at the developments.[9] As part of HUD's efforts to alter the public perception of residents, Assistant Secretary Joseph Shuldiner announced plans to start a resident-written newspaper. *Residents' Journal's* editor Ethan Micheali stipulated that the newspaper was going to be exactly as its name suggests: a journal for public housing residents and *not* a political forum for the CHA:

> I was immediately intrigued by the idea (of *Residents Journal*), having heard often from residents that the mainstream media misrepresented them and failed to provide them with useful information ... Before accepting the position, I asked the CHA for a written guarantee they would not censor or otherwise shape the editorial content of the publication. I felt that editorial independence would be a critical component of the publication's ability to attract and retain residents to its ranks.[10]

Responding to residents' frustrations regarding their misrepresentation in the mainstream news media, for the past 13 years *Residents' Journal* has been at the forefront of an effort to re-present Chicago's public housing in the American imagination. In contrast to the dystopian interpretations and imagined reputations traditionally shackled to representations of the "ghetto" or "slum," *Residents' Journal* appreciates the actual daily practices of those who inhabit this environment: The neighbor*hood* (home) of public housing becomes a specific space of place-based attachments and spatial mobilization. *Residents' Journal* illustrates the ways in which some inhabitants represent their own lives, thereby challenging the static conceptual limitations of Wilson's "neighborhood effects" model. In depicting Chicago's public housing as a psychotopographical landscape where sociospatial divides *can* be conquered, *Candyman* and *Residents' Journal* demythologize the one-dimensional terrain of stereotypes, assumptions, and moral panics presented in *Judgment Night*.

Death: *Judgment Night*

Director Mario Van Peebles fired the starting gun for the filmic "death" of public housing with the violent project-based film *New Jack City* (1991). Since then, dramatic scenes from the hood have become a commonplace feature on our screens. In representing public housing as a divided space – zoned according to incidents of alcoholism, street crime, and drug addiction – *Menace II Society* (1993), directed by Albert and Allen Hughes, set in the Jordan Downs project in Los Angeles; and *Clockers* (1995), directed by Spike Lee, situated in the Gowanus projects in Brooklyn, were joined by the less critically successful drama *Judgment Night* (1993), set in the Robert Taylor Homes in Chicago. Where Stephen Hopkins' film differs from its contemporaries is in its harshly drawn distinction between the utopian suburban home of the middle-class central characters and the nightmarish inner city they unwillingly venture into en route to a boxing match. The film's strict topographical binary opposition invokes and justifies the late-twentieth-century moral panic over the inner city, helping to seal the fate of public housing in the American visual imagination.

This social polarization is established in the film's first few minutes when we find our suburban heroes – Frank (Emilio Estevez), John (Stephen Dorff), Ray (Jeremy Piven), and Mike (Cuba Gooding, Jr) – in an idyllic autumnal landscape of middle-class familiarity. Scenes of kids riding bicycles and a man with a briefcase coming home from work are accompanied by a symbolic hip-hop soundtrack which pulses in the background like a mounting heartbeat, hinting at the urban fate that awaits them. After hugging his wife on the stoop of their home, Frank and his friends take to the road in a luxurious RV that Ray has secured on loan for the night. The calm before the storm is swiftly cut short, however, when a traffic jam forces the group to make a detour into an area of Chicago recognizable as the concrete towers of the Robert Taylor Homes.

As the RV careens off the Dan Ryan Expressway and into a dimly lit tunnel exit, the camera cuts to a high-angle crane shot that highlights the dystopian gravity of this spatial decision. In stark topographical contrast to the raised street and florescent lights of the freeway, the dark, decayed, burrowed tunnel they turn into leaves the viewer in no doubt that the suburbanites' have made a wrong turn. Finding themselves on the proverbial wrong side of the tracks, the group enters a terrifying urban landscape of litter-filled vacant lots and omnipresent graffiti. Against a cacophony of complaints, Ray brings the RV to a grinding halt in front of a group of homeless men loitering around a burning oil barrel in the middle of the street. Seizing a chance to humiliate the men from the raised safety zone of the RV, Mike beckons them over to ask for directions, "We're the welcome wagon; can you come here for a minute, please?" Under the beam of the headlights, a homeless man stumbles into the frame mumbling the partly discernable line, "Let them have it, Earl." Cue dramatic music as Earl reaches into his pocket, rummaging for the ultimate come back to Mike's provocation: a gun. As the horrified friends dive to the floor of the RV and Ray attempts to retrieve his gun from the glove compartment, the camera reveals that the "weapon" is just a harmless bottle of booze. With his pride thoroughly dented, Ray steps on the gas, ordering his friends to lock the doors and reassuring them that if anything like that happens again, "We'll just blow *them* away."

Judgment Night's representation of urban existence satisfies the image of "underclass" life postulated by William Julius Wilson. Wilson contends that although the lack of jobs and poverty was the ultimate cause behind inner-city destitution, behavioral deficiencies amongst predominantly African-American communities create a "tangle of pathology" – a term borrowed from former Senator Daniel Patrick Moynihan to describe the social traits that perpetuate the conditions of the poor. Wilson argues that since the 1970s, structural changes in the economy – such as the shift from manufacturing to service industries and the departure of low skilled jobs from city centers – rendered the remaining non-working inner-city families "socially isolated" from role models and job networks, and mired in concentrated poverty, crime, single motherhood, and welfare dependency. With this social transformation of the ghetto, "joblessness as a way of life takes on a different social meaning ... a vicious cycle is perpetuated."[11]

Hopkins' camera articulates Wilson's critical stance by framing the Robert Taylor Homes as the social equivalent of a black hole. Through textual references to its cartography, the film constructs public housing as a site of repression and social isolation. "One Way," "Do Not Enter," and red "Stop" signs appear throughout the film, signifying the various pathologies that Wilson argues separate housing project residents from the wider metropolitan matrix (see Fig 12 & 13). Within this filmic road to perdition, residents are trapped in a vicious cycle that offers them one choice: murder or be murdered. Frank, John, Ray, and Mike's repeated cries of "We have *never* been here" and "I don't see a sign or *anything* here," add weight to the sense that public housing is a sociospatial dead end. Ensuring that citizenship exists solely within the mobile territory of the RV, the vehicle comes to symbolize America's investment in individualist home ownership as a marker of national

Figure 12: *Judgment Night*, Dir: Stephen Hopkins, Largo Entertainment, 1993.

belonging. The film's stark comparison between the "respectability, diligence and moral superiority of (white) homeowner" and the "disreputableness, slothfulness, and property endangering" black project tenants renders citizenship an ideological construction and a type of control.[12] As Seyla Benhabib writes in *The Rights of Others*, "Citizenship and practices of political membership are the rituals through which the nation is reproduced spatially. The control of territorial boundaries ... seeks to ensure the purity of the nation *in time* through the policing of its contacts and its interactions *in space* ... Every nation has its others, within and without."[13] In this sense, the vehicle's windshield becomes a literal and metaphorical frontier demarcating those *in* the modern spaces of order (those "within") and those *outside* (those "without"). Rendering the underclass "socially isolated" from the safe, comfortable lifestyle coded within the interior of the RV, the planar frame of the windshield confines modernity and power within the closed limits of middle-class white suburbia (see Fig 14). This representation of the underclass as a separate group reinforces the discourses of urban decline widespread in American culture during the late twentieth century.

In addition to Wilson's critique, during the 1980s and 1990s numerous cultural commentators traced the troubles of US cities to the growth of an alien and dysfunctional urban core. A *Time* magazine story from 1977 stated: "Behind (the ghetto's) crumbling walls lives a large group of people who are more intractable, more socially alien and more hostile than almost anyone had imagined. They are the unreachables: the American underclass."[14] This statement isolates the "underclass" as a disconnected group implicitly responsible for its members' misery and "unreachability." As Steve Macek notes in his book *Urban Nightmares*, "With such an 'Other,' no commonality, no communication, no shared experience is desirable or even possible; the only possible relation decent (white, suburban) people can have to such Others is to exclude, control, and confine them."[15]

Figure 13: "Station closed."

Figure 14: The windshield.

Reared on this ideology, when the suburbanites look down at the projects' residents though the picture frame of the windshield, they are certain that mockery and objectification is all that the poor *deserve*. Thus, when the RV pulls away from the homeless men and Ray reassures his friends, "Look, don't worry, when the guys built the expressway they did it *logically*. When we hit the next intersection, we'll cut over," he is convinced that "the guys" (Chicago Aldermen Richard Daley and John J. Duffy) had it right: *logic* will prevail and the paranoid political establishment that constructed the expressway barrier will protect him and his friends from the *illogical* urban "other." Ray underlines this sense of intractable difference between himself and the urban dweller when he expects the homeless man to be armed. To Ray, because of *where* he is, the man must be a criminal, a social and spatial pariah who exists outside of or, in the case of the screen metaphor, on the other side of the public sphere. Through this representation of spatial duality – of inside and outside, of self and "other" – the film portrays social barriers, or in the words of Kenneth B. Clark "invisible walls" which "confine those who have no power, and…perpetuate their powerlessness."[16] However, after becoming involuntary witnesses to a drug hit, the group is forced to breach Clark's "invisible wall," leaving the safe confines of the mobile home behind in order to run for their lives.

As gunshots ring out in their wake Ray cries, "Where's the cops, man?," to which Mike responds, "We could dynamite the whole city block and no one would come." "That's *criminal*" decides John. In the next moment, John stumbles across a vandalized payphone. In the few seconds between John uttering "It's criminal" and picking up the abused phone – a democratic feature of urban civilization – the film spatially designates public housing as a "criminogenic" environment.[17] John's critique refers not only to police negligence but also, through the scene's spatio-temporal association, links project residents with the decrepitude of their living environment. This scene provides "a spatial fix" for "generalized insecurities

Figure 15: Robert Taylor Homes.

and complaints" about U.S. society, conveniently blaming local residents for the despicable conditions they are forced to endure on a daily basis.[18] The sense that life in public housing is a *self-made* misery extends to the film's close attention to the bounded iconography of its architecture.

Lured by the deceptively welcoming sight of twinkling Christmas lights in a window, the suburbanites finally arrive at the front door of the foreboding Robert Taylor Homes. Shot from a low angle and illuminated by sultry lighting, the red brick buildings rise up ignobly like a volcano ready to erupt. Iron security fences throw jagged slices of shadow against its side, entombing the high-rise in claw-like silhouettes that look similar to the dark bars of a prison cell (see Figure 15). This abstract geometry magnifies the image of criminality, localizing transgressions within the space, while simultaneously hinting at the perceived destiny of many of its young inhabitants. An exchange between Frank and Ray articulates this sense of social separation:

Frank: We've got to make one of these people let us use their phone.
Ray: Do you really think one of these freaks is going to let us use their phone?!
Frank: These freaks are our neighbors Ray!
Ray: They're not my neighbors.
Frank: I bet we haven't been further than ten miles from your front door this whole night.

Ray's disavowal of his "neighbors" draws attention to how social differences are all the more evident when we live in close proximity to one another. Today, as the Plan for Transformation calls for half million-dollar condominiums to be constructed adjacent to yet-to-be-demolished public housing high-rises, observers are asking: "how the twain will meet."[19] Doug Van Dyke, a white homeowner in a new mixed-income development admits, "People on both sides have looked at each other with more than a little suspicion."[20] Ray's dismissal of public housing, then, parallels Van Dyke's thinly veiled anxiety about living next door to ex-project residents. This film's theme of spatial dread continues unabated when the pursuing felons force Frank, John, Ray, and Mike to negotiate a rickety ladder that transects two tenement rooftops.

Shot from above, the next sequence frames Robert Taylor Homes as a predatory Venus Flytrap threatening to engulf the suburbanites at every turn. Other elements of the *mise-en-scène*, such as ominous silhouettes and shadows, reinforce the overriding impression that subsidized housing is a hazardous place to visit, or worse still, to live. This disconcerting topography reflects aspects of Ray's troubled subjectivity. Thus, when the suburbanite declares, "Nothing about tonight makes much sense," he is at once disconnected in the space of public housing yet comfortable in his own understanding of it – "They're *not* my neighbors, man." For Ray, the projects will always be viewed through a social barrier, whether it's a windshield or the veiny green veil of the overused hundred dollar bills with which he unsuccessfully tries to buy his life. His viewpoint is geographically and culturally unyielding. The gang leader punishes Ray for his views by tossing him off the roof and into the misty orange netherworld below, dismissing him with the line "You think you can buy me off? Ten thousand dollars might buy you out of North Shore. Here, that means shit. This is my fucking world."

The film's climactic final scene takes place in a South Side grocery store where Hopkins leaves the family man Frank to fight it out with the gang leader alone. After the criminal threatens to hurt the suburbanite's wife and child, a fistfight ensues and "normal" middle-class Frank heroically outwits the deviant public housing resident. As a squad car and ambulance arrive and the final credits roll, the final verdict is in. By framing the projects as a deviant, wild core populated by a hopelessly pathological "other" – the moral inverse of the noble, victorious suburbs – public housing is sentenced to death in the viewer's imagination. If we are not already convinced that public housing is, in Ray's words "hell," then the visual and sonic ferocity of the film's final minutes leaves us in no doubt. Hurricane-force winds whip through the air, slapping the building's exterior and choking the air with trash – giving visual form to the notion that public housing is a lost cause. The portrayal of public housing as a descending spiral of physical disintegration and mental immiseration, from which there is *absolutely* no hope of recovery, reflects the hegemonic mythology surrounding the implementation of the Plan for Transformation.

The Plan's myth-making tactics are effectively articulated in a report from mixed-income property developers, The North Town Community Partnership, which states that, "seen from 40 floors up in a luxury tower across town, Cabrini-Green's apartment slabs brood like tombstones on quarantined turf."[21] The report continues with metaphors of disease and decay that characterize public housing as "warehouses of terminal poverty, crime plagued, prowled by dope gangs." Yet, this report, like the visual propaganda on offer in the film, conveniently ignores historical fact. By failing to articulate the government's culpability in the establishment of urban problems – the denial of social services, the failing public school system, and sweeping disinvestment – the ninety-minute cultural narrative distorts the meaning of Chicago's inner-city troubles and narrows the complexity of project life. Instead, public housing exists as a problem in itself, and a burden to the world. By presenting inner-city Chicago as a degenerate space rife with poverty, lack of policing, dead ends, and cultural aliens, *Judgment Night* supports the government's implosion of public housing and conveniently ignores the generations of law-abiding residents who, against the odds, made this place their home. Indeed, in spite of their difficult living conditions, many residents have spent years trying to improve their built environment, and create a nurturing place of upward social mobility and hope.

In the following section I offer a reading of real-life community mobility, *Residents' Journal*, via the spatial re-conceptualizations offered in *Candyman*. Building on Anne Buttimer's assertion that "The observer who explores place speaks of housing, whereas the resident of that place lives the process of dwelling," I contrast the differing sociospatial landscapes presented in *Judgment Night* and *Candyman* as a way to highlight the difference between an *outsider's* way of describing public housing and an *insider's* way of experiencing dwelling.[22] The "outsider's trap," continues Buttimer "is that one looks at places, as it were, from an abstract sky."[23]

Resurrection: *Candyman*

Candyman's credit sequence opens with overhead shots of Chicago's traffic-laden expressways, which lace through the city streets like overly clogged bodily arteries. Accompanied by the dramatic tones of a Philip Glass soundtrack, the camera weaves through every inch of this heaving city mass, taking us on a journey from the Kennedy Expressway, to the "Red" and "White" buildings of the Cabrini-Green housing project in the city's Near North Side, and onwards to the high-rise condominiums of the glittering Gold Coast. By opening *Candyman* in this ethnographic manner, Bernard Rose signifies how public housing has been mapped *onto* and *into* the vocabulary of the American popular imagination. As the camera pans across this landscape, Candyman's austere voice articulates this infamy: "*They will say* that I have shed innocent blood … I came for *you*." Candyman's threat to the collective "you" is, in effect, addressed to the collective "us" – the people who live in the condominiums and work out at the gyms below – the white middle-class movie-goer. Filmed in 1992 when Cabrini-Green was reeling from the gang wars of the late 1980s, *Candyman* emerged during the height of white middle-class paranoia about the threat of housing project crime spilling into *their* communities. In this sense, *Candyman* joins *Judgment Night* in its theme of sociospatial dread. Yet, while *Judgment Night* presents the city's borders through a strict suburban/utopia vs. urban/dystopia binary, *Candyman* offers a more nuanced social analysis of these divisions.

Rose critiques Chicago's border-filled city space in the film's opening sequence. Maps show a comprehensive overview of the city, yet, through abstraction and one-dimensionality they also eliminate qualities of urban experience and street life. As Michel de Certeau has argued, the planner's bird's-eye viewpoint fails to map the point of view of personal itineraries in space by which pedestrians actualize sites through their "narrative footsteps."[24] However, by lingering over Chicago's inner-city space for a full six minutes, Rose's opening sequence signals a call to arms – a rallying cry for a reanalysis of this space. We are forced to look past the "grid" of the map to the spaces in-between the buildings, at the "narrative footsteps" on the sidewalks where the potential for new thoughts and realities emerge. While acknowledging the limits of filmic representation, this sequence emphasizes the power of film to resist symbolization and to redraw the city's topography. This objective begins when Rose's camera departs its spectral vantage point, swooping down to street level amongst the "narrative footsteps" of Chicago.

Here, *on the ground*, we find Helen interviewing a teenager who has heard about Candyman from a "friend of a friend who knew someone." This, importantly, is the first of three back-to-back versions of the legend the film will offer. Through a female voice-over we learn that Candyman is a bogeyman who can be invoked by the ritual of saying his names five times in front of a mirror. As the retelling goes, in a white picket-fenced suburban house, Clara dares her amorous boyfriend Billy to perform the incantation. Too cowardly to complete the mantra in full, Billy pronounces the name four times before retreating downstairs. Alone, Clara stares at her reflection in the mirror and, in a demonstration of supernatural curiosity, utters the final "Candyman." With this last word, Candyman's figure (Tony Todd) flashes behind her, followed by a shot of the living-room ceiling from the boyfriend's viewpoint, punctured by a hook seeping with blood. A little later in the film, Helen and Bernadette light-heartedly replay the teenager's version of the story by beginning the invocation, which only Helen completes.

The second version of the Candyman legend emerges when, seeking further verification of the legend, Helen consults with her academic rival, Philip Purcell (Michael Culkin), who provides a historicized version of the Candyman story:

Candyman was the son of a slave. His father had amassed a considerable fortune from designing a device for the mass-production of shoes after the Civil War. Candyman had been sent to all the best schools and had grown up in polite society where he was a prodigious talent as an artist. He was much sought after when it came to documenting one's wealth and position in society in a portrait and it was in this latter capacity that he was commissioned by a wealthy landowner to capture his daughter's virginal beauty. When a relationship developed between the young man and woman, the father executed a terrible revenge. He paid a pack of brutal hooligans to chase Candyman through the town to Cabrini Green, where they sawed off his right hand with a rusty blade. They proceeded to smash nearby beehives and smear his body with honey, causing him to be stung to death, and nobody came to his aid. They burnt his body on a giant pyre and scattered his ashes over Cabrini-Green. As a result, Candyman is said to haunt Cabrini-Green.

Following this professorial interpretation, the film shifts to the academic interior of a classroom at the University of Illinois. Here, Helen replays a Dictaphone recording of the teenager's interview, which invites the interest of nearby African-American janitors, Henrietta and Kitty. Intrigued by their knowledge of the Candyman tale, Helen asks the women to give her their version of a recent murder at the projects that had been linked to the legend:

Kitty:	Well all I know is that there was some lady in her tub and … and she heard a noise. I think her name was Ruthie-Jean … And she heard this banging and smashing like someone was trying to make a hole in the wall - so Ruthie called 911 and she said somebody coming through the walls. And they didn't believe her … But when they finally got there she was dead.
Helen:	Was she shot?
Kitty:	No. Umm, she was killed with a hook. Sch'tz (slicing movement with her hand) Yeah.
Henrietta:	It's true. Yeah, it is. I read it in the papers. Candyman killed her.

Taken together, the three accounts of the legend can be read as a paradigm of *Candyman's* thematic concerns, since they establish the interrogation of the credibility of myth. From the teenager's tale of white suburban horror to Purcell's academic account to Henrietta and Kitty's urban reality, *Candyman* offers three contradictory versions of the legend that cross class, race, and educational boundaries. Through its sociocultural plurality, *Candyman* deconstructs the one-dimensional white, male, middle-class interpretation of urban life we are offered in *Judgment Night*. This diversity highlights the futility of Helen's quest for a singular definition of the legend and, in a broader sense, public housing as a whole.

Moreover, this sequence draws attention to the fact that *Candyman* is a story *about* storytelling. This self-reflexive technique underscores the film's examination of representational modes of truth as well as our spectatorial role in the consumption of myths related to life in public housing. *Candyman* exposes not only how representations traffic between the screen and the viewer but also lays bare the manipulative power inbuilt in all representations. This exploitation is apparent when we consider the way in which Helen is framed as the conduit for the film's narrative. As the teenager regales Helen with her version of the legend, the academic looks imploringly out of the screen as if directly into the eyes of the viewer. Centrally locating her in the frame, Helen's only prop is a cigarette, which sends curlicues of smoke about her head, framing her in the gauzy ocher tones of a 1940s Hollywood heroine. This aestheticized close-up effectively foregrounds the following sequences' investigations into voyeuristic fascination, placing Helen and, through its spectatorial identifications, the viewer as central figures within this examination. This theatrical close-up problematizes the relationship between subject and object, underscoring how we exoticize and abstract the inner-city as a space of "otherness" and pathologize it as a subject for academic study.

The subjective potential inherent in all representations is critically evaluated through the absence of the film's central object: the figure of Candyman. While he enters our mental consciousness from the beginning of the film through childish gossip, academic scholarship, and newspaper headlines, it is not until over halfway through the movie that Tony Todd enters the physical action. As Candyman admits, he exists only through "the writing on the wall," "the whisper in the classroom," and "the rumor on the street corner." Moreover, as trailers for the film hauntingly plead, "What's behind the mirror?" and maintain that, "You don't have to believe, just beware," the question must be asked: beware of what exactly? If the teenager, the academic, and the cleaners are to be believed, what we need to be fearful of is Candyman and what he most powerfully signifies, of course, is the archetypical figure of the "underclass": the angry black man.[25] Candyman's exclusion from the physical action for all but a couple of final scenes critiques the way in which *Judgment Night* profiles public housing residents' as a vaguely threatening but nonetheless nameless group of "others." Candyman's corporal absence deconstructs our naive but willing consumption of orally circulated and written gossip centered on African-American males in Chicago's public housing. This naiveté is apparent when Henrietta and Kitty reassure Helen about the reliability of their version of events not through the accuracy garnered of personal experience but with the guarantee, "It's true. Yeah, it is. I read it in the papers."

Long tainted with the dubious honor of being "America's most notorious housing development," over the years Cabrini-Green has been subject to damning headlines.[26] Typical captions during the late twentieth century read: "Suspects Sought in Cabrini Death" (*Chicago Defender*, 1974) and "Cabrini-Green Area Thieves Prey on Women Drivers in Daylight" (*Chicago Tribune*, 1982).[27] The film acknowledges this infamy when Helen browses through newspaper microfiche of the death of Ruthie Jean only to discover the derogatory headline, "What killed Ruthie-Jean?: Life in the Projects." By asking "what" and not "who" killed the public housing resident, the film suggests that some news media, far from being passive heuristic devices of verifiable truths, are destructive forces willing to construct fear and pathology around the material conditions of urban communities. In this sense, fear coalescences, not only in the invisible figure of Candyman, but in public housing as a whole. Therefore, when Candyman admits "I am Rumor. It is a blessed condition to live in other people's dreams, but not have to be," he acknowledges the phantasmatic importance attached not only to his existence but also to the fictive nature of some news stories centered in Cabrini-Green. Indeed, CHA figures during the late 1990s indicated that Cabrini-Green was not an especially violence-prone area. As Larry Bennett and Adolph Reed Jr. write, "Between 1992 and 1993 Cabrini Green's incidence of crime (that is, annual homicides, criminal sexual assaults, serious assaults, robberies, burglaries, thefts, and vehicle thefts per one hundred residents) fell from 10.3 to 8.2."[28] The film's opening theme of narrative interrogation emphasizes that, unlike *Judgment Night*, *Candyman* does not simply endorse media-based "truths" but, as these figures suggest, presents them as misleading representations generating fear and maintaining social tensions.

Through its critical examination of the reception and transmission of stories centered in public housing, *Candyman* engages in some of the same disputes as *Residents' Journal*. The newspaper recently criticized a story promoted in the mainstream media that increased violence in the city could be linked to CHA leaseholders. In fact, based on an analysis of Chicago Police Department data, *Residents' Journal* responded that there are no concrete links between the demolition of high-rise public housing buildings and the perceived increase in crime.[29] In order to tackle what Micheali calls the "falsification" of public housing in the television news media, since 2000 *Residents' Journal* has transmitted a weekly live call-in television show on the Cable Access Network (see Figure 16).[30] With a potential audience of millions, *RJ TV* highlights the journal's Urban Youth International Journalism Program, an initiative that aims to "broaden the intellectual, educational and career horizons of youths who live in public housing and other low-income neighborhoods by training them to communicate their perspectives and priorities in print news and feature articles and other positive examples of community action in the city's public housing."[31] In this sense, *Residents' Journal* provides an oppositional discourse to mainstream media representations of project life that conjoins practice (life in the projects) with (re)presentation. *Candyman*'s analogous (re)visioning is on offer for all to see as Helen and her academic partner Bernadette (Kasi Lemmons) make their fateful *crossover* into Cabrini-Green in search of the site of Ruthie-Jean's murder.

Having parked their car at what Helen refers to as a "safe" distance, the scholars climb the dilapidated stairwell of the red brick building, where the director's camera reveals filthy walls, graffiti-stained with Candyman's name. Perched atop Helen's shoulder, the camera pans all

Figure 16: Mary C. Johns on RJTV, the *Residents' Journal* television show. Cable Access Network, March, 2008.

Figure 17: Helen Lyle (Virginia Madsen) with Bernadette (Kasi Lemmons) recording the "writing on the wall." *Candyman*, Dir: Rose, Bernard. U.S.A.: Polygram Filmed Entertainment/Propaganda Films, 1992.

around, scanning this "writing on the wall" and reflecting Helen's desire for knowledge of the Candyman myth (see Figure 17). Rather than being confused or horrified at what she finds, the academic is delighted; "This is great!" Helen tells a skeptical Bernadette. Arriving at the front door of Ruthie-Jean's vacant apartment, Helen proceeds to violate several boundaries in the space of a few minutes. After climbing over yellow crime scene tape, Helen enters the murdered woman's bathroom (the reported "scene of the crime"), only to discover a hole in the wall where a mirrored medicine cabinet used to be, which marks an entryway into the next apartment. Despite Bernadette's suspicions, Helen crosses the mirrored *border* to see what lies on the "other side."

As Helen scrambles through the hole in the wall, the camera is, again, positioned by her head thereby forcing the viewer to assume the same investigative role. Our pointed identification with the scholar as boundary-breaking "investigator" places the anxious white middle-class movie-goer within an analogous field of mediation. As spectators we also look into the mirror and consequently we too are susceptible to the discoveries that lie on the other side.[32] The viewer, now positioned on the opposite side of the wall to Helen, sees that she is entering through a huge graffitied image of a black face (Candyman's), whose gaping mouth is the hole through which the academic is scrambling. Before Helen has a chance to appreciate the sight in front of her, she lifts her camera and proceeds to take photographs of the graffiti on the walls. As the academic reaches the end of the camera film, the scene is suddenly plunged into darkness; in the few seconds it takes for her eyes to readjust to the varied light conditions, and for the soundtrack to build to a deafening climax, a graffitied black scream fills the cinema screen referencing the "writing on the wall" that sustains Candyman's notoriety (Figure 18). This sequence marks an important filmic shift in terms of how we – Helen and the viewer – *see* public housing.[33] First, in their simplest and most literal form, mirrors act as tools with which to reflect objective truth. Therefore, by looking *into* and *through* the mirror, we are asked to take responsibility for the act of *seeing*. Thus far, *Candyman* has provided dubious vehicles for "truth" – newspapers, oral interviews – but a mirror, as we all know, never lies. Stripped bare of hysteria and academic competition, the mirror comes to symbolize a collective plea to reassess interpretations of public housing. Second, the absence of her photographic shield forces the academic to confront the subject of her study. Helen's direct exposure to public housing, as opposed to reading about Cabrini-Green in a sensationalist media report, marks the film's first symbolic stage towards recognizing the "other."

Promising to return to Cabrini-Green with extra film for her camera, Helen and Bernadette leave Ruthie-Jean's apartment only to be met with a young housing tenant. "You don't belong here, lady, going through people's apartments and things," Ann-Marie McCoy (Vanessa Williams) tells Helen. Ignoring McCoy's chastisement, Helen is excited by the prospect of interviewing the murdered woman's neighbor, and wrangles herself an invitation into her home. Irritated by Helen's snooping, the public housing resident compares the academics to prior visitors – "newspapers, cops, caseworkers, they all want to *know*" – and boldly confronts her inquisitors: "So you say that you doing a study? What are you going to say? That we rob, we steal, that we gang bang: we're all on drugs right? We're

Figure 18: Helen confronts "Candyman."

not all like those downstairs. I just want to raise my son good." Taken aback by McCoy's list of racist stereotypes, Helen is further mystified by an apartment that is warm, comfortable and far removed from the apocalyptic domestic interior that confronted the suburbanites in *Judgment Night*. Here, Helen is forced to meet head-on her academic preconceptions about what the home of a single mother from public housing *should* look like. Raised in an era of public demonizations of inner-city single motherhood, exemplified by Charles Murray's *Losing Ground* (1984), which attacked liberal welfare programs like Aid for Dependent Children for fostering dependency on government handouts, Helen had *expected* McCoy to be an unmitigated failure.[34] In her unrelenting quest to frame Cabrini-Green in a way that supports her thesis, Helen fails to reflect upon the everyday lives of those who don't fit into this narrow idea of project life. By daring to *crossover* into the private domestic space of public housing as opposed to just reading about Cabrini-Green in an academic study, however, *Candyman* exposes the misunderstanding upon which Helen builds her thesis. In this sense, both McCoy and Helen "perform" Brumley and Gotham's conceptual tool "using space." The public housing resident "uses space" to resist her marginal economic position and Helen "uses space" by "witnessing" McCoy's struggle and beginning her journey towards recognizing the "other." McCoy's and Helen's mobility defies the static interpretation of project life offered in *Judgment Night* and unmoors Wilson's "neighborhood effect" significations – "One Way," "Do Not Enter," "Stop" – which firmly situate social pathologies on the back stoops of public housing apartments. Furthermore, in defiance of Murray's report, McCoy is an employed single mother – cleverly revealed through her supermarket worker's uniform – who only wants the best for her young son. In this sense, *Candyman* frames McCoy as a "spatial actor" who negotiates the space around her, enabling her to become an agent of, rather than subject to, her own destiny.[35] Michaeli articulates this need to re-conceptualize single mothers from public housing:

> Once I started covering public housing, I started to see that people were really different from how I had been led to believe. They were not lazy at all. They were incredibly hardworking, for the most part. Really, really diligent in making sure that their kids were dressed and fed and went to school, and that their apartments were clean.[36]

Written *by* and *for* public housing residents, *Residents' Journal* presents a "mobile" take on life in the projects thereby challenging academic and mainstream-media ascribed degradations, which, if they acknowledge residents' at all, frame them as lethargic and ambivalent about their situation. Michaeli stresses the important role of the mass media in this re-imagining:

> *Residents' Journal's* very presence among other media contradicts recurring images of public housing tenants as lazy, illiterate, and unconnected to broader communities ... Mainstream media are sometimes frustratingly reluctant to include the perspectives of public housing tenants in articles and discussions about the future of public housing communities. Media organizations tend to accept assumptions about the behavior

of public housing tenants, the need for mixed-income communities, and the effect of certain types of architecture on the lifestyles of public housing residents. Mainstream media simultaneously tend to ignore and accept the second-rate services provided to public housing residents. I believe this skewed coverage is a direct result of our failure as a society to address issues of race, gender, and poverty.[37]

The neglect of public housing is an issue addressed later in the film when Helen returns to the comfort of her Lincoln Park apartment with the photographic slides of her visit to Cabrini-Green (see Figure 19). Pulling shut the drapes in her living room, Helen projects the stills onto her velvet curtains. In the background emerges the silhouette of Cabrini-Green. It then dawns on the academic that the structure of the building that she had "investigated" that afternoon is *exactly* the same as her own condominium. Helen's building was originally intended to be public housing, but was transformed into expensive apartments in the 1960s due to the lack of structural barrier separating it from the wealthier Gold Coast. Helen reveals this fact to a shocked Bernadette: "They covered the cinder blocks in plaster, and they sold them off as condos." Just as Rose's filmic story-within-a-story exposes the limits of mental subjective representation, so Helen's discovery of an invisible house exposes the physical traces of her building's link to past and present oppression and denial. Indeed, while the academic rightly notes that her building is an architectural replica of Ruthie-Jean's, she ignores the historical and economic factors separating these structures; while one reflects the comfort of gentrification, the other embodies decay. Recalling Kenneth B. Clark's discussion of the formation of "invisible walls," the "invisible walls" in Helen's apartment suggest her alienation from the bureaucratic structures that constructed the projects, and yet her, and our own, implication in its history and present situation. Just as the windshield in *Judgment Night* became a literal and metaphorical frontier demarcating a definitional boundary between those *in* the modern spaces of order and those *outside*, so the plaster walls in Helen's apartment constitute a planar frame that confines power, money, and luxury within the closed limits of white middle-class existence. As Helen peers through the looking glass of her penthouse widow onto the public housing complex beyond, she performs the same action we all do when we turn on the news at night to consume images of the inner-city. This spectacle, experienced from a spectral point-of-view of detachment and assumed authority, can be turned on and off at will. Skewed, flexible framing allows us, as Michaeli points out, to "accept the second-rate services provided to public housing residents" and to protect oneself from the presence of the "other."

It is only when Helen removes the mirrored disguise in Ruthie-Jean's apartment and in her own that she exposes herself to a reality that had otherwise been, quite literally, covered up. By collapsing this spatial boundary, Helen undermines the social and ideological differences separating public housing from the rest of the city. While Ray breaches the "invisible wall" of the RV's windshield thereby confronting the world *outside*, so Helen violates the liminal space of the mirror consequently facing alterity for the first time. The

Figure 19: Inside Helen's apartment on the Gold Coast.

mirror reflections and border-crossings in *Candyman* invite Helen to a critical reversal, to realize the limits that define bourgeois subjectivity, to experience, what Laura Wyrick terms a revelatory "aporia."[38]

The high-speed, violence-ridden climax of *Candyman* begins when the academic encounters the fantastical Candyman in an empty parking garage where he tells her, "I came for you." Overcome, Helen loses consciousness and wakes up to find herself in McCoy's apartment, holding a meat clever and completely drenched in blood. The blood belongs to Anne-Marie's dog, which lies decapitated on the floor – and the single mother's baby, Anthony, is missing. Following this bizarre turn of events, she is arrested for the abduction and assumed murder of McCoy's baby. Henceforth, Helen also becomes the prime suspect for the grisly murders of Bernadette and a psychiatrist at the hospital where she is committed. Helen finally gains the fame she covets, not by publishing her research on Candyman, but through an unexpected kind of infamy. The "recording" materials that the researcher used to decipher the projects are now turned on her; as she is taken away for questioning, the police car's headlights project onto her frame like a Broadway stage-light, while the buzzing flashlights from journalists' cameras snare like a drum roll announcing the academic's entry onto a stage of notoriety normally reserved for the inner-city public housing resident.

After escaping from the asylum by jumping through the window of her psychiatrist's office, Helen returns to Cabrini-Green where she discovers Candyman who tells her, "Our names will be written on a thousand walls, our crimes told and retold by our faithful followers. Surrender to me now and he will be unharmed. We'll be infamous." Helen, hypnotized by Candyman's offer of immortality, falls into his arms, effectively sacrificing herself for the sake of the missing baby. As she wanders through Cabrini-Green in the next scene, Helen hears a faint cry and realizes that Candyman has placed Anthony in a woodpile, which the residents have prepared for a bonfire. After rescuing the baby from the burning pyre, the scholar both supersedes and becomes Candyman, or as film scholar Kirsten Moana Thompson has suggested "Candywoman": the white female academic and the African-American legend forever tied in a coalition of myth.[39] No longer able to separate herself from the "other" through her academic research, Dictaphone, newspaper headlines, or the plaster walls of her apartment, Helen becomes part of Candyman's "congregation, the community of believers."

In the film's final sequence, the camera returns to Candyman's dilapidated residence and hovers over a new graffiti image on the wall. Here, Helen has been immortalized as the reincarnation of Caroline, Robitaille's original lover, pictured in white surrounded by flames with the words, "IT WAS ALWAYS YOU HELEN" scrawled on the wall. Helen's death marks a shift in her narrative function; she is now "the writing on the wall," the demonized spirit once embodied in the singular figure of the African-American man. In finding herself in the same helpless position as the nineteenth-century Candyman, modern-day Helen is held accountable for the errors perpetrated by her white ancestors against the "other." By setting Helen on fire (albeit inadvertently) in a pyre at the same place where the white people had burned Candyman one-hundred years before, an understated exchange of imperialist violence occurs - the discriminated dwellers of Cabrini-Green become the vigilantes.[40] This spatiotemporal link highlights the way in which space bears the memorial scars of historical traumas rooted in America's history of violence against African-Americans. Moreover, the film reminds the viewer that Cabrini-Green is a "memory palace," a space loaded with representational surfaces like streets and buildings which function as visual cues, reminding the residents of their past.[41]

Through her recognition of the lives of public housing residents Helen establishes a framework within which we can contemplate the work of the *Residents' Journal*. If *Candyman* tells a story of demythology, then *Residents' Journal* subverts the conventional paradigm of Chicago's public housing space, and reimagines its space. This subversion surfaces in its pages through opposition to the Plan for Transformation.

We can interpret *Residents' Journal*'s response to public housing demolition as, what Gotham refers to, as a form of "'institutional distanciation'[42] whereby residents attempt to distance themselves from…the contemptuous perceptions of project life" by cultivating "an attachment to place that allows them to salvage dignity and personal autonomy."[43] Gotham continues, "resistance to public housing demolition is not an incidental mechanism of defense against a threat to living space, but is an essential constituent of place identity."[44] Tenants who work on the *Residents' Journal* "use" their project identity to express their meaningful attachment to place, and to challenge displacement and the resulting disruption of friendship ties and social networks (Gotham, 2003: 730). For example, in a recent article titled "Who could Miss the Hole?" Michaeli describes how some residents of Robert Taylor Homes construct their "place identity" through "Old School" parties:

> On a warm Saturday this August, hundreds of former Robert Taylor residents set up tents and booths and gathered in an empty field where the Hole once stood. Giant speakers belted out dusties, hip hop, R & B and jazz music. Food and drink were plentiful and mostly free. At a few tents, people sold t-shirts emblazoned with photographs of the high rises and the addresses of the now-demolished buildings. Many people wore home-made T-shirts commemorating friends who had died too young. In one spot, old friends posed for photographs in front of a colorful mural of the buildings.[45]

Contrary to its oppressive nickname and its harsh representation in *Judgment Night*, Robert Taylor Homes was not a dead-end space that residents struggled to get "out" of but, rather, a place to which some tenants make a concerted effort to stay connected to. According to a recent study, displaced residents maintain their association with their old neighborhoods by returning every year for specially organized "birthday" parties that celebrate the construction date of their old public housing buildings.[46] In fact, 76 percent of all public housing tenants' social network is comprised of other public housing inhabitants and, if they could, roughly 75 percent of all displaced CHA families would return to their old neighborhood.[47] Former public housing tenant, Ray Ward, describes his attachment to the Robert Taylor Homes: "When I left, the buildings were still standing … When I drove by now, I almost cried. There was so much memory here. It's a whole life you can't get back."[48] As noted by Sudhir Alladi Venkatesh and Isil Celimli, while nostalgia may be a component of this attachment, the "social supports residents spent years, if not decades, building up are not easy to cast aside" (Venkatesh & Celimli, 2004). As a former resident, Ward understands public housing as a site of spatial contiguity, interdependence and entailment, and place-based identity. To theorize Ward's experience in public housing it is useful to call upon Bourdieu's place-based concept, habitus.

Bourdieu has described habitus as a "sense of one's place … a sense of the other's place" in the world of one's lived environment and is concerned with how these "senses" affect our interactions with places and people.[49] Habitus is a "system of durable, transposable disposition, structured structures predisposed to function as structuring structures, that is, as principles which generate and organize practices and representations."[50] In other words, habitus provides the individual with the dispositions to navigate within different environments – in Ward's case, public housing – and determines decision-making strategies. The habitus is an evolving phenomenon motivated by past and present actions and reactions. The concept of habitus articulates not only Ward's inherent bond with his community (the "structured structures"), but also the improvised "maneuvers" and adaptations of residents to different circumstances.

A prime example of such an adaptation arose in 2003 when, as reported in a joint investigation by *Residents' Journal* and *The Chicago Reporter*, some residents filed a class-action lawsuit against the CHA alleging that the housing authority violated the Federal Fair Housing Act as well as contractual obligations to tenants when it moved 78 percent of all involuntarily displaced families to census tracts that were more than 95 percent African-American and with more than 16.6 percent of the population living in poverty.[51] In 2005, the lawsuit was settled; the CHA agreed to modify its relocation procedures for families yet to be moved and to "retrofit" relocation for families already moved by offering them better mobility counseling (Polikoff: 319).[52] The judge also required that the CHA preserve two buildings slated for demolition for public housing residents who wanted to stay in the community during the implementation of the initiative. Waging political battles of resistance for full recognition of rights, some residents assert that they are not only citizens but politically mobile agents capable of altering the current course of public housing redevelopment in Chicago. Charting a decisive blaze across the city's public sphere, the residents' sociospatial exercises of power concur with Brumley and Gotham's concept of "using space."

Moving beyond Wilson's "neighborhood effects" model, *Residents' Journal* highlights the spatial characteristics of human agency, and the attempts of some residents to contest their so-called social marginality. As I have discussed at other points in this chapter, "using space" may involve several different social activities from the creation of informal social networks to class action lawsuits. The "performance" of these activities creates a counter-knowledge network, which operates in contrast to the discourses that the mainstream print, television, and film media use to construct their reality. By depicting the "spatial acting" of housing project residents within their locale, *Candyman* frees the space of public housing from points of fixity by emphasizing the "spatiality of poor people's agency."[53]

Residents' Journal, like Rose's filmic critique of outsider's social designations, illustrates the ways in which inhabitants represent their own lives and, importantly, *imagine themselves*. In doing so, *Residents' Journal* puts faces on countless unsung heroes who in their day-to-day lives puncture misconception after misconception about the habitus of public housing dwellers. Recasting the prevailing view that public housing was an unmitigated failure, *Residents' Journal* reminds us that while public housing may have been flawed, that does not always mean that those who lived there were failures. *Candyman* and *Residents' Journal* offer important lessons as I, a white graduate student, follow Helen's path into Cabrini-Green: Listen, never pre-judge, and most importantly of course, do not believe the hype.

Notes

1. Janine Jackson and Jim Naureckas, "Crime Contradictions: US News Illustrates Flaws in Crime Coverage," *Extra! Fairness and Accuracy in Reporting*, May/June 1994: 10.
2. Ibid.
3. Social science research focusing on residents' experiences of public housing also tends to be unfavorable and most often concentrates on urban high-rise developments. Often cited studies of life in subsidized housing depict residents as threatened, attempting to protect themselves from internal human and physical threats (Newman, 1972; Popkin et al., 2000; Rainwater, 1970). More generally, social scientists typically characterize low-income people as apathetic victims of despair (reviewed in Kieffer, 1984; Naples, 1988; also see Rappaport, 1981). Roberta Feldman and Susan Stall, *The Dignity of Resistance: Women Residents Activism in Chicago's Public Housing*, Cambridge, UK: Cambridge University Press, 2004: 7.
4. William Julius Wilson, "The Ghetto Underclass: Social Science Perspectives," *The Annals of The American Academy of Political and Social Sciences*, vol. 501, January 1989.
5. Robert Beauregard, *Voices of Decline: The Postwar Fate of U.S. Cities*, Oxford: Blackwell, 1993: 6.
6. Clive Barker, "The Forbidden," *Books of Blood*, vol. 5, New York City, NY: Time Warner Paperbacks, 1988.
7. Kevin Fox Gotham & Krista Brumley. "Using Space: Agency and Identity in a Public Housing Development," *City & Community*, 1: 3 September 2002.
8. Pierre Bourdieu, "*Droit et passé-droit. Le champ des pouvoirs territoriaux et la mise en oeuvre des reglements,*" *Actes de la Recherche en Sciences Sociales*, 81/82, 1990: 53.
9. According to Sudhir Alladi Venkatesh, these include rodent infestations, broken elevators, high crime rates, a corrupt and inefficient bureaucracy, and a hostile relationship with other city agencies.
10. Sudhir Alladi Venkatesh, "Residents' Journal: By and For Public Housing Residents: An Interview with Ethan Michaeli," *Souls 4*, 2002: 90–93.
11. William Julius Wilson, *The Truly Disadvantaged, The Inner City, the Underclass and Public Policy*, Chicago, IL: University of Chicago Press, 1987: 57.
12. David Theo Goldberg, "Polluting the Body Politic," *Racism: The City and the State*, Eds. Malcolm Cross & Michael Keith, London & New York: Routledge, 1993: 55.
13. Seyla Benhabib, *The Rights of Others: Aliens, Residents and Citizens*, Cambridge, MA & New York: Cambridge University Press, 2004: 18.
14. "The American Underclass." *Time*, August 29. 1977: 14–15.
15. Steve Macek, *Urban Nightmares: The Media, The Right, and the Moral Panic Over the City*, Minneapolis and London: University of Minnesota Press, 2006: 133.
16. Kenneth B. Clark, *Dark Ghetto: Dilemmas of Social Power*. New York: Harper & Row, 1965: 11.
17. William Bennett, John Dilulio, and John Walters. *Body Count: Moral Poverty and How to Win America's War Against Crime and Drugs*, New York: Simon and Schuster, 1996: 28.
18. Beauregard: 22.
19. Brian Smith, "The Store in the Middle." *Chicago*, February. 2004: 75.
20. Ibid.
21. Larry Bennett and Adolph Reed Jr., "The New Face of Urban Renewal: The Near North Redevelopment Initiative and the Cabrini Green Neighborhood," *Without Justice for All: The New Liberalism and our Retreat from Racial Inequality*, ed. Adolph Reed Jr. Boulder: Westview Press, 2001: 183.

22. Anne Buttimer, "Home, Reach, And the Sense of Place," *The Human Experience of Space and Place*, Ed's David Seamon and Anne Buttimer, Oxford: Taylor and Francis, 1980: 171.

23. Ibid.

24. Michel de Certeau, "Walking in the City," *The Practice of Everyday Life*, Berkeley, California: University of California Press, 2002.

25. Kim D. Hester-Williams, "Neo-Slaves: Slavery, Freedom, and the African-American Apotheosis in Candyman, The Matrix, and The Green Mile," *Genders*, Issue 40, 2004 http://www.genders.org/g40/g40_williams.html (accessed 12 April 2008).

26. John McCormick, "Can Chicago Beat the Odds," *Newsweek*, February 1, 1989: 25.

27. Ibid.: 24–26.

28. Bennett & Reed: 202.

29. Mary C. Johns, "U.S. Reps Call for Moratorium on Public Housing Demolitions," *Residents' Journal*, Fall 2008.

30. Informal interview conducted with Ethan Micheli and Mary C. Johns on August 25, 2008 at the *Residents' Journal* offices in Chicago.

31. "Urban Youth International Journalism Program," *Residents' Journal: We the People Media*, 2009 <http://www.wethepeoplemedia.org/Home/UYIJP/About.htm.

32. Kirsten Moana Thompson, "Strange Fruit: Candyman and Supernatual Dread," *Apocalyptic Dread: American Film at the turn of the Century*, Albany, New York: SUNY Press, 2007: 63.

33. Antonis Balasopoulos, "The Demon of (Racial) History: Reading Candyman," *Gramma: Journal of Theory and Criticism 5*, Aristotle University of Thessaloniki, 1997: 38.

34. Charles Murray, *Losing Ground: American Social Policy, 1950–1980*, New York: Basic Books, 1984.

35. Kevin Fox Gotham, "Toward an Understanding of the Spatiality of Urban Poverty: The Urban Poor as Spatial Actors," *International Journal of Urban and Regional Research*, vol. 27 (3), September 2003: 724.

36. Steve Rhodes, "News From Home," *Chicago*, June 2003: 99.

37. Venkatesh, 2002: 91.

38. Laura Wyrick, "Summoning Candyman: The Cultural Production of History," *Arizona Quarterly*, vol. 54, (3), Autumn 1998: 99.

39. Thompson: 72, 80.

40. Balasopoulos: 39.

41. In 1596 Matteo Ricci devised the technique of the "memory palace." It is a mnemonic link system based on places and the architecture in places that allows a person the means of committing large quantities of information to memory. Francis A. Yates, *The Art of Memory*, Chicago: Chicago University Press, 1966.

42. David A. Snow and Leon Anderson, "Identity Work among the Homeless: The Verbal Construction and Avowal of Personal Identities," *American Journal of Sociology 92*, 1987: 1336–71.

43. Gotham, 2003: 731.

44. Ibid.

45. Ethan Michaeli, "Who Could Miss the Hole?" *Residents' Journal*, Winter 2008, no. 44.

46. Jennifer Sushinsky, "The Neighborhood Project: A Cabrini Green Youth Perspective in Photographs and Words," http://www.neighborhoodproject.org/web_pages/about_us.html.

47. Sudhir Venkatesh & Isil Celimli, "Tearing Down the Community," *Shelterforce Online*, Issue: 138, November/December 2004.

48. Michaeli: 2008.

49. Bourdieu: 53.

50. Ibid.
51. Sudhir Venkatesh, Isil Celimli, Douglas Miller, Alexandra Murphy, & Beauty Turner, *Chicago Public Housing Transformation: A Research Report*, New York: Center for Urban Research and Policy, Columbia University, February 2004.
52. Alexander Polikoff, *Waiting for Gautreaux: A Story of Segregation, Housing and the Black Ghetto*, Evanston, IL: Northwestern University Press, 2006.
53. Gotham, 2003: 724.

Chapter 14

From the Bronx to Berlin: Hip-Hop Graffiti and Spatial Reconfigurations of the Hood

David Drissel

For decades, modern urban graffiti has been damned by some and praised by others. Few art forms have generated as much overt derision and acclaim, disgust and respect, and intolerance and reverence, as urban graffiti. The aerosol-painted "tag" names, iconoclastic slogans, and billowing cartoon-like images plastered on warehouses, subway cars, freight trains, bus stations, highway overpasses, bridges, basketball courts, skateboard parks, sidewalks, and other public venues have elicited contrasting appraisals from a wide variety of observers. While critics have contended that the presence of graffiti is incontrovertible evidence of urban decay and delinquent vandalism gone rampant (Wilson & Kelling, 1982), sympathetic observers have described the practice as a youth-based alternative genre of inner-city folk art, designed to "reclaim public space" from hegemonic elites (Lynn & Lea, 2005, p. 40).

Though graffiti has existed in various forms for centuries, the origins of modern urban graffiti can be traced back to the predominately low-income, African-American and Hispanic neighborhoods of Philadelphia and New York City in the 1960s. It was within a climate of dwindling economic opportunities, rising crime rates, and the racialized stigmatization of "ghetto youth" that the phenomenon of modern urban graffiti first emerged. Initially, local street gangs played a major role in disseminating urban graffiti by utilizing group symbols as a means for marking off territory. Subsequently, youthful graffiti "crews," lacking explicit gang affiliations and generally avoiding violent confrontations, picked up on the trend and began displaying their uniquely designed graffiti both within and outside of their neighborhood turf (Austin, 2001).

The advent of hip hop in the South Bronx of the mid-1970s dramatically transformed urban graffiti by aligning it symbolically with a dynamic new subculture, based in large measure on the lived experiences of inner-city youth, coupled with a street-based code of respect and authenticity ("keeping-it-real"). In the new alternative argot of hip hop, the discursive frame of the "hood" (slang for neighborhood) largely replaced the more pessimistic and exclusionary term, "ghetto." In contrast to the impersonal spatial idiom of the ghetto, the hood was framed as the actual home/habitat of people facing major challenges in their daily lives. According to Murray Forman (2002), "As a discursive shift, the turn to the hood involves an intentional, engaged process of cultural recuperation of African-American and Latino dominated space enacted primarily by contemporary urban minority youth" (p. 65).

Hip hop, via the oppositional discourse of rap music in particular, effectively has transmitted the subterranean concept of the hood into mass public consciousness. Thus, the hood has been framed not simply as "urban" or "black," but more specifically as "the urban space occupied by black working-class and poor people" (Ogbar, 2007, p. 6). As a cultural product of the hood, graffiti has been touted as one of the four original "pillars" of hip hop, which along with rapping, deejaying, and breakdancing, initially gained widespread acceptance and popularity among minority youth in the South Bronx (George, 1998). As an integral component of hip hop's "cross-cultural communication network," graffiti has been widely disseminated from its original metropolitan base to other American cities in which "marginalized black and Hispanic communities … picked up on the tenor and energy in New York hip hop" (Rose, 2008, p. 26). In effect, graffiti has become linked to hip-hop subcultural identities (Castlemen, 1984; Iveson, 2007; Macdonald, 2001; Rahn, 2001) and youthful rebellion in various urban locales around the world (Austin, 2001; Sanders, 2007).

This chapter examines the sociospatial origins of hip-hop graffiti in New York City and its subsequent development in Berlin, Germany – two global cities that have undergone dramatic sociospatial transformations over the past several years. Significantly, Berlin is known as "the graffiti capital of Europe" (Tzortzis, 2008), due to the city's spatial cornucopia of tenement buildings, train stations, vacant lots, sidewalks, and concrete walls literally covered with balloon-lettered tags, bulbous graphics, cartoonish characters, hip-hop jargon, and political slogans. In particular, the chapter analyzes the unique sociospatial milieu and dissemination of graffiti in Berlin's ethnically diverse Kreuzberg borough. Known as "Little Istanbul," Kreuzberg includes thousands of Turkish migrants and their descendants, who are often stereotyped, stigmatized, and marginalized by majority-group residents.

Figure 20: Kreuzberg graffiti in hip-hop style, with New York City train imagery and crew tag (detail).

Figure 21: Kreuzberg graffiti in hip-hop style, with New York City train imagery and crew tag.

Hip-hop graffiti is portrayed in this chapter as a distinct type of spatial performance and subcultural discourse, which involves social actors contesting urban social spaces and negotiating place-specific collective identities. Applying various sociopolitical theories of space, Berlin's graffiti subculture is examined for evidence of dialectical dispositions and subversive, nonconformist challenges to dominant social structures in the urban field. The subjective meaning of the hood to Berlin's hip-hop graffiti writers is addressed in this context and compared to the South Bronx archetype. The reasons why young people of various ethnicities engage in the practice of graffiti writing in Kreuzberg and other parts of Berlin, given legal and social sanctions, are investigated. The chapter includes ethnographic observations and open-ended interviews conducted by the author in Kreuzberg and other Berlin neighborhoods in 2004. In order to insure confidentiality, pseudonyms are used for all respondents.

Contesting urban space

Space is a social construction that "shapes social action and guides behavior," including the practices and activities of everyday life (Gotham, 2003, p. 723). Put simply, "space is a practiced place" (de Certeau, 1984, p. 117). The physical place of the street, for instance, becomes a space only when people are actually engaged in social practices such as walking, running, driving, or conversing on or near the street. Social theorists often emphasize the dynamic, stratified character of public space in cities, thus contending that power is spatially constructed and wielded through an economy of discourse. As Michel Foucault (1984) observes, "Space is fundamental to any form of communal life; space is fundamental to any exercise of power" (p. 252). Rather than depicting marginalized groups as being contained spatially in fixed ghettoized stasis, such groups possess social agency. As a result, various groups act to ameliorate or even overcome social constraints through the productive use of space (Gotham, 2003).

Major reconfigurations of urban space, such as the gentrification of low-income residential areas, tend to spark spatial contestations between antithetical social actors. Long-term residents frequently seek to "preserve" their neighborhood by organizing anti-gentrification campaigns, lobbying elected officials, and resorting to property destruction in extreme cases. Even the inner-city ghetto, once the reputedly otherworldly bastion of sociocultural insularity, increasingly has found itself under siege by yuppies (young urban professionals) and related groups. As Lance Freeman (2006) observes in *There Goes the Hood:* "Walls that were formerly solid seem porous now, at least from the perspective of who is moving into the ghetto" (p. 16).

Empirical studies (e.g., Hendry et al., 1993; Pearce, 1996) have revealed that urban youth in particular tend to have strong emotional attachments to local spaces and places, which often serve as a major source of collective identity, group cohesion, and intergroup conflict. The neighborhood is especially important as an identity marker for youth, as localized spatial orientations tend to depict non-residents as suspicious or unwelcome outsiders. Such territoriality is "best understood as a spatial strategy to effect, influence, or control resources and people by controlling area" (Sack, as quoted in Hesse et al., 1992, p. 172).

Young people frequently utilize public space to subvert and resist various hegemonic standards of behavior; despite periodic attempts by adult regulatory regimes to control, marginalize, or even prohibit their presence in particular urban areas. Teenagers often find themselves subjected to police harassment, public and private surveillance, and temporal and spatial curfews in public spaces (Valentine, 1996), as a result of being depicted as "a potential threat to public order" (Baumgarnter, 1988; Cahill, 1990). Urban "revitalization" schemes in North American and European cities tend to involve the *de facto* privatization of public space; i.e., unofficially excluding "undesirables" such as loitering teens in general and minority youths in particular from newly gentrified locales (Berman, 1986; Fyfe & Bannister, 1996). Nonetheless, the act of entering various urban spaces – even restricted or forbidden ones – is pivotal to the youthful negotiation of collective identities. As Sheena

McGrellis (2005) observes, "Central to these negotiations is the creation, transgression and sometimes evasion of boundaries. Such boundaries not only mark where it is possible to go, but also who it is possible to be" (p. 517).

Origins of hip-hop graffiti

By the time of hip hop's advent in the mid-1970s, New York City had undergone massive urban renewal projects aimed at radically transforming the spatial cityscape. Beginning in the fifties, a series of large-scale public renovation schemes in Manhattan sharply raised property values, consequently dislocating many long-time residents from their neighborhoods and dramatically reducing economic opportunities for poor people and non-whites in particular. Such urban renewal projects, accompanied by the gentrification of many low-income neighborhoods, resulted in a modern-day exodus of minorities from Manhattan's reconstructed areas to outlying ghettos located in the Bronx and Brooklyn (Gonzalez, 2004).

Accompanying this wave of metropolitan migration was a massive loss of blue-collar jobs and higher levels of income polarization between the rich and poor. Though the Bronx had never been affluent, "it went into a sudden decline" in the 1960s and became "the poorest, toughest neighborhood in the whole of New York" by the end of the decade (Hebdige, 1987, p. 137). In particular, the South Bronx – with its "blighted" housing projects, vacant tenement buildings, and crime-ridden streets – came to symbolize the worst possible conditions of "contemporary urban decay" (Forman, 2002, p. 89). As Joe Austin (2001) asserts, "A major renegotiation of the racialized urban social hierarchy had taken place" (p. 24).

From its inception in the mid-1970s, hip hop has been characterized as a distinct youth subculture with strong spatial connections to the South Bronx. Originally based on an underground network of alienated, impoverished young people and highly competitive disc jockeys spinning records on the streets of the South Bronx, hip hop was highly defiant and controversial from the start. As a street-level neighborhood experience, hip hop was inherently interactive, involving networked audiences of mostly friends and acquaintances. Though the roots of hip-hop are primarily African-American, the subculture has always included important hybridized influences from migrant Jamaicans and Puerto Ricans, who interacted with their subcultural cohorts in the same urban spaces (Forman, 2002). Far removed from the relatively exclusionary spaces of Manhattan's upscale concert halls and discothèques, hip hop was shaped by the common experiences of its localized seminal participants. Indeed, hip-hop aficionados openly interacted in neighborhood block parties, community centers, parks, and nightclubs. As Todd Boyd (2003) observes:

At some overt level, hip-hop has always been about the cultural identity of those who perform the music, and those who constitute its core audience. This concern over identity is generally bounded by two other primary issues: a politics of location and an overall search for that which is considered authentic.

(p. 18)

Like the broader hip-hop subculture, the origins of urban graffiti are directly linked to contestations over space and place, coupled with the negotiation and construction of "authentic" collective identities. In many respects, graffitists are reacting to the visible and invisible partitioning of public space in urban settings. Frequent semiotic struggles are waged between graffitists and other actors (including dominant institutions and rival crews) over segmented urban assets. Accordingly, graffiti writers often seek to establish spatial parameters for their territory, while transgressing rival spatial domains with their own distinct signage. In point of fact, much of the earliest New York graffiti emphasized specific street names. "Johnny of 93" was a common example of this style, which included the writer's name and shortened street address (93rd Street). Street designations in graffiti effectively aligned the writer with a distinct neighborhood, thus affirming a particular collective identity (Austin, 2001).

Beginning in early 1970s, graffiti crews tacitly negotiated their identities by challenging hegemonic spatial boundaries throughout New York City. Not surprisingly, the most obvious target was the city's subway system. The subways, which transcended spatial boundaries and were used extensively by both the "haves" and "have-nots," appeared to be a logical venue in which to plaster one's mark. After all, relatively affluent subway travelers typically would shun so-called "bad" neighborhoods, but were unable to avoid seeing symbolic representations of the ghetto painted on the universal subway trains and tracks. With literally millions of New Yorkers riding the rails each day, subway graffiti presented a new and unique means for visibly challenging the racialized urban social hierarchy.

During the same period, graffitists also began "tagging" (writing one's name or crew moniker) in other public spaces, such as train stations and yards, thus expanding exposure for their personalized art to the widest possible audience. The "Fabulous Five," a Bronx-based hip-hop graffiti crew, became widely known throughout New York City by the late 1970s due to their provocative graffiti "pieces" (elaborate, highly stylized, colorful masterpieces) that extended over the entire length of subway trains (Castleman, 1982).

To the mainstream New Yorker, such graffiti was vandalism – pure and simple. The presence of graffiti only served to reinforce existing fears concerning the omnipresent danger of ghetto youth and the threatening presence of such delinquents in shared public spaces. The capitalist value system, based in large measure on the sanctity of property rights, seemed suddenly under assault by this ubiquitous and burgeoning phenomenon. Ironically, capitalist-sponsored advertising billboards had intruded into public spaces long before the graffiti boom. But from the capitalist vantage point, there was no comparison. Graffiti essentially was a ritualized assault on property rights, with the communal comfort zones of the bourgeoisie suddenly invaded. Class and racial divisions had leapt from the shadows of the hood and seized the collective walls and windows of "The Man." The ostensible invisibility of poverty and racism had been shattered, while the communal canvas of the city was now marked and re-marked with seemingly indecipherable statements of insolence and rebellion.

Within a decade of its genesis, hip-hop graffiti had "dramatically reinscribed the graphic space of wall writing" around the world (Chmielewska, 2007, p. 147), thus gaining devotees from among young people of virtually all nationalities, races, ethnicities, and social classes in cities as diverse and far-flung as Los Angeles, London, Montreal, Paris, Sao Paulo, and Barcelona. As a synthesis of both written language and picturesque art designed to communicate particular messages and ideas, hip-hop graffiti has evolved into a highly competitive yet clandestine form of global subcultural expression.

The aesthetic heterodoxy of graffiti

The French social theorist, Pierre Bourdieu, asserts that various fields are established and contested in social space, with adversarial agents producing "place-specific forms of identity, consciousness, and knowledge" (as quoted in Gotham, 2003, p. 724). The field, which is defined for analytical purposes as a "network, or a configuration, of objective relations between positions" (Bourdieu and Wacquant, 1992, p. 97), is akin to a game with various players competing with each other to achieve particular objectives such as power (capital) accumulation. Bourdieu describes art as a distinct field, which has its own rules, social positions, and taste preferences. Within the art world and other fields of cultural production, elites rigidly define aesthetic concepts such as "good taste" and "bad taste." As Bourdieu observes in *Distinction: A Social Critique of the Judgment of Taste* (1984): "It must never be forgotten that the working-class 'aesthetic' is a dominated 'aesthetic', which is constantly obliged to define itself in terms of the dominant aesthetics" (p. 41).

Therefore, hip-hop graffiti can be described as an aesthetic heterodoxy originating among the lower classes, effectively dominated by the orthodox establishment within the field of art. Indeed, the theoretical juxtaposition of art-versus-vandalism is a common theme in various academic and public policy debates. The "graffiti as vandalism" thesis is based on allegations of illegal, antisocial behavior by wall-writing perpetrators, who reputedly have caused significant damage to the image (and property values) of particular neighborhoods. From this dominant vantage point, graffiti signifies "danger" by encouraging various forms of criminal behavior in dilapidated urban spaces (Brantingham & Brantingham, 1993; Eck & Weisburd, 1995; Reynald & Elffers, 2009). Conversely, the "graffiti as art" thesis maintains that such displays can have a positive impact on neighborhoods by enhancing the overall aesthetic appeal of otherwise drab or blighted streetscapes. Hence, hip-hop graffiti is distinguished from indiscriminate acts of vandalism, since its practitioners utilize an "abstract highly-stylized art form" (Lynn & Lea, 2005, p. 41), which is designed to generate emotional responses from significant others (Halsey & Young, 2006).

According to Bourdieu (1977), the roles and activities of actors within a given field are somewhat ordered and constrained by their distinctive habitus; that is, "a system of durable, transposable dispositions, that are structured, inculcated and generative" (p. 53). Actors who occupy a similar structural position in social space are provided by their habitus with a long-lasting (though not permanent) set of principles, representations, sensibilities, tastes, perceptions, experiences, understandings, beliefs, lifestyles, and patterns of behavior, which exist in contradistinction to other sociospatial schema. Simply put, the habitus is "a sense of one's and others' place and role in the world of one's lived environment" (Hillier & Rooksby, 2008, p. 21). Within any given field, subordinate groups will seek to overturn the spatial order, while dominant groups will actively defend their structural position with whatever resources best exemplify their habitus. "As a space of forces or determinations, every field is inhabited by tensions and contradictions which are at the origin (basis) of conflicts," Bourdieu (2008) observes. "This means that it is simultaneously a field of struggles or competitions which generate change" (p. 47).

Subversive subcultural communication

Within the habitus of the hood, modern urban graffiti has emerged not only as a heterodox art form, but also as a subversive means of subcultural communication. This is evident by the common practice of graffitists referring to themselves as "writers." Indeed, graffiti includes not only images but also highly stylized words, thus reflecting identity-laden, linguistic forms of expression that often are unintelligible to the uninitiated. Different perceptions of graffiti are the result of varying socialization experiences and dispositions, which depend on one's "information habitus;" that is, "the schemata of perception, thought and action that relate to access to, acquisition of, and uses of information" (Bock, 2004, p. 284). Those people who exist apart from the graffiti subculture's information habitus frequently lack both the dispositional understanding and aesthetic appreciation of such unorthodox communication repertoires, thereby utilizing their own power resources to work against such practices.

Tellingly, hip-hop graffiti has developed its own esoteric patterns of field-like behavior akin to a game – both externally and internally. According to Nancy MacDonald (2001), the graffiti subculture is extremely hierarchical and tightly regulated. "It operates its own governing system and its own set of rules and guidelines," she observes. "These may be unwritten, but they are clear" (p. 184). For example, rules of etiquette governing the positioning and size of writers' names are generally understood within the subculture. Repeated violations of such rules are viewed as intensely disrespectful, which can lead to so-called "cross out wars" between rival crews (MacDonald, pp. 210–211). Bourdieu would describe such social situations and dialogic interactions among competing social actors as "codes of spatial performance" (as quoted in Gotham, 2003, p. 724).

The symbolic "game" of graffiti often pits crew against crew within the habitus of a particular cityscape or neighborhood. Nonetheless, crews tend to share a similar structural position in social space and react analogously to hegemonic forms of spatial domination or oppression. Moreover, crews frequently have similar informal organizational structures. For instance, each crew typically is composed of around four or five loosely organized friends that pool resources (e.g., paint, markers, and drawings), exchange information, travel together, and disseminate their tags throughout the community and beyond. In addition, crews are responsible for socializing novices into the practice. As Austin (2001) observes,

"The crew developed as a kind of social hybrid, combining the informal organization of a peer group, the shared-goal orientation of a sports team, and the collective identity and protective functions of a gang" (p. 64).

Rap music has consistently embraced the enduring mythos of the hood, which has been adopted vicariously by young people from a wide variety of racial and socioeconomic backgrounds. The lived environment of homeboys and homegirls has been transmitted across space and time, prompting youths in various geo-cultural locales to become rappers, graffiti writers, and breakdancers. The perceived personal benefits for tagging and spray-painting pieces include the opportunity to engender respect among subcultural peers, assert independence, develop a "strong" or "masculine" identity, achieve "a sense of accomplishment" and pride, participate in "gregarious" group activities, and engage in covert forms of sociopolitical rebellion (MacDonald, 2001; Halsey & Young, 2006). In addition, many graffitists reportedly derive "pleasurable" sensations from the act of writing; for example, "the intensity of feeling which, for instance, accompanies the motioning of the aerosol can" (Halsey & Young, 2006, p. 279).

Given the oppressive habitus of the hood, graffitists may lack adequate access to stocks of economic, social, and cultural capital. As an alternative, Bourdieu (1985) refers to "symbolic capital," which includes honor and prestige within society, as recognized by authoritative institutions or elite standards. However, under hegemonic circumstances, graffitists are unlikely to acquire symbolic capital, unless their artwork has achieved "official" recognition by museums or other orthodox institutions. Consequently, Sarah Thornton (1997) has expanded upon Bourdieu's concept of symbolic capital to include "subcultural capital," which refers to the interactive process of achieving in-group prestige or honor within a particular youth subculture. Simply put, subcultural capital "confers status on its owner in the eyes of the relevant beholder" (p. 202). Accruing subcultural capital involves spurning both high-culture standards and the pop-culture mainstream, while maintaining personal tastes deemed to be "authentic" by one's subcultural peers (Weinzierl & Muggleton, 2003).

Correspondingly, graffiti writers rise or fall within the subcultural hierarchy ("the new prestige economy of writing") based on their works' relative merit and visibility to relevant beholders (Austin, 2001). Individual writers and crews who have garnered widespread respect or fame within the subculture are considered to be the most successful. But the kind of fame graffitists achieve differs dramatically from the elitist or mass-mediated form accorded to celebrated artists. Rather, the graffitist tends to receive notoriety, and in the process accrue subcultural capital, in a mostly covert alter-ego (tagging) method. Admiration by others of his writing style generates recognition that is bounded by fairly specific subculture-based criteria. Such fame is earned in the process of "bombing" or "getting up" a tag in as many locations as possible. Rewarded by a subcultural status-hierarchy that informally recognizes such achievements, the novice "toy" writer (or crew) aspires to move up the ladder and eventually become a highly respected "king."

Sociospatial change in Berlin

Berlin has undergone an enormous amount of sociospatial change since the end of World War II, with four decades of Cold War bifurcation profoundly altering the city's urban landscape. In the immediate postwar era, the victorious allied powers separated Germany into occupation zones that eventually resulted in the country's bipolar partition. From 1949 to 1989, Berlin was divided into two *de facto* cities; with Soviet forces dominating the eastern half, while the western sector was a virtual capitalist "island" surrounded by hostile communist territory (Glaeser, 2000, p.105). East Berlin became the capital of the new Soviet-dominated German Democratic Republic (GDR), founded as a Marxist-Leninist state in 1949. West Berlin, occupied by the United States, Great Britain, and France in the immediate aftermath of World War II, became an integral part of the new pro-Western Federal Republic of Germany (FRG).

For years afterward, Cold War tensions remained very high in Berlin, leading in 1961 to the construction of the Berlin Wall by East Germany. The Wall did much more than simply partition Berlin geopolitically and militarily; it also dramatically transformed the "routines of everyday life" for virtually everyone living in the city (Moran, 2004, p. 217). In this respect, the Wall's presence fractured neighborhoods, shattered public parks, separated families, disrupted train routes and highways, and severed economic ties between various firms and individuals. Both "sides" of Berlin developed their own unique business practices, education systems, media outlets, public utilities, mass transit, cultural facilities, health care systems, legal statutes, and more. According to Boris Gresillon (1999), "This dual structure was given official sanction and perpetuated the division of the city between 1949 and 1989" (p. 290).

The fall of the Berlin Wall in November 1989 and the subsequent reunification of Germany (and Berlin) in October 1990 dramatically altered the spatial status quo. In epochal terms, Germans began referring to this transitional period as the *Wendezeit* ("the time of the turning"). The incredibly swift pace of political reunification reflected the widespread "presupposition of an essential unity of the German people" (Glaeser, 2000, p. 2). Streaming by the thousands through what was left of the Wall, East Berliners appeared eager to experience the freedom, abundance, opulence, sensuality, and crass commercialism of a seemingly utopian West Berlin (Veenis, 1999). Young people, in particular, embraced reunification, especially "in relation to leisure, entertainment, new consumption patterns and the extent of foreign travel" (Smith, 1998, p. 297).

However, the tearfully jubilant euphoria of reunification proved to be short-lived. Indeed, the reunification process was decidedly lopsided, with the GDR absorbed politically by the hegemonic FRG (Glaeser, 2000, p. 95). The social-psychological "burden" of transition clearly was on the backs of Easterners, who were expected to adopt the West's political and economic system very swiftly. In effect, "West-shock" occurred for many in the East, who were apparently unprepared for the onslaught of a highly competitive market economy (Fischer et al., 2007). Western investors quickly privatized or closed many enterprises in the former East Berlin; thus causing unemployment rates to skyrocket and anti-Western resentment to percolate. Suddenly, East Berliners had to abandon virtually their entire daily routine and embrace revised, Western-imposed versions of everything from street signs and billboards to phone booths, youth organizations, school textbooks, and university curricula (Moran, 2004; Smith, 1998). In effect, "former GDR citizens had been involuntarily relocated – not geographically, but culturally and politically" (Kahn, 2000).

Moreover, reports throughout the 1990s indicated that a psychological-cultural "wall in the head" (*Mauer im Kopf*) had replaced the geopolitical Berlin Wall (Burns, 1999; Graff, 2000; Kahn, 2000; Fischer et al., 2007). Though the physical barricades had fallen, stereotypical portrayals of East and West Germans, known as *Ossis* and *Wessis* respectively, soon became prevalent (Glaeser, 2000). As the dominant group in the newly "united" Berlin, *Wessis* often portrayed *Ossis* in a decidedly negative light. "They are not like us" was a common *Wessi* refrain about *Ossis*, often stereotyped as "backward" and "provincial" in contradistinction to the reputedly more "advanced" and "sophisticated" *Wessis*. In West German popular discourse, the "other" Germans were "whining Easterners" (*Jammer Ossis*). Such stereotypes often focused on the alleged "weak" work ethic and ineptitude of *Ossis*, with the former GDR's lack of incentives usually blamed (Glaeser, 2000; Kahn, 2000).

The post-reunification migration of relatively prosperous *Wessis* into several of the former East Berlin's traditional working-class districts has further exacerbated sociospatial tensions. This trend has resulted in low- and middle-income *Ossis* being displaced from their homes, shops, businesses, and neighborhoods. New "islands of wealth" have been created in many frontier-style "Wild East" neighborhoods, resulting in significant population exchanges. For instance, approximately 70,000 new residents entered the (former East) Berlin district of Prenzlauer Berg between 1991 and 1997, while around 65,000 left during the same period. The new residents tended to be "younger, better educated, and form more single households than those who left" (Mayer, 2006).

Such gentrification-style economic restructuring in Berlin is an intensely localized manifestation of neoliberal globalization and its hegemonic processes of uneven development, which has had a predominantly deleterious impact on working-class communities within various post-communist societies (Smith, 1996). Indeed, the massive exodus of *Ossis* from traditional working-class neighborhoods is a direct manifestation of the post-reunification transition from state-socialism to capitalism in the former East Berlin. Having paid fixed rental rates that were heavily subsidized by the communist state for decades, *Ossis* were unaccustomed to negotiating leases with individual landlords. Though the Berlin city government had instituted rent controls for relatively impoverished neighborhoods in the immediate post-reunification era, such regulations were easily circumvented and weakened by various legal loopholes utilized by innovative and unscrupulous landlords, mostly from the West. By the late 1990s, city officials had mostly abandoned the enforcement of rent control mechanisms and instead embraced policies favoring homeowners over renters (Mayer, 2006). Thus, ever-higher rental fees were a byproduct of "the gradual retreat of the state," which facilitated major spatial dislocations for disadvantaged residents and the relatively rapid deterioration of traditional neighborhood social structures (Holm, 2006).

Numerous nondescript, multi-occupant tenement buildings and storefronts in Prenzlauer Berg, Mitte, and other Eastern Berlin boroughs have undergone massive renovation by entrepreneurs and firms in recent years, which has led to the proliferation of single-ownership townhouses, luxurious apartments, trendy cafes, and cosmopolitan boutiques, catering to an upscale clientele. Such "international earmarks of gentrification," based on "the infrastructure of conspicuous consumption," have become dominant and ubiquitous in Berlin's new frontier (Holm, 2006). Due to the increasingly visible role of yuppies, Germans have begun referring to gentrification as *Yuppisierung*. Echoing southern criticism of northern-sponsored "reconstruction" and attendant carpetbaggers in the aftermath of the American Civil War, many *Ossis* view *Yuppisierung* by *Wessis* as "unwelcome, post-unification pillage" (Ozment, 2004, p. 312).

Berlin graffiti origins

Berlin's hip-hop graffiti scene first emerged in the early 1980s, primarily in the Western district of Kreuzberg – which bordered the Berlin Wall and offered several miles of open wall space and very little police surveillance at the time. While the East German *Stasi* dealt harshly with graffitists and were able to virtually eliminate the practice in the communist sector, Western authorities reacted mostly with indifference, tacitly allowing unfettered artistic expression for several years. Consequently, the western side of the Berlin Wall was often filled with graffiti, while the eastern side was vacant and painted white. During the

Figure 22: Mahatma Gandhi depicted with hip-hop imagery in Berlin automotive repair lot.

1980s, graffitists slowly progressed in their tactics from writing tag names on the Wall to spray-painting political slogans and other phrases a few years later. By 1984, elaborate pieces were covering much of the Wall and had turned it into an ironic tourist attraction (Tillman, 1990).

One of the main factors initially fueling graffiti production in Berlin was the rising global popularity of hip hop – including American rap music and related films such as *Wild Style* (1983) and *Beat Street* (1984). Both documentaries were filmed in the South Bronx and featured rappers, graffiti writers, and competitive breakdancers. Paradoxically, *Beat Street* was shown openly in East Berlin cinemas – with the communist authorities touting it as a searing indictment of American capitalism. However, the film apparently had the opposite effect, since many East German young people "tended to see a real parallel between ghetto life and their oppression as citizens of a communist dictatorship" (Brown, 2006, p. 139). Lamar, a 32-year-old young man who grew up in East Berlin, told me in a 2004 interview that his first real exposure to hip-hop culture was through *Beat Street*. As a result of seeing the film, he tried his hand at graffiti writing and later became a breakdancer (and instructor) in a Berlin crew of B-boys.

Figure 23: Berlin B-Boys and graffitists from the hood, pictured in Berlin public square.

While the immense popularity of American hip hop was a significant factor in the global diffusion of urban graffiti in Berlin, an eclectic mode of multicultural syncretism occurred simultaneously. In various cultures, hip hop has been modified to reflect localized needs and concerns, thus exhibiting *glocalization*; that is, crosscultural interactions synthesizing the global with the local. Reflecting the "hybridization" and "indigenization" of hip hop (Lull, 1995), American rap and graffiti often fuse with various local/national discourses to produce distinctly new style formations. According to Todd Boyd (2003), "It is precisely this series of moves from the local, to the regional, to the national, and even to the global that demonstrate this expression of hip hop's cultural identity in the broadest sense, confounding any attempts to read blackness as monolithic" (p. 19).

Accordingly, the German hip-hop subculture has become increasingly indigenized since the first German rap music was recorded in the mid-1980s. Initially, German rap was performed almost exclusively in English and was obviously derivative of the African-American prototype. But by the early 1990s, German hip-hop artists were not only rapping in German, but also addressing specific German issues and concerns. In effect, hip hop

Figure 24: Graffiti piece critical of moneyed interests and gentrification in Berlin.

had been "recontextualized" by borrowing cultural objects from one setting for the purpose of applying them in a different social context (Androutsopoulos & Scholz, 2002); thus facilitating the elaboration of urban graffiti themes that reflect both American and German influences.

With the fall of the Berlin Wall and subsequent reunification of Germany, hip-hop graffiti quickly spread throughout the city, with a new generation of writers incessantly splattering words and images on numerous dilapidated tenement façades in Friedrichshain, Mitte, and other eastern boroughs. Since that time, Berlin has become "the most 'bombed' – slang for graffiti-covered – city in Europe" (Tzortzis, 2008). Though municipal authorities have conducted major anti-graffiti campaigns in Berlin since the early 1990s, the city remains adorned with seemingly ubiquitous tags and pieces. According to Marko Moritz, head of Berlin's anti-graffiti task force, approximately fifteen graffiti offenders are arrested each week. "We know we'll never be able to completely eliminate graffiti," Moritz concedes. "The property damage caused by graffiti is estimated at 35 million to 50 million euros a year" (as quoted in Tzortzis, 2008).

Spatial contestations in Little Istanbul

An important source of sociospatial stratification within contemporary Berlin is the distinction that exists between ethnic Germans and non-ethnic Germans. Notably, twelve percent of Berlin's population is described officially as "foreign" – that is to say, immigrants and their descendants. Approximately two million people of Turkish ancestry live in Germany and more than 115,000 live in Berlin. Turkish residents, many of whom have never become German citizens, comprise four percent of Berlin's population. The vast majority of Turkish youth in Berlin are the children or grandchildren of Turkish migrants who settled in West Germany (and West Berlin) in the 1960s as so-called "guest workers" (*Gastarbeiter*). Notably, approximately 36 percent of Berlin Turks are between the ages of 10 and 25 (Soysal, 2001, p. 9). Compared to the general German population, Turkish youth tend to have much higher rates of unemployment and high school noncompletion (Schneider, 2005). Negative depictions of Turkish youth are commonplace throughout German society and particularly in Berlin, including stereotypes describing them as "unskilled or semi-skilled" (Petzen, 2004, p. 22) and "essentially criminal elements" (Soysal, 2001, p. 9).

Berlin's Turkish population is heavily concentrated in the mostly low-income neighborhoods of Kreuzberg. The district is known locally as "Little Istanbul," due to its relatively large population of Turkish-Germans. Kreuzberg also includes large numbers of college students, anarchists, hippies, punks, metal heads, breakdancers, and gay men and lesbians. Though Kreuzberg has undergone substantive changes in recent years, it has retained its own distinct *kiezkultur* ("neighborhood culture"), which includes a strong communal orientation. Several young people told me that Kreuzberg is one of Berlin's "hippest" or "coolest" hoods, in part because it includes various nightclubs and alternative music venues. In contrast, many German media sources and conservative politicians have depicted Kreuzberg in highly negative terms, often describing it ominously as a dangerous "no-go area" that is fraught with high rates of crime, drug abuse, gangs, and other deviant behaviors. Such observers frequently describe the district as having a very large number of chronically unemployed people and "foreigners" on welfare (Mayer, 2006).

Prior to reunification, Kreuzberg was on the geographic periphery of West Berlin and included many derelict buildings and barren tracks of land, which often attracted youthful squatters and graffitists from West Germany. As an occupied city, West Berlin had a special exemption for military service that was mandatory for young men elsewhere in the country. Consequently, West Berlin became a bohemian magnet for antiauthoritarian, radical youth during the Cold War who often settled in communal squats (previously abandoned houses occupied by non-proprietary residents), located mostly in Kreuzberg. In fact, militant anti-government rebellions and riots have occurred in Kreuzberg for several years, often sparked by May Day commemorations and reactions to unpopular urban renewal initiatives and encroaching gentrification. German anarchists, many of whom call themselves *Autonomen* (participants in the "autonomous movement"), have often instigated such riots, going back to the early 1980s (Leach, 2009).

The rapid deindustrialization of Kreuzberg since reunification has resulted in a glut of abandoned buildings, many of which have been filled by middle- and lower-income families fleeing from newly gentrified eastern neighborhoods. Compared to Prenzlauer Berg and Mitte, Kreuzberg initially experienced a somewhat slower rate of post-reunification gentrification. But yuppie-style development increasingly has been occurring in larger swathes of Kreuzberg, much to the chagrin of long-time residents. Not surprisingly, the relatively low rents, underdeveloped properties, legendary club culture, and "authentic" bohemian atmosphere of Kreuzberg have attracted yuppie-colonists from other parts of the city and country. In turn, resistance to creeping gentrification has assumed many forms over the past several years, including peaceful protest marches, massive sit-ins at development sites, and acts of vandalism. Most provocatively, unidentified arsonists with reputed ties to anarchist groups have torched hundreds of expensive automobiles owned by yuppies in Kreuzberg and other boroughs (Waleczek, 2009).

Turkish Boyz in the hood

Over the past few decades, Turkish-German performers in Kreuzberg and other urban ethnic enclaves have become central figures in the German rap music industry, devising their own distinct style. Known as "Oriental Hip Hop," this subgenre of German rap includes Turkish language lyrics and incorporates elements of *Arabesk* (traditional Turkish) folk music. Thus, the German hip-hop scene has become a syncretistic multicultural hybrid, one that effectively blends diasporic African-American culture with diasporic Turkish-German culture (Brown, 2006).

Tellingly, the Berlin rapper Sido describes public housing projects in Kreuzberg and other Berlin hoods as "concrete prisons" (Roxborough, 2005). As he raps in "Mein Block," the "air is thick – the buildings are high/few trees – people on drugs/this is where dreams die." The Turkish-German filmmaker, Neco Celik, depicts the everyday lives of troubled youth on the streets of Kreuzberg in his 2002 film, *Alltag* ("Daily Life"). The movie includes many aspects of hip-hop, including Turkish-German rap music, breakdancing, and graffiti crews. Celik, who was born in 1972 and grew up in Kreuzberg, is most often compared to Spike Lee, due to his cinematic emphasis on the oppositional milieu of the hood. As a youth, Celik sought to emulate the "gangsta rap" lifestyle as a member of the Turkish street gang, the Thirty-Sixers – named for the last two digits of Kreuzberg's postal code (Berstein, 2003). Discussing the hybridized, black-inflected identities of Turkish-German youths as portrayed in *Alltag*, Timothy Brown (2006) observes:

> The German-born children of these immigrants occupy a place between the worlds; neither fully Turkish nor fully German, they identify more with the specific culture of their own neighborhood than with either of their two "parent" cultures. But the neighborhood culture itself, as Celik shows, is a mixture, not only of Turkish and German cultures, but of U.S. culture – or perhaps more accurately, African-American culture.
>
> (p. 137)

Turkish-German rap music lyrics and related graffiti slogans often directly and indirectly confront racism, xenophobia, and other forms of social exclusion, which evidently resonate with hip-hop fans of various ethnicities and social classes. One notable example is the Turkish-German rap song, "The Life of a Stranger," by King Size Terror, which focuses on the "otherness" of Turks in German society. As Brown (2006) explains, "Hip hop offers a ready-made model of underdog ethnic nationalism that is highly appealing to groups who have to deal with being 'strangers in a strange land'" (p. 147). Significantly, many Turkish-German youths and assorted ethnic-German hip-hop aficionados speak the creolized ethnic dialect of *Kanak Sprak* ("nigga speak") – at least when among themselves. In recent years, this term has been modified (from the original anti-Turkish/racist term, *Kanake*) and rehabilitated by Turkish-German literary figures and hip-hop activists (Byrd, 2009).

Writing on the walls of Berlin

While exploring various neighborhoods in Berlin for two weeks in the summer of 2004, I observed elaborate graffiti displayed on numerous warehouses, tenement walls, squats, park enclosures, public transit yards, trains, monuments, office buildings, and train stations. In particular, I focused my research on the largely residential neighborhoods of Kreuzberg and Friedrichshain (which were officially consolidated into a single municipal district in 2001). Before the Wall's fall, Kreuzberg had been on the western side and Friedrichshain on the east. The longest section of the Berlin Wall still in existence, the graffiti/mural-laden Eastside Gallery, runs through the heart of this area. Paradoxically, graffiti pieces in this outdoor "gallery" have achieved some degree of respectability and status within the orthodox field of art; thus circumventing the normal dismissal of such works by art critics, politicians, and law enforcement officers.

Soon after entering Kreuzberg, I observed crude English- and German-language graffiti covering the concrete base of a historic monument on the public square. In large bold letters, the nonsensical phrase, "Make my baby or even kill me," is scrawled. In addition, several hip-hop tags are plastered on the base of the statue. A few blocks away, I walked around a public housing complex populated mostly by low-income families. Within the complex, I found several highly detailed mural-style graffiti pieces depicting everyday life in the hood – including people of various races, ethnicities, ages, and genders, in portrait-style settings. One of the most striking pieces depicts the American rock legend, Jimi Hendrix, smiling amid a backdrop of rainbow colors spray-painted on a tenement wall.

In the courtyard of the apartment complex, I interviewed Omer, a 19-year-old Turkish Muslim dressed in hip-hop attire, who occasionally dabbles in graffiti writing. Omer explains that the apartment complex is filled almost completely with people of Turkish descent. The apartments are located next-door to a Turkish grocery store and down the street from a trendy Turkish dance club. "I don't really feel as though I belong in the West or the East," he states. "I'm Turkish, but was born in Berlin; so I'm a Berliner too." It is noteworthy that Omer does not claim to be German, though he professes a localized collective identity and is particularly proud of his ethnic neighborhood enclave in Kreuzberg. He explains that his parents migrated to West Germany from Turkey as "guest workers" in the mid-1960s and relocated to West Berlin in the late 1980s, arriving in the city a few months before the Wall's fall. "We aren't really accepted by most Germans, who see us as foreign rather than people of the same country," he remarks.

Omer's story is not particularly unique, given the marginalized status of Berlin's Turkish "immigrant" community, which is a product of the Turkish Diaspora. He observes that Germans in the former East Berlin have acquired a nefarious reputation for being inhospitable to so-called "foreigners." He recounts that neo-Nazi skinheads attacked two of his friends in Brandenburg (eastern Berlin) a few years ago. "There are certain parts of Berlin that are dangerous for Turks and other Muslims, but my neighborhood is usually not affected by racists directly," he states. Noting that several of his friends are graffiti writers, Omer explains that being surrounded by hip-hop graffiti written by fellow Turks actually makes him feel safe. "When I see new graffiti tags, I know that my friends are nearby," he says. "The graffiti helps remind me that this is my home and that Kreuzberg is different from the rest of Berlin."

Later in the day, I witnessed Omer and several other Turkish youths conversing with two ethnic Germans who are members of a local breakdancing crew. "I love rap and that's gotten me interested in breaking too," Omer says. "I wanted to do something different and meet people from other neighborhoods." He reveals that his interest in breaking and graffiti has been fueled not only by American rap music, but also by the Turkish-language genre of Oriental hip hop.

I talked briefly with several B-boys (breakdancers) interacting with Omer, who informed me that they are avid fans of rap music – including both American and German-Turkish varieties of the genre. Alvin, a 17-year-old blond breaker with a sinewy athletic frame, clad in baggy gray sweatpants and a stylish German-language hip-hop t-shirt, contends that breakdancing actually breaks down barriers between different types of people. Born and raised in a nearby Kreuzberg neighborhood, he has been breaking since he was twelve years of age. Though he is familiar with many of the negative stereotypes of both *Ossis* and Turks, he states that the location of a person's birthplace or ethnicity should be irrelevant – especially if you are a skillful, talented B-boy. As he explains:

> Anybody can dance, but having a great style is what's really important. Sure, there's a difference between *Ossis* and *Wessis,* or at least that's what I've been told, but when you have the right style that's what matters most. When you see a B-boy breaking, you can tell what he's like inside as a person. Then, nothing else is important, since respect can be earned, even if people don't like what hood you're coming from.

Walking further into Kreuzberg I spied a multi-storey squat/live music venue, which has an impressive, vibrant facade covered with various anarchist-influenced murals and hip-hop graffiti. The building is visible for several blocks away as it juts defiantly into the air, appearing to pulsate in an effervescent kaleidoscope of aerosol-painted neon colors. One side of the structure features a large elongated worm coiling and ascending from the ground level to the top floor, while the rest of the exterior is filled with various smaller graphics, including the red-lettered anarchy ("A") symbol and a depiction of the famous Argentinean revolutionary, Ernesto "Che" Guevara. Revealing African-American hip-hop influences, a painted sign near the front entrance, declares boldly in English, "Fuck the Police." On an adjoining wall there is a large graffiti piece depicting a black B-boy gesturing defiantly, standing in front of two streaming New York subway cars, emblazoned with the crew tag, "The Nasty Boys."

In the same vicinity, I talked to Tim, a 25-year-old graffitist who recently moved to Kreuzberg from his "native" Eastern Berlin neighborhood, due to escalating rents. He expressed great pride in pointing out several of his elaborate, multicolored graphics in the area – including one work bearing the iconic heading of *Der Berliner Mauer* ("The Berlin Wall"). The piece includes a grumpy-looking Karl Marx grasping an aerosol can in one hand, preparing to spray paint into the faces of unsuspecting passersby. Unemployed for over a year, Tim seemed visibly disheartened while discussing his personal life, yet animated and enthusiastic when discussing graffiti. When asked why he writes on the walls of Berlin, he states:

Bombing the city with graffiti is my way of having my voice heard. Everyone who walks by can't help but see what I'm thinking. I've been unemployed for quite a while and weary of the promises made by politicians. It's difficult to secure a decent job these days, especially when you're from the East. When I'm back in my old neighborhood, I bomb even more.

While on foot in Friedrichshain, I encountered a four-person graffiti crew composed of hip hop-loving German youths who had recently finished painting graffiti on a nearby park wall. Within a few minutes of my arrival, the crew had completed a large piece that featured an anime-style rabbit licking an ice cream cone seductively, next to the German-language name of their crew illustrated in brightly colored, billowing spray-painted letters. The piece was highly reminiscent of the graffiti style of tagging first popularized on the streets of the South Bronx in the seventies, yet incorporating a distinctive German ambience.

Members of the crew were visibly exhausted from several hours of difficult artistic work and seemed uncomfortable at first in acknowledging the existence of any sociocultural tensions within Berlin. "Yes, there are differences, but only narrow-minded people focus on things like that," 18-year old Louis states reluctantly. "Actually, many West Berliners visit Friedrichshain in the East to experience the coolest nightclubs. And the presence of Turkish people in Kreuzberg helps to make things interesting and fun," he adds enthusiastically. Berta, a 16-year-old member of the crew agrees, noting that *Wessis* tend to perceive *Ossis* much more positively if they happen to live in certain urban areas. As she states:

From a *Wessi's* point of view, you are hardly an *Ossi* when you're living in Friedrichshain or Kreuzberg. This is because the area is so trendy and has population exchanges happening all the time. But we don't approve of poor people being forced out of their housing. One reason why we write graffiti is because we oppose such things happening in our neighborhood.

In addition to hip-hop-style writing and pieces, I observed a great deal of graffiti that featured themes and slogans associated with anarchism, anti-gentrification protests, environmentalism, anti-nuclear sentiments, and anti-globalization viewpoints. For instance, one brightly colored graffiti piece located on a wall enclosure in an automotive repair lot has an illustration of a sedate Mahatma Gandhi spray-painted with the English words, "Truth is God." Gandhi appears to be staring at a US dollar sign defaced with a red mark, above the phrase, "Don't Believe the Hype." These two pieces were both designed apparently to be a critique of Western capitalist values such as materialism, greed, and conspicuous consumption, juxtaposed with Eastern (alternative) values symbolized by Gandhi – including asceticism, selflessness, and altruism.

As I explored Kreuzberg and Friedrichshain, I came across numerous graffiti slogans and graphics that directly questioned or opposed gentrification. Such messages often were very explicit in their verbiage, including the English phrase "Yuppies Fuck Off" and German slogans such as *Kein Spekulant* ("No Speculators") and *Yuppies auf's Maul* ("Hit Yuppies in the Mouth").

One notable graffiti slogan spray-painted on a tenement wall in a Friedrichshain neighborhood compares Berlin's gentrification projects to South Africa's past system of racial segregation, with the phrase: *Yuppisierungist Apartheid* ("Yuppie Gentrification is Separateness").

Conclusion

The sociospatial milieus of New York City and Berlin have undergone dramatic, revolutionary changes over the past several decades. Though the historic, political, and social circumstances of the two cities vary substantially, each metropolitan environment has experienced significant reconfigurations of social space and related restructurings of the economy. In particular, major urban renewal and gentrification projects have occurred in both cities, resulting in the massive displacement and intra-urban migration of long-term residents to ghettoized neighborhoods. In the case of New York, the South Bronx has become a less expensive alternative for impoverished African-American and Hispanic residents, many of whom could no longer afford the skyrocketing rents of Manhattan. In the case of Berlin, Kreuzberg has become a relatively low-rent multicultural refuge, not only for immigrant Turks and their families, but also for college students, bohemian youths, and displaced families fleeing from recently gentrified neighborhoods.

Paradoxically, the particular spatial environments of New York and Berlin are empowering for some groups, while stifling and oppressive for others – particularly those who have been relegated to a lower-status position within the field of social relations. Such a "spatial ordering of the city" (Sandercock, 2008, p. 222) is prone to hegemonic discourses of otherness and marginalization, articulated by dominant urban actors whose dispositions and communicative repertoires have been shaped largely by their habitus. Politicians, the mass media, and other orthodox elites have labeled both Kreuzberg and the South Bronx as "blighted" and "dangerous" ghettos, even though the deleterious condition of such living spaces is due primarily to institutional discrimination and deindustrialization.

In reaction to the marginalization of subordinated groups in New York and Berlin, subcultural counter discourses of innovation and rebellion have emerged, particularly among youth. Such dissident campaigns have sought to transform or overturn the dominant spatial order by engaging in various aesthetic heterodoxies in fields such as art, music, and dance. Most notably, within the South Bronx of the mid-1970s, hip hop crystallized as an oppositional youth-based phenomenon, which effectively challenged the racialized urban social hierarchy. Modern urban graffiti, in particular, became largely subsumed within the hip-hop rubric; thus evolving into a major discursive toolkit for countless thousands – if not millions – of semiotic urban-guerrillas "bombing" hoods around the world.

The globalization of market forces has helped to spark new spatial contradictions that are particularly acute within transitional societies such as post-reunification Germany. During the past two decades, urban spaces in the former East Germany and East Berlin have undergone an incredibly swift pace of marketization and gentrification. Struggles between the dominant *Wessis* and the largely subordinate *Ossis* have generated new dialectical dispositions, tensions, and conflicts. Dramatic changes in the spatial patterns of social interaction have directly influenced the collective identities of young people living in Berlin. With new forms of stratification and rampant inequality impacting many neighborhoods, alternative means for accumulating stocks of capital – including the nonmaterial form of subcultural capital – have become appealing to youth. As several respondents in this study have implied, the underground prestige economy of graffiti has provided new opportunities for gaining a modicum of respect and even fame – at least within the hip-hop subculture.

The original hip-hop generation, composed primarily of African-American and Hispanic youth, has effectively disseminated rap music, graffiti, and breakdancing into not only America's predominately white suburbs, but also the contested urban domains of Berlin and other multicultural global locales. By reframing the ghetto as the hood, hip-hoppers have sought, at least implicitly, to rebut the negative stigma of impoverished-racialized neighborhoods everywhere. Within the field of urban conflict, the distinctive habitus of the hood has metastasized, first in the South Bronx and later in Kreuzberg. Contestations of urban space have become particularly acute in Kreuzberg, as recent encroachments by gentrifying pioneers continue to escalate, threatening to displace long-time residents.

In the course of my interviews in Berlin, I discovered that young people who identify with modern urban graffiti or other aspects of hip hop tend to have a strong vicarious affinity with African-American culture – at least when it comes to their collective identity and mode of public expression among peers. The inherent "blackness" of hip hop evidently resonates with many respondents, several of whom claim to have encountered comparable forms of social exclusion and marginality in their own lives – due to factors such as ethnicity, social class, or residential locale. Most respondents displayed African-American fashion styles, though often mixed with German or Turkish brands or slogans. In exploring Kreuzberg and other neighborhoods, I observed graffiti written in English, German, and the Turkish-German dialect of *Kanak Sprak* (or some combination thereof), which often included black-inflected hip-hop expressions and imagery. In this respect, Berlin youths are negotiating and constructing hybridized collective identities by essentially synthesizing various global and local discourses through everyday spatial practices.

As revealed in this study, the common discursive theme for Berlin youth is the importance of "home" or "neighborhood," which is often framed by low-income residents as somehow under siege or assault by external urban forces. Many Berlin young people have embraced hip-hop graffiti as a subversive discursive strategy designed to challenge and contest hegemonic social structures within the urban field. Rather than living in fixed ghettoized stasis, Berlin graffitists are using public space to overcome contradictory sociospatial constraints. In this respect, youthful graffitists and their supporters possess social agency, operating within the adversarial context of their neighborhood habitus. In sum, the decades-old hip-hop narrative of poor/black opposition to wealthy/white subjugation in the American hood has been recontextualized to reflect the beleaguered yet defiant existence of alienated young people living in Berlin.

References

Androutsopoulos, J. and Scholz, A. (2002). On the Recontextualization of Hip Hop in European Speech Communities: A Contrastive Analysis of Rap Lyrics. Retrieved from www.fu-berlin.de/phin/phin19/p19t1.htm

Austin, J. (2001). *Taking the Train: How Graffiti Art Became an Urban Crisis in New York City*. New York: Columbia University Press.

Baumgarnter, M. E. (1988). *The Moral Order of the Suburbs*. New York: Oxford University Press.

Berman, M. (1986). Take it to the Streets: Conflict and Community in Public Space. *Dissent*, Fall: 470–94.

Bernstein, R. (2003). A Bold New View of Turkish-German Youth. *The New York Times* (April 12).

Bock, M. (2004). Family Snaps: Life-World and Information Habitus. *Visual Communication*, 3, 281–293.

Bourdieu, P. (1977). *Outline of a Theory of Practice*. Cambridge, United Kingdom: Cambridge University Press.

Bourdieu, P. (1984). *Distinction: A Social Critique of the Judgment of Taste*. London: Routledge.

Bourdieu, P. (1985). The Forms of Capital. In J. G. Richardson (Ed.), *Handbook of Theory and Research for the Sociology of Education*. New York: Greenwood.

Bourdieu, P. (2008). Habitus. In J. Hiller & E. Rooksby (Eds), *Habitus: A Sense of Place*. Padstow, UK: Ashgate Publishing.

Bourdieu, P. and Wacquant, L. (1992). *An Invitation to Reflexive Sociology*. Chicago: University of Chicago Press.

Boyd, T. (2003). *The New H.N.I.C. (Head Niggas in Charge): The Death of Civil Rights and the Reign of Hip Hop*. New York University Press: New York and London.

Brantingham, P. and Brantingham, P. (1993). Nodes Paths and Edges: Considerations on the Complexity of Crime and the Physical Environment, *Journal of Environmental Psychology*, 1, 3–28.

Brown, T. (2006). "Keeping it Real" in a Different Hood: (African-) Americanization and Hip Hop in Germany. In D. Basu and S. J. Lemelle (Eds), *The Vinyl Ain't Final: Hip Hop and the Globalization of Black Popular Culture*. London: Pluto Press.

Burns, C. (1999). Germans Now Divided by the "Wall in the Head." *CNN.com* (November 9).

Byrd, B. (2009). Media Representations of Turkish-German and Hip-Hop Language as a Uniform Ethnolect. *Texas Linguistic Forum*, 53, 72–78.

Cahill, S. (1990). Childhood and Public Life: Reaffirming Biographical Divisions. *Social Problems*, 37, 390–402.

Castleman, C. (1982). *Getting Up: Subway Graffiti in New York*. Cambridge, Massachusetts: MIT Press.

Chmielewska, E. (1984). Framing (Con)text: Graffiti and Place. *Space and Culture*, 2, 145–169.

De Certeau, M. (1984). *The Practice of Everyday Life*. Berkeley and Los Angeles: University of California Press.

Eck, J. and Weisburd, D. (1985). *Crime and Place*, New York: Criminal Justice Press.

Fischer, R., Maes, J., & Schmitt, M. (2007). Tearing Down the "Wall in the Head"? Culture Contact between Germans. *International Journal of Intercultural Relations*, 31, 163–179.

Forman, M. (2002). *The Hood Comes First: Race, Space, and Place in Rap and Hip-hop*. Middletown, Connecticut: Wesleyan University Press.

Foucault, M. (1984). Space, Knowledge, and Power. In P. Rabinow (Ed.), *The Foucault Reader*. New York: Pantheon.

Freeman, L. (2006). *There Goes the Hood: Views of Gentrification from the Ground Up*. Philadelphia: Temple University Press.

Fyfe, N., & J. Bannister. (1996). City Watching: Closed Circuit Television Watching in Public Spaces. *Area*, 28(1), 37–46.

George, N. (1998). *Hip Hop America*. New York: Penguin Books.

Glaeser, A. (2000). *Divided in Unity: Identity, Germany, and the Berlin Police*. Chicago and London: University of Chicago Press.

Graff, J. (2000). Germany's Youth across the Divide. *CNN.com* (October 4).

Gonzalez, E. (2004). *The Bronx*. New York: Columbia University Press.

Gotham, K. F. (2003). Toward an Understanding of the Spatiality of Urban Poverty: The Urban Poor as Spatial Actors. *International Journal of Urban and Regional Research*, 27(3), 723–737.

Gresillon, B. (1999). Berlin, Cultural Metropolis: Changes in the Cultural Geography of Berlin Since Reunification. *Cultural Geographies* 3. 284–294.

Halsey, M. and Young, A. (2006). "Our Desires are Ungovernable": Writing Graffiti in Urban Space. *Theoretical Criminology*, 3, 275–306.

Hebdige, D. (1987). *Subculture: The Meaning of Style*. London and New York: Routledge.

Hendry L., Shucksmith, J., Love, J.G. & Glendinning, A. (1993). *Young People's Leisure and Lifestyles*. London: Routledge.

Hesse, B., Rai, D. K., Bennett, C., & McGilchrist, P. (1992). *Beneath the Surface: Racial Harassment*. Alderhot: Avebury.

Hiller, J. and Rooksby, E. (2008). Introduction to First Edition. In J. Hiller and E. Rooksby (Eds), *Habitus: A Sense of Place*. Padstow, UK: Ashgate Publishing.

Holm, A. (2006). Urban Renewal and the End of Social Housing: The Roll Out of Neoliberalism in East Berlin's Prenzlauer Berg: Urban Renewal, Urban Policy, and Modes of Regulation. *Social Justice*, (September 22).

Iveson, K. (2007). *Publics and the City*. Oxford: Wiley-Blackwell.

Kahn, C. (2000). *Ten Years of German Unification: One State, Two Peoples*. Westport, Connecticut and London: Praeger.

Kelling, G. I., & Wilson, J. Q. (1982). Broken Windows: The Police and Neighborhood Safety. *The Atlantic Magazine*. Retrieved from http://www.theatlantic.com/magazine/archive/1982/03/broken-windows/4465/

Leach, D. (2009). An Elusive "We": Antidogmatism, Democratic Practice, and the Contradictory Identity of the German Autonomen. *American Behavioral Scientist*, 7, 1042–1068.

Lull, J. (1995). *Media, Communication, Culture: A Global Approach*. Cambridge: Policy Press.

Lynn, N. and Lea, S. J. (2005). "Racist" Graffiti: Text, Context and Social Comment. *Visual Communication*, 4(1), 39–63.

MacDonald, N. (2001). *The Graffiti Subculture: Youth, Masculinity and Identity in London and New York*. Bassingstoke, UK and New York: Palgrave Macmillan.

Mayer, C. (2009). Germany's Election: Divided They Stand. *Time.com* (September 21).

McGrellis, S. (2005). "Pure and Bitter Spaces: Gender, Identity and Territory in Northern Irish Youth Transitions. *Gender and Education* 5, 515–529.

Moran, J. (2004). November in Berlin: The End of the Everyday. *History Workshop Journal*, 1, 216–234.

Ogbar, J. (2007). O.G. *Hip-hop Revolution: The Culture and Politics of Rap*. Lawrence, Kansas: University Press of Kansas.

Ozment, S. (2004). *A Mighty Fortress: A New History of the German People*. New York: Perennial Press.

Pearce, J. (1996). Urban Youth Cultures: Gender and Spatial Forms. *Youth & Policy*, 52, 1–11.

Petzen, J. (2004). Home or Homelike? Turkish Queers Manage Space in Berlin. *Space and Culture*, 1, 20–32.

Rahn, J. (2001). *Painting without Permission: Hip-Hop Graffiti Subculture.* Basingstoke, UK: Palgrave Macmillan.

Reynald, D., & Elffers, H. (2009). The Future of Newman's Defensible Space Theory and the Routine Activities of Place. *European Journal of Criminology,* 1, 25–46.

Rose, T. (2008). Rap Music. In T. Strode and T. Wood (Eds), *The Hip-Hop Reader.* New York: Pearson Longman.

Roxborough, S. (2005). Almost Like Real Gangstas. This Time German Rap is Coming from the Streets. *The Atlantic Times* (February). Retrieved from http://www.atlantic-times.com/archive_ detail.php?recordID=128.

Sack, R. (2003). *A Geographers Guide to the Real and the Good.* New York and London: Routledge.

Sandercock, L. (2008). Difference, Fear and Habitus: A Political Economy of Urban Fears. In J. Hiller and E. Rooksby (Eds), *Habitus: A Sense of Place.* Padstow, UK: Ashgate Publishing.

Sanders, B. (2005). *Youth Crime and Youth Culture in the Inner City,* London: Routledge.

Schneider, P. (2005). The New Berlin Wall. *The New York Times* (December 4).

Smith, F. (1998). Between East and West: Sites of Resistance in East German Youth Cultures. In T. Skelton & G. Valentine (Eds), *Coolplaces: Geographies of Youth Cultures.* London and New York: Routledge.

Smith, N. (1996). *The New Urban Frontier: Gentrification and the Revanchist City.* New York: Routledge.

Soysal, L. (2001). Diversity of Experience, Experience of Diversity: Turkish Migrant Youth Culture in Berlin. *Cultural Dynamics* 5.

Thornton, S. (1997). The Social Logic of Subcultural Capital. In K. Gelder & S. Thornton (Eds), *The Subcultures Reader.* London and New York: Routledge.

Tillman, T. (1990). *The Writings on the Wall.* Santa Monica, California: Publishing Company.

Tzortzis, A. (2003). "Bombing" Berlin, the Graffiti Capital of Europe. *The New York Times* (March 3). Retrieved from http://www.nytimes.com/2008/03/03/travel/03iht-04graffiti.10654044.html.

Valentine, G., Skelton, T., & Chambers, D. (1998). Cool Places: An Introduction to Youth and Youth Cultures. In T. Skelton & G. Valentine (Eds), *Coolplaces: Geographies of Youth Cultures.* London and New York: Routledge.

Veenis, M. (1999). Consumption in East Germany: The Seduction and Betrayal of Things. *Journal of Material Culture,* 4(1).

Waleczek, T. (2009). An Arson a Day: Car Conflagrations Ignite Political Row in Berlin. *Spiegel Online International* (June 19). Retrieved from http://www.spiegel.de/international/ germany/0,1518,631435,00.html.

Weinzierl, R. & Muggleton, D. (2003). What is "Post-Subcultural Studies" Anyway? In D. Muggleton and R. Weinzierl (Eds), *The Post-Subcultures Reader.* Oxford and New York: Berg.